Feminism and Sexuality
A Reader

GENDER AND CULTURE
Carolyn G. Heilbrun and Nancy K. Miller, EDITORS

A Gender and Culture Reader

A Series of Columbia University Press
edited by Carolyn G. Heilbrun and Nancy K. Miller

Previously published in the series:

Modern Feminisms: Political, Literary, Cultural
Edited and Introduced by Maggie Humm

FEMINISM AND SEXUALITY

A READER

Edited by
Stevi Jackson and Sue Scott

COLUMBIA UNIVERSITY PRESS
New York

Columbia University Press
New York   Chichester, West Sussex

Library of Congress Cataloging-in-Publication Data

Feminism and sexuality: a reader / edited by Stevi Jackson
   and Sue Scott.
        p.   cm.
   Includes bibliographical references and index.
   ISBN (invalid) 0231-10708-0 cl 0-231-10709-9-pa
   1. Feminism.   2. Sex.   I. Jackson, Stevi.   II. Scott, Sue.
HQ1150.F453 1996
   305.42 -- dc20   96-16020
                                                     CIP

Casebound editions of Columbia University Press books are printed on
permanent and durable acid-free paper.

Printed in the United States of America
c 10 9 8 7 6 5 4 3 2 1

CONTENTS

This book is dedicated to our mothers,
Frances Jackson and Olive Scott

Acknowledgements

We would like to thank all those who helped to bring this book into being, in particular Jackie Jones and Nicola Carr at Edinburgh University Press. We are particularly grateful to Ruby Bashir who provided invaluable help with many of the routine tasks such as photocopying, cutting and pasting, as well as re-ordering the footnotes and references in the readings. Finally many thanks to Shaun Moores for giving up access to the kitchen table – except when he was providing food to put on it.

SEXUAL SKIRMISHES AND FEMINIST FACTIONS
Twenty-Five Years of Debate on Women and Sexuality

Stevi Jackson and Sue Scott

Sexuality has become a central political issue for feminists and also a source of divisions amongst them. This is perhaps not surprising given that sexual activities and identities are more generally controversial within Western societies and are issues around which there has been a great deal of public discussion. Feminists have developed their own distinctive perspectives on these public issues, for example, on pornography, prostitution, sexual violence, and homosexuality and lesbianism as well as their own private practices. We have rarely, however, been able to present a united front. Indeed sexuality has been contested terrain amongst feminists since the nineteenth century. No sooner had it been identified as a major area of concern by the modern movement, than significant disagreements began to emerge.

Our aim in compiling this reader is to provide a guide to the development of feminist debates on sexuality since the early 1970s. Although constrained by the space available, we have endeavoured to reproduce material which is representative of the diversity of feminist theory and politics and illustrative of some of the shifts in perspective which have occurred over the last two-and-a-half decades.[1] While we have our own opinions about the issues we will be discussing here, and will make it clear where we stand, we will also attempt to explain other views as clearly and fairly as we can. Making this selection has by no means been easy, given the sheer volume of work feminists writing in this area have produced. A glance at any publisher's catalogue reveals that sexuality is now a major issue within and across many academic disciplines. The growth of interest in this area can be traced back to the beginning of 'second wave' feminism,[2] and had its origins in the political aims of the Women's Liberation Movement (WLM) and the movement for gay liberation. In recent years feminist and gay scholars have taken the lead in putting sexuality on the academic agenda and in developing research, theory and teaching in this field. This new scholarship on sexuality differs radically from the older, sexological tradition. Sexology treated sexuality as a biological and psychological phenomenon, often drawing on a medical model which regarded differences from a narrowly defined heterosexual norm as pathological.[3] More recent approaches have given far higher priority to the social and cultural shaping of human sexuality. Instead of treating male-dominated heterosexual relationships as an unproblematic norm, these perspectives have subjected it to critical scrutiny. In this book we are concerned primarily with feminist rather than gay perspectives, and will deal with the latter only where the relationship between the two has been identified as an issue by feminists.[4]

In this introduction we explain how and why sexuality became a political issue for feminists and explore the different strands of thought which have subsequently emerged. First, however, we should define the terms we are using. Feminists frequently distinguish between sex, gender and sexuality, although there is by no means a consensus on how these terms should be used. The words 'sex' and 'sexual', so basic to these debates, have, in common usage, two meanings. They can refer both to the physical distinction between male and female and to intimate erotic activity. Ann Oakley (Reading 1.1) accounts for this double meaning by suggesting that what is sexual in the second sense concerns relations between the sexes in the first sense. In so doing she reinforces the heterosexist thinking, common in Western cultures, which many other feminists have gone on to challenge: the tendency to define 'sex' as 'the sex act', and this in turn as heterosexual coition. The term 'sexuality' is generally broader in meaning, encompassing erotic desires, practices and identities. Sometimes this term, too, is used to include our sense of ourselves as women or men. We prefer to use the term 'gender' to cover all aspects of what it means to be a woman or a man and to refer to the social and cultural distinctions between women and men. 'Sexuality' is then reserved for aspects of personal and social life which have erotic significance. In this sense, the concept of 'sexuality' remains somewhat fluid, in part because what is deemed erotic, and hence sexual in this sense, is not fixed. What is erotic to one person might be disgusting to a second and politically unacceptable to a third. Indeed, competing ideas about eroticism have underpinned many of the fiercest controversies among feminists around such issues as pornography. In using this rather slippery term, we wish to convey the idea that sexuality is not limited to 'sex acts', but involves our sexual feelings and relationships, the ways in which we are or are not defined as sexual by others, as well as the ways in which we define ourselves.

The term 'gender' was adopted by feminists to emphasise the social shaping of femininity and masculinity, to challenge the idea that relations between women and men were ordained by nature. Sometimes a distinction is made between 'sex' as the biological differences between male and female and 'gender' as the cultural distinction between femininity and masculinity along with the social division between women and men.[5] Not all feminists accept this distinction. Some think that it denies the importance of the physical body, while others argue that our understanding of the anatomically sexed body is itself socially constructed.[6] We ourselves endorse the latter view.

While making an analytical distinction between gender and sexuality, we recognise that the two are empirically related. Indeed it is the relationship between the two which makes sexuality a crucial issue for feminists and which is the focus of many of the readings we have included in this volume. The social distinction and hierarchical relationship between men and women profoundly affect our sexual lives. This is true not only for those of us who are heterosexual: lesbian and gay sexualities are also shaped by wider understandings of masculinity and femininity, as are heterosexual attitudes to other sexualities – for example, the idea that lesbians are not 'real women'. Gender and sexuality intersect with other social divisions such as those based on 'race' and class, so that we each live our sexuality from different locations within society. Hence women's experiences of both gender and sexuality are highly variable. Feminists have sought to understand both what we share in common as women and the differences between us. In the context of the women's movement, which aims to advance the interests of all women, these differences have become a crucial, and often highly contentious, issue.

POLITICISING THE PERSONAL

It is not difficult to see why sexuality should be a major feminist issue. Historically enormous efforts, from chastity belts to property laws, have been made to control female sexuality and to tie women to individual men through monogamous heterosexual relationships. The double standard of morality has entitled men to sexual freedoms denied to women. It has also divided women themselves into two categories: the respectable madonna and the rebarbative whore. Women's sexuality has been policed and regulated in a way which men's has not: it is the woman prostitute who is stigmatised and punished, not her male clients. Heterosexual activity has always been risky for women, associated as it is with loss of 'reputation', with unwanted pregnancy and with diseases which threaten fertility. Women have also been vulnerable to male sexual violence and coercion, yet held responsible for both their own and their assailants' behaviour.

First wave feminists campaigned around many of these issues, but the ways in which they did so were constrained by the material circumstances in which they lived – such as limited opportunities for economic independence and control of their own fertility – and the prevailing sexual morality. Hence, for example, the most immediately feasible strategy for opposing the sexual exploitation of women and the double standard of morality was to argue for greater chastity for men rather than greater sexual freedom for women.[7] The social and political context which gave rise to second wave feminism was very different and created new possibilities for feminist approaches to sexuality.

In the era following the Second World War, more women than ever before entered the labour market and they had greater opportunities for education. None the less they remained disadvantaged in both spheres, and the ideology of woman's place being in the home was still firmly entrenched. The 1960s were years of relative affluence and full employment in the West, but also of major political upheavals. Economic prosperity was not equally available to all: poverty was 'rediscovered' at this time, while members of ethnic minorities in many countries were excluded from full citizenship rights. In the southern United States, black voters remained disenfranchised; the civil rights movement, aimed at counteracting this, became an important training ground for young American political activists, both black and white. More generally, there was a resurgence of Left politics among the young in Western nations as a whole, mobilised through opposition to the Vietnam War and a host of other examples of injustice and imperialism. In Europe the year 1968 saw two major upheavals: the quashing of a new, more liberal, socialist government in Czechoslovakia by the Soviet Union and a major student uprising and general strike in Paris. From the late 1960s and into the early 1970s Left activism, especially among students, remained at a high level. It was largely from among the ranks of this 'New Left' that the new generation of feminist activists came. Having become politicised through these movements, many women became aware that they were marginalised within them, relegated to secondary supporting roles, while men made the decisions. While combating all other forms of inequality, that between women and men was largely neglected: it was ignored altogether, treated as trivial or, later, diagnosed as a problem to be solved 'after the revolution'.

The 'New Left' and 'Old Left' shared this insensitivity to women's oppression, but they differed in many other respects. Crucially for the direction which feminist politics was to take, the 'New Left' was far more libertarian and specifically opposed to the authoritarian regimes of the Eastern Bloc, state socialist, nations. This entailed, among other things, a greater receptivity to ideas about the possibility and desirability of change in personal life, and a vision of individual fulfilment, pleasure and freedom as legitimate revolutionary goals.[8] A further influence at this time, evident within the Left and more generally, was the so-called 'sexual revolution' of the 1960s. The extent to which this was a revolutionary change or merely a continuation of trends evident long before has been called into question.[9] There were some developments during this which did seem to presage an era of greater sexual freedom, such as the wider availability of contraception, particularly the oral contraceptive pill. In many Western countries, permissive legislation around sexual issues was also a feature of this period. In Britain, for example, the abolition of theatre censorship, the liberalisation of abortion and divorce laws and the decriminalisation of homosexual acts between consenting men over 21 were all enacted in the later years of the decade. It took some time before the effects of such changes became evident in the population as a whole, but for those who were young, independent and politicised, they were part of a broader social context in which sexually libertarian ideas were current. These ideas certainly had an impact on women in Left groups and played a part in the subsequent development of a feminist analysis of the sexual revolution.

The new ideals of sexual liberation circulating within the Left, and in various counter-cultural movements of the time, promised new freedoms. 'Free love' was promoted while marriage was condemned as a bourgeois institution which reduced people to possessions. These ideas potentially put men and women on an equal footing, challenging the old double standard and presenting sex as something to be enjoyed for its own sake. In practice, however, they had different consequences for women and men. In retrospect many women felt that 'sexual liberation' meant greater access for men to women's bodies and the removal of their right to say 'No' to sex, lest they be damned as 'unliberated'.[10] As a feminist cartoon of the time put it: 'They used to call me a frigid bitch – now I'm a bourgeois individualist.' All this, combined with the marginalisation of women, and women's issues, within Left organisations, provided the impetus for feminist critique. Marge Piercy described the situation as follows:

> A man can bring a woman into an organization by sleeping with her and remove her by ceasing to do so. A man can purge a woman for no other reason than that he has tired of her, knocked her up, or is after someone else.[11]

This is not as far-fetched as it might sound. Stokely Carmichael, of the Student Nonviolent Co-ordination Committee (SNCC)[12] is on record as announcing that 'the only position for women within the SNCC is prone'.

By the end of the 1960s it is surprising neither that many women felt that they needed an autonomous movement of their own, nor that they should have identified sexuality as a key issue. While some of the effects of the so-called sexual revolution can be seen as having been problematic for women, it did open up sexuality as a political issue. Even its more negative consequences had the effect of producing the possibility of resistance, and the development of alternative, feminist, perspectives. Many feminists tried to preserve what they saw as the positive elements within the libertarian ideas of the New Left – the dissociation of sex from reproduction, the emphasis on sexual pleasure and freedom, the critique of marriage and monogamy – while also challenging the coercive and predatory aspects of male sexuality. It was not simply that women were questioning men's rights of sexual access; they also began to express dissatisfaction with the quality of their relationships with men, both in bed and out.

Feminists also retained the New Left idea that our political analysis should be carried through to the way we live our personal lives. The slogan 'The personal is political', however, meant much more than this. Women discovered that many of their individual problems and anxieties were shared by others and concluded that they were more than merely personal, they derived from our social situation and were characteristic of our oppression as women. Since they were social in origin they required political solutions. In coming to see our personal troubles as political issues we redefined the boundaries of politics itself. Women-only groups and the practice of consciousness-raising were central to this process. Consciousness-raising was not, then, a self-indulgent collective act of introspection. On the contrary, the purpose of talking about our personal lives was to pool our experiences, to discover common ground among us and to use this as the basis of political analysis and action.

Aspects of life which had previously been seen as outside the public realm of politics were placed on the political agenda. It became possible to talk, for example, about the 'politics of housework' or 'the politics of orgasm'.[13] Many aspects of sexuality were opened up for discussion and analysis. Feminists continued to attack the double standard, to challenge the view that sexuality was bad for women and that only 'bad' women were sexual. They began to demand the right to define their own sexuality, to seek forms of sexual pleasure not constrained by the set heterosexual pattern of foreplay (if you were lucky) followed by penetration, to see themselves as sexually active rather than passive objects of male desire. At the same time, women's shared experience of pressured sex with men led to new analyses of sexual coercion and violence which drew parallels between 'normal' heterosexuality and rape. Feminists also attacked the sexual objectification of women in beauty contests, pin-ups and pornography and the commodification of sexuality through prostitution. All this contributed to a fundamental critique of heterosexual practice and ultimately of the institution of heterosexuality itself.[14]

Most of the issues which have been the focus of later feminist debates were already being discussed within a few years of the WLM coming into being. Many of the tensions which were to give rise to political differences within feminism were also evident at this time. Feminists began from a common point of departure: that the current ordering of heterosexual relations was detrimental to women and implicated in our subordination. We subsequently followed divergent paths, guided by differing priorities for change and strategies for action. Some of these key areas of debate have guided our organisation of the book: whether women's sexuality is repressed or socially constructed; the differences between heterosexual and lesbian feminists; the tension between sex as pleasure and sex as power; the extent to which pornography and prostitution can be considered oppressive to women.

CHALLENGING BIOLOGICAL DETERMINISM

In making sexuality a political issue feminists conceptualised it as changeable and therefore challenged the prevailing assumption that sexual desires and practices were fixed by nature. This challenge was being made across a range of issues. The WLM aimed to change the conditions which produce women's subordination. If those conditions were natural it would have been futile to try to change them; conversely trying to change them implied that they were understood as social in origin. As Christine Delphy puts it:

> People do not revolt against what is natural, therefore inevitable; or inevitable, therefore natural. Since what is resistible is not inevitable; what is not inevitable could be otherwise – it is arbitrary therefore social. The logical and necessary implication of women's revolt, like all revolts, is that the situation can be changed. Belief in the possibility of change implies belief in the social origins of the situation.[15]

Challenging biological determinism is therefore an important political strategy for feminists and not just an academic matter. A related issue here is that of agency and structure. In arguing that sexuality is social, it is important that we do not replace biological determinism with another form of determinism. We need to take account of the social structures and cultural practices which constrain our sexuality, but we should also consider the ways in which we actively construct our own understanding of sexuality and negotiate sexual activities within these constraints. Without an understanding of the interrelationship between the structures we inhabit and ourselves as agents, there can be no conceptualisation of strategies for change. While feminist sexual politics has been concerned with choice and taking personal responsibility for our conduct, feminists have also been aware of the complexity of social and cultural influences on our sexuality and aware of the dangers of overly individualistic solutions to the problems women face.

This belief in the social origins of women's oppression was and is common to all shades of feminist opinion, but there have always been different forms of analysis arising from this shared assumption. Moreover, these analyses have evolved further over the last few decades. Where sexuality is concerned, the idea that its current form is oppressive and needs to be changed does not always lead to a fully developed analysis of sexuality itself. For feminists with reformist aims, the focus is more likely to be legislative or bureaucratic change relating to issues such as the treatment of rape victims or responses to sexual harassment. These issues are also important to feminists seeking more radical change, but are likely to be integrated into an understanding of sexuality as more fundamentally embedded in the social and cultural order. It is these more radical tendencies which have generated most feminist theorising on sexuality. The majority of these theorists have conceptualised sexuality as socially constructed, but precisely how this process occurs has been the focus of much debate. There has also, always, been a minority position arguing that women have an authentic sexuality which is repressed or suppressed within patriarchal societies.

Contrary to what is suggested in many women's studies texts, this difference does not map neatly on to a division between socialist, poststructuralist and postmodernist feminists on the one hand and radical feminists on the other.[16] There is, for example, a tradition in Marxist thought within which sexuality is seen as repressed by capitalism. Some Marxist and socialist feminists have turned to psychoanalysis – a theory within which repression is a central concept – in order to explore female sexuality.[17] Radical feminists are often misrepresented as essentialist, as believing in an essential female nature and female sexuality. While there are, no doubt, some radical feminists who embrace these views, the majority are opposed to them.[18] We have already quoted Christine Delphy, who is part of a French radical feminist tradition which has always stood against the doctrine of women's 'difference'.[19] In Britain, too, there is a strong anti-essentialist radical feminist current.[20] Some North American feminists have been particularly badly misrepresented in this respect, Andrea Dworkin being one case in point. She is on record as being fundamentally opposed to the idea that women are innately 'better' than men (see Reading 1.4), yet she is frequently labelled essentialist.[21]

Differing opinions on whether female sexuality is socially constructed or is an innate potential cut across other theoretical and political divisions. So too do other differences of emphasis to be found in feminist work. Among those who see sexuality as socially constructed there are three main strands of analysis, each focusing on a different aspect of social construction. The first of these foregrounds the issue of male dominance, analysing sexuality in relation to patriarchal structures; the second concentrates on the construction of our sexual desires at the level of individual subjectivity, in other words on how we come to be sexual in particular ways; and the third seeks to demonstrate the variability and malleability of human sexual desires. Although feminists have contributed to these strands from many different perspectives, particular groups of theorists are often associated with each of them, for example, radical feminists primarily with the first and psychoanalytic feminists with the second. There are, however, some who seek to establish connections between all three aspects of sexuality, and this we consider to be the best way forward for feminist theory.

Many feminist interests coalesce around the third strand we have identified – the malleability of human sexuality – since the idea that sexuality is historically and culturally variable is fundamental to all forms of social constructionism. If we can demonstrate that sexuality is not the same in all cultures and that historically it has been subject to change, then we have an effective counter-argument to biological determinism. Moreover, if something can be shown to have changed, this indicates a potential for future transformations. It is not surprising then that feminists of many different theoretical and political persuasions have contributed to the accumulation of knowledge about the diverse forms which sexuality has taken in different historical and cultural contexts. The first three readings in this volume are illustrative of this shared concern on the part of feminists who offer very different perspectives.

Those concerned with understanding the position of women in Western societies have been examining the organisation of gender and sexuality in other societies at least since the 1930s. Margaret Mead, for example, sought to demonstrate that the traits which were deemed to be masculine or feminine – including the ways in which men and women express their sexuality – varied from one society to another. She studied three New Guinea societies and concluded that each of them had very different ideas about femininity, masculinity and sexuality.[22] It is this tradition of work which Ann Oakley draws on (Reading 1.1) Anthropologists have since begun to raise more fundamental questions about Western conceptualisations of gender and sexuality, suggesting that not all cultures regard gender as a set of binary opposites permanently embodied in men and women. Nor do other cultures necessarily see gender and sexuality as parts of our inner being.[23] Where early anthropologists catalogued an enormous array of diverse sexual practices existing in human societies,[24] more recent work has suggested that there is no reliable way of deciding in advance what constitutes a sexual act. What counts as sexual depends on the meanings of specific acts in both their wider cultural and immediate interpersonal contexts.[25]

Such analyses suggest that we can no longer regard sexuality as an inner drive which we express – or which is repressed. Similar conclusions have emerged from historical work on sexuality. It has been commonplace to regard the Victorian era as one in which sex was repressed, later to be released from constraint as sexual mores became more permissive in the latter part of the twentieth century. This view presupposes a given, natural sexuality kept in check by moral convention and restraint. While some theorists were already questioning this view,[26] the publication of Michel Foucault's work in the late 1970s inspired a widespread rethinking of the history of sexuality.[27] Foucault suggests that sexuality is not regulated only through proscription and prohibition, but produced through prescription and incitement. In other words, it is not simply a matter of being told what not to do, but being shown what it is possible to do and what should be done. He argues that the nineteenth century was not a period of silence around the sexual, but one in which there was a 'discursive explosion' around sexuality, a cataloguing and categorising of individual acts and proclivities which gave rise to a new sexual lexicon. This brought into being the concept of sexuality as we understand it today, and made it possible to name a diverse range of sexualities, such as nymphomania, homosexuality or necrophilia. These were thought of as properties of persons, intrinsic to one's inner being, rather than merely a description of specific acts. Hence it became possible, for example to *be* a homosexual. Sexology came into being as a mode of regulation, a means of controlling through classifying, distinguishing 'normal' sexuality from 'pathological' forms. Thus sexuality was increasingly subject to medical gaze, and was no longer merely a matter of morality. At the same time, making sexuality a basis for the ascription of identities made it possible for those so identified to resist negative definitions and develop alternatives. For example, there could be no movement for homosexual liberation without a past history which defined homosexuals as a social category.

Although Foucault himself pays little attention to gender and regards the regulation of women's sexuality as only one form of regulation amongst many, feminists have found much in his work useful.[28] In particular, it allows us to see female sexuality as socially constructed and reconstructed in complex and often contradictory ways rather than as simply being repressed. This facilitates a more nuanced understanding of the changes which took place in the nineteenth century, when earlier ideas of women as lustful temptresses gave way to a notion of women as 'naturally' pure. Seeing this as a repression of earlier free expression is overly simplistic. In the first place it ignores the forms of regulation which were imposed on women in earlier centuries, and, secondly, it disguises the multiplicity of meanings which accreted around female sexuality in the Victorian era. Women were thought to be asexual in the sense of having no autonomous desire, but saturated with sexuality in that they were governed by their sexual organs. Having no desires of their own, they were none the less supposed to be susceptible to seduction and thus could easily be dislodged from their pedestal, becoming 'fallen women'. Even in their 'pure' state women's bodily functions – such as menstruation – were seen as polluting, their reproductive organs as drains which needed to be sluiced out at regular intervals.[29]

This appreciation of the complexities of female sexuality underpins Poovey's account of medical intervention in childbirth in the nineteenth century (Reading 1.2). From a different, but equally social constructionist, understanding of this period, Sheila Jeffreys offers an account of the invention of lesbianism and the subsequent pathologising of women's close friendships (Reading 1.3). Jeffreys emphasises the co-option of women into heterosexuality as a manifestation of patriarchal power. This differentiates her perspective from a Foucauldian one: the latter conceptualises power as more diffuse, multi-faceted and located in diverse discursive practices. Poovey, while influenced by Foucault's historical analysis also pays attention to the material underpinnings of power in specific sets of social relations.

If, as these arguments suggest, sexuality is a social construct and ideas about female sexuality shift historically, how does this affect our individual desires and conduct? Do we simply internalise and express forms of sexuality appropriate to our culture and time or is the relationship between cultural mores and individual subjectivity less mechanistic and more open? Feminists have long been aware that our individual sexualities are profoundly influenced, yet not wholly determined, by the cultures we inhabit. Developing a means of theorising this, accounting for both socio-cultural structures and individual agency, is an ongoing project for feminists. One obvious and established body of theory which addresses this issue is psychoanalysis. Feminists originally found Freud's view of female sexuality – as shaped by penis envy, as inevitably passive and masochistic – both implausible and misogynist (see Reading 1.5). Later, less literal and more symbolic readings of Freud, inspired by the French psychoanalyst Jacques Lacan, found favour among some feminists.[30] The attraction of this perspective is its emphasis on the cultural and linguistic structures in which we are positioned in becoming sexed subjects, and its representation of feminine sexual identity as a precarious accomplishment (see Reading 1.6). The Lacanian version of psychoanalysis remains androcentric, placing the symbolic phallus – if not the literal penis – at the centre of culture. This has led some feminists influenced by Lacan to seek alternative formulations. One possibility is to challenge phallic privilege by exploring the possibility of a female sexuality founded on women's bodily specificity rather than defining it in terms of male sexuality. It is this project which is particularly associated with Luce Irigaray (Reading 1.7).[31]

Many feminists, however, remain sceptical of the entire psychoanalytic enterprise. Since it offers a universalistic theory of subjectivity, it is very difficult to reconcile with historical understandings of sexuality as changing over time. Even in the Lacanian version, which suggests that sexed, desiring subjects are constituted through their entry into language and culture, this refers not to a specific language and culture, but to the very process of becoming a 'speaking subject'. It is difficult to challenge its phallocentricity without assuming some essential pre-cultural female sexuality. Because psychoanalysts conflate gender and sexuality, reducing both to the gender of our 'object choice', they cannot adequately account for lesbian and homosexual desire without falling back on ideas about masculinised women and effeminate men. In psychoanalytic theory, being a woman means desiring a man: where does this leave women who desire women?

Despite these and many other criticisms, psychoanalysis retains a strong foothold within feminist theorising on sexuality. It is still often treated as if it were the only perspective which can explain our individual sexual desires. Its influence may be due, in part, to the lack of viable alternatives. It is not that there are no other theories, but that they are either inadequate or underdeveloped. Traditional social scientific theories of socialisation have generally been abandoned as far too mechanistic and deterministic. A few feminists have drawn on the interactionist tradition which focuses on the negotiation of sexual meanings and posits individual subjects as active agents in the construction of their own sexual identities (see Reading 1.5). Others have brought Foucauldian perspectives to bear on the problem of subjectivity. Wendy Hollway, for example, analyses the ways in which men and women can position themselves as sexual subjects and objects within the discourses available to them (Reading 1.8). Neither of these perspectives has been fully developed and both share a major conceptual problem: they are not conducive to a structural analysis of the power relations between men and women in relation to their understandings of subjective and intersubjective processes. The lack of a convincing alternative to psychoanalysis is a major gap in feminist theory and one which, in our view, deserves more attention.

We are now entering a phase in which feminists are re-evaluating past work on the social construction of gender and sexuality and assessing its strengths and weaknesses. One question which has been raised, in particular by Diana Fuss, is whether it is possible to escape entirely from essentialist thinking and whether we are in danger of posing a false dichotomy between essentialism and constructionism.[32] Similarly, Carole Vance has drawn our attention to different degrees of social constructionism and asks whether those theories which conceptualise sexual desires themselves as constructed are in danger of ignoring the body, treating sexuality as disembodied.[33] The challenge which faces us here, and which feminists are now taking up, is to develop a theory of the body as itself socially constructed while being experienced as a material, physical presence.[34] A related issue is the way in which feminists have developed their arguments about the social construction of gender and sexuality by drawing contrasts between humans as social and animals as natural. In the final reading of this section, Lynda Birke suggests that we think again about our depiction of animals and that this could serve to strengthen, rather than weaken, social constructionist theory.

We remain firmly committed to the social constructionist project, which we see as both theoretically and politically necessary for feminism. There are a number of problems with essentialism. In the first place, it rests on something unknowable, a hypothesised 'natural' sexuality somehow uncontaminated by cultural influences. As a result, it cannot adequately explain cultural and historical variations in human sexuality – differential repression is too crude a concept to capture the complexities of such variations. Furthermore, it conceptualises the social regulation of sexuality as a negative force and hence does not allow for the productive deployment of power in the shaping of sexuality. It cannot account for differences in masculine and feminine sexuality except in terms of 'natural' differences or differential repression. Either women and men are innately different and nothing can change this, or women's sexuality is seen as more repressed than that of men. This latter view takes current definitions of male sexuality as the bench-mark of unrepressed sexuality, in other words what sexuality should be like. Few feminists would find the political consequences of this acceptable. Subsumed within this paradigm is an equation of normal sexuality with heterosexuality, thus its assumptions are both sexist and heterosexist.

It may be tempting to imagine an innate female potential for sexual pleasure, which is denied to us within patriarchal societies,[35] but this presupposes that there is such a thing as an innate sexuality which can be freed from social constraints. Clearly, no such sexuality can ever exist, since we have no way of conceptualising it outside of language and culture. Human sexuality has always been a social product and will continue to be so, in whatever form of society comes into being in the future. The appeal of the concept of repression is that it can carry a sense of the damage and danger women have experienced in the sexual arena. However, this idea is better expressed as oppression rather than repression. Whereas the concept of repression suggests the holding back of some underlying force, oppression focuses attention on social relations of power and domination.

HETEROSEXUALITY AND LESBIANISM

An incipient critique of heterosexuality was evident in discussions among feminists from the earliest years of WLM, and it was not long before lesbianism began to be seen as both a viable alternative and a form of resistance to patriarchal domination. Debates on lesbianism and heterosexuality subsequently proved to be a source of tension within the WLM. This tension has at times been destructive, in that it caused major rifts within the women's movement, but it has also proved productive in that it has forced us to theorise heterosexuality more adequately.

In the early days of second wave feminism, discussions of sexuality took it to be synonymous with heterosexuality and focused on women's struggles to derive satisfaction from relationships with men. It was argued that heterosexuality, as currently practised, prioritised male pleasure in stressing penetrative sex as 'the real thing' and perpetuating the myth of the vaginal orgasm. Anne Koedt's article (Reading 2.1) was particularly influential at that time in alerting women to the ways in which they had been duped into expecting to derive maximum pleasure from minimal clitoral contact.[36] Although the basis of the argument – that female orgasm was centred on the clitoris rather than the vagina – derived from mainstream sexological research[37] feminists were able to appropriate it for their own purposes. Koedt and others argued that this 'discovery' called for a rethinking of sexual practice, a deprioritising of penetrative sex, and that it rendered the penis more or less irrelevant to women's sexual satisfaction. Koedt's critique was well aimed. For many women, steeped in the mythology of male sexual needs and female sexual obligations, the idea that they had a right to pleasure at all was relatively new. By the 1970s, the knowledge that sex could and should be pleasurable for women had seeped into mainstream culture, but many young women outside feminist circles remained in ignorance of their own sexual anatomy and orgasmic potential.[38] Even now, when such knowledge circulates widely in the pages of magazines such as *Cosmopolitan*, young heterosexual women still have difficulty in defining and demanding their own pleasure (see Reading 2.2).

Koedt suggested that men might not be necessary to women's sexual pleasure, but she did not extend this to advocacy of lesbianism. Over the next few years, however, feminist debates became increasingly focused on lesbianism and lesbian sexuality. Lesbians had been visible in WLM from the beginning but the role they played depended on their own political commitments and the response to them on the part of heterosexual feminists. The precise details of the relationship between lesbian and heterosexual feminists varied from one country to another. In Britain and the USA, the gay and feminist movements emerged more or less simultaneously, at the end of the 1960s, and the more radical elements of both movements saw themselves as facing a common enemy: the patriarchal establishment. In both countries the Gay Liberation Front (GLF) sought to establish alliances with other oppressed groups and identified 'the roots of women's oppression as in many ways similar to [their] own'.[39] Many lesbians became active in sexual politics through the GLF, or combined involvement in both gay and feminist politics. Before long, however, the male-dominated agenda of gay politics led to widespread disillusionment.[40] Nor were lesbians universally accepted in the women's movement. In the USA, the movement had a strong reformist current represented by the National Organization of Women (NOW). Although lesbians joined, they were not made welcome in an organisation seeking to represent the 'respectable' face of feminism. Betty Friedan, a prominent member of NOW, dubbed them the 'lavender menace', provoking a demonstration of lesbians at the second NOW congress in 1970.[41] While this led to a change of policy within NOW and an affirmation of women's right to define their own sexuality, lesbianism continued to be regarded as problematic within this liberal feminist tendency. It was largely radical feminists, in the USA and elsewhere, who made lesbianism a central political issue. Those New York women who had protested at the marginalisation of lesbians formed the Radicalesbians who, in 1970, produced a paper entitled 'Woman-identified woman', one of the first statements which located lesbianism as a form of resistance to patriarchy. 'A lesbian is the rage of all women condensed to the point of explosion',[42] they wrote, and went on to argue that as long as women put their energies into relationships with individual men, this held back their own liberation and the liberation of all women. Lesbians, by contrast, gave all their energies to their sisters rather than their oppressors. In the years which followed, many feminists in North America, Europe and Australasia developed this stance, which came to be known as political lesbianism.

Outside the USA, the reformist, liberal variant of feminism was less developed and there was less overt opposition to lesbians within the movement. In Britain, for example, the main currents in the WLM were radical and socialist feminism, and lesbians were prominent in both groupings. None the less, there was still some unease about lesbianism and a tendency for heterosexual feminists to resist the derogation of feminists as 'a bunch of man-hating dykes' by insisting on their own 'normality'. The early agenda of the WLM in Britain, as elsewhere, excluded specifically lesbian concerns, and it was not until 1974 that the right to a self-defined sexuality and the end of discrimination against lesbians was added to the list of the movement's demands.[43] By this time, lesbian feminism had become a vocal tendency within the British movement. Many hitherto heterosexual women came out as lesbians in this period, defining themselves as such in terms of their politics and lifestyle rather than as a result of some innate predisposition.[44] Thus lesbianism was seen by some as a choice any woman could make, as in the slogan 'any woman can'. None the less, there was also a recognition of the many constraints which kept women heterosexual. The critique of heterosexuality went much further than discontent with male sexual ineptitude. Heterosexuality was seen as an institution through which men appropriated women's bodies and their labour. Romantic attachment to men led only to exploitation. As another popular slogan put it: 'It starts when you sink into his arms and ends with your arms in his sink.' Political lesbianism was thus an escape from and a challenge to patriarchal domination.

Political lesbianism in this sense was most commonly found among those who already held radical feminist views, who saw patriarchy as a system of male dominance. Some of these women became 'separatist' in orientation, rejecting all personal contact and political alliances with men. It was tensions between these radical lesbians and other feminists which, by the end of the 1970s, were to prove particularly disruptive for the WLM. The rifts thus created, alongside other divisions, made a unified women's movement increasingly difficult to sustain.[45] However, there was no simple split between lesbian and heterosexual women. Many lesbian feminists rejected separatism as a political solution, especially where it implied criticism of those women who remained heterosexual. Those who had been lesbians before the rise of the WLM, so-called 'real lesbians', were often sceptical of the zeal of recent converts, and concerned about the authenticity of their desires.[46] Lesbian socialist feminists, for whom sexuality was a less central political issue, largely remained aloof from disputes about political lesbianism. Lesbian radical feminists were to be found on both sides of the divide, causing acute and painful splits within radical feminism. More positively, the debate this engendered produced a fuller theorisation both of the critique of heterosexuality and of the politics of lesbianism.

One of the landmark publications of this period was Adrienne Rich's 'Compulsory heterosexuality and lesbian existence' (Reading 2.3). Rich focused on the institutionalisation of heterosexuality, arguing that what was assumed to be a 'natural' choice was in fact imposed upon women. Rather than emphasising the differences between lesbian and heterosexual women, she posited the existence of a lesbian continuum on which all women could be placed. Some other lesbians felt that Rich's notion of a continuum denied the specificity of lesbian sexuality and lesbians' oppression as lesbians. On the other hand, those identifying themselves as radical lesbians thought that Rich did not go far enough, that she focused too much on women's coercion into heterosexuality rather than on the oppressive nature of the institution itself.[47]

Rich's critique of heterosexuality in no way implied a personal criticism of heterosexual feminists – indeed this is one reason why radical lesbians objected to it. Sheila Jeffreys claims that it 'seems to allow heterosexual women to continue their relationships with men while feeling politically validated in sharing a lesbian continuum'.[48] Other analyses being produced at that time were certainly far more discomfiting for heterosexual feminists, as well as for those lesbians who did not want to dissociate themselves from their heterosexual sisters. The idea that heterosexual feminists were traitors to the cause had been in circulation since the early 1970s, but gained momentum in Europe towards the end of the decade. The final WLM conference in Britain in 1978, disintegrated into chaotic warring factions over this issue. The following year a group known as the Leeds Revolutionary Feminists circulated a paper entitled 'Political lesbianism: the case against heterosexuality', which strongly implied that heterosexuality and feminism were mutually exclusive.[49] This provoked further heated debate and served to draw a sharp demarcation between radical and revolutionary feminists.[50] Radical feminists, whether lesbian or heterosexual, insisted that the WLM was for all women and that all women shared a common oppression.

An equally acrimonious dispute occurred in France, where public debate on radical lesbianism was sparked off by the publication of Monique Wittig's 'The straight mind' in *Questions Féministes* early in 1980 (see Reading 2.4), followed by a further article 'One is not born a woman' in the next issue of the journal. Lesbians, according to Wittig, were fugitives from the patriarchal class system in which women are defined by their subordination to men, hence her conclusion that 'lesbians are not women'. In Parisian feminist circles during that year, heterosexual women found themselves castigated as collaborators, while those lesbians who defended them were damned as 'kapos'[51] and even denied the status of lesbians by being referred to as 'homosexual women'. Many radical feminists, both heterosexual and lesbian, took an opposing stance, including Marie-Jo Dhavernas (Reading 2.5). Like their sisters in Britain they were highly critical of the vanguardist stance taken by radical lesbians and saw them as turning the women's movement against women, of seeing heterosexual women – rather than men or patriarchy – as the enemy.[52]

These debates were almost exclusively conducted without reference to other divisions between women. In posing men as the class enemy, class in its wider social sense was ignored as were racial divisions. The ways in which women are located within the intersection between various forms of oppression profoundly influence their experience of both lesbianism and heterosexuality (see Readings 2.6 and 2.9). As a black lesbian, Cheryl Clarke (Reading 2.6), finds herself fighting on several fronts, against homophobia and sexism in both black and white communities, as well as against white racism. This issue raised questions of difference within feminism more widely, causing feminists to reassess theories of male domination, to look for ways of taking account of the complexities and contradictions inherent in women's lives.[53] One result of this was an exploration of the potential for feminist theorising within poststructuralism and postmodernism.[54]

Among Left academics in particular, disillusionment with traditional Marxism rendered poststructuralist and postmodernist perspectives attractive. Once appropriated by feminist and gay theorists, and applied to sexuality, this tendency ultimately led to the development of Queer theory.[55] Rather than setting up categories such as 'lesbian' as the basis of political identities, Queer sought to destablise the binary oppositions between men and women and straight and gay. Such identities were not seen as authentic properties of individual subjects, but as fluid and shifting, to be adopted and discarded, played with and subverted, strategically deployed in differing contexts (see Reading 2.7). Radical lesbian perspectives were regarded as essentialist in that they cast lesbianism as a fixed point outside of, and in opposition to, patriarchal relations.[56] Politically the aim of Queer theory is to demonstrate that gender and sexual categories are not given realities but are 'regulatory fictions', products of discourse.[57] Here Queer theory converges with Queer politics, in the latter's playing out of parodic performances at street level, for example holding public 'kiss-ins' and mock weddings, and the notion of 'gender fuck' – challenging gender categories through dress and transgressive sexual performance.[58]

> Queer means to fuck with gender. There are straight queers, bisexual queers, tranny queers, lez queers, fag queers, SM queers, fisting queers in every single street in this apathetic country of ours.[59]

This quotation says two things about Queer. First, that the label does not attach exclusively to lesbians and gay men, but can include bisexuals – previously excluded from both lesbian feminism and gay activism. It can encompass heterosexual activity between lesbians and gay men and even between heterosexuals if their practices are sufficiently disruptive of straight sexual conventions.

> Heterosexual behaviour does not always equal 'straight'. When I strap on a dildo and fuck my male partner, we are engaged in 'heterosexual' behaviour, but I can tell you it feels altogether queer, and I'm sure my grandmother and Jessie Helms would say the same.[60]

So, no doubt, would Mary Whitehouse! This further illustrates a second key feature of Queer, implicit in both the above quotations, that the transgression of moral and gender boundaries is seen as subversive. Claire Hemmings argues that, in the context of bisexuality, such performances destablise the hierarchical ordering of heterosexuality.[61] Elizabeth Wilson contests Hemmings's interpretation, arguing that such acts could easily be incorporated into a conventional, if 'kinky', heterosexual couple's repertoire without having any such destablising consequences.[62]

Queer politics also entails a realigning of lesbians with gay men rather than with feminism. In the context of AIDS and attacks on gay men and lesbians by the moral Right, many lesbian feminists felt that the old alliance with gay men should be resurrected. Not all of these women identified with Queer, but this alliance, combined with a dissatisfaction with the prescriptiveness of radical lesbianism, led many lesbians to engage with these new forms of political activism. Others remained more sceptical. Rather than the radical departure it purports to be, Queer can be seen as just another identity politics. Moreover, although it claims to be a means of working across differences and disrupting boundaries, it can turn out to be yet another means by which white gay men impose their agenda upon sexual politics, and ignore the constraints imposed by institutionalised racial and sexual oppression. This point has been made by a number of prominent black lesbian activists.[63]

Queer theory and Queer politics are not entirely synonymous. In so far as Queer activism affirms a new oppositional identity, it conflicts with the emphasis in Queer theory on deconstructing all such identity categories. While academic theorists are engaged in challenging the 'compulsory order of sex/gender/desire',[64] much of the blurring of gender categories within gay culture is occurring at the level of style rather than politics.[65] We ourselves doubt whether wearing a tutu with Doc Martins will bring patriarchy to its knees. Moreover, the prominence of Queer theory may have more to do with the making of academic reputations than with furthering grass-roots struggles, and may be explicable in terms of academic rather than street politics (see Reading 2.8). Much of this theory is couched in a language inaccessible to those outside the intellectual clique which produces it.

> As one lesbian femme explained, she likes her boys to be girls, meaning that 'being a girl' contextualizes and resignifies 'masculinity' in a butch identity. As a result, that masculinity, if that it can be called, is always brought into relief against a culturally intelligible 'female body.' It is precisely this dissonant juxtaposition and the sexual tension that its transgression generates that constitute the object of desire.[66]

It is doubtful whether those depicted here would recognise themselves.

In the meantime older debates have not gone away, although the recent spate of writings on heterosexuality engage to some extent with Queer theory and politics.[67] The questions of whether heterosexual sex is necessarily oppressive for women, and whether heterosexuality is a tenable practice for feminists is still under discussion. Heterosexuality does not necessarily have the same meaning for all women. Just as black lesbians, who have always allied with black men against racism, are less impressed with Queer's transgression of women-only politics than their white sisters, so black heterosexual women do not necessarily see relationships with men as politically reactionary (see Reading 2.9). Heterosexual feminists more generally are still struggling to retain a critical stance on the institution of heterosexuality while engaged in redefining its practices and renegotiating relationships with men (Reading 2.10). This raises a number of questions about the pleasures and dangers of sexuality for women.

POWER, PLEASURE AND THE SEX WARS

There has long been a tension in feminist thinking about sexuality between the potentially pleasurable aspects of sex and its dangers. Heterosexuality has always been risky for women, whether in terms of the double standard and fears of loss of 'reputation' or of pregnancy, disease, violence and coercion. At the same time, as discussed in the previous section, there has been a concern with pleasure and the lack of it. All this is bound up with the larger issue of power: heterosexuality is constructed around a hierarchy of gender evident in its specifically sexual practices as elsewhere. Lesbianism is a potential escape from this, a more pleasurable and less risky alternative, yet lesbians are not immune from the heterosexual ordering of desire which shapes all our sexualities. What counts as erotic is itself socially constructed in terms of relations of dominance, to the extent that it is difficult even to think of sex outside of the patriarchal language and culture which shape our thoughts, desires and fantasies.

Much of feminist critique has been concerned with heterosexuality as a locus of male power, with the policing of women through coercive sex, with the continuities between 'normal' heterosexual practice and sexual violence and abuse. One strand of radical feminism identifies sexuality as a key site of women's oppression. Kate Millett, for example, in one of the earliest radical feminist texts, argued that women's oppression began in the bedroom and from there infected all aspects of social life.[68] One of the strongest theoretical elaborations on the centrality of sexuality in maintaining women's subordination is that developed by Catharine MacKinnon (Reading 3.1). MacKinnon draws upon Marxist class analysis in arguing that, just as the exploitation of labour is the root of capitalist class relations, so sexual exploitation is fundamental to male dominance, hence to the unequal relations between women and men.[69]

Many feminists have developed analyses of sexual violence which have underlined the ways in which it serves as a mechanism of social control, keeping women in their place.[70] One key theme which has emerged from much of this work is the linkage between the standard pattern of heterosexual encounters and coercive and violent sex. Within dominant cultural discourses, men are cast as the active initiators of sexual activity and women as passive recipients of male advances; men's desires are seen as uncontrollable urges which women are paradoxically expected both to satisfy and to restrain. These dynamics have been analysed in relation to a range of phenomena from everyday sexual harassment on the streets or at work, to rape, murder and the sexual abuse of children.[71] The parallels between these various forms of coercive sexuality and 'normal' heterosexuality have led a number of feminists to think in terms of a continuum of violence (see Reading 3.2).[72]

Feminists have seen sexual violence as an enactment of male power. In order to counteract the tendency to see acts such as rape as simply a form of seduction using undue force, feminists have tended to emphasise the power relations rather than sexual relations in this context. The regularity with which male sexuality finds violent expression has, however, led many feminists to consider the ways in which power is itself eroticised within contemporary culture.[73] Deborah Cameron and Elizabeth Frazer illustrate the ways in which this eroticisation of power can lead to the extreme of murder (Reading 3.3). Their analysis is particularly interesting in that they argue that such acts are not the result of a generalised misogyny, but are enacted as a result of the specific ways in which masculine subjectivity is constructed in modern societies.

Sexual violence has been a major focus of feminist activism. On the surface it would appear to be an issue around which feminists could unite, since all women, whatever their class, 'race' or sexual orientation can be subject to violence or the threat of violence. In practice, however, this has proved a thorny issue, especially in terms of the intersections between racial and sexual oppression (Reading 3.4). Sexual violence has very specific meanings for black women, since routine sexual exploitation, coercion and brutality towards women have been very much a part of the history of slavery and colonialism. This renders it inseparable from racism: enslaved and colonised women have been subject to specific racialised forms of patriarchal oppression and sexualised forms of racial oppression.[74] This is complicated by the ways in which black masculinity under colonial and slave regimes has been constructed as a threat to white women, which was used to legitimate forms of control and punishment from lynchings and beatings through to legislation limiting black men's access to white women.[75] Historically white men's 'protection' of 'their' women has existed side by side with their gross exploitation of black women. The forms of activism engaged in by white feminists have often been attacked on the grounds of insensitivity to these issues. For example 'reclaim the night' marches, which called for a curfew on men, failed to acknowledge that black men do not have the same freedom of the streets enjoyed by white men, that they have been vulnerable to both police harassment and racist attacks.

Another source of dissent from feminist activism and scholarship around sexual violence is voiced by those who feel that too much emphasis has been placed on sexual danger at the expense of sexual pleasure. The point has been made particularly strongly by feminists with a libertarian perspective on sexuality.[76] The issue of sexual pleasure is taken up by Amber Hollibaugh in Reading 3.5. Hollibaugh does not only argue for a recognition of sexual pleasure, but suggests that power itself can be a source of eroticism and that we should not deny this potential in ourselves. This is taken further in Pat Califia's explicit defence of sadomasochism (Reading 3.6). These articles exemplify one of the opposing positions in what became known as the 'feminist sex wars'. Other feminists strongly object to this rehabilitation of power as a source of pleasure (see Readings 3.3 and 3.7).

The libertarian stance has primarily been adopted by those lesbian feminists who have maintained allegiances with gay men.[77] For these theorists the emphasis has moved from gender oppression to sexual oppression. This is coupled with a desire to re-eroticise lesbian sex, to challenge what is seen as a puritanical orthodoxy with lesbian feminism, summed up by the term 'vanilla' sex.[78] In casting themselves as 'outlaw' lesbians, libertarians such as Gayle Rubin have defended other so-called sexual minorities and in so doing have denied the importance of gender hierarchy.[79] The whole range of outlaw sexualities are seen as equally worthy of protection from oppression and opprobrium, without any apparent awareness that there is a world of difference between a street prostitute and a millionaire pornographer or between a man who has sex with a child and that child. This defence of sexual pluralism loses sight of the basis on which feminists originally developed their critique of power and dominance in sexual relations, through questioning the hierarchical basis of heterosexuality. Many of the sexualities currently being defended or promoted reproduce these hierarchies whether in the form of sado-masochism or 'cross-generational relations' (Rubin's euphemism for pederasty). Generally such practices are defended only in the context of lesbian and gay relationships – libertarian feminists refrain from suggesting that, for example, heterosexual sado-masochism is acceptable. They maintain that sado-masochistic practices do not have the same meaning where they are not part of the institutionalised hierarchy, and moral privileging, of heterosexuality (see Reading 3.6). As Deborah Cameron and Elizabeth Frazer point out, this argument fails to ask where these desires come from and therefore assumes that they are 'natural' or given (Reading 3.3). Those critical of the libertarians do not deny that we all experience desires which entail the eroticisation of power, but suggest that we should subject such desires to critical scrutiny rather than simply celebrate them.

These debates have been occurring in the context of increasing concern about AIDS and therefore about the potential dangers attached to certain sexual practices.[80] Fear of the risk of HIV transmission might seem to close down the potential for sexual pleasure and exploration, but some feminists have argued that safer sex could be better sex, especially in the heterosexual context. While libertarian lesbians have been seeking to bring power back into sex, including penetrative sex, other feminists have sought to increase women's pleasure through decentring penetration and arguing for more egalitarian forms of heterosexual practice. While safer sex in government health campaign literature has tended to mean sex as before,[81] but with a condom, some feminists have drawn on earlier critiques of heterosexuality in order to promote alternative sexual practices (see Reading 3.8).[82] The reality of heterosexual relationships, however, works against women redefining sexual practices. The balance of power in such relationships, along with wider cultural discourses and the sexual scripts which men and women draw on, militate against women negotiating safer sex (Reading 3.9).

The final readings in this section deal with what counts as sex and what counts as pleasure in the 1990s, with the ways in which eroticism is discursively constructed and produced in practice (Readings 3.10 and 3.11). In discussing lesbian sex, Diane

Richardson raises the issue of the lack of a language with which to describe both practices and pleasures (Reading 3.11). This lack is also evident in heterosexual relations, where pleasure has long been defined from a masculine perspective (Reading 3.9). While we have been critical of libertarian perspectives, we believe that the pursuit of pleasure is a positive goal for feminists. In pursuing this goal, however, we need to retain a critical stance on the ways in which our desires have been constructed within a heterosexually ordered patriarchal society, and remain aware of the material constraints which limit the pleasure we can currently attain. The polarisation of the debate between libertarian and anti-libertarian feminists has made it difficult to theorise a space between these two positions in which we can explore both power and pleasure and their interconnections. Linda Singer expresses some similar misgivings about the terms of current debates, arguing for a new sexual politics which takes account of the specific local and global contexts within which our sexual practices are located (Reading 3.10). In accepting the need to contextualise specific sexual practices and relationships, however, we would not want to lose sight of the broader, structural inequalities within which we live out our sexual lives.

SELLING SEX

In many respects feminist debates on pornography and prostitution mirror those we outlined in the previous section. Pornography is another central issue in the 'sex wars'; on one side are those who see pornography as centrally implicated in women's oppression and who campaign vigorously against it, while on the other are those who seek to appropriate erotic imagery for women, and who oppose any move towards tighter regulation of pornography.[83] Pornography and prostitution are linked in a variety of ways. Both involve the commodification of sexuality within the marketplace where the buyers are predominately men. In both cases the appropriation of women's bodies by men occurs through the medium of a cash nexus. This also raises questions about the social construction of male sexuality, of why men are the main buyers of sex, since both male and female prostitution exist largely for men. Men are seen as having sexual 'needs' which must be met. If they do not have access to a regular sexual partner, then an 'outlet' must be found elsewhere. Therefore prostitution is often explained as providing a necessary service. It is this hydraulic model of male sexuality which feminist analysis has sought to challenge.[84]

Both prostitution and pornography provide employment for women and raise more general questions about the exploitation of women in the labour market and also about the conditions under which this particular group of women work. Women's involvement in sex work is directly related to their lack of economic opportunities elsewhere. We need, then, to consider what is general to women as workers and what is specific to work within the sex industries. When we consider women's position as workers in this way, we should recall that feminists have always made connections between women's paid work in the labour market and their unpaid work in the home. The cash nexus disguises the continuities between commercialised sex and the private unpaid sexual services women routinely provide for men. In the case of prostitution in particular parallels can be drawn with marriage, since marriage has traditionally given men 'conjugal rights' over their wives' bodies in exchange for maintenance. Thus a wife can be seen as having a single employer while a prostitute works on freelance terms. In an early feminist analysis of prostitution, Ellen Strong, herself previously a hooker, argued this case. Having pointed out that all women learn to trade their sexual attractions and favours for economic support, she comments:

> all the hustler has done is to eliminate the flowery speeches and put things where they're really at. Without the games, she will trade what is regarded as a commodity anyway, for what she wants.[85]

Sex work, however, involves more than market relations. It entails specifically sexual forms of exploitation and depends upon the commodification of women's sexuality. It is not just exploitation *per se* which is addressed by feminist critiques of pornography and prostitution, but the ways in which this intersects with other oppressive aspects of sexuality, in particular with sexual violence and the prioritisation of male sexual 'needs'.

Feminists have been addressing these issues for over a century. Judith Walkowitz (Reading 4.1) draws out connections between Victorian campaigns around prostitution and the politics of pornography today. What makes these particularly tricky issues for feminists is that they are also the focus of attention from the moral Right. It is therefore imperative that the feminist aim of liberating women is differentiated from the moralists' goal of reinforcing the patriarchal family. Feminists campaigning against pornography have often found themselves in uneasy alliances with the Right, leaving them open to attack from other feminists, particularly those arguing from socialist or libertarian positions.[86] Walkowitz shows how these problems have bedevilled feminists since the nineteenth century, when those who sought an end to sexual exploitation found their campaigns hijacked by those moralists who wanted to keep women in a 'protected', and hence subordinate, place within the family.[87]

Whereas the moral Right's objections to pornography are framed in terms of 'obscenity', a specifically feminist critique of pornography arises from wider concerns about women's control of their own bodies. It entails women's refusal to be reduced to their physical sexuality and resistance to our subordination as objects for male use and pleasure. The appropriation of women's bodies by men is a fundamental feminist issue,[88] which is why some feminists have put so much energy into combating pornography, sexual exploitation and violence. Andrea Dworkin, a prominent campaigner against pornography, draws our attention to the connections between pornography and prostitution, through the representation of woman as whore who exists only to serve men's sexual 'needs' (Reading 4.2). The whore can only figure in male imagination under patriarchal domination, within which women are reduced to their sex.

One feminist response to women being reduced to sexual objects is to turn the tables on men, to argue that heterosexual women can gain pleasure from looking at representations of the male body, that if each sex objectifies the other then the situation is no longer one of inequality. Even if it were possible to reorder our desires so that women gained the same pleasure from the act of looking, to overcome the centuries of male dominance within which the male and female gaze have been differently constructed, and to counter the economic domination which ensures that the mass production of representations remains under male control, the idea that objectifying men solves the problem is fatally flawed. Susanne Kappeler addresses this problem in Reading 4.3, analysing what it means to turn people into objects, to thus rob them of the status of subjects. Kappeler is not saying that other sexual practices can simply be 'read off' from pornography, or that pornography has specific effects outside of engagement with it. Rather representation and the act of looking are themselves material practices, and these material practices are themselves objectificatory. The objectification which is produced through these practices can only exist within a system of inequality and would be inconceivable if such inequality did not exist. While we accept that women can look at male bodies, and may even desire them, they do not look from a position of authority, and hence their looking lacks the sexual frisson men gain from power. Truly to objectify men would be to subordinate them, a goal which, in our view, is both unrealistic and undesirable.

Other forms of inequality can also lead to objectification and to the material appropriation of human bodies. This has been the case under systems of slavery and colonialism, where the bodies of the enslaved and colonised are variously used as instruments of labour, cleared from land wanted by the coloniser or ultimately physically destroyed and annihilated. As we argued in the previous section, enslaved and colonised women have been subjected to specific forms of subjugation in which racial and sexual oppression intersect in complex ways. The racism which is often a feature of pornography is not accidental, but is the product of the double objectification of black women as objects to be used by their white masters. The master–slave imagery so often used in pornography, and which positions the male spectator as master of what he surveys, would have no cultural or erotic significance without the history of white imperialism. Thus racism is not an accidental feature of pornography but is deeply embedded in symbolic repertoire. Hence Patricia Hill Collins argues that an analysis of racism is central to a full understanding of pornography (Reading 4.4). The reduction of black women to the status of whore is likewise central to prostitution.

The widespread availability of pornography within modern societies results from the development of mass media and communications technologies. It is no longer the property of the privileged, literate few. Dianne Butterworth discusses the most recent medium through which pornography is disseminated, through computer-generated imagery and the internet (Reading 4.5). In all the discussion about virtual reality and virtual sex, it is easy to forget that the production of pornography still ultimately involves real women and that it cannot have any meaning outside of power relations between men and women. Butterworth forcefully reminds us of this. What goes on in cyberspace, however 'virtual' it is, does interconnect with a web of material social practices. However, this should not be taken to imply a simple causal model in which pornography is held responsible for men's abuse and exploitation of women. One common criticism of anti-pornography feminists is that they see pornography as causing sexual violence and that they confuse what goes on at the level of fantasy with real social practices – as in the slogan 'Pornography is the theory, rape is the practice.'[89] There are problems with any attempt to 'prove' a causal link of this kind, as many feminists on both sides of the debate recognise. Most research which claims to do so, measures changes in men's attitudes after exposure to pornographic material under artificial conditions which bear little relation to the complexities of human actions in concrete social situations. Moreover, it is impossible to read off behaviour from beliefs and attitudes.[90] It is equally misguided to draw on research of this kind to demonstrate the absence of any relationship between pornography and the abuse of women – which some feminists opposed to anti-pornography campaigns try to do.[91] Deborah Cameron and Elizabeth Frazer argue that we should move beyond these disputes about causality and develop a more sophisticated understanding of the relationship between representations and behaviour (Reading 4.6). Rapists, murderers and abusers must derive the ideas for the scenarios they enact from somewhere; while pornography does not cause violence it does provide scripts which violent men can utilise. As Cameron and Frazer point out, human action, including sexual violence, is always meaningful for the actor; it always entails processes of interpretation in which human beings represent their actions to themselves. In so doing they make use of the forms of cultural representation available to them.

It is clear that neither male violence nor the production of pornography occur in a social vacuum: both depend upon the ideas circulating within a culture at any given time. Pornography draws on the wider cultural narratives through which masculinity and male sexuality are constructed and itself contributes to their construction and reconstruction. It helps to circulate and perpetuate particular versions of these narratives such as the mythology of women as sexually available, deriving pleasure from being dominated and possessed and a model of masculinity validated through sexual mastery over women. A man does not rape as a direct reaction to a pornographic stimulus; rather pornography contributes to the cultural construction of a particular form of masculinity and sexual desire which make rape possible and which script the possibilities for its enactment. Pornography is not, of course, the only form of representation implicated in these processes.

Pornographic representations are also produced and consumed within historically specific contexts. This point is made both by Cameron and Frazer and by Mary McIntosh (Reading 4.7). Whereas Cameron and Frazer locate pornography within modernist ideals of masculine transcendence,[92] McIntosh analyses the historical construction of the concept of pornography and the social contexts in which it became available. It was originally defined, in the nineteenth century, in terms of the then current norms of obscenity and the capacity of erotic material to deprave and corrupt. Only bourgeois men were deemed fit to be exposed to such material, protected from its purportedly deleterious effects by a supposed scholarly interest. Hence both the definition of, and access to, pornography were rooted in gender and class distinctions. McIntosh argues against the anti-pornography movement, suggesting that feminists should seek to subvert the morality through which pornography is defined. She exhorts us to adopt a politics of transgression and to develop our own alternative practices of erotic representation.

Pornography entails more than just representations since it involves the employment of women as models and actors. This is also a central issue in relation to prostitution. Indeed there is some overlap between those employed in these two forms of sex work, and in associated occupations such as stripping and hostessing. Anti-pornography campaigners tend to focus on the violence and degradation which women in the sex industry are subject. Others are wary of seeing prostitutes only as victims and are more concerned with conditions which might enable women to ply this trade in greater safety and exert more control over their working conditions and earnings. These are complex issues given the variety of forms prostitution takes, the varying social and economic context in which it occurs and cross-national variations in legislation surrounding it (see Reading 4.8).

Prostitution can be seen as a job like any other which women choose because it gives them a better deal than the available alternatives. Such a choice is clearly made within certain constraints and in some circumstances women, especially those from poorer countries, are coerced into prostitution. The term 'prostitutes' encompasses women commanding high fees from a select clientele, young homeless escapees from abuse living and working on the streets and Third World women ensnared into working in brothels all over the world.[93] It is not surprising then that women who have experience of this work can define it very differently. Some prostitutes' organisations, such as The English Collective of Prostitutes seek recognition as workers:

> The sex industry is not the only industry which is male dominated and degrades women, but it is the industry where the workers are illegal and can least defend publicly our right to our jobs.[94]

The emphasis here is on women's poverty, on prostitutes' need to work and the illegality which both limits where and how they can work and increases the dangers associated with the job. Prostitution is seen primarily as a class issue rather than a matter of specifically sexual exploitation, a position which aligns the English Collective of Prostitutes with certain forms of socialist feminist analysis. Thus feminist campaigns to limit kerb-crawling are seen as a threat to prostitutes' right to work. On the other hand, some ex-prostitutes organise around enabling women to escape from the abuse and coercion entailed in sex-work. This is more in keeping with a radical feminist analysis of the sexual subjugation of women. This is the line taken by WHISPER (Women Hurt by Systems of Prostitution Engaged in Revolt):

> We have chosen the acronym WHISPER because women in systems of prostitution do whisper among ourselves about the coercion, degradation, sexual abuse and battery in our lives . . . Our purpose is to make the sexual enslavement of women history.[95]

The diverse individual experiences of sex-work do not invalidate structural analyses of it. A feminist perspective should encompass both the economic relations which shape women's position within the sex industry and the patriarchal relations which make this particular form of exploitation possible. Central to the latter is the differential social construction of male and female sexuality which positions women as providers of sexual services and men as the purchasers. The research carried out in Norway by Cecilie Høigård and Liv Finstad provides a revealing account of the mismatch between prostitutes' feelings about commercial sexual relations and their clients' desires and fantasies (Reading 4.9). While the women distanced themselves from the sexual acts they engaged in, men often assumed that they were giving the women pleasure. Whatever their reading of the women's experience, men were able to gain pleasure from these encounters. Women who work as prostitutes may also, of course, engage in non-commercial sex for pleasure or as part of a valued relationship. For prostitutes who are heterosexual in their non-working lives, this entails marking a boundary between sex as work and sex as sex. In a study of London prostitute women Sophie Day and Helen Ward illustrate this distinction in relation to the use of condoms (Reading 4.10). A condom creates a physical barrier between the prostitute and her client's penis, whereas latex-free sex with a partner connotes intimacy and trust.

Our final reading (Reading 4.11) brings us back to the economic structures which underpin prostitution. The economics of prostitution involves not only local labour markets, but the global division of labour. Sexual tourism promises jaded business men 'exotic' women in exotic locations, and should once more alert us to the intersections between gender, 'race' and class. Third World women are constructed as exotically other, as docile and hospitable waiting to welcome the traveller. This imagery pervades much of the marketing of regular tourism in South East Asia,[96] and is easily transferred to commercial sex – the more so since it mirrors the wider market relationship between rich and poor nations. In the local context where young women are recruited, poverty is a major motivating factor for entry into sex-work.[97]

A final issue which deserves consideration here, which is raised in Reading 4.10, is that prostitution can expose women to the risk of infection with HIV and other sexually transmitted diseases (STDs). Prostitutes have, since the nineteenth century, been blamed for carrying disease and infecting men – thus absolving men from having infected them in the first place.[98] In the current context, prostitutes are among those held responsible for the spread of AIDS. In the West, prostitutes now routinely expect their clients to use condoms, but many men are still reluctant to do so and some will pay more, or resort to violence, to obtain unprotected sex. In an age of international travel a man can carry HIV from one side of the world to the other, thus subjecting women thousands of miles apart to a shared risk which is itself a product of male expectations of heterosexual practice.[99] The link this creates between such women does not, however, erase the vast inequality between a British middle-class wife and a Thai prostitute: the life expectancy of such women once infected with HIV is likely to be dramatically different, one product of the social and economic advantages of the former over the latter. Thus while male heterosexual practice may have globalising effects, these effects are mediated by the local contexts where their impact is felt.

CONCLUSION

Differences amongst women have emerged as a major issue in feminist theory in recent years, and there is still a great deal of work to be done in drawing out the consequences of these differences for women's experience of sexuality. Many feminist analyses of sexuality have tended to homogenise women as a category. The differences which have surfaced in this area of debate have often had more to do with differences in sexual practices and theoretical perspectives than with the different positions women occupy in local and global structures of inequality. If we are to appreciate the complexity and diversity of women's sexual lives and the relationship of sexuality to other aspects of women's subordination, a great deal more work needs to be done.

Feminist debates around sexuality have been framed from a Western perspective and the forms they have taken – and the heat they have generated – owe a great deal to the cultural significance of sexuality in modern Western societies. Sexuality is conventionally singled out as a 'special' area of life: it has been variously romanticised and tabooed, seen as a threat to civilisation or the route to social revolution, as a source of degradation and a means of personal growth. Whichever meanings it is accorded it is made to carry the burden of a host of aspirations and anxieties. Gayle Rubin calls this 'the fallacy of misplaced scale' and associates it with 'sex negativity', the ways in which our culture has associated sex with heinous sins.[100] We see this as a feature of positive attitudes to sex as well as negative ones. Sexuality may be feared as a source of dirt, disease and degradation, but it is equally revered as a gateway to ecstasy, enlightenment and emancipation. Feminists need to give more critical attention to this cultural obsession with sexuality, including the ways in which it shapes the discourses that we ourselves have produced.

We are not saying that sexuality is unimportant or an insignificant aspect of women's subordination. Rather we are suggesting that the material appropriation of women's bodies and the cultural significance accorded to sexuality are interrelated. We cannot afford to leave either of these aspects of sexuality unexamined since they only exist in relation to each other. If we concentrate on the appropriation of women's bodies without paying attention to the cultural meanings mapped on to these bodies, we are in danger of assuming some given male desire to possess women and risk succumbing to the essentialism which feminists have tried so hard to resist. If, on the other hand, we focus exclusively on the cultural meanings of sex, we are in danger of ignoring the material inequalities with which our sexual desires and practices are enmeshed.

NOTES

1. There are, however, two serious omissions: the work of Gayle Rubin and Carole Vance, which we had hoped to include in the collection. Unfortunately, both of these influential theorists refused us permission to reproduce extracts from their work.
2. The term 'second wave feminism' refers to the Women's Liberation Movement which emerged in most Western countries at the end of the 1960s and beginning of the 1970s. 'First wave feminism' generally means the feminism of the nineteenth and early twentieth century – although some would locate its origins earlier. Although usually associated with the demand for women's suffrage, first wave feminism encompassed a wide range of political campaigns.
3. For critical gay and feminist perspectives on the history of sexology see Jeffrey Weeks, *Sex Politics and Society: The Regulation of Sexuality Since 1800*, 2nd ed, London: Longman, 1989; and Margaret Jackson, *The Real Facts of Life: Feminism and the Politics of Sexuality c1850–1940*, London: Taylor & Francis, 1994.
4. For a selection of writings on gay and lesbian perspectives see Henry Abelove, Michèle Aina Barale and David Halperin (eds), *The Lesbian and Gay Studies Reader*, London: Routledge, 1993.
5. This distinction was first made by Robert Stoller in *Sex and Gender: On the Development of Masculinity and Femininity*, New York: Science House, 1968. Ann Oakley took up this distinction in *Sex, Gender and Society*, Oxford: Martin Robertson, 1972. It has since become commonplace in much feminist social scientific writing in English-speaking countries. An alternative formulation, that of a sex-gender system, was made by Gayle Rubin in a classic article entitled 'The traffic in women: notes on the "political economy" of sex', in R. Reiter

(ed.), *Towards an Anthropology of Women*, New York: Monthly Review Press, 1975. The term 'gender' is less often used by speakers of other European languages.

6. For overviews of these debates see Sue Scott and D.H.J. Morgan, 'Bodies in a social landscape', in Sue Scott and David Morgan (eds), *Body Matters*, London: Falmer Press, 1993; and Stevi Jackson, 'Gender and heterosexuality: a materialist feminist analysis', in Mary Maynard and June Purvis (eds), *(Hetero) sexual Politics*, London: Taylor & Francis, 1995.

7. For differing interpretations of first wave campaigns around sexuality, see Judith Walkowitz, 'The politics of prostitution', in Catherine R. Stimpson and Ethel Spector Person (eds), *Women, Sex and Sexuality*, Chicago: University of Chicago Press, 1980 (reprinted from *Signs*, 1980), and her *City of Dreadful Delight: Narratives of Sexual Danger in Late-Victorian London*, London: Virago, 1992; Ellen DuBois and Linda Gordon, 'Seeking ecstasy on the battlefield: danger and pleasure in nineteenth century feminist thought', in Carole S. Vance (ed.), *Pleasure and Danger: Exploring Female Sexuality*, London: Routledge, 1984; Sheila Jeffreys, *The Spinster and her Enemies*, London: Pandora 1985.

8. In terms of the intellectual influences of the time, there was an interest in Marx's early work on alienation, in existential philosophy and in the work of Frankfurt School theorists such as Reich and Marcuse.

9. See Weeks, *Sex Politics and Society*; Sheila Jeffreys, *Anti-Climax: A Feminist Perspective on the Sexual Revolution*, London: The Women's Press, 1990.

10. See Jeffreys, *Anti-Climax*; and the introduction to Ann Snitow, Catherine Stansell and Sharon Thompson, *Desire: The Politics of Sexuality*, London: Virago, 1984.

11. Marge Piercy, 'The Grand Coolie Damn', in Robin Morgan (ed.), *Sisterhood is Powerful: An Anthology of Writings from the Women's Liberation Movement*, New York: Vintage Books, 1970, p. 483.

12. The SNCC was a civil rights organisation, particularly active in registering black voters in the southern United States in the 1960s.

13. There were articles with these titles in one of the earliest North American collections of feminist writing, Robin Morgan's *Sisterhood is Powerful*.

14. All of these issues are covered in Morgan, *Sisterhood is Powerful*, with the exception of rape. One of the earliest discussions of rape is Susan Griffin's, 'Rape: the All American Crime', *Ramparts*, 10(3), 1971, pp. 2–8.

15. Christine Delphy, *Close to Home: A Material Analysis of Women's Oppression*, London: Hutchinson, 1984, p. 211.

16. The practice of classifying feminist thought into such categories as radical feminism, socialist feminism and liberal feminism is itself problematic for a number of reasons. In particular it tends to treat these categories as static and overemphasises the differences between them while ignoring differences within each of them. The result is often a set of unhelpful stereotypes. For an excellent discussion of these problems see Mary Maynard, 'Beyond the big three: the development of feminist theory into the 1990s', *Women's History Review*, 4(3), 1995, pp. 269–81.

17. See, for example, Juliet Mitchell, *Psychoanalysis and Feminism*, Harmondsworth: Penguin, 1975, or many of the articles in the journals *mf* and *Feminist Review*. In France, the group known as 'Psych et Po' has explicitly used psychoanalysis to argue that women's difference is suppressed and have also allied themselves to proletarian class struggle. See Simone de Beauvoir, 'Feminism – alive, well and in constant danger', in Robin Morgan (ed.), *Sisterhood is Global*, Harmondsworth: Penguin, 1985.

18. This is a widespread misapprehension, but some of those guilty of perpetuating it include Lynne Segal, *Is the Future Female?*, London: Virago, 1987; and Chris Weedon, *Feminist Practice and Poststructuralist Theory*, Oxford: Blackwell, 1987. An American version of this myth is to be found in Alice Echols, 'The taming of the id: feminist sexual politics, 1968–83', in Carole S. Vance (ed.), *Pleasure and Danger: Exploring Female Sexuality*. London: Routledge & Kegan Paul, 1984. Echols maintains that radical feminism, with its emphasis on gender and sexuality as socially constructed has given way to 'cultural feminism' which sees women's oppression as stemming from the repression of female values and which assumes that female sexuality is inherently different from that of men.

19. This view has been clearly expressed in their journals *Questions Féministes* and *Nouvelles Questions Féministes*.

20. This tendency is represented, for example, in the publication *Trouble and Strife* and by writers such as Deborah Cameron, Diane Richardson, Susanne Kappeler and Diana Leonard – as well as ourselves. Some of these writers have produced critiques of this misrepresentation. See Maynard, 'Beyond the big three'; Debbie Cameron, 'Telling it like it wasn't: how radical feminism became history', *Trouble and Strife*, no. 27, 1993, pp. 11–15; and Diane Richardson, 'Representing other feminisms', *Feminism and Psychology*, forthcoming.

21. To take one particularly gross example, Lynne Segal informs us – on two occasions – that Dworkin 'states with finality' and is 'insistently certain' that 'male power "authentically originates in the penis"', (Segal, *Is the Future Female* p. 103 and in her *Straight Sex: The Politics of Pleasure*, London: Virago 1994, p. 61). If we trace the quote from Dworkin back to its source, we find that it appears in a discussion of the ways in which patriarchal culture constructs sexuality in terms of male power. Her complete sentence reads as follows: 'The seventh tenet of male supremacy is that sexual power authentically originates in the penis.' Dworkin is not saying that the penis as a physical organ is the source of this power, but that it is culturally endowed with power and actually used as a weapon against women. In other words, in taking Dworkin's words out of context, Segal radically alters their meaning. See Andrea Dworkin, *Pornography: Men Possessing Women*, London: The Women's Press, 1981, p. 24.

22. Margaret Mead, *Sex and Temperament in Three Primitive Societies*, London: William Morrow, 1935.
23. See Anna Meigs, 'Multiple gender ideologies and statuses', in P. Reeves Sanday and R. Goodenough (eds), *Beyond the Second Sex: New Directions in the Anthropology of Gender*, Philadelphia: University of Pennsylvania Press, 1990; Gilbert Herdt, 'Mistaken sex: culture, biology and the third sex in New Guinea, in Gilbert Herdt (ed.), *Third Sex. Third Gender: Beyond Sexual Dimorphism in Culture and History*, New York: Zone Books, 1994; Frederick Errington and Deborah Gewertz, *Cultural Alternatives and a Feminist Anthropology: An Analysis of Culturally Constructed Gender Interests in Papua New Guinea*, Cambridge: Cambridge University Press, 1987. Whereas some of Mead's critics claim that she overestimated cultural differences, Errington and Gewertz suggest that her analysis was too deeply rooted in Western ideas about gender as a quality intrinsic to the self.
24. See, especially C.S. Ford and F.A. Beach, *Patterns of Sexual Behaviour*, London: Eyre & Spottiswood, 1952.
25. See, for example, Meigs, 'Multiple gender ideologies and statuses'; and Herdt 'Mistaken sex', and his *Guardians of the Flutes*, New York: McGraw Hill, 1981. Both Meigs and Herdt describe societies in which young boys must ingest semen through ritual acts of fellatio in order to attain manhood. A Western observer might see this a homosexual act, but to participants its meaning is understood in terms of acquiring the necessary attributes of masculinity which are in no way antithetical to heterosexual activity.
26. See particularly John Gagnon and William Simon, *Sexual Conduct*, London: Hutchinson, 1974. Gagnon and Simon criticised the notion of repression from an interactionist perspective, arguing that nothing is sexual in itself, that acts and relationships come to be sexual only through being defined as such. This argument was developed from a feminist perspective in S. Jackson, *Childhood and Sexuality*. Oxford: Blackwell, 1982 and Reading 1.5.
27. See especially Michel Foucault, *The History of Sexuality, vol. 1, An Introduction*, trans. Robert Hurley, Harmondsworth: Allen Lane, 1979.
28. For positive feminist appropriations of Foucault see Jana Sawicki, *Disciplining Foucault: Feminism, Power and the Body*, New York: Routledge, 1991; and Carol Smart, 'Disruptive bodies and unruly sex: the regulation of reproduction and sexuality in the nineteenth century' in Carol Smart (ed.), *Regulating Womanhood: Historical Essays on Marriage, Motherhood and Sexuality*, London: Routledge, 1992. For more critical engagements see Nancy Fraser, *Unruly Practices: Power, Discourse and Gender in Social Theory*, Oxford: Polity Press, 1989; and Caroline Ramazanoglu (ed.), *Up Against Foucault: Explorations of Some Tensions Between Foucault and Feminism*, London: Routledge, 1993.
29. See Sally Shuttleworth, 'Female circulation: medical discourse and popular advertising in the mid-Victorian era', in M. Jacobus, E. Fox-Keller and S. Shuttleworth (eds), *Body/Politics: Women and the Discourses of Science*, London: Routledge, 1990. See also Reading 1.2.
30. For Lacan's own work see his *Écrits: A Selection*, London: Tavistock, 1977; and J. Mitchell and J. Rose (eds), *Feminine Sexuality: Jacques Lacan and the École Freudienne*, London: Macmillan, 1982. Lacan is renowned for the impenetrability of his writing. For more accessible discussions of his work see Stephen Frosh, *The Politics of Psychoanalysis: An Introduction to Freudian and Post-Freudian Theory* London: Macmillan, 1987 and Elizabeth Grosz, *Jacques Lacan: A Feminist Introduction*, London: Routledge, 1990.
31. A further feminist approach to psychoanalysis is to be found in the work of American object-relations theorists such as Nancy Chodorow. See her *The Reproduction of Mothering: Psychoanalysis and the Sociology of Gender*, Berkeley: and Los Angeles University of California Press; *Feminism and Psychoanalytic Theory*, New Haven: Yale University Press, 1989. We have not included a reading from Chodorow's work since her earlier, and most influential, writings were concerned with the construction of gender rather than sexuality. More recently, however, she has turned her attention to sexuality, in *Femininities, Masculinities, Sexualities: Freud and Beyond* London: Free Association Books, 1994.
32. Diana Fuss, *Essentially Speaking: Feminism, Nature and Difference*. New York: Routledge, 1989.
33. Carole S. Vance, 'Social construction theory: problems in the history of sexuality', in D. Altman *et al.* (eds), *Which Homosexuality?*, London: Gay Men's Press, 1989. We had hoped to include this piece in this volume, but were denied permission to do so by the author.
34. See, for example, Scott and Morgan, 'Bodies in a social landscape'; Judith Butler, *Bodies that Matter*, New York: Routledge, 1993; Caroline Ramazanoglu, 'Why men stay on top', in M. Maynard and J. Purvis, (eds), *(Hetero)sexual Politics*, London: Taylor Francis, 1995.
35. This was argued by some early feminists, for example, Mary Jane Sherfey, *The Nature and Evolution of Female Sexuality*, New York: Random House, 1972. Sherfey argued that women's insatiable sexual appetite and capacity for multiple orgasm had been suppressed since the dawn of human civilization.
36. Although Koedt's statement is the best known exposition of these ideas, she was not alone in expressing them. Another article, contemporaneous with Koedt's and making similar points is Susan Lydon's 'The politics of orgasm', in R. Morgan (ed.), *Sisterhood in Powerful*. These issues had also been tackled, over two decades previously in Ruth Herschberger's ground- breaking book *Adam's Rib*, New York: Harper & Row, 1970, originally published in 1948 when there was no women's movement to receive it.
37. William Masters and Virginia Johnson, *Human Sexual Response*, New York: Bantam Books, 1981. This work, originally published in the 1960s, purported to prove that female orgasm, however it was induced, was centred on the clitoris, not the vagina.

38. See, for example, Stevi Jackson, 'Girls and sexual knowledge', in D. Spender and E. Sarah (eds), *Learning to Lose*, London: The Women's Press, 1982.

39. London Gay Liberation Front broadsheet, 1970, reproduced in David Evans, *Sexual Citizenship: The Material Construction of Sexualities*, London: Routledge, 1993.

40. See Liz Stanley, 'Male needs' the problems and problems of working with gay men', in S. Friedman and S. Sarah (eds), *On the Problem of Men: Two Feminist Conferences*, London: The Women's Press, 1982; Jeffreys, *Anti-Climax*; Snitow *et al.*, *Desire*. For views of this split from gay men see Evans, *Sexual Citizenship* and Tim Edwards, *Erotics and Politics: Gay Male Sexuality, Masculinity and Feminism*, London: Routledge, 1993.

41. For a discussion of these events and the relationship between lesbians and the women's movement at this time see Del Martin and Phyllis Lyon, *Lesbian/Woman*, New York: Bantam Books, 1972.

42. Quoted in Jeffreys, *Anti-Climax*, p. 290. See also Snitow *et al.*, *Desire*; and Martin and Lyon, *Lesbian/Woman*.

43. The original four demands of the British movement, formulated at the Oxford conference in 1970, were equal pay; equal education and opportunity; free 24 hour nurseries; and free contraception and abortion on demand. Four years later at the national conference in Edinburgh, two more demands were added: legal and financial independence, and an end to discrimination against lesbians and a right to a self-defined sexuality. Later a further demand, for freedom from male violence, was added.

44. For a discussion of lesbian feminism in Britain during the 1970s see E.M. Ettorre, *Lesbians, Women and Society*, London: Routledge & Kegan Paul, 1980.

45. Class, and more crucially racial, divisions among feminists were also increasingly apparent at this time.

46. See Ettorre, *Lesbians, Women and Society*; and Snitow *et al.*, *Desire*. Many lesbians were later to comment that their sexual practices had been de-eroticised by the emphasis on lesbianism as a political choice. See Joan Nestle, *A Restricted Country*, London: Sheba, 1988; and Wendy Clark, 'The dyke, the feminist and the devil', *Feminist Review*, 11, 1982, pp. 30–39.

47. See Jeffreys, *Anti Climax*; and also Louise Turcotte's introduction to Monique Wittig, *The Straight Mind and Other Essays*, Hemel Hempstead: Harvester Wheatsheaf, 1992. For a more positive appraisal of Rich's work see Debbie Cameron, 'Old hat?', *Trouble and Strife*, no. 24, 1992, pp. 41–5.

48. Jeffreys *Desire*, p. 297.

49. This paper, along with other contributions to the ensuing debate, is published in Onlywoman Press (eds), *Love Your Enemy: The Debate Between Heterosexual Feminism and Political Lesbianism*, London: Onlywoman Press, 1981.

50. The term 'radical feminism' is now often used to include revolutionary feminism although the distinction between them is a politically important one. Both analyse patriarchy as a system of male domination and are critical of heterosexuality. Revolutionary feminists, however, give far greater causal priority to sexuality in explaining women's subordination. While radical feminists see lesbianism as a potential form of resistance to patriarchy, it is only revolutionary feminists who feel that political lesbianism is a *necessary* strategy for feminists. Hence it is the latter who are critical of those feminists who remain heterosexual. Sheila Jeffreys is the best known exponent of revolutionary feminism. Others currently writing in this tradition include Sue Wilkinson and Celia Kitzinger. See, for example, the introduction to their edited collection *Heterosexuality: A 'Feminism & Psychology' Reader*, London: Sage, 1993. The radical feminist magazine *Trouble and Strife* was founded in 1983 to counter this tendency and explicitly opposed the radical lesbian position in its first issue. Feminists who have been associated with this magazine include Jalna Hanmer, Diana Leonard, Sophie Lawns, Lynne Alderson (the founder members) and more recently Susanne Kappeler, Liz Kelly, Deborah Cameron and Stevi Jackson.

51. Kapos were prisoners in Nazi concentration camps who acted as guards under the authority of their captors.

52. The dispute also split the editorial collective of *Questions Féministes*, the French radical feminist theoretical journal. Those who opposed the radical lesbian line – Christine Delphy, Emmanuèle de Lesseps and Simone de Beauvoir – went on to found *Nouvelles questions féministes*, amid legal battles in the courts with the radical lesbian members of the original collective. See Claire Duchen, 'What's the French for political lesbian?', *Trouble and Strife*, no. 4, 1984., pp. 24–34; Claire Duchen (ed.), *French Connections*, London: Hutchinson, 1987; Stevi Jackson, *Christine Delphy*, London: Sage, 1996.

53. For a general discussion of these issues see Caroline Ramazanoglu, *Feminism and the Contradictions of Oppression*, London: Routledge, 1989.

54. These two interconnected perspectives derive from a tradition in French thought. Poststructuralism developed out of the structuralist tradition established in linguistics by Ferdinand de Saussure, which looks for structures underlying all human language and culture. Where structuralists see language and meaning as arbitrary but patterned, poststructuralists see meanings are far more fluid, as constantly shifting and discursively constituted. Postmodernism represents a critical stance on the modernist project of the Enlightenment, in particular the idea that there are objective truths which reason can uncover. Postmodernists are sceptical of all 'metanarratives', or grand explanatory theories, and also of the idea of history as progress. For a summary of these ideas, see Mandan Sarup, *An Introductory Guide to Poststructuralism and Postmodernism*, Hemel Hempstead: Harvester Wheatsheaf, 1988.

55. The term 'Queer' is not meant in the old pejorative sense. It can be seen as a continuation of an older

political strategy, found in feminist and anti-racist politics of 'reclaiming' names previously used against oppressed groups. This is summed up by the phrase 'Queers bash back'. 'Queer' is thus confrontational and is used in this sense to cover all kinds of transgressive sexual activities.

56. See particularly the critique of Monique Wittig in Diana Fuss, *Essentially Speaking*, New York: Routledge, 1989.
57. The phrase 'regulatory fictions' is Judith Butler's. See her *Gender Trouble*, New York: Routledge, 1990.
58. For a discussions of Queer politics, see Cherry Smyth, *Lesbians Talk Queer Notions*, London: Scarlet Press, 1992. For a critique see Julia Parnaby, 'Queer straights', *Trouble and Strife*, no. 26, 1993; pp. 13–16.
59. Anonymous leaflet, 'Queer Power Now', London, 1991, quoted in Smyth, *Lesbians Talk Queer Notions* p. 17.
60. Carol Queen, quoted by Claire Hemmings, 'Re-situating the bisexual body', in Joseph Bristow and Angelia R. Wilson (eds), *Activating Theory: Lesbian, Gay, Bisexual Politics*, London: Lawrence & Wishart, 1993, p. 132.
61. *Ibid.*
62. Elizabeth Wilson, 'Is transgression transgressive?' in Joseph Bristow and Angelic R. Wilson (eds), *Activating Theory: Lesbian, Gay, Bisexual Politics*, London: Lawrence & Wishart, 1993.
63. See, for example, the contributions made by Inge Blackman and Pratibha Parmar to Smyth, *Lesbians Talk Queer Notions*.
64. Butler, *Gender Trouble*, p. 6.
65. For an ascerbic critique of Queer style from a gay male perspective see Stephen Maddison, 'A Queered pitch', *Red Pepper*, February 1995, p. 27.
66. Butler, *Gender Trouble*, p. 123.
67. See, for example Wilkinson and Kitzinger, *Hetero Sexuality*, especially the contributions by Mary Gergen and Alison Young; see also Segal, *Straight Sex*.
68. Kate Millett, *Sexual Politics*, New York: Doubleday, 1969. The idea that sexuality is central to women's subordination goes back well before the rise of second wave feminism. For sources on first wave feminism see note 7. Between 'the waves', issues of sexuality were given considerable attention by both Herschberger, *Adam's Rib*; and Simone de Beauvoir, *The Second Sex*, Harmondsworth: Penguin, 1972 (originally published in 1949).
69. Here she differs from other radical feminists. French radical feminists, and those British feminists influenced by them, see sex-classes as themselves economic, as based on male exploitation of women's labour as well as their bodies. For examples of French feminism see Delphy, *Close to Home*; Wittig, *The Straight Mind*; Colette Guillaumin, *Racism, Sexism, Power and Ideology*, London: Routledge, 1995. For British appropriations see Diana Leonard, *Gender and Generation*, London: Tavistock, 1980; Sylvia Walby, *Patriarchy at Work*, Oxford: Polity, 1986; Jackson, 'Gender and heterosexuality'.
70. For a range of perspectives on this issue see, Susan Brownmiller, *Against our Will: Men, Women and Rape*, Harmondsworth: Penguin, 1976; Stevi Jackson, 'The social context of rape: sexual scripts and motivation', *Women's Studies International Quarterly*, 1(1), 1978; pp. 27–38; Susan Edwards, *Female Sexuality and the Law*. Oxford: Martin Robertson, 1981; Carol Smart, *Feminism and the Power of Law*, London: Routledge, 1989.
71. There is a vast literature on these themes. A few examples follow. On sexual harassment see Catharine MacKinnon, *Sexual Harassment of Working Women*, New Haven: Yale University Press, 1979; Liz Stanley and Sue Wise, *Georgie Porgy*, London: Pandora, 1984. On rape see Griffin, 'Rape'; Brownmiller, *Against our Will*; Jackson, 'The social context of rape'. On sexual murder see Jane Caputi, *The Age of the Sex Crime*, London: The Women's Press, 1988; Deborah Cameron and Elizabeth Frazer, *The Lust to Kill: A Feminist Investigation of Sexual Murder*, Oxford: Polity, 1987. On child sexual abuse see Emily Driver and Audrey Droisen, *Child Sexual Abuse: Feminist Perspectives*, London: Macmillan, 1989; Judith Herman, *Father-Daughter Incest*, Cambridge, Mass.: Harvard University Press, 1981; Florence Rush, *The Best Kept Secret*, Maidenhead: McGraw-Hill, 1980.
72. For other examples of the use of the idea of a continuum of violence see Jackson, 'The social context of rape'; Andra Medea and Kathleen Thompson, *Against Rape*, New York: Noonday Press, 1974.
73. This has been a consistent theme in Sheila Jeffreys writing. See Jeffreys, *Anti-Climax*. For a more sophisticated analysis see Susanne Kappeler, *The Pornography of Representation*, Oxford: Polity, 1986, and *The Will to Violence: The Politics of Personal Behaviour*, Oxford: Polity, 1995. For a discussion of rapists' accounts of the ways in which power intersects with sexual desire see Diane Scully, *Understanding Sexual Violence: A Study of Convicted Rapists*, London: Unwin Hyman, 1990.
74. See also Patricia Hill Collins, Reading 4.4.
75. See, for example Amirah Inglis, *The White Woman's Protection Ordinance*, London: Sussex University Press, 1975.
76. This was a particular focus of the controversial conference on the politics of sexuality held at Barnard College, New York in 1982. See the papers from that conference collected in Carole S. Vance (ed.), *Pleasure and Danger: Exploring Female Sexuality*, London: Routledge, 1984.
77. There are also links between libertarians and Queer, although by no means all Queer theorists endorse libertarian perspectives.
78. 'Vanilla' sex is generally used as a pejorative term, although some do use it to describe their own practices. It refers to egalitarian sexual practices in which neither partner takes a dominant role, which

usually excludes penetrative sex, and certainly the use of sex toys. It is sweet and cuddly sex, rather than passionate raunchy sex. See Reading 3.11.

79. Gayle Rubin, 'Thinking sex: notes for a radical theory of the politics of sexuality', in Carole S. Vance (ed.) *Pleasure and Danger: Exploring Female Sexuality*, London: Routledge, 1984. We had initially hoped to include extracts from this article in this volume, but were denied permission to do so by the author.

80. Some lesbians have defended sado-masochistic practices on the part of gay men on the grounds that they can be 'safer' than penetrative sex. They may be safer with regard to HIV transmission, but whether they are safer in any other sense is open to question.

81. See Janet Holland, Caroline Ramazanoglu and Sue Scott, 'Managing risk and experiencing danger: tensions between government AIDS education policy and young women's sexuality', *Gender and Education*, 1(4), 1990; Sara Scott, 'Sex and danger: feminism and AIDS', *Trouble and Strife*, no. 11, 1987; pp. 13–17.

82. See also the final chapter of Diane Richardson, *Women and the AIDS Crisis*, London: Pandora, 1989.

83. In Britain these debates are reflected in the activities of two opposing campaigning groups. The Campaign Against Pornography (CAP) and Feminists Against Censorship (FAC). A third group the Campaign Against Pornography and Censorship, largely shares CAP's analysis of the harm done by pornography but also resists censorship. It should be noted that feminists in CAP do not necessarily support censorship. They are more likely to favour direct action against purveyors of porn and to support the sort of civil liberties legislation favoured by Andrea Dworkin and Catharine MacKinnon in the USA.

84. Mary McIntosh was one of the first to question this model of male sexuality in 'Who needs prostitutes? The construction of male sexual needs', in Carol Smart and Barry Smart (eds), *Women, Sexuality and Social Control*, London: Routledge & Kegan Paul, 1978. Feminists have also made the same point in relation to rape, which is often excused in terms of men being unable to 'help themselves'.

85. Ellen Strong, 'The hooker' in Robin Morgan (eds), *Sisterhood is Powerful. An Anthology of Writings from the Women's Liberation Movement*, New York: Vintage Books, 1970.

86. For anti-pornography perspectives on these issues see the essays in Dorchen Leidholdt and Janice Raymond (eds), *The Sexual Liberals and the Attack on Feminism*, New York: Pergamon, 1990; For libertarian arguments against anti-pornography campaigners see Gillian Rodgerson and Elizabeth Wilson (eds), *Pornography and Feminism: The Case Against Censorship*. London: Lawrence & Wishart, 1991.

87. For further sources on these issues, see note 7

88. For an insightful analysis of the individual and collective appropriation of women's bodies see Colette Guillaumin, 'The practice of power and the belief in nature, part 1: the appropriation of women', in Colette Guillaumin, *Racism, Sexism, Power and Ideology*, London: Routledge, 1990.

89. See, for example, Rodgerson and Wilson, *Pornography and Feminism*.

90. For a discussion of such studies and a critique of their methods, see Alison King, 'Mystery and imagination: the case of pornography effects studies' in Alison Assiter and Avedon Carol (eds), *Bad Girls and Dirty Pictures*, London: Pluto Press, 1992.

91. For an example of this see Lynne Segal, 'Pornography and violence: what the "experts" really say', *Feminist Review*, 36, 1990 pp. 29–41.

92. See also Reading 3.3.

93. For a discussion of some different forms of prostitution in relation to the difficulties of defining it see Jo Phoenix, 'Prostitution: problematizing the definition', in M. Maynard and J. Purvis (eds), *(Hetero) Sexual Politics*, London: Taylor & Francis, 1995.

94. Nina Lopez-Jones 'Workers: introducing the English Collective of Prostitutes', in Frédérique Delacoste and Priscilla Alexander (eds), *Sex Work: Writings by Women in the Sex Industry*, London: Virago, 1988, p. 273.

95. Sarah Wynter, 'WHISPER: Women Hurt by Systems of Prostitution Engaged in Revolt', in Frédérique Delacoste and Priscilla Alexander (eds), *Sex Work: Writings by Women in the Sex Industry*, London: Virago, 1988 p. 270.

96. For example, see advertisements for many of the airlines based in South East Asia.

97. For a further discussion of sex tourism see Julia O'Connell Davidson, 'British sex tourists in Thailand', in M. Maynard and J. Purvis (eds), *(Hetero) Sexual Politics*, London: Taylor & Francis, 1995.

98. A well-known historical example, The Contagious Diseases Acts which subjected prostitutes working in English garrison towns in the 1860s to punitive forms of surveillance, is discussed in some detail in Judith Walkowitz, *Prostitution and Victorian Society*, Cambridge: Cambridge University Press, 1980.

99. See Sue Scott and Richard Freeman, 'Prevention as a problem of modernity: the case of HIV and AIDS', *Sociology of Health and Illness*, 1995.

100. Gayle Rubin, 'Thinking Sex', p. 278.

PART ONE

ESSENTIALISM AND SOCIAL CONSTRUCTIONISM

1.1

SEXUALITY

Ann Oakley

Our first reading comes from Ann Oakley's groundbreaking book, Sex, Gender and Society. This was one of the earliest attempts to argue that femininity and masculinity are socially constructed. In this extract, Oakley draws on cross-cultural evidence to argue that differences between male and female (hetero)sexuality are products of culture, rather than nature.

As a leading anthropologist once observed, 'sex' is not a particularly useful word in the analysis of cultures. To survive, a culture must reproduce, and copulation is the only way. But what is defined as 'sexual' in content or implication varies infinitely from one culture to another or within the same culture in different historical periods.

In Victorian times for instance, a large group of Western females were denied their sexuality altogether, but the twentieth century has seen the emergence (or re-emergence, after the inhibitions of the eighteenth and nineteenth centuries) of the female's right to sexuality, which has come to be defined at least partly in terms of her own sexual needs. The Victorian lady was not supposed to have sexual desires – hence her paradoxical use as a sexual object for the man's satisfaction. Her twentieth-century counterpart, however, has considerable auras of sexuality, extending beyond the bedroom into an entire world of commercially-oriented sex and erotic meaning.

These terms 'sex' and 'sexual' are subject to constant confusion. The dictionary gives, under 'sexual', 'Of, pertaining to, or based on, sex or the sexes, or on the distinction of sexes; pertaining to generation or copulation'. Perhaps it is not surprising that the confusion exists: 'sex' (biological maleness or femaleness) and 'sexuality' (behaviour related to copulation) are very closely connected. Behaviour is 'sexual' if

From A. Oakley, *Sex, Gender and Society*, London: Maurice Temple Smith, 1972.

it refers to the kind of relationship between male and female in which copulation is, or could be, or is imagined to be, a factor. 'Sexuality' describes the whole area of personality related to sexual behaviour.

Both male and female must have some propensity for sexual behaviour if copulation is to occur, but this propensity is usually held to be different in male and female. Along with the male's greater aggression in other fields, goes his aggression in the sphere of sexuality: males initiate sexual contact, and take the symbolically, if not actually, aggressive step of vaginal penetration – a feat which is possible even with a frigid mate. They assume the dominant position in intercourse. Males ask females to go to bed with them, or marry them, or both: not vice versa.

The female's sexuality is supposed to lie in her receptiveness and this is not just a matter of her open vagina: it extends to the whole structure of feminine personality as dependent, passive, unaggressive and submissive. Female sexuality has been held to involve long arousal and slow satisfaction, inferior sex drive, susceptibility to field dependence (a crying child distracts the attention) and romantic idealism rather than lustful reality. Women are psychologically, no less than anatomically, incapable of rape.

That these stereotypes persist can be seen from any woman's magazine and almost any fiction dealing with sexual relationships.

[. . .]

What do we know about the sex drive in men and women, about the physiological processes involved in copulation and orgasm? Are we able to say that in these things men and women are biologically different?

[. . .]

The theory that male sexuality arises spontaneously and is specifically genital while the female's is not, is simply not borne out by the behaviour of males and females in other cultures – for instance by the Brazilian tribe studied by Jules Henry. . . . or the Trobriand islanders studied by Malinowski[1] [. . .]. The differences in the emotional meaning of puberty to male and female in our cultures, are not necessarily universal either, any more than are the social differences influencing the ways in which they gain their sexual experience.

[. . .]

Because puberty is a bridge between childhood and adulthood, and because the adult roles of the sexes are significantly differentiated in our society both inside and outside the home, the climate in which male and female pass through puberty tends to stress rather than ignore sex differences in the physiological process itself. An additional factor is perhaps our cultural emphasis on the importance of sexuality. The Arapesh, who as a culture devalue sexuality and develop tenderness and parental responsibility in both males and females, do not treat the adolescent girl as in need of protection from the male's exploitation of her as a sexual object.[2] Menstruation is therefore not the signal of danger it is in our society. Arapesh males simply do not regard females as vessels for their own sexual satisfaction, but as individuals whose desirability as spouses is related to the culture's primary work of child-rearing. The sexual feeling that exists between spouses is not fundamentally different from the other feelings or affections that tie siblings, or parents and children, together – it is just a more complete expression of it. In this context, adolescence is not a period of fervent mating choice either: by the age of nine or ten girls are already betrothed, and the adolescent male's task is to prepare his own betrothed for the responsibilities of parenthood which they will both share. The Arapesh have no fear that adolescents left to themselves will copulate, nor do the adolescents themselves expect that they will. Margaret Mead [. . .] explains:

> . . . the Arapesh further contravene our traditional idea of men as spontaneously sexual creatures, and women as innocent of desire, until wakened, by denying spontaneous sexuality to both sexes and expecting the exceptions, when they do occur, to occur in women. Both men and women are conceived as merely capable of response to a situation that their society has already defined for them as sexual . . . with their definition of sex as response to an external stimulus rather than as spontaneous desire, both men and women are regarded as helpless in the face of seduction . . . Parents warn their sons even more than they warn their daughters against permitting themselves to get into situations in which someone can make love to them.[3]

Puberty for the Arapesh is therefore hardly a physiological situation at all, although it remains a sign of maturation and of readiness for the adult role.

Anthropology shows that the whole area of human sexuality is subject to tremendous cultural variation. The following are among the many features of human sexual behaviour which vary: sexual play between children (which may be specifically genital and widely permitted throughout childhood, as among the Trobrianders, or heavily discouraged and repressed, in middle childhood especially, as in our own society); intercourse between immature adults (which may be a common occurrence unrelated to marriage and procreation, as in Samoa, or discouraged, as again in Western culture); the importance of sexual activity itself (which may be defined as the appropriate preoccupation for an entire society to the exclusion of other interests, as among the Truk, or may take a very secondary place indeed as among the Arapesh); the extent to which sexual desire is dangerous and needs curbing, as among the Manus, or is weak and uncertain and likely to fail altogether, as in Bali.[4]

The idea that the female's sexuality is qualitatively different from the male's, and in particular that it is slow to mature and in need of intensive stimulation, is not universal in all cultures. In the Southwest Pacific society described by William Davenport [. . .] sexual intercourse is assumed to be highly pleasurable (and deprivation harmful) for both sexes.[5] During the early years of marriage men and women are reported to have intercourse twice a day, with both reaching orgasm simultaneously. Intercourse is defined as a prolonged period of foreplay, during which there is a mutual genital stimulation by both partners, and a short period of copulation lasting fifteen to thirty seconds. It is firmly believed that, once stimulated during foreplay, neither male nor female can fail to reach orgasm, and women unable to reach orgasm are unheard of. Either husband or wife can break up the marriage if sexual intercourse is infrequent (that is, about every ten days).

In this society children beyond the age of three or four are discouraged from genital play, and all sex play between children is frowned upon: there is a latency period from about five or six until puberty when sexual behaviour is not in evidence. Beyond puberty and before marriage both males and females are urged to masturbate to orgasm in order to relieve sexual tension, which is assumed to be as great in females as in males.

Malinowski reported a similar convergence of male and female sexual behaviour among the Trobriand Islanders.[6] Like many other people, the Trobrianders appear to do without latency – there is no period of childhood during which sexual interests and activities are absent. Small children play sexual games together; genital manipulation and oral genital stimulation are frequent. By the age of four or five children are mimicking intercourse, and girls of six to eight have intercourse with penetration. (This experience is delayed for boys, presumably until they are able to achieve full intercourse at the age of ten or twelve.) These sexual activities continue unabated throughout childhood, but at adolescence become more serious – the subject of great endeavour and absorbing preoccupation.

[. . .]

Amongst the Trobrianders, as also among the Lesu, Kurtatchi, Lepcha, Kwoma and Mataco, women frequently take the initiative in sexual relationships. Indeed, in the last two societies, sexual initiatives are taken by the female exclusively.[7]

The positions used in intercourse by the Trobrianders omit the usual dorsal-ventral (man on top of woman) position [. . .] which they dislike because the woman is hampered by the weight of the man and cannot be sufficiently active. The expression for orgasm means 'the seminal fluid discharge' and is used of both sexes, referring also to the nocturnal emission of seminal and glandular secretions in male and female. Masturbation is looked on by the Trobrianders as the practice of an idiot, one who is unable to indulge in heterosexual intercourse. It is unworthy of both men and women, whose proper sexuality is bound up with their mutual relationship. Malinowski, in comparing the sexuality of the Trobrianders with that of his own culture, concluded that there were qualitative differences between them.

[. . .]

Differences in the sexuality of male and female have been variously attributed to differences in (a) their anatomies (b) the functioning of their hormones (c) their psychologies (d) their personalities and (e) the cultural learning processes to which they are subjected.

Of these five, only the first two and the last are contrasting explanations, since the psychology and personality of male and female largely depend on culture. In fact the role of anatomy in determining sexuality must remain a purely hypothetical one until some explanation is given on how the two connect. As it stands the statement 'anatomy is destiny' offers no real explanation. Freudian theory can be interpreted as a massive attempt to take on the one hand distinctions of anatomy and on the other distinctions of 'destiny' (or social role) and propose a series of processes by which one might lead to the other.

[. . .]

In industrial cultures (and in some others too) the sexual relationship between male and female has been subsumed in the general power relationship of the sexes. This – the thesis of Kate Millett's 'Sexual Politics'[8] – has far-reaching implications for many areas of sex differentiation, including sexuality itself.

NOTES

1. J. Henry, *Jungle People*, New York: Vintage Books, 1964; B. Malinowski, *The Sexual Lives of Savages*, London: Routledge & Kegan Paul, 1932.
2. M. Mead, *Sex and Temperament in Three Primitive Societies*, London: William Morrow, 1935.
3. *Ibid.*
4. See C.S. Ford and F.A. Beach, *Patterns of Sexual Behaviour*, London: Eyre & Spottiswood, 1952.
5. W. Davenport, 'Sexual patterns and their regulation in a society of the Southwest Pacific', in F.A. Beach (ed.), *Sex and Behaviour*, London: John Wiley, 1965.
6. Malinowski, *The Sexual Lives of Savages*.
7. Malinowski, *The Sexual Lives of Savages*; Ford and Beach, *Patterns of Sexual Behaviour*.
8. K. Millett, *Sexual Politics*, New York: Doubleday, 1971.

SCENES OF AN INDELICATE CHARACTER
The Medical Treatment of Victorian Women

Mary Poovey

Feminists have also used historical evidence to demonstrate that human sexuality is not fixed by 'nature'. Mary Poovey explores shifts in the construction of female sexuality in the nineteenth century, in particular the contradictions underlying medical and other scientific ideas. At this time women were defined as both asexual and saturated with sexuality, incapable of autonomous desire yet almost helplessly susceptible to sexual stimulation, as morally pure but physically impure. In this extract Poovey uses the debate about the use of chloroform during childbirth as one instance of these contradictions. This practice was pioneered in Scotland by James Young Simpson, but met considerable opposition from other doctors, especially in England.

[. . .]

By contrast to its rapid adoption in surgery, chloroform encountered vehement opposition in midwifery, and practitioners remained divided over the advisability of its use.[1] Instead of the physiological explanations a twentieth-century obstetrician might offer for employing or rejecting the anodyne, mid-nineteenth-century medical men implicitly or explicitly formulated their positions in relation to two issues that had less to do with the scientific properties of the anodyne than with the ontological nature of woman and medicine's proper relation to her.[2] The first of these issues was whether the woman in labor came under God's jurisdiction or man's.[3]

[. . .]

The second issue raised in the chloroform debate was the epistemological and practical question of how a doctor could read, so as to master, a woman's body, which was so different from his own.

From M. Poovey, *Uneven Developments*, London: Virago, 1989.

[. . .]

Whether they borrowed or contested the theological terms in which woman's nature had traditionally been formulated, nineteenth-century medical men constructed their arguments about anesthesia on the same contradictory assumptions about female nature that dominated religious discourse. That these assumptions preceded rather than followed from physiological evidence can be seen in an [. . .] issue that surfaced repeatedly in the chloroform debates. One version of this issue appears in a report Simpson delivered to the Medico-Chirurgical Society in July 1848, nine months after his enthusiastic adoption of chloroform. In this report, Simpson attributed the failure of English practitioners to achieve the same kind of success that Scottish doctors had achieved to a misreading of the anesthetized body. 'Immediately before the chloroform produced anaesthesia,' Simpson is reported as saying,

> more especially if there was any noise or disturbance, it not unfrequently excited the patient, who would talk incoherently for a moment or two, beg the inhalation to be suspended, perhaps struggle to get free of it, and have his [sic] arms and legs thrown into a state of strong clonic spasms . . . In the English Journals such cases have been repeatedly and gravely recorded as instances of delirium, and spasms, and convulsions, and failure. They are not more anxious, or deserving of attention, than the same symptoms would be in a case of hysteria, and are quite transient if the inhalation is only persevered in.[4]

Simpson's passing reference to hysteria is telling, for what English journals repeatedly reported were not simply random 'instances of delirium, and spasms, and convulsions,' but specifically female displays of *sexual* excitation. Those few spasms that were reported in males were universally described as signs of fighting. These reports had been appearing ever since the first successful inhalation of anesthesia, for ether, chloroform's immediate predecessor, had an even greater tendency than chloroform to stimulate motor and verbal responses. In an article published in 1847 [. . .] W. Tyler Smith, a young practitioner from Bristol who was to become one of the founders of the Obstetrical Society, cited this excitation as a decisive barrier to ether's use. Smith claims to judge ether on a 'physiological and pathological basis,' but when he comes to 'the occasional incitement of the sexual passion,' it becomes clear that this, not physiology, is the heart of his objection.

> In one of the cases observed by Baron Dubois, the woman drew an attendant towards her to kiss, as she was lapsing into insensibility, and this woman afterwards confessed to dreaming of coitus with her husband while she lay etherized. In ungravid women, rendered insensible for the performance of surgical operations, erotic gesticulations have occasionally been observed, and in one case, in which enlarged nymphae were removed, the woman went unconsciously through the movements attendant on the sexual orgasm, in the presence of numerous bystanders . . . I may venture to say, that to the women of this country the bare possibility of having feelings of such a kind excited and manifested in outward uncontrollable actions, would be more shocking even to anticipate, than the endurance of the last extremity of physical pain.[5]

As Smith continues, his interpretation of such displays becomes more elaborate. 'In many of the lower animals, we know that an erotic condition of the ovaria is present during parturition, and that sexual congress and conception may take place immediately upon delivery. It was, however, reserved for the phenomenon of etherization to show that, as regards sexual emotion, the human female may possibly exchange the pangs of travail for the sensations of coitus, and so approach to the level of the brute creation.' [. . .] 'May it not be,' Smith writes in this early lecture, 'that in woman the physical pain neutralizes the sexual emotions, which would otherwise probably, be present, but which would tend very much to alter our estimation of the modesty and retiredness proper to the sex, and which are never more prominent or more admirable than on these occasions?'

Implicit in Smith's description is the fear that, under ether, women would regress to brute animals, a state in which they would be beyond the doctor's control. It was to counter this possibility that Smith offered his paradoxical theory of a propriety 'naturally' induced by pain – a theory, not incidentally, that ensured the doctor's ability to know what the woman really felt even when she 'prominently' displayed its opposite: 'admirable' modesty and retiredness. In this argument, [. . .] protect[s] the doctor against being implicated in what he says the patient feels. Once more, Smith attributed this protectiveness to the 'naturally' compliant woman: 'chastity of feeling, and, above all, emotional self-control, at a time when women are receiving such assistance as the accoucheur can render, are of far more importance than insensibility to pain. They would scarcely submit to the possibility of a sexual act in which their unborn offspring should take the part of excitor; and as the erotic condition has been chiefly observed in patients undergoing operations on the sexual organs, we must assign as the exciting cause, either the manipulations of the attendant or the passage of the child.'[6]

Paradoxically, Smith is representing woman as both an innately sexual creature and a being whose natural modesty and emotional self-control prevent her sexuality from obtruding on the medical men. One source of the confusion here is whether – or to what extent – physiology, which is indisputably the medical man's terrain, is the natural basis for morality, the domain that has previously been claimed by clergymen. Another is what definition of woman will prevail *whoever* acquires the authority to govern her: Is woman primarily a sexual or a moral creature? Is she man's temptress or his moral guide? These contradictory representations of female nature were inherited from the eighteenth century; they marked the contest between an earlier representation of woman as sexual and the domestic ideal that gradually displaced this image in the course of the century in a variety of discourses ranging from sermons to conduct books to novels.[7] [. . .] What is important to my argument is the way in which the seventeenth-century representation of woman as essentially sexual was precipitated back out of the domestic ideal in the medical debates I am discussing. [. . .] I want to show the form in which the sexualized woman returned and the anxieties she aroused. The key to the latter is Smith's last phrase. If women are primarily reproductive, hence sexual, animals, then childbearing itself might be a sexually exciting experience in which no man is necessary at all. Smith's objection to anesthesia was that it would remove from female sexuality the only check to which it would submit, the 'modesty and retiredness proper to her sex,' but whether this 'check' was 'natural' or 'proper' remains unclear and therefore problematic for Smith's argument.

Smith's concern reappears repeatedly in the chloroform debate. Dr G.T. Gream, physician-accoucheur to Queen Charlotte's Lying-in Hospital and one of the most fashionable obstetricians in London's West End, was particularly outspoken on this point, but he was certainly not alone. One of his lengthy complaints before the Westminster Medical Society in 1849 prompted a fellow medical man, Dr Tanner, to cite an operation 'in King's College Hospital on the vagina of a prostitute, in which ether produced lascivious dreams.'[8] So clamorous was the response that both John Snow and James Simpson rose to counter this charge. Snow simply pointed out that all 'unpleasantness' could be avoided if a specialist administered chloroform; Simpson flatly denied that such scenes could exist.[9] 'He had never seen, nor had he ever heard of any other person having seen, any manifestation of sexual excitement result from the exhibition of chloroform,' he is reported to have said. 'The excitement, he was inclined to think, existed not in the individuals anaesthetized, but was the result of impressions harboured in the minds of the practitioners.' Collapsing Dr Tanner's report with that of Baron Dubois, Simpson remarks that the experience of one 'Parisian prostitute' with 'lascivious dreams' should not be generalized to all women. 'Surely it was,' he retorted, 'to say the least, very unbecoming to say that most English ladies should have sexual dreams (like one French prostitute) when under the influence of chloroform.'[10]

In this exchange, Simpson was enlisting his listeners' assumptions about class and national character to bolster what he presented as a physiological argument: surely whatever 'lascivious dreams' anesthetized patients might report were confined to those lower-class French women who dreamed such things anyway. But Simpson was unwilling to abandon the notion that, in childbirth at least, all women were more alike than different or to risk the success of his discovery to his claim that English ladies would display no compromising reactions. Instead of pursuing the argument about class (as some practitioners did), Simpson recommended a 'large, overwhelming dose' of the anodyne as a precaution against the excitation that was so unpredictable and so easily misconstrued. By 1855, Dr James Arnott had the temerity to suggest that Simpson's putatively scientific mode of application – the so-called Edinburgh method – had been developed not for the patient's safety but precisely to protect the practitioner from such '"involuntary confidences" and emotions' as light anesthesia was apt to produce.[11] Whether Arnott was correct or not, his charge points out the extent to which Simpson and Smith actually agreed about one essential fact: such 'scenes of an indelicate character' were undesirable and possibly dangerous for the patient, the practitioner, and the medical profession as a whole.[12] I suggest that this shared preoccupation with propriety reveals that, in at least one important sense, the chloroform debate was not really a debate at all. Or – more precisely – it *was* a debate but *not* about the issues it purported to address. Instead of disputing the nature or position of woman with each other or with religious authorities, obstetricians on both sides agreed that woman was a reproductive creature who was, by nature, socially dependent on man but somehow morally superior to him. From this perspective, medical arguments can be seen as elaborations of the theological position, which refined – and provided a new language for – social practices that remained essentially unchanged. Nevertheless, the disagreement among medical men was fiercely argued because important issues were at stake: these included both the authority of individual medical men within the profession and the social status of all medical men. The real issue under dispute, then, was tactics: doctors argued about what treatment of women would consolidate the obstetricians' position within the profession and in society as a whole.

NOTES

1. The *OED* cites instances of the adjective *obstetric* (or *obstetrical*) from the seventeenth and early eighteenth centuries. Interestingly, these early uses are almost all metaphorical and refer to a man aiding in the 'delivery' of an idea, text, or event. Examples include: 'there all the Learn'd shall at the labour stand, And Douglas lend a soft, obstetric hand' (1742; Pope, *Dunciad*, 4, p. 394); 'this you protect their pregnant hour; . . . Exerting your obstetric pow'r' (*c.* 1750; Shenstone, *To the Virtuosi*, vii). One non-metaphorical use depicts a male frog, the 'obstetrical toad' (Alytes obstetricians), who aids the female in birth. 'They spawn like frogs; but what is singular, the male affords the female obstetrical aid' (1776; Pennant, *Zoology*. 3: 17). By the end of the eighteenth century, the word was generally used in its medical sense: 'The obstetric art . . . began to emerge from its barbarity during the sixteenth century' (*Medical Journal*. 2, 1799, pp. 453). Instances of figurative usages continue to appear, however, as when Bryon wrote to Scott in 1822 that 'Mr Murray has several things of mine in his obstetrical hands.' The word *obstetrician* first first appears in 1828, when Dr Michael Ryan calls attention to its novelty: 'it may be necessary to say a few words apologetic, for my adoption of the word obstetrician' (1828; *Man Midwifery*, p. v). In 1819, the word *obstetrics* already referred to a medical practice more extensive than the simple delivery in which even untrained women could assist: '*Obstetrics*, the doctrines or practice of midwifery . . . Employed in larger signification than midwifery in its usual sense' (1819; *Pantalogia*). The *OED* cites the first appearance of *accoucheur* as Laurence Sterne's *Tristram Shandy* (1759–67): 'Nothing will serve you but to carry off the man-midwife,' says Tristam's father. '*Accoucheur*, – if you please,' responds Dr Slop (2: xii). W. Tyler Smith was intent on eliminating the very word *midwife* from medical language and in sharply distinguishing between scientific, male-adminstered obstetrics and unscientific, female-dominated 'midwifery': 'We may confidently hope,' he states in his first obstetric lecture, 'that hereafter the sign of the escape of midwifery from the midwife will be . . . obscure and insignificant, and that the very term *midwifery* will be rejected on account of its derivation' (*Lancet*, 2, p. 371). See also 'Obstetrics a science, midwifery an art,' *British and Foreign Medico-Chirurgical Review*, 4, 1849, pp. 501–10.

2. See Margaret Sandelowski, *Pain, Pleasure, and American Childbirth: From Twilight Sleep to the Reed Method, 1914–1960*. Westport, Conn.: Greenwood Press, 1984, pp. 29–30. Simpson also acknowledges this when he stated that 'the application of anaesthesia to midwifery involves many more difficult and delicate problems than its mere application to surgery' (quoted in Sandelowski *Pain, Pleasure, and American Childbirth* p. 28).

3. See Ann Oakley, *Women Confined: Towards a Sociology of Childbirth*, New York: Schocken Books, 1980, pp. 8–9.

4. James Young Simpson, *Anaesthesia: or the Employment of Chloroform and Ether in Surgery, Midwifery, etc.*, Philadelphia. Lindsay & Blackiston, 1849, p. 189.

5. *London Lancet* 1, 1847, p. 377, 'Smith allows a disturbing ambiguity to insinuate itself into his account when he fails to report that Dubois specified that the attendant the woman kissed was female. Dubois's account also emphasizes the woman's modesty. "What did you dream of" was my question; but the patient turned up her face aside with a smile, the peculiarity of which having drawn my particular attention, I renewed my question; but on her having again refused to let me know the nature of her dream, I had recourse, in order to ascertain it, to the intermediary communication of a respectable person of her own sex, and who was present at the operation of inhaling ether. To the same question being renewed, she answered, she had dreamt she was beside her husband, and that he and herself had been simultaneously engaged, going through those preliminaries which had led her to the state in which we now beheld her' (*London Lancet*, 1859, pp. 411–12). W. Tyler Smith, who had arrived in London in 1840 after scanty education in Bristol, had no influence or connections, yet he rose to such prominence that in 1859 he became one of the founders of the Obstetrical Society. His degree was an MB; he was not a member of the Royal Colleges. See A. J. Youngson, *Scientific Revolution in Victorian Medicine*, New York: Holmes & Meier, 1979, pp. 77–8; and W. Tyler Smith, 'On the founding of the obstetrical society of London (1859),' *Transactions of the Obstetrical Society of London*, 1859, pp. 5–4.

6. *London Lancet*, 1, 1847, p. 377.

7. For discussions of the domestication of this image, see Nancy Armstrong, *Desire and Domestic Fiction: A Political History of the Novel*, New York: Oxford University Press, 1987, esp. ch. 2; Susan Staves, *Players'*

Scepters: Fictions of Authority in the Restoration, Lincoln, Nebr.: University of Nebraska Press, 1979, ch. 3; and Mary Poovey, *The Proper Lady and the Woman Writer: Ideology as Style in the Works of Mary Wollstonecraft, Mary Shelley, and Jane Austen*, Chicago: University of Chicago Press, 1984, ch. 1.

8. *Lancet*, 1, 1849, p. 212. In 1853, Dr Robert Lee and Dr Gream were still making this point. See *Lancet*, 1, 1853, p. 611.

9. *Lancet*, 1, 1849, p. 212.

10. *Ibid.*, pp. 39, 5. Dr Syme added that 'he had never witnessed any sexual excitement produced by the exhibition of chloroform, but that he and others had frequently heard patients in the operating theatre swearing, when excited by chloroform, and that, sometimes, in patients whose friends had seldom or never heard using such language. Possibly these improper expressions were only a true exhibition of the state of the patient's mind, and it was always stopped by throwing him deeply asleep' (p. 395).

11. *Lancet*, 1, 1855, p. 499. One way of construing the quarrel about how to administer chloroform is to see it as part of an ongoing debate about whether Edinburgh-trained medical men were superior or inferior to London-trained men. The 'Edinburgh method' of chloroform application was considered by many English doctors as irresponsible and unsafe; in England, lighter doses were applied, and often doctors used an inhaler – not a rag or handkerchief – to administer the anodyne. In Edinburgh, all medical men were trained in surgery and pharmacy and were therefore what would be called general practitioners in England. When they began coming to England in large numbers in the second half of the eighteenth century, they helped swell the ranks of general practitioners, many of whom wanted – but were denied – representation in the Royal Colleges. Scottish physicians were not formally recognized in England, but the Royal Colleges had no mechanism for effectively limiting their practice. See Noel Parry and José Parry, *The Rise of the Medical Profession: A Study of Collective Social Mobility*, London: Croom Helm, 1976, pp. 105–7.

12. This phrase appears in *Lancet*, 1, 1856, p. 424.

1.3

WOMEN'S FRIENDSHIPS AND LESBIANISM

Sheila Jeffreys

Sheila Jeffreys also takes an historical perspective in order to illustrate changing perceptions of close relationships between women. She argues that redefinitions of female sexuality in the late nineteenth and early twentieth centuries, along with the construction of the category 'lesbian', resulted in the outlawing of passionate friendships.

In the eighteenth and early nineteenth centuries many middle-class women had relationships with each other which included passionate declarations of love, nights spent in bed together sharing kisses and intimacies, and lifelong devotion, without exciting the least adverse comment. Feminist historians have explained that the letters and diaries of middle-class women in America in the first half of the nineteenth century frequently contain references to a passionate same-sex friendship.[1] Lillian Faderman's book *Surpassing the Love of Men* details innumerable such friendships between women which met with such social approval that a woman could cheerfully write to the male fiancé of the woman she loved, saying that she felt exactly like a husband towards her and was going to be very jealous.[2] Women so involved with one another might, if they got married, refuse to be parted from their loved one, so that the husband would have to honeymoon with two women instead of one. Such friendships were seen by men as useful because they trained women in the ways of love in preparation for marriage.

These women wrote about their feelings to each other in ways which would nowadays seem quite inappropriate to same-sex friendship. Faderman describes the friendship between Jane Welsh Carlyle and the novelist and spinster Geraldine

From S. Jeffreys, *The Spinster and her Enemies*, Hammersmith. HarperCollins Publishers Ltd, 1985.

Jewsbury. Jewsbury sought to sustain her friend through her difficult marriage to the foul-tempered philosopher Thomas Carlyle. In their correspondence they expressed their passionate emotional attachment. The following extracts from Jewsbury's letters show how she felt:

> O Carissima Mia . . . you are never out of either my head or my heart. After you left on Tuesday I felt so horribly wretched, too miserable even to cry, and what could be done? (July 1841); I love you my darling, more than I can express, more than I am conscious of myself, and yet I can do nothing for you. (October 29 1841); I love you more than anything else in the world . . . It may do you no good now, but it may be a comfort some time, it will always be there for you. (May 1842); If I could see you and speak to you, I should have no tragic mood for a year to come, I think, and really that is saying no little, for I have had a strong inclination to hang myself oftener than once with the last month. (c. 1843)[3]

Historians could not fail to notice the expression of such sentiments. They have tried to ignore them or explain them away so that they could not be allowed to challenge their heterosexual account of history. The commonest approach has been to say that such romantic expressions were simply the normal form of friendship at that time. They say that it was fashionable to be effusive. Precisely the same explanation has been given for the romantic emotional expression between men of the sixteenth century. In this way historians have tidied away what they found incongruous and wiped the history of homoeroticism from the slate of heterosexual history.

The American feminist historian Carroll Smith-Rosenberg has given passionate friendships between women the attention they deserve in her essay 'The Female World of Love and Ritual'. She does not underestimate the importance of passionate friendships but by concentrating on explaining why women might have found such friendships necessary at the time she implies that such expression between women is somehow deviant and needs more explanation than heterosexuality. She explains that such relationships between women were a vital support for women who were likely to marry virtual strangers, for whom they were unlikely to feel great emotional or physical attachment. She sees these women as having needed the comfort of female friends through the difficult and gruelling lives of constant childbearing. She explains that men and women were brought up in quite separate, homosocial worlds so that women were most likely to rely on same-sex relationships for support and nurturance. The implication of such an explanation might be that such same-sex friendships are obsolete today. It is not the existence of love between women that needs explaining but why women were permitted to love then in a way which would encounter fierce social disapproval now.

The feminist historians who have been uncovering these relationships have assumed that they were devoid of genital sexual expression on the grounds that the repression of women's genital sexuality in the nineteenth century would have made spontaneous genital expression unlikely. Whether or not these women expressed themselves genitally there is no doubt that physical excitement and eroticism played an important part in their love. This is clear from the way Sophia Jex-Blake describes her relationship with Octavia Hill in the following quotation from her diary of 1860. The two women are negotiating the spending of a holiday together:

> Told Octa about Wales, – sitting in her room on the table, my heart beating like a hammer. That Carry [Sophia's sister] wanted to go to Wales and I too, and most convenient about the beginning of July, so . . . 'Put off my visit?' said Octa. 'No, I was just going to say . . . if you wish to see anything of me, you must come too, I think and not put off the mountains until heaven.' She sunk her head on my lap silently, raised it in tears, and then such a kiss.[4]

It is not a platonic peck on the cheek which is being described here. On the grounds of the absence of genital contact alone, some contemporary feminist writers have sought to establish a clear distinction between these passionate friendships, even in the case of spinsters like Jex-Blake and Hill who were in passionate friendships with women all their lives, and 'lesbianism'.[5] Such a distinction is very difficult to draw. The conventions which govern the expression of erotic love may change, but the emotions and the physical excitement may have felt the same.

Today intense emotional and sensual interaction between women friends in the West is not seen as socially acceptable. Faderman illustrates this change with an experiment which was carried out at Palo Alto High School in 1973:

> For three weeks the girls behaved on campus as all romantic friends did in the previous century: They held hands often on campus walks, they sat with their arms around each other, and they exchanged kisses on the cheek when classes ended. They expressly did not intend to give the impression that their feelings were sexual. They touched each other only as close, affectionate friends would. But despite their intentions, their peers interpreted their relationship as lesbian and ostracised them.[6]

In contemporary society women are only expected to feel a controlled and non-physical level of fondness for their women friends and to wonder if they are 'lesbian' if they feel more. Why and how did this change occur?

Faderman explains that women's same-sex friendships came to be seen as a threat in the late nineteenth century as the women's movement developed to challenge men's dominance and new social and economic forces presented middle-class women with the possibility of choosing not to marry and be dependent on men. She sees the sexologists who classified and categorised female homosexuality, including within it all passionate friendships, as having played a major role in discouraging love between women for all those who did not want to adopt the label of homosexuality. Another American feminist historian, Nancy Sahli, shows how the outlawing of women's friendships was put into operation.[7] In American women's colleges up until the late nineteenth century, the practice of 'smashing', in which young women would pursue their beloveds with gifts and declarations until their feelings were returned and they were 'smashed' was perfectly acceptable. These friendships were gradually outlawed and rendered suspicious by college heads who were often living with women they loved in passionate unions themselves. By the 1890s it was seen as necessary to root out these friendships as unhealthy practices.

As part of their self-imposed task of categorising varieties of human sexual behaviour, the sexologists of the late nineteenth century set about the 'scientific' description of lesbianism. Their description has had a momentous effect on the ways in which we, as women, have seen ourselves and all our relationships with other women up until the present. They codified as 'scientific' wisdom current myths about lesbian sexual practice, a stereotype of the lesbian and the 'pseudohomosexual' woman, categorising women's passionate friendships as female homosexuality and offered explanations for the phenomenon. Male writers of gay history have tended to see their work as sympathetic and helpful to the development of a homosexual rights movement since they explained male homosexuality in terms of innateness or used psychoanalytic explanations which undermined the view of male homosexuality as criminal behaviour.[8] Female homosexual behaviour was never illegal in Britain, though there were attempts to make it so in 1921, so the sexologists' contribution cannot be seen as positive in that way.

Havelock Ellis provided a classic stereotype of the female homosexual in his *Sexual Inversion*:[9]

> When they still retain female garments, these usually show some traits of masculine simplicity, and there is nearly always a disdain for the petty feminine artifices of the toilet. Even when this is not obvious, there are all sorts of instinctive gestures and habits which may suggest to female acquaintances the remark that such a person 'ought to have been a man'.

[. . .]

Feminists were neatly slotted into a picture of lesbian women who were really pseudomen. Using the accusation of lesbianism to subvert women's attempts at emancipation is a form of attack with which women involved in the contemporary wave of feminism are all too familiar. Ellis's *Sexual Inversion* was the first volume in his *Studies in the Psychology of Sex*. Contemporary male gay historians have seen him as performing a service to male homosexuals by breaking down the stereotype that they were effeminate. For women the service he performed was quite the reverse.

[. . .]

As a counterpart to the 'butch' masculine stereotype of the lesbian which the sexologists were creating, they provided a model for the 'pseudohomosexual'. They made it clear that their concern about the pseudohomosexual stemmed from what they saw as the spread of homosexuality within the feminist movement. Edward Carpenter expressed in 1897 his alarm at the phenomenon of lesbianism within the women's movement, combined with a quite obvious horror at the extent to which feminists were abandoning the constraints of the feminine sex role.

[. . .]

Such women do not altogether represent their sex; some are rather mannish in temperament; some are 'homogenic', that is inclined to attachments to their own sex rather than the opposite sex; such women are ultra-rationalising and brain-cultured.

[. . .]

Edward Carpenter, like Havelock Ellis, is currently seen as a founding father of sexual enlightenment, and as a male homosexual who, in writing about men's love for each other positively, was an inspiration to the burgeoning male homosexual rights movement. In the light of his reputation as a homosexual revolutionary, as well as a friend to feminism, such comments on lesbians and feminists strike a rather discordant note. What they suggest, like the rest of his writings, is that his view of women's emancipation was that women should have equal rights so long as they remained different, feminine and passionately attached to men.

[. . .]

The pseudohomosexual was characterised as a woman who did not necessarily fit the masculine stereotype, had been seduced by a 'real homosexual' and led away from a natural heterosexuality, to which it was hoped that she would return. Real homosexuality was seen to be innate, and pseudohomosexuality a temporary divergence. Ellis described pseudohomosexuality as a 'spurious imitation'.

[. . .]

The pseudohomosexual is shown to be not just easily led but intellectually inferior which should be enough to discourage women from 'imitation'.

[. . .]

One of Ellis's case studies illustrates how this confusion around self-definition was operating amongst women at the time that Ellis was writing. The case study is of a woman who specifically denied herself genital sexual expression with the woman she lived with and loved in order to avoid having to fit herself into the definition of homosexuality being offered in the sexological literature of the 1890s. She writes that her woman friend had been having a 'trying time' and moved into her bed on the advice of a doctor so that she would not have to sleep alone:

> One night, however, when she had had a cruelly trying day and I wanted to find all ways of comforting her, I bared my breast for her to lie on. Afterwards it was clear that neither of us could be satisfied without this . . . Much of this excitement was sexually localised, and I was haunted in the daytime by images of holding this woman in my arms. I noticed also that my inclination to caress my other women friends was not diminished, but increased. All this disturbed me a great deal. The homosexual practices of which I had read lately struck me as merely nasty; I could not imagine myself tempted to them.[10]

The woman continues by saying that she consulted an older man friend who advised her to be very careful and not give in to her impulses. She told her friend of her anxiety and of her decision, which was clearly to forego genital sexual expression. The friend was unhappy, none the less they went on sleeping together. The result was that they continued to have a passionate emotional and physical relationship which merely omitted genital contact:

> in the day when no one was there we sat as close together as we wished, which was very close. We kissed each other as often as we wanted to kiss each other, which was many times a day.
>
> The results of this, so far as I can see, have been wholly good. We love each other warmly, but no temptation to nastiness has ever come, and I cannot see now that it is at all likely to come. With custom, the localised physical excitement has practically disappeared, and I am no longer obsessed by imagined embraces. The spiritual side of our affection seems to have grown steadily stronger and more profitable since the physical side has been allowed to take its natural place.[11]

This woman's precautions did protect her from being classified as a true invert in Ellis's studies. It would be interesting to see how contemporary lesbians would define this woman today. The case study demonstrates the effect which sexological literature was already having upon what was in the 1890s probably only the very small group of women who had access to this literature. These women were having to make choices and instead of living out their love for other women in whatever ways seemed appropriate to them, they had to decide whether they were female homosexuals or just friends.

American lesbian feminist historians suggest that female homosexuality and all strong emotional expression between women was stigmatised by the sexologists in the late nineteenth and early twentieth century in response to a concatenation of social and economic circumstances which offered a real threat to men's domination over women.[12] Increased job opportunities for middle-class women in the steadily growing spheres of education, after the 1870 Education Act in Britain, in clerical work and shop work, provided opportunities for women to maintain themselves independently of men. Changes in social attitudes allowed for single women to live together outside their families without being regarded with suspicion. Suitable living space in the form of rooms and flatlets was becoming available in the 1890s.

[. . .]

A section of Radclyffe Hall's *The Unlit Lamp* in which she describes a circle of women engaged in passionate friendships with each other living in rooms in London in the 1890s, suggests that opportunities for women to live together existed at that time.

[. . .] [T]he number of women in excess of men in the population was steadily rising in the last half of the nineteenth century. When this 'surplus' of women had the possibility of living and working outside the structures of heterosexuality they became a threat to the maintenance of men's control. This threat was particularly serious when independent women were engaged in passionate friendships with each other and were in a position to form a strong female network which could bond against men. It was this last danger that the development of a strong feminist movement appeared to be creating in the late nineteenth century. It is clear from the writings of the sexologists that they were far from enthusiastic about feminism, and particularly its lesbian manifestations. An attack upon passionate emotional involvement between women served to undermine the link between them and dilute their potential strength.

[. . .]

Two explanations for homosexuality were advanced in the period. One form of explanation was to attribute homosexuality to a hereditary, unchangeable cause. Havelock Ellis saw homosexuality as innate, Krafft-Ebing cited a hereditary taint and Edward Carpenter favoured the theory of a third or intermediate sex. The other form of explanation, developed in the work of the psychoanalysts from Freud onwards, was to see homosexuality as a result of childhood trauma. Lillian Faderman explains how the first form of explanation was more attractive to lesbians in the period, because it offered no possibility of a 'cure', and attributed no blame or individual responsibility. She suggests that, as a result, those women who were determined to assume a lesbian identity, based upon the sexological definitions, could do so and demand public tolerance on the grounds that they could not help themselves. As an example of this process Faderman cites Radclyffe Hall's *The Well of Loneliness* as an impassioned plea for tolerance in which the heroine is fashioned into a 'masculine' homosexual as in Ellis's definition.

[. . .]

Some historians suggest that explanations in the form of innateness helped in the formation of a proud self-conscious homosexual sub-culture in the post-First World War period. But we must remember that the necessity for this form of 'defence' was the result of the sexologists' work in stigmatising and isolating the lesbian in the first place.

The changing climate in attitudes to lesbianism is illustrated by the way in which female homosexuality was almost made illegal in 1921. An amendment to the [UK] bill to make the age of consent 16 for indecent assault was added in committee and subsequently passed in the house. The amendment read as follows: 'Any act of gross indecency between female persons shall be a misdemeanour and punishable in the same manner as any such act committed by male persons under section 11 of the Criminal Law Amendment Act 1885.'[13]

The amendment failed to pass into law because the bill to which it was attached was an 'agreed' bill, meaning that the government would only find time for it if it was not significantly altered. The amendment destroyed the bill. The debate gives us an opportunity to sample the attitudes of MPs towards lesbianism at this time. All who spoke purported to be equally disturbed at having to mention such a noxious subject, and they were united in their condemnation. Those who opposed the amendment did so on the grounds that making lesbianism illegal would only spread the offence by giving it publicity. Colonel Wedgwood declared, 'it is a beastly subject, and it is being better advertised by the moving of this Clause than in any other way.'[14] Lieutenant Moore-Brabazon suggested that there were three possible ways of dealing with the 'pervert'. The death penalty would 'stamp them out', and locking them up as lunatics would 'get rid of them' but the third way, ignoring them, was best:

> The third way is to leave them entirely alone, not notice them, not advertise them. That is the method that has been adopted in England for many hundred years, and I believe that it is the best method now, these cases are self-exterminating. They are examples of ultra-civilisation, but they have the merit of exterminating themselves, and consequently they do not spread or do very much harm to society at large . . . To adopt a Clause of this kind would harm by introducing into the minds of perfectly innocent people the most revolting thoughts.[15]

Lesbianism, then, did not escape legal penalty in Britain for so long simply because of Queen Victoria's fabled refusal to believe lesbians existed, or because the legislature regarded lesbianism as less 'beastly' than male homosexuality. Lesbianism was an alarming phenomenon to these MPs because they thought it would spread like wildfire if women even heard of it. Silence, and every attempt to make lesbianism invisible, was the only effective weapon.

One reason the MPs gave for the great dangerousness of lesbianism was its purported role in destroying civilisations:

> These moral weaknesses date back to the very origin of history, and when they grow and become prevalent in any nation or in any country, it is the beginning of the nation's downfall. The falling away of feminine morality was to a large extent the cause of the destruction of the early Greek civilisation, and still more the cause of the downfall of the Roman Empire.[16]

It could, according to another MP, cause 'our race to decline'.[17] Another reason given was the danger posed to husbands who might lose their wives to the 'wiles' of the lesbian. Most cogent of all was the fact that lesbianism 'saps the fundamental institutions of society' since 'any woman who indulges in this vice will have nothing whatever to do with the other sex'.[18] The MPs were aware that the spread of lesbianism could undermine the institutions of marriage and the heterosexual family through which male dominance over women was maintained.

It would be a shame to leave this debate without mentioning the great solicitude shown by ex-public school MPs towards their colleagues in the Labour party. Colonel Wedgwood explained, 'I do not suppose that there are any members of the Labour party who know in the least what is intended by the Clause.'[19] Wedgwood claimed that they would not know because they would not have studied the classics, and it was only from such study that MPs could know anything of homosexuality.

Stella Browne and Marie Stopes are two women who are recognised as having made very significant contributions to the history of sex reform. Stella Browne was a socialist feminist who campaigned for birth control and abortion from the period immediately before the First World War to the 1930s. She was a member of the British Society for the Study of Sex Psychology founded in 1914. [. . .] Marie Stopes began her career in the writing of sex advice books and the promotion of birth control information with the publication of *Married Love* in 1918. Both women helped to popularise the ideas of the male sex reformers. [. . .] The promotion of heterosexuality by sex advice writers was invariably combined with the stigmatising of lesbianism. If women were to be encouraged into active participation in heterosexual sex then they had to be persuaded that there was no reasonable alternative by the negative portrayal of love between women. Stopes and Browne both exhibited great anxiety about lesbianism and sought, with great difficulty, to distinguish between innocent affectionate friendships and inversion. There are indications that both these women had experience of passionate friendships with women which they felt forced to redefine or reject when they adopted the ideology of the male sexologists.

[. . .]

Browne distinguished between pseudohomosexuality and real lesbianis: 'Artificial or substitute homosexuality – as distinct from true inversion – is very widely diffused among women, as a result of the repression of normal gratification and the segregation of the sexes, which still largely obtains.'[20] She further distinguished between pseudohomosexuality, which she went so far as to say might be 'entirely platonic', and 'true affectionate friendship' between women: 'Sometimes its only direct manifestations are quite noncommittal and platonic but even this incomplete and timid homosexuality can always be distinguished from true affectionate friendship between women, by its jealous, exacting and extravagant tone.'[21] Browne gives women a clue about how to classify the nature of their feelings for other women. Homosexual love is 'jealous, exacting and extravagant', i.e. unpleasant. She offers no clearer distinction and it would not be surprising if women remained confused. The dividing line between friendship and pseudohomosexuality is clearly artificial given that pseudohomosexuality can be 'platonic' anyway. She compounds the confusion by saying that women need not doubt their heterosexuality even if they experience no attraction towards men until late in life and have felt devotion and intense desire for women friends. [. . .] It is possible to infer from the way in which Browne writes about passionate friendships between women that her sympathetic knowledge comes from her own experience.

[. . .]

She backs up her assertion that women require men with a list of the dreadful physical consequences which will befall them if they are independent:

> I would even say that after twenty-five, the woman who has neither husband nor lover and is not under-vitalised and sexually deficient, is suffering mentally and bodily – often without knowing why she suffers; nervous, irritated, anaemic, always tired, or ruthlessly fussing over trifles; or else she has other consolations, which make her so-called 'chastity' a pernicious sham.[22]

[. . .]

Suffragists were singled out for attack. 'I am sure that much of the towering spiritual arrogance which is found, e.g. in many high places in the Suffrage movement . . . is really unconscious inversion.'[23] She thought that it was repressed inversion which fuelled feminism, and that the women's feminist zeal would be undermined if they had sexually fulfilling relationships with each other [. . .] It seems that Browne was in a real agony of mind. She was unable to condemn love affairs between women, perhaps because she was one of the women of 'fine brains' who were forced into them, but she saw them as really inferior to heterosexuality. She could only justify such relationships on the grounds that genital contact was involved so that they might serve to undermine the aggressive feminism which she saw as based on women's frigidity.

[. . .]

Marie Stopes was a fervent missionary in the cause of heterosexual love and sex. [. . .] Stopes invested heterosexual sex and specifically sexual intercourse, with mystical, religious exultation in *Married Love* she wrote when she had not even experienced sexual intercourse herself . . . One might well be tempted to think that the lady did protest too much.

[. . .]

Married Love was written after Stopes engaged in a detailed study of sexological literature through which she hoped to find the answer to the frustrations she felt in her unconsummated marriage. From that literature she would have received an alarming picture of the dangers of intense female friendship from the sexologists' classifications and vilifying of lesbianism.

Stopes exposed the intensity of her anxiety about lesbianism in *Enduring Passion* in 1928. She was worried because she believed women would prefer lesbian sex if they tried it, and might abandon their marriages:

> If a married woman does this unnatural thing she may find a growing disappointment in her husband and he may lose all natural power to play his proper part . . .
> No woman who values the peace of her home and the love of her husband should yield to the wiles of the lesbian whatever her temptation to do so.[24]

She considered that lesbianism was spreading, especially among 'independent' women, and was moved to exclaim, 'This corruption spreads as an underground fire spreads in the peaty soil of a dry moorland.'[25] Having already admitted the strong and possibly superior attractions of lesbian sex, she was forced to find a reason for the importance of sexual intercourse which had nothing to do with enjoyment. Stopes believed, though no scientific proof was forthcoming for her hypothesis, that secretions from the man's penis were necessary to women's bodily health, and that these passed through the walls of the vagina during sexual intercourse. She explained, 'The bedrock objection to it [lesbianism] is surely that women can only *play* with each other and *cannot* in the very nature of things have natural union or supply each other with the seminal or prostatic secretions they ought to have.'[26] This was bad news for celibate women and women whose male lovers wore condoms as well as for lesbians. Stopes was forced to invent a mythical dependence of women on sexual intercourse for their physical health for want of any more cogent arguments against lesbianism. Women were asked to have faith and carry on with heterosexuality.

The writings of Stella Browne and Marie Stopes, since they are by women at a time when the vast majority of literature prescribing how women should relate to men was by men, could be seen as validating the prescription of the sexologists. Stopes and

Browne could be regarded as promoting what women 'really' wanted, what was 'really' in women's interests. This cannot be a realistic picture. They were writing at a time which was a watershed in the history of the construction of women's sexuality. It was a time when the male sexologists were calling upon women to repudiate their love for each other and pour their energies into men. Browne and Stopes form part of a generation of women who had to twist themselves into knots by rejecting their own experience of loving women. From this time on the sex reformers would have had a less difficult task. In later generations women's love for women would not appear as a conceivable choice, which they would then have to reject.

NOTES

1. Caroll Smith-Rosenberg, 'The female world of love and ritual: relations between women in the nineteenth century America', in N.F. Cott and E.H. Pleck (eds), *A Heritage of Her Own*, New York: Touchstone Books, Simon & Schuster, 1979.
2. Lillian Faderman, *Surpassing the Love of Men: Romantic Friendship and Love between Women from the Renaissance to the Present*, London: Junctions, 1981.
3. *Ibid.*, p. 164.
4. Smith-Rosenberg, 'The female world of love and ritual'.
5. Rosemary Auchmuty, 'Victorian spinsters', unpublished Ph.D. thesis, Australian National University, 1975.
6. Faderman, *Surpassing the Love of Men*, p. 312.
7. For an example of criticism of Faderman see Sonia Ruehl, 'Sexual theory and practice: another double standard', in Sue Cartledge and Joanna Ryan (eds), *Sex and Love: New Thoughts on Old Contradictions*, London: The Women's Press, 1983.
8. Jeffrey Weeks, *Coming Out: Homosexual Politics in Britain from the Nineteenth Century to the Present*, London: Quartet Books, 1977.
9. Havelock Ellis, *Sexual Inversion: Studies in the Psychology of Sex*, vol. 2, Philadelphia, F.A. Davis, 1927, first published 1897, p. 221.
10. *Ibid.*, p. 200.
11. *Ibid.*, p. 221.
12. H. Faderman, *Surpassing the Love of Men*, Nancy Sahli, 'Smashing: women's relationships before the Fall', *Chrysalis*, no. 8.
13. Parliamentary Debates, Commons, 1921, vol. 145, 1799.
14. *Ibid.*, 1800.
15. *Ibid.*, 1805.
16. *Ibid.*, 1799.
17. *Ibid.*, 1804.
18. *Ibid.*, 1804.
19. *Ibid.*, 1800.
20. Shelia Rowbotham, *A New World for Women: Stella Browne, Socialist Feminist*, London: Pluto Press, 1977, p. 102.
21. *Ibid.*, p. 102.
22. *Ibid.*, p. 101.
23. *Ibid.*, p. 57.
24. Marie Stopes, *Enduring Passion*, London: Hogarth Press, 1953 (first published 1928), p. 29.
25. *Ibid.*, p. 30.
26. *Ibid.*

1.4

BIOLOGICAL SUPERIORITY
The World's Most Dangerous and Deadly Idea

Andrea Dworkin

Andrea Dworkin's critique of essentialism rests on its potential political consequences. Writing in 1978, when some feminist activists were attracted to the idea that women were naturally superior to men, Dworkin argues that this view is just as mistaken as that which asserts that women are naturally subordinate. Taking a radical feminist perspective she suggests that any form of biological determinism is ultimately Fascist in its implications.

I

All who are not of good race in this world are chaff.

Hitler, Mein Kampf

It would be lunacy to try to estimate the value of man according to his race, thus declaring war on the Marxist idea that men are equal, unless we are determined to draw the ultimate consequences. And the ultimate consequence of recognising the importance of blood   that is, of the racial foundation in general – is the transference of this estimation to the individual person.

Hitler, Mein Kampf

Hisses. Women shouting at me: slut, bisexual, she fucks men. And before I had spoken, I had been trembling, more afraid to speak than I had ever been. And, in a room of 200 sister lesbians, as angry as I have ever been. 'Are you a bisexual?' some woman screamed over the pandemonium, the hisses and shouts merging into a raging noise. 'I'm a Jew,' I answered; then, a pause, 'and a lesbian, and a woman.' And a coward. Jew was enough. In that room, Jew was what mattered. In that room, to answer the question 'Do you still fuck men?' with a No, as I did, was to betray my deepest convictions. All of my life, I have hated the proscribers, those who enforce sexual conformity. In answering, I had given in to the inquisitors, and I felt ashamed. It humiliated me to see myself then: one who resists the enforcers out there with militancy, but gives in without resistance to the enforcers among us.

The event was a panel on 'Lesbianism as a Personal Politic' that took place in New York City, Lesbian Pride Week 1977. A self-proclaimed lesbian separatist had spoken. Amidst the generally accurate description of male crimes against women came this ideological rot, articulated of late with increasing frequency in feminist circles: women and men are distinct species or races (the words are used interchangeably); men are biologically inferior to women; male violence is a biological inevitability; to eliminate it, one must eliminate the species/race itself (means stated on this particular evening: developing parthenogenesis as a viable reproductive reality); in eliminating the biologically inferior species/race Man, the new *Ubermensch* Womon [. . .] will have the earthly dominion that is her true biological destiny. We are left to infer that the society of her creation will be good because she is good, biologically good. In the interim, insipient SuperWomon will not do anything to 'encourage' women to 'collaborate' with men.

[. . .]

The audience applauded the passages on female superiority/male inferiority enthusiastically. This doctrine seemed to be music to their ears. Was there dissent, silent, buried in the applause? Was some of the response the spontaneous pleasure that we all know when, at last, the tables are turned, even for a minute, even in imagination? Or has powerlessness driven us mad, so that we dream secret dreams of a final solution perfect in its simplicity, absolute in its efficacy? And will a leader someday strike that secret chord, harness those dreams, our own nightmare turned upside down? Is there no haunting, restraining memory of the blood spilled, the bodies burned, the ovens filled, the peoples enslaved, by those who have assented throughout history to the very same demagogic logic?

In the audience, I saw women I like or love, women not strangers to me, women who are good not because of biology but because they care about being good, swept along in a sea of affirmation. I spoke out because those women had applauded. I spoke out too because I am a Jew who has studied Nazi Germany, and I know that many Germans who followed Hitler also cared about being good, but found it easier to be good by biological definition than by act. Those people, wretched in what they experienced as their own unbearable powerlessness, became convinced that they were so good biologically that nothing they did could be bad. As Himmler said in 1943:

> We have exterminated a bacterium [Jews] because we did not want in the end to be infected by the bacterium and die of it. I will not see so much as a small area of sepsis appear here or gain a hold. Wherever it may form, we will cauterize it. All in all, we can say that we have fulfilled this most difficult duty for the love of our people. And our spirit, our soul, our character has not suffered injury from it.[1]

So I spoke, afraid. I said that I would not be associated with a movement that advocated the most pernicious ideology on the face of the earth. It was this very ideology of biological determinism that had licensed the slaughter and/or enslavement of virtually any group one could name, including women by men. ('Use their own poison against them,' one woman screamed.) Anywhere one looked, it was this philosophy that justified atrocity. This was one faith that destroyed life with a momentum of its own.

[. . .]

II

I am told that I am a sexist. I *do* believe that the differences between the sexes arc our most precious heritage, even though they make women superior in the ways that matter most.

George Gilder, *Sexual Suicide*

Perhaps this female wisdom comes from resignation to the reality of male aggression; more likely it is a harmonic of the woman's knowledge that ultimately she is the one who matters. As a result, while there are more brilliant men than brilliant women, there are more good women than good men.

Steven Goldberg, *The Inevitability of Patriarchy*

As a class (not necessarily as individuals), we can bear children. From this, according to male-supremacist ideology, all our other attributes and potentialities are derived. On the pedestal, immobile like waxen statues, or in the gutter, failed icons mired in shit, we are exalted or degraded because our biological traits arc what they are. Citing genes, genitals, DNA, pattern-releasing smells, biograms, hormones, or whatever is in vogue, male supremacists make their case which is, in essence, that we are biologically too good, too bad, or too different to do anything other than reproduce and serve men sexually and domestically.

The newest variations on this distressingly ancient theme centre on hormones and DNA: men are biologically aggressive; their fetal brains were awash in androgen; their DNA, in order to perpetuate itself, hurls them into murder and rape; in women, pacifism is hormonal and addiction to birth is molecular. Since in Darwinian terms (interpreted to conform to the narrow social self-interest of men), survival of the fittest means the triumph of the most aggressive human beings, men are and always will be superior to women in terms of their ability to protect and extend their own authority. Therefore women, being 'weaker' (less aggressive), will always be at the mercy of men. That this theory of the social ascendancy of the fittest consigns us to eternal indignity and, applied to race, conjures up Hitler's identical view of evolutionary struggle, must not unduly trouble us. 'By current theory,' writes Edward O. Wilson reassuringly in *Sociobiology: The New Synthesis*, a bible of genetic justification for slaughter, 'genocide or genosorption strongly favouring the aggressor need take place only once every few generations to direct evolution.'[2]

III

I have told you the very low opinion in which you [women] were held by Mr Oscar Browning. I have indicated what Napoleon once thought of you and what Mussolini thinks now. Then, in case any of you aspire to fiction, I have copied out for your benefit the advice of the critic about courageously acknowledging the limitations of your sex. I have referred to Professor X and given prominence to his statement that women are intellectually, morally and physically inferior, to men ... and here is a final warning ... Mr John Langdon Davies warns women 'that when children cease to be altogether desirable, women cease to be altogether necessary.' I hope you will make note of it.

Virginia Woolf, *A Room of One's Own*

In considering male intellectual and scientific argumentation in conjunction with male history, one is forced to conclude that men as a class are moral cretins. The vital question is: are we to accept *their* world view of a moral polarity that is biologically fixed, genetically or hormonally or genitally (or whatever organ or secretion or molecular particle they scapegoat next) absolute; or does our own historical experience of social deprivation and injustice teach us that to be free in a just world we will have to destroy the power, the dignity, the efficacy of this one idea above all others?

Recently, more and more feminists have been advocating social, spiritual, and mythological models that are female-supremacist and/or matriarchal. To me, this advocacy signifies a basic conformity to the tenets of biological determinism that underpin the male social system. Pulled toward an ideology based on the moral and social significance of a distinct female biology because of its emotional and philosophical familiarity, drawn to the spiritual dignity inherent in a 'female principle' (essentially as defined by men), of course unable to abandon by will or impulse a lifelong and centuries-old commitment to childbearing as *the* female creative act, women have increasingly tried to transform the very ideology that has enslaved us into a dynamic, religious, psychologically compelling celebration of female biological potential. This attempted transformation may have survival value – that is, the worship of our procreative capacity as *power* may temporarily stay the male-supremacist hand that cradles the test tube. But the price we pay is that we become carriers of the disease we must cure. It is no accident that some female supremacists now believe men to be a distinct and inferior species or race. Wherever power is accessible or bodily integrity honoured on the basis of biological attribute, systematised cruelty permeates the society and murder and mutilation will contaminate it. We will not be different.

It is shamefully easy for us to enjoy our own fantasies of biological omnipotence while despising men for enjoying the reality of theirs. And it is dangerous – because genocide begins, however improbably, in the conviction that classes of biological distinction indisputably sanction social and political discrimination. We, who have been devastated by the concrete consequences of this idea, still want to put our faith in it. Nothing offers more proof – sad, irrefutable proof – that we are more like men than either they or we care to believe.

NOTES

1. Jeremy Noakes and Geoffrey Pridham (eds), *Documents on Nazism 1919–1945*. New York: The Viking Press, 1975, p. 493.
2. Edward O. Wilson, *Sociobiology: The New Synthesis*, Cambridge, Mass.: The Belknap Press of the Havard University Press, 1975, p. 573.

THE SOCIAL CONSTRUCTION OF FEMALE SEXUALITY

Stevi Jackson

In seeking to explain the construction of our individual sexualities, some feminists have turned to psychoanalysis, but others have been wary of it. This critique of Freud, written in the late 1970s, goes on to offer an alternative perspective on female sexuality derived from sociological perspectives.

Sexuality cannot be treated in isolation: it cannot be understood [as] if it is separated from [. . .] such things as the relations between the sexes, the cultural ideals of 'love', or the institution of marriage. Sexual behaviour is social behaviour; it is not just the consummation of some biological drive.

[. . .]

We cannot define anything as sexual in an absolute sense, for what is 'sexual' in one society may not necessarily be sexual in another. An act is not sexual by virtue of its inherent properties – [. . .] [but] becomes sexual by the application of socially learned meanings. Sexual behaviour is in this sense 'socially scripted' in that it is a 'part' that is learned and acted out within a social context, and different social contexts have different social scripts. In using the term 'sexuality', then, I am referring not just to genital sexual activity, but to all the attitudes, values, beliefs and behaviours which might be seen to have some sexual significance in our society. From this starting point it is possible to establish a theoretical framework in which female sexuality – and its implications – may be better understood.

THE DETERMINANTS OF HUMAN SEXUALITY: BIOLOGY VERSUS CULTURE

The idea that there is somehow some pure and uncontaminated 'human nature' underlies many theories about humanity but nowhere has it been given more prominence than in the area of sexuality. By classifying the version of sexuality in our own society as 'natural', typically masculine and feminine forms of sexuality are assumed to be part of the natural order of things and not therefore open to negotiation. Sexual attitudes and behaviour are still often thought of as preordained and the historical and cultural contributions to this form of activity ignored.

[. . .]

Sexual acts are classified as biological functions and it is naively assumed that the whole of human sexuality must be governed by something often referred to as 'instinct'.

These assumptions have been allowed to go unchallenged, despite the contradictory evidence which has accumulated. Biological factors do NOT determine the forms which sexuality takes, but merely set parameters within which other influences operate. Although women and men may differ genetically, hormonally, and physiologically, it is not possible to leap to the conclusion that they therefore also differ in terms of personality or behaviour. Biology is not destiny in any absolute sense; it only comes to be so through the qualities which are assigned to members of each gender within society.

The argument that specific forms of human behaviour, especially sexual behaviour, are 'natural' is often based on comparisons with animals, particularly other primates. As a species we do share some characteristics and fundamental needs with other mammals, but to apply evidence from animal observation directly to human behaviour is to ignore crucial differences. For human beings exist in a social environment structured through language and symbols, and this plays a much more influential role in determining how we behave than do the biological factors which we share with other animals. [. . .] But it is this very social environment and its crucial role that is likely to be forgotten in discussions of the sexual. For some reason the sexual is thought to be peculiarly representative of the 'animal' side of human nature.

> Committing the ethological fallacy, wherein we are warned that our hunting-gathering natures are the central themes around which modern man must organize his marriage and reproductive life or in which we are instructed to consider our common attributes with other primates, is an example of an unwillingness to live with the existential and changing nature of man (sic) at an individual and collective level.[1]

[. . .]

The form that sexual behaviour takes in our own society cannot be taken as a universal norm. Far from being fixed and immutable, human sexuality takes widely diverse forms and changes over time.

[. . .]

We cannot regard our own patterns of sexual activity as 'natural' and dismiss all else as the bizarre predilections of 'primitive' peoples. No one society can be taken as the norm. The message of anthropology is clear: there is an enormous range of possible styles of sexuality within our species, and the attitudes and behaviour found in any society are produced by social learning.

Within our own society women are assumed to be sexually passive and in general less sexual than men. [. . .] To understand why female sexuality takes the form that it does we need to examine cultural notions of femininity, attitudes to sexuality, and the whole interrelationship between our private lives and the structure of our society – an enormous task which is outside the scope of this paper. To understand how female sexuality develops we need to explore the ways in which the process of sexual learning operates and how this is related to other aspects of social learning. It is on this that I will now focus attention.

THE CULTURAL SHAPING OF THE SEXUAL: REPRESSIVE OR CONSTRUCTIVE?

How, then, does culture create the sexual? The process whereby an individual is socialized into particular modes of sexuality may be conceptualized in two essentially oppositional ways. We might begin by positing the existence of some form of innate sexual drive which is then moulded, modified, or repressed by the operation of social forces: i.e. that learning involves the curbing of instinctual urges. In terms of this model it could be argued that a particularly severe repression of libido undergone by women accounts for the form female sexuality takes. Alternatively we might postulate a process of learning through social interaction whereby the sexual is assimilated into the individual's self-concept. According to this view, psychosexual development is not contingent upon biological determinants, but on the milieu and content of social learning. The feminine mode of sexual expression would then be explained as the outcome of a particular form of learning rather than the repression of some quantifiable sexual energy.

The former premise is the basis on which Freudian theory was founded. Later work in this area, even when repudiating Freudianism, has tended to adopt the concept of the libido or at least the assumption that some basic sexual drive exists. This has tended to favour a rather over-determined view of sexuality as an innate force emanating from the individual. The alternative approach, as outlined by Gagnon and Simon attempts to counter these tendencies.[2]

The latter approach has several advantages. In the first place, by disallowing the primacy of biological drives, it permits a more positive conception of the socio-cultural influences involved, providing a sense of the social construction of sexuality rather than viewing the learning process as a negative tampering with innate biological mechanisms – even supposing that it is possible to identify an inborn, unsocialized drive. Secondly, this approach lends itself to a more sophisticated handling of the concept of socialization. To view this as the repression of innate drives is to present the individual as the passive product of a struggle between biological and social forces. Even if the latter are declared the victors of the battle, there is a danger of replacing biological determinism with an equally rigid and oversimplified sociologistic explanation. [. . .] Gagnon and Simon provide an interactionist framework within which the subject may be seen as active in her or his socialization: in the construction of the sexual self.

Finally, and perhaps most importantly, this perspective avoids the difficulties posed by the heritage of Freudian phallocentricity. It has been argued that

> . . . the fact is that the male sex is not only considered relatively superior to the female, but it is taken as the universal human norm.[3]

This assumption is an integral part of Freudian theory – the libido is seen as an active, masculine force. If female sexuality is assumed to be the product of a repressed libido, there is a danger of perceiving it as either a distorted version of the masculine (and therefore evaluating male sexuality as 'better') or as a functional complement to it. Most of the theorizing in this area has been done by men who have indeed conceptualized female sexuality in these terms. Gagnon and Simon's model enables us to see masculine and feminine forms of sexuality as the results of differing learning experiences rather than as the outcome of differential repression. Hence the problem of treating the feminine as merely the negation of the masculine is avoided.

Although Freud's theory may be rejected on these grounds, it cannot easily be dismissed as not worth discussing, for his massive contribution to theories of sexuality should not be ignored. His work represents the first comprehensive theory of psychosexual development and is a most impressive attempt to come to terms with the complexities of the problem, to understand the inter-relationship between biological, psychological and environmental influences and to relate sexuality to the rest of personality. Freud's theory assumes further importance by virtue of the great impact it has had upon everyday thinking about the sexual. Not only did it provide a starting point for the development of later theories, but it has filtered into the folk-knowledge of our society and helped to shape common-sense conceptions of sexuality. An examination of Freud's ideas and of the criticisms Gagnon and Simon offer will illuminate some of the problems involved in discussing the emergence and development of sexuality.

TALES OF TRAUMA AND TRANSFERENCE: FREUD ON FEMININITY AND SEXUALITY

[. . .]

Freud traces the development of the libido, an inborn sexual energy, through various stages which condition the final form of adult sexuality. But the significance of this development is not only sexual: for him the whole human personality is determined by a series of crises assailing the libido. He hopes to find the key to the 'mystery' of femininity and female sexuality in such phenomena as penis envy, the Œdipal situation, and the clitoral–vaginal transference. Of these it is the 'genital trauma' which is apparently the major influence upon the female psyche.

When a little girl of three or four years of age first sets eyes upon the male organ, Freud informs us, she immediately overcome by an intense envy from which she will never recover. On the basis of her own experience of clitoral activity she will make a correct judgement of the sexual, or at least masturbatory function of this organ and will 'realize' that her own is inadequate for the purpose. She will see herself as castrated. This traumatic discovery, Freud argues, is responsible for the greater degree of envy in the mental life of women and for their 'extraordinary vanity', the latter being a compensation for their anatomical 'deficiency'. Babies, too, are compensation: a male baby is particularly desired since he brings with him the 'longed-for penis'.[4]

Yet why should the little girl covet the boy's penis in the first place? At this age children positively evaluate the like-self[5] and it is therefore more likely that she will regard the male genitals as an ugly protuberance than as something desirable. Her own body she sees as whole and complete. Again, why should she then decide that her own organ is inferior for masturbatory purposes? It is unlikely that she will see her clitoris as a truncated penis, even if she is aware of its existence, which she need not be to engage in infantile styles of masturbation. In all likelihood she will come to the conclusion that the penis is simply a urinary organ, and in respect of this function it is true she may feel some envy. Simone de Beauvoir argues that, since at this age children are fascinated by their excretory functions, the girl may envy the boy's practical advantage in this matter. There is nothing to suggest, however, that this envy assumes the obsessive proportions Freud attributes to it. Moreover, this feeling would evaporate once the child outgrew her interest in such things.[6] It is possible that the anatomical difference comes to be symbolic of male prestige. So perhaps in this sense the penis may become an object of envy – not for what it is, but for what it has come to represent.

Freud makes much of the ideas that in the course of her psychic development a girl has to change both her object choice – from her mother to her father, and her leading erotic zone – from the clitoris to the vagina. The energy absorbed in this process is supposed to lead to an arrest of psychic development, and hence to a psychic rigidity and lack of creativity. Furthermore, because the girl, lacking a penis to begin with, has no castration fears, she remains in the Œdipal situation indefinitely. In not being forced to abandon it, she fails to develop the strong superego characteristic of the male and her mental life therefore remains closer to the instinctual level: she is somehow less civilized than the male.

Her situation is the reverse of his: whereas the male's castration complex drives him away from the Œdipal situation, the girl's genital trauma prepares her for it. It is her envy of the penis that enables the girl to transfer her object choice from her mother to her father. She blames her mother for her lack of penis and therefore feels hostility towards her. She realizes, too, that her mother shares her 'inferiority' since castration is a fate common to all women, and so she comes to devalue all that is feminine, including her mother. No explanation is given to why a child should blame her mother for this cruel fate. Nor is it by any means obvious that she will see that her mother's body is like her own. It is after all, as unlike hers as that of her father if presence or absence of a penis is not taken to be the sole criterion by which such comparisons are made.

Penis envy, Freud argues, also prepares the way for the clitoral–vaginal transference which is crucial in the development of 'normal' femininity and mature, passive, narcissistic and masochistic sexuality. It is now known that physiologically such a transference is a myth and that orgasms are not vaginally, but clitorally centred.[7] Juliet Mitchell suggests that we interpret this transference as being a change in mental attitude. In this sense the idea retains some validity.[8] Women in Western societies are expected to be sexually passive, to think of sexuality as synonymous with coitus, and to associate coitus with reproduction. Hence they must abandon the pursuit of sexual pleasure associated with the clitoris, and prepare for the passive, receptive, reproductive role consistent with vaginal penetration. If it is viewed in this way, however, this transference cannot be 'constitutionally prescribed' or as determining (in the sense that Freud used the term) the final form of sexuality. Rather, the transference itself depends upon expectations concerning the form that adult female sexuality ought to take.

In making pronouncements on femininity, Freud never looked beyond the fixed concepts and categories he imposed upon his observations. His obvious prejudices, made clear in his use of language, distort his analysis. The female is a mutilated male; that which is masculine is normal and unmysterious, while things feminine are seen as aberrations, as enigmas. Underlying all this, however, are the more basic problems concerning the nature of sexual drives, the idea of infantile sexuality, and lack of appreciation of the influence of social factors on the moulding of the personality.

In formulating his theories on sexuality, Freud interprets a wide range of infant behaviour as being inherently sexual, as prototypical of adult sexuality, and as determining its character. Though social factors are assumed to play some part, it is doubtful whether Freud would concede their primacy, for he seems to regard 'inhibitions' as being as much constitutionally determined as culturally imposed. He conceptualizes these as 'dams . . . restricting the flow . . . of sexual development':

> One gets the impression from civilized children that the construction of these dams is the product of education, and no doubt education has much to do with it. But in reality this development is organically determined and fixed by heredity . . . Education [is] following the lines already laid down organically and . . . impressing them somewhat more clearly and deeply.[9]

So education (or socialization) plays only a secondary part in the process; that of furthering 'nature's' ends.

Freud's use of the term 'repression' is also ambiguous. He states for instance, that puberty leads to an accession of libido in boys, but it is 'marked in girls by a fresh wave of repression'.[10] His words seem carefully chosen, here and elsewhere, to leave us in ignorance of the source of this repression. It is to be viewed as originating from within the individual or from without, as innate or acquired, as constitutional or imposed? Since this repression provides the impetus for the clitoral vaginal transference which Freud perceives as essential to the development of normal femininity, it must be assumed that he considers it to be an integral part of psychic development. He seems, in effect, to be assuming that organic factors take precedence over socio-cultural ones.

It is with Freud's conception of these innate sexual drives that Gagnon and Simon take issue. They argue that he has mistakenly imposed the language of adult sexual experience on the behaviour of children and has imputed sexual motives to them solely on the basis of the meaning their behaviour would have if performed by an adult actor. No act, in their terms, is sexual in itself, but only if it is defined as such. A child's behaviour cannot be construed as sexual since it does not, as yet, carry such meaning for the child. If this is accepted then there is little basis for assuming that sexual drives exist.

> Sexual behaviour is socially scripted behaviour and not the . . . expression of
> some primordial drive.[11]

It is not until the onset of puberty in our society that these social-sexual scripts are
learnt, for it is not until then that the subject comes to be defined as a potential
sexual actor and to accept herself or himself as such. An emphasis on continuity with
childhood is, from this perspective misleading. Obviously sexual learning does not
happen all at once with no reference to previous experience, but the aspect of pre-
adolescent development that has greatest relevance for sexuality is the learning of
gender roles. It is the feminine or masculine self-identity acquired through this process
which provides the framework within which the learning of sexual scripts occurs.

> . . . the crucial period of childhood has significance not because what happens is
> of a sexual nature, but because of the non-sexual development that will condition
> subsequent encounters with sexuality.[12]

Gagnon and Simon are, in effect, reversing Freud's conception of the inter-
relationships between sexuality and sex role behaviour. Whereas Freud sees the sexual
as determining all other areas of personality development, they view the emergence of
sexuality as contingent upon the development of other, non-sexual, aspects of gender
identity. For Freud the feminine character is created by the pattern of female sexual
development, while for Gagnon and Simon female sexuality is itself built upon an
earlier foundation of gender role learning.

The latter theory stresses the importance of adolescence as the crucial turning point
in the development of the sexual self. The onset of this period is heralded by the
physical changes of puberty, but it is not these changes in themselves which determine
the development of sexuality, but the meaning which is attached to them. They serve,
in effect, as signals to others, indicating that the child may be defined as a potential
sexual actor and will be expected to learn the scripts which govern adult sexual
behaviour. In the course of this new phase of learning the individual assimilates
the sexual into her or his self-identity and comes to see herself or himself as capable
of playing a sexual role. Previous to these developments, before learning the scripts
of socio-sexual behaviour and casting themselves in them, an individual's behaviour
cannot be said to be sexual.

> It is in the process of converting external labels into internal capacities for
> naming that activities become more precisely defined and linked to a structure
> of socio-cultural expectations and needs that define the sexual.[13]

PERCEPTIONS OF CHILDHOOD EROTICISM: PLEASURE AND THE SEXUAL

These theoretical frameworks raise two inter-related and inter-dependent questions
concerning the process of sexual learning. First, to what extent can the development
of sexuality in adolescence be seen as continuous or discontinuous with childhood
experience? And secondly, what is the nature of those childhood experiences which
might be perceived as having implications for the emergence of sexuality?

I would argue, with Gagnon and Simon, that in terms of sexual learning in our society adolescent experiences do involve a significant break with the past. It is in this period of life that the individual becomes fully aware of the sexual meanings attached to certain aspects of her or his social environment, comes to be defined as a sexual actor, and begins to build an image of herself or himself as such. It is the time when conscious sexual learning begins, when new discoveries are made and novel experiences undergone that are not always easy to relate to childhood experience.

This is not say that all this occurs totally independently of any former influences. Some continuity must exist, for during childhood the basis of the individual's self identity to which the sexual is assimilated, is established. Also certain childhood experiences may, when combined with the new knowledge gained in adolescence, contribute to the individual's understanding of sexuality. There is an implicit distinction here between two categories of learning which have implications for later psycho-sexual development. The first involves the creation of a larger framework of self-identity of which gender identity is an essential component, and in terms of which sexual scripts are learnt and interpreted. The second arises out of behaviour which, though not intrinsically sexual, is likely to be labelled as such and which might therefore be retrospectively interpreted as sexually relevant in the light of later experience and thus provide a more direct link between childhood and adolescence. By positing the possible existence of such a link I do not wish to attribute some sort of causal precedence to this variety of childhood experience. Their importance lies not in determining later sexual development, but in providing the adolescent with data that she or he may be able to build into her or his emerging conception of the erotic, or which may provide moral categories for sexual activities.

This in no sense, then, implies an acceptance of Freud's interpretations of children's sexuality. Whether based on observations of children or psychoanalytical case studies, his conclusions are somewhat suspect. In the former case he tends to arrive at somewhat absurd conclusions, not simply because he apprends the behaviour of young children with the vocabulary of adult sexual experience, but because, in doing so, he imputes specifically sexual motives to them. He does not simply note the affinities between infant behaviour and adult sexual acts, but regards them as being manifestations of the same primordial drive, as satisfying the same need. So, for example, he holds that the child's flushed cheek and contented sleep after being fed is analogous to the adult post-orgasmic state.[14] That these two varieties of contentment may have something in common is no grounds for arguing as Freud does, that one is an early expression of the other, a manifestation of infantile sexuality.

The other source of 'evidence', involving retrospective interpretation of childhood experiences, may also be distorting.

As Simon and Gagnon argue:

> . . . rather than the past determining the present it is possible that the present re-shapes the past, as we reconstruct our autobiographies in an effort to bring them greater congruence with our present identities, roles and available vocabularies.[15]

It is such biographical reconstruction, attempting to explain the present by reference to the past, that forms the basis of the psychoanalytical method. Freud, reasoning from the premised existence of the libido as a powerful sexual drive determining human personality, may then interpret adult behaviour in terms of inferred childhood sexual experiences. In the process the child's behaviour, responses and affections are infused with sexual meaning. It is the nature of psychoanalysis that it imposes preconceived categories onto behavioural phenomena and then purports to have explained them.

Freud, having stated (correctly) that we must not confuse the sexual with the genital, proceeds to interpret a wide range of behaviour and responses as sexual, as satisfying some drive. He argues that the child *needs* to have such sensations repeated, rather than she or he finds them simply pleasurable and therefore enjoys their repetition. He notes the rhythmical nature of activities such as thumb sucking and regards them as proof of their sexual nature. This is a prime example of the mis-labelling of childhood experiences: could it not be that the child simply finds this activity pleasurable? That sexual acts may also incorporate this characteristic may only mean that rhythmical stimuli in general are found to be pleasurable, rather than such sensations are inherently sexual. It is, says Freud the quality of stimuli that determines whether or not they are sexual, but apart from offering the example of rhythmical sensations he declines to elaborate further. Apparently the ineffable wisdom of psychoanalysis can uncover sexual motives underlying such apparently innocent childish activities and desires as playing on swings or wanting to be an engine driver.

By such arguments as these, Freud contrives to label as sexual almost anything a child apprehends as pleasurable. It might be argued against this that anything we perceive as sexual in children's behaviour is, for them, merely a pleasurable experience. If sexuality lies not in the quality of an act but in the meaning given to it, then a child's behaviour or responses cannot be interpreted as being sexual when the child has not yet learnt the vocabulary of motives through which sexual activity is mediated.

[. . .]

ADOLESCENCE: THE PERIOD OF SEXUAL DISCOVERY

Adolescence is the period of life when conscious sexual learning begins. At this time children make discoveries concerning the facts of sex and reproduction, experience changes in their bodies, and begin to learn the socio-sexual scripts that govern adult sexual behaviour. These scripts are not just guidelines for sexual action, but also the means by which the individual comes to understand and come to terms with sexuality. In effect they provide a sexual vocabulary of motives.

> Elements of such scripting occur across many aspects of the sexual situation. Scripts are involved in learning the meaning of internal states, organizing the sequences of specifically sexual acts, decoding novel situations, setting the limits on sexual responses, and linking meanings from non-sexual aspects of life to specifically sexual experience.[16]

The ways in which these scripts are learnt is profoundly affected by the gender-role learning of childhood, so that girls and boys learn to be sexual in different ways. These diverging lines of development are not the results of repression or accession of libido, but of differential learning experiences built onto a firmly established sense of gender identity.

[. . .]

The acquisition of biological facts comprises only a small part of adolescent sexual learning. In order to become a competent actor within socio-sexual dramas and to develop a sexual commitment, the individual needs to be able to interpret her or his own emotions in sexual terms, to recognize potentially sexual situations, and to be able to make decisions on how to act in them.

> Without the proper elements of a script that defines the situation, names the actors and plots the behaviour, nothing sexual is likely to happen . . . combining such elements as desire, privacy and physically attractive person of the appro-
> priate sex, the probability of something sexual happening will, under normal circumstances, remain exceedingly small until either one or both actors organize these behaviours into an appropriate script.[17]

Before an adolescent girl can begin to participate fully in sexual scenes she must become familiar with the scripts that govern them and be able to locate her own actions within them.

Girls learn to enact sexual scripts within the milieu of their peer group, an environment which may be characterized as homo-social and heterosexual.[18] So although their sexual interest is focused on the opposite sex, it is primarily to their same-sex peers that adolescents will look for validation of their sexual attitudes and accomplishments. In such a situation, girls and boys develop markedly different sexual expectations and hence continue their psychosexual development along the divergent paths that have already been mapped out.

Among their peers, boys' sexual commitment, gained early through the practice of masturbation, will be reinforced as a result of the social validation accorded to male sexual exploits. [. . .] But although the sexual world is a major preoccupation of boys in their early teens, it is not until later that they become adept at the social skills necessary to the establishment and maintenance of relationships with girls. For a girl, however, this pattern is reversed, she acquires a socio-sexual commitment before developing a specifically sexual one. Each sex, then, has only partial knowledge of sexual scripts, and girls are best trained in precisely those areas for which boys are least well prepared. While girls are learning the language of romantic love, the boys are concerning themselves with rather more directly sexual interests. It is not until the later years of adolescence that they are able to negotiate socio-sexual relationships with each other. In meantime it is likely that girls' romantic interests will be focused on more distant fantasy figures – until such time as their male counterparts are able to behave in a manner that is congruent with feminine expectations.

[. . .]

Early in their teens girls begin to evaluate boys as sexual partners and to compete for their attention. Yet, while they are trying out their skills as seductresses [. . .] and may be admired and envied for popularity with boys, they will find they receive no social support for sexual activity *per se*. A girl has nothing to gain and her 'reputation' to lose if she is too sexually active.

The maintenance of a positive feminine self-concept depends on the successful management of romantic relationships, rather than on specifically sexual achievement. So girls carefully guard their reputations and with the help of a sexual response tuned to romantic stimuli, endeavour to establish ongoing relationships as a precondition for sexual activity. Most girls pass into adulthood still unsure of their sexual identity and with a romantic, passive and dependent orientation towards erotic activity. They enter into adult sexual careers governed by scripts which deny them the possibility of a self-defined sexuality in a world in which the sexual is partitioned off from the rest of everyday life.

THE END PRODUCT: FEMALE SEXUALITY IN A CHANGING EROTIC ENVIRONMENT

[. . .]

It is far too simplistic to argue that [. . .] women's sexuality is repressed by the demands of a patriarchal capitalist society. It is preferable to conceptualize the relationship between society and sexuality in terms of the latter being socially constructed through the processes of learning to fit in with the current institutions, ideology and morality of that society.

The advance of capitalism has created a gulf between the public sphere of production and exchange and the private sphere of the family and personal relationships. Within the latter, sexuality has become so extremely privatized and exclusively personal that it constitutes a world apart from the rest of our lives even in their most intimate aspects. It is a subject set aside to be learnt at a particular time and in unique ways. Whether this separateness leads to a guilty, negative orientation to the sexual or to ideals of specialness and spontaneity, it results in problems of communication. Even within the privacy of the sexual dyad, sex itself is rarely discussed. Sexual activity is usually initiated by and proceeds through innuendo and gesture rather than open talk. Hence sexual interaction is characterized by a degree of confusion and doubt about the intentions and interpretations of the other which is not typical of more routine forms of interaction.

Such problems are heightened by the fact that men and women have learnt to be sexual in different ways, that sexual dramas are scripted for actors who have different sexual vocabularies of motive and different orientations to and expectations of sexual relationships. Feminine and masculine sexual roles are popularly believed to fit together and be complementary, but in reality the relation between them is more often one of disjunction. Each gender is, as Gagnon and Simon point out, estranged from the existential nature of the other's sexual experience. [. . .] For women, all this is further complicated by the superiority of men which is carried over into the bedroom (and not the other way around as some radical feminists would have us believe). As a result the most widely disseminated ideas and ideals of sexuality are masculine ones and sexual relationships are male dominated. The heterosexual marriage bed becomes a scene of confusion and deception rather than of conjugal bliss. It is hardly surprising that lesbian women appear more at home in their sexual lives than their heterosexual sisters.[19]

[. . .]

NOTES

1. J.H. Gagnon and W. Simon *Sexual Conduct*, London: Hutchinson, 1974, p. 3.
2. *Ibid.*
3. George Simmel, quoted in V. Klein, *The Feminine Character*, London: Routledge & Kegan Paul, 1946, p. 82.
4. S. Freud, 'Some physical consequences of the anatomical distinction between the sexes' (1925), *The Standard Edition of the Complete Works of Sigmund Freud*, ed. J. Strachey vol. XIX (London: Hogarth Press, 1961); Freud, 'Female sexuality' (1931) vol. XXI; Freud, 'Femininity' (1933) vol. XXII.
5. L. Kohlberg, 'A cognitive development analysis of children's sex-role concepts and attitudes', in E. Maccoby (ed.), *The Development of Sex Differences*, London: Tavistock, 1967.
6. S. de Beauvoir, *The Second Sex*, London: New English Library, 1969.
7. W.H. Masters and V. Johnson, *Human Sexual Response*, Boston: Little, Brown & Co., 1966.
8. J. Mitchell, 'Female sexuality', Marie Stopes Memorial Lecture, University of York, 1972.
9. S. Freud, 'Three essays on sexuality' (1905), *Standard Edition*, vol. VII, 1953.
10. *Ibid.*, p. 220.
11. W. Simon, and J.H. Gagnon, 'On psychosexual development', in Goslin (ed.), *Handbook of Socialization Theory and Research*, Chicago: Rand McNally, 1969, p. 736.
12. *Ibid.*, p. 741.
13. *Ibid.*, p. 734.
14. Freud, 'Three essays on sexuality'.
15. Simon and Gagnon, 'On psychosexual development', p. 734.
16. Gagnon and Simon, *Sexual Conduct*, p. 19.
17. *Ibid.*
18. Simon and Gagnon, 'On psychosexual development'.
19. P. Whiting, 'Female sexuality: its political implications', in M. Wandor (ed.), *The Body Politic*, London: Stage 1, 1972; Gagnon and Simon, *Sexual Conduct*.

1.6

FEMININE SEXUALITY

Jacqueline Rose

The reading of Freud provided by the French psychoanalyst Jacques Lacan is thought by some feminists to overcome the problems of a more literal interpretation of Freud. Here Jacqueline Rose explains some of Lacan's ideas and argues that they offer crucial insights into female sexuality. From this perspective desire is constituted through our entry into language and culture, through submission to the 'law of the father'.

Re-opening the debate on feminine sexuality must start [. . .] with the link between sexuality and the unconscious. No account of Lacan's work which attempts to separate the two can make sense. For Lacan, the unconscious undermines the subject from any position of certainty, from any relation of knowledge to his or her psychic processes and history, and *simultaneously* reveals the fictional nature of the sexual category to which every human subject is none the less assigned. In Lacan's account, sexual identity operates as a law — it is something enjoined on the subject. For him, the fact that individuals must line up according to an opposition (having or not having the phallus) makes that clear. But it is the constant difficulty, or even impossibility, of that process which Lacan emphasised.

[. . .]

Lacan's account of subjectivity was always developed with reference to the idea of a fiction. Thus, in the 1930s he introduced the concept of the 'mirror stage',[1] which took the child's mirror image as the model and basis for its future identifications. This image is a fiction because it conceals, or freezes, the infant's lack of motor co-ordination and the fragmentation of its drives. But it is salutary for the child, since it gives it the first sense of a coherent identity in which it can recognise itself. For Lacan, however, this is already a fantasy — the very image which places the child divides its identity into two. Furthermore, that moment only has meaning in relation to the presence and the look of the mother who guarantees its reality for the child. [. . .] The mirror image is central to Lacan's account of subjectivity, because its apparent smoothness and totality is a myth. The image in which we first recognise ourselves is a *misrecognition*. Lacan is careful to stress, however, that his point is not restricted to the field of the visible alone: 'the idea of the mirror should be understood as an object which reflects – not just the visible, but also what is heard, touched and willed by the child'.[2]

For Lacan the subject is constituted through language – the mirror image represents the moment when the subject is located in an order outside itself to which it will henceforth refer. The subject is the subject *of* speech (Lacan's 'parle-être'), and subject *to* that order. [. . .] Language can only operate by designating an object in its absence. Lacan takes this further, and states that symbolisation turns on the object *as* absence. He gives as his reference Freud's early account of the child's hallucinatory cathexis of the object for which it cries,[3] and his later description in *Beyond the Pleasure Principle*[4] of the child's symbolisation of the absent mother in play. In the first example, the child hallucinates the object it desires; in the second, it throws a cotton reel out of its cot in order to symbolise the absence and the presence of the mother. Symbolisation starts, therefore, when the child gets its first sense that something could be missing; words stand for objects, because they only have to be spoken at the moment when the first object is lost. For Lacan, the subject can only operate within language by constantly repeating that moment of fundamental and irreducible division. The subject is therefore constituted in language *as* this division or splitting (Freud's *Ichspaltung*, or splitting of the ego).

Lacan termed the order of language the symbolic, that of the ego and its identifications the imaginary.

[. . .]

Lacan's account of childhood then follows his basic premise that identity is constructed in language, but only at a cost. Identity shifts, and language speaks the loss which lay behind that first moment of symbolisation. When the child asks something of its mother, that loss will persist over and above anything which she can possibly give, or say, in reply. Demand always 'bears on something other than the satisfaction which it calls for',[5] and each time the demand of the child is answered by the satisfaction of its needs, so this 'something other' is relegated to the place of its original impossibility. Lacan terms this 'desire'. It can be defined as the 'remainder' of the subject, something which is always left over, but which has no content as such. Desire functions much as the zero unit in the numerical chain – its place is both constitutive *and* empty.

The concept of desire is crucial to Lacan's account of sexuality. He considered that the failure to grasp its implications leads inevitably to a reduction of sexuality back into the order of a need (something, therefore, which could be satisfied). Against this, he quoted Freud's statement: 'we must reckon with the possibility that something in the nature of the sexual instinct itself is unfavourable to the realisation of complete satisfaction'.[6]

At the same time 'identity' and 'wholeness' remain precisely at the level of fantasy. Subjects in language persist in their belief that somewhere there is a point of certainty, of knowledge and of truth. When the subject addresses its demand outside itself to another, this other becomes the fantasied place of just such a knowledge or certainty. Lacan calls this the Other – the site of language to which the speaking subject necessarily refers.

[. . .]

Sexuality belongs in this area of instability played out in the register of demand and desire, each sex coming to stand, mythically and exclusively, for that which could satisfy and complete the other. It is when the categories 'male' and 'female' are seen to represent an absolute and complementary division that they fall prey to a mystification in which the difficulty of sexuality instantly disappears: 'to disguise this gap by relying on the virtue of the "genital" to resolve it through the maturation of tenderness . . ., however piously intended, is nonetheless a fraud'.[7] Lacan therefore, argued that psychoanalysis should not try to produce 'male' and 'female' as complementary entities, sure of each other and of their own identity, but should expose the fantasy on which this notion rests.

[. . .]

Lacan [. . .] considered that it was the failure to grasp the concept of the symbolic which has led psychoanalysis to concentrate increasingly on the adequacies and inadequacies of the motherchild relationship, an emphasis which tends to be complicit with the idea of a maternal role. The concept of castration was central to Lacan because of the reference which it always contains to paternal law.

[. . .]

Lacan argued [. . .] for a return to the concept of the father, but this concept is now defined in relation to that of desire. What matters is that the relationship of the child to the mother is not simply based on 'frustration and satisfaction' ('the notion of frustration (which was never employed by Freud)',[8] but on the recognition of her desire. The mother is refused to the child in so far as a prohibition falls on the child's desire to be what the mother desires (not the same, note, as a desire to possess or enjoy the mother in the sense normally understood):

> What we meet as an accident in the child's development is linked to the fact that the child does not find himself or herself alone in front of the mother, and that the phallus forbids the child the satisfaction of his or her own desire, which is the desire to be the exclusive desire of the mother.[9]

The duality of the relation between mother and child must be broken, just as the analytic relation must be thrown onto the axis of desire. In Lacan's account, the phallus stands for that moment of rupture. It refers mother and child to the dimension of the symbolic which is figured by the father's place. [. . .] For Lacan, it takes on this value as a function of the androcentric nature of the symbolic order itself.[10] But its status is in itself false, and must be recognised by the child as such. Castration means first of all this – that the child's desire for the mother does not refer *to* her but *beyond* her, to an object, the phallus, whose status is first imaginary (the object presumed to satisfy her desire) and then symbolic (recognition that desire cannot be satisfied).

The place of the phallus in the account, therefore, follows from Lacan's return to the position and law of the father, but this concept has been reformulated in relation to that of desire. Lacan uses the term 'paternal metaphor', metaphor having a very specific meaning here. First, as a reference to the act of substitution (substitution is the very law of metaphoric operation), whereby the prohibition of the father takes up the place originally figured by the absence of the mother. Secondly, as a reference to the status of paternity itself which can only ever logically be *inferred*. And thirdly, as part of an insistence that the father stands for a place and a function which is not reducible to the presence or absence of the real father as such. [. . .] Finally, the concept is used to separate the father's function from the idealised or imaginary father with which it is so easily confused and which is exactly the figure to be got round, or past.

[. . .]

Thus when Lacan calls for a return to the place of the father he is crucially distinguishing himself from any sociological conception of role. The father is a function and refers to a law, the place outside the imaginary dyad and against which it breaks.

[. . .]

The concept of the phallus and the castration complex can only be understood in terms of this reference to prohibition and the law, just as rejection of these concepts tends to lose sight of this reference. The phallus needs to be placed on the axis of desire before it can be understood, or questioned, as the differential mark of sexual identification (boy or girl, having or not having the phallus). By breaking the imaginary dyad, the phallus represents a moment of division (Lacan calls this the subject's 'lack-in-being') which re-enacts the fundamental splitting of subjectivity itself. And by jarring against any naturalist account of sexuality ('phallocentrism . . . strictly impossible to deduce from any pre-established harmony of the said psyche to the nature it expresses'[11]), the phallus relegates sexuality to a strictly other dimension – the order of the symbolic outside of which, for Lacan, sexuality cannot be understood. The importance of the phallus is that its status in the development of human sexuality is something which nature *cannot* account for.

When Lacan is reproached with phallocentrism at the level of his theory, what is most often missed is that the subject's entry into the symbolic order is equally an exposure of the value of the phallus itself. The subject has to recognise that there is desire, or lack in the place of the Other, that there is no ultimate certainty or truth, and that the status of the phallus is a fraud (this is, for Lacan, the meaning of castration). The phallus can only take up its place by indicating the precariousness of any identity assumed by the subject on the basis of its token.

[. . .]

The subject then takes up his or her identity with reference to the phallus, but that identity is thereby designated symbolic (it is something enjoined on the subject). [. . .] 'Any speaking being whatever'[12] must line up on one or other side of the divide.

Sexual difference is then assigned according to whether individual subjects do or do not possess the phallus, which means not that anatomical difference *is* sexual difference (the one as strictly deducible from the other), but that anatomical difference comes to *figure* sexual difference, that is, it becomes the sole representative of what that difference is allowed to be. It thus covers over the complexity of the child's early sexual life with a crude opposition in which that very complexity is refused or repressed. The phallus thus indicates the reduction of difference to an instance of visible perception, a *seeming* value.

Freud gave the moment when boy and girl child saw that they were different the status of a trauma in which the girl is seen to be lacking (the objections often start here). But something can only be *seen* to be missing according to a pre-existing hierarchy of values ('there is nothing missing in the real'[13]). What counts is not the perception but its already assigned meaning – the moment therefore belongs in the symbolic.

[. . .]

Three points emerge from what has been described so far:

1. anatomy is what figures in the account: 'for me "anatomy is not destiny", but that does not mean that anatomy does not figure',[14] but it *only figures* (it is a sham);
2. the phallus stands at its own expense and any male privilege erected upon it is an imposture 'what might be called a man, the male speaking being, strictly disappears as an effect of discourse, . . . by being inscribed within it solely as castration';[15]
3. woman is not inferior, she is *subjected*.

NOTES

1. J. Lacan, 'Le Stade du mirroir comme formateur de la fonction du Je', in *Écrits* Paris: Seuil, 1936.
2. J. Lacan, 'Cure psychanalytique à l'aide de la poupée fleur', Comptes rendus, reunion 18 Octobre, *Revue française de la psychanalyse*, 4 (October–December), 1949, p. 1567.
3. S. Freud, 'Project for scientific psychology', in S. Freud with J. Breuer, *Studies of Hysteria* (1893); reprinted in *The Standard Edition of the Complete Psychological Works of Sigmund Freud*, vol. II, London: Hogarth, 1953–74, p. 319.
4. S. Freud, *Beyond the Pleasure Principle* (1920), *Standard Edition*, WI. XVIII, p. 14.
5. J. Lacan, 'The meaning of the phallus', in *Jacques Lacan & the École Freudienne: Feminine Sexuality*, ed. Juliet Mitchell and Jacqueline Rose, London: Macmillan, 1982, p. 80.
6. S. Freud, 'On the universal tendency to debasement in the sphere of love', (1912) (Contributions to the Psychology of Love, II) *Standard Edition*, vol. XI, pp. 188–9; J. Lacan, 'The phallic phase and the subjective import of the castration complex', in *Feminine Sexuality*, p. 113.
7. Lacan, 'The meaning of the phallus', p. 81.
8. *Ibid.*, p. 80.
9. J. Lacan, 'Les formations de l'inconscient', *Bulletin de Psychologie*, 2, 1957–8, p. 14.
10. J. Lacan, 'D'une question preliminaire à tout traitment possible de la psychose', *Écrits*, 1966, pp. 554–5, 198.
11. J. Lacan, *Encore*: Le séminaire XX, 1972–3, Paris: Seuil, 1975, p. 150.
12. Lacan, 'The phallic phase and the subjective import of the castration complex'.
13. *Ibid.*, p. 113.
14. M. Safouan, *La Sexualité féminine dans la doctrine Freudienne* (le champ freudien), Paris: Seuil, 1976).
15. J. Lacan, 'Le Séminaire XVIII 1969–70', unpublished typescript, p. 4.

1.7

THIS SEX WHICH IS NOT ONE

Luce Irigaray

An alternative psychoanalytic perspective is provided by Luce Irigaray. While she shares Lacan's emphasis on the importance of language in the construction of subjectivity, she vigorously contests the phallocentrism of Freudian and Lacanian perspectives, arguing that they deny women's difference and are implicated in the suppression of our sexuality.

Female sexuality has always been conceptualized on the basis of masculine parameters. Thus the opposition between 'masculine' clitoral activity and 'feminine' vaginal passivity, an opposition which Freud – and many others – saw as stages, or alternatives, in the development of a sexually 'normal' woman, seems rather too clearly required by the practice of male sexuality. For the clitoris is conceived as a little penis pleasant to masturbate so long as castration anxiety does not exist (for the boy child), and the vagina is valued for the 'lodging' it offers the male organ when the forbidden hand has to find a replacement for pleasure-giving.

In these terms, woman's erogenous zones never amount to anything but a clitoris-sex that is not comparable to the noble phallic organ, or a hole-envelope that serves to sheathe and massage the penis in intercourse: a non-sex, or a masculine organ turned back upon itself, self-embracing

About woman and her pleasure, this view of the sexual relation has nothing to say. Her lot is that of 'lack,' 'atrophy' (of the sexual organ), and 'penis envy,' the penis being the only sexual organ of recognized value. Thus she attempts by every means available to appropriate that organ for herself: through her somewhat servile love of the father-husband capable of giving her one, through her desire for a child-penis, preferably a boy, through access to the cultural values still reserved by right to males alone and therefore always masculine, and so on. Woman lives her own desire only as the expectation that she may at last come to possess an equivalent of the male organ.

Yet all this appears quite foreign to her own pleasure, unless it remains within the dominant phallic economy. Thus, for example, woman's autoeroticism is very different from man's. In order to touch himself, man needs an instrument: his hand, a woman's body, language . . . And this self-caressing requires at least a minimum of activity. As for woman, she touches herself in and of herself without any need for mediation, and before there is any way to distinguish activity from passivity. Woman 'touches herself' all the time, and moreover no one can forbid her to do so, for her genitals are formed of two lips in continuous contact. Thus, within herself, she is already two – but not divisible into one(s) – that caress each other.

This autoeroticism is disrupted by a violent break-in: the brutal separation of the two lips by a violating penis, an intrusion that distracts and deflects the woman from this 'self-caressing' she needs if she is not to incur the disappearance of her own pleasure in sexual relations. If the vagina is to serve *also*, but *not only*, to take over for the little boy's hand in order to assure an articulation between autoeroticism and heteroeroticism in intercourse (the encounter with the totally other always signifying death), how, in the classic representation of sexuality, can the perpetuation of autoeroticism for woman be managed? Will woman not be left with the impossible alternative between a defensive virginity, fiercely turned in upon itself, and a body open to penetration that no longer knows, in this 'hole' that constitutes its sex, the pleasure of its own touch? The more or less exclusive – and highly anxious – attention paid to erection in Western sexuality proves to what extent the imaginary that governs it is foreign to the feminine. For the most part, this sexuality offers nothing but imperatives dictated by male rivalry: the 'strongest' being the one who has the best 'hard-on,' the longest, the biggest, the stiffest penis, or even the one who 'pees the farthest' (as in little boys' contests). Or else one finds imperatives dictated by the enactment of sadomasochistic fantasies, these in turn governed by man's relation to his mother: the desire to force entry, to penetrate, to appropriate for himself the mystery of this womb where he has been conceived, the secret of his begetting, of his 'origin.' Desire/need, also to make blood flow again in order to revive a very old relationship – intrauterine, to be sure, but also prehistoric – to the maternal.

Woman, in this sexual imaginary, is only a more or less obliging prop for the enactment of man's fantasies. That she may find pleasure there in that role, by proxy, is possible, even certain. But such pleasure is above all a masochistic prostitution of her body to a desire that is not her own, and it leaves her in a familiar state of dependency upon man. Not knowing what she wants, ready for anything, even asking for more, so long as he will 'take' her as his 'object' when he seeks his own pleasure. Thus she will not say what she herself wants; moreover, she does not know, or no longer knows, what she wants.

[. . .]

Within this logic, the predominance of the visual, and of the discrimination and individualization of form, is particularly foreign to female eroticism. Woman takes pleasure more from touching than from looking, and her entry into a dominant scopic economy signifies, again, her consignment to passivity: she is to be the beautiful object of contemplation. While her body finds itself thus eroticized, and called to a double movement of exhibition and of chaste retreat in order to stimulate the drives of the 'subject,' her sexual organ represents *the horror of nothing to see*. A defect in this systematics of representation and desire. A 'hole' in its scoptophilic lens. It is already evident in Greek statuary that this nothing-to-see has to be excluded, rejected, from such a scene of representation. Woman's genitals are simply absent, masked, sewn back up inside their 'crack.'

[. . .]

Whence the mystery that woman represents in a culture claiming to count everything, to number everything by units, to inventory everything as individualities. *She is neither one nor two.* Rigorously speaking, she cannot be identified either as one person, or as two. She resists all adequate definition. Further, she has no 'proper' name. And her sexual organ, which is not *one* organ, is counted as *none.* The negative, the underside, the reverse of the only visible and morphologically designatable organ (even if the passage from erection to detumescence does pose some problems): the penis.

But the 'thickness' of that 'form,' the layering of its volume, its expansions and contractions and even the spacing of the moments in which it produces itself as form – all this the feminine keeps secret. Without knowing it. And if woman is asked to sustain, to revive, man's desire, the request neglects to spell out what it implies as to the value of her own desire. A desire of which she is not aware, moreover, at least not explicitly. But one whose force and continuity are capable of nurturing repeatedly and at length all the masquerades of 'feminity' that are expected of her.

[. . .]

Perhaps it is time to return to that repressed entity, the female imaginary. So woman does not have a sex organ? She has at least two of them, but they are not identifiable as ones. Indeed, she has many more. Her sexuality, always at least double, goes even further: it is *plural.* Is this the way culture is seeking to characterize itself now? Is this the way texts write themselves/are written now? Without quite knowing what censorship they are evading? Indeed, woman's pleasure does not have to choose between clitoral activity and vaginal passivity, for example. The pleasure of the vaginal caress does not have to be substituted for that of the clitoral caress. They each contribute, irreplaceably, to woman's pleasure. Among other caresses . . . Fondling the breasts, touching the vulva, spreading the lips, stroking the posterior wall of the vagina, brushing against the mouth of the uterus, and so on. To evoke only a few of the most specifically female pleasures. Pleasures which are somewhat misunderstood in sexual difference as it is imagined – or not imagined, the other sex being only the indispensable complement to the only sex.

But *woman has sex organs more or less everywhere.* She finds pleasure almost anywhere. Even if we refrain from invoking the hystericization of her entire body, the geography of her pleasure is far more diversified, more multiple in its differences, more complex, more subtle, than is commonly imagined – in an imaginary rather too narrowly focused on sameness.

'She' is indefinitely other in herself. This is doubtless why she is said to be whimsical, incomprehensible, agitated, capricious . . . not to mention her language, in which 'she' sets off in all directions leaving 'him' unable to discern the coherence of any meaning. Hers are contradictory words, somewhat mad from the standpoint of reason, inaudible for whoever listens to them with ready-made grids, with a fully elaborated code in hand. For in what she says, too, at least when she dares, woman is constantly touching herself. She steps ever so slightly aside from herself with a murmur, an exclamation, a whisper, a sentence left unfinished . . . When she returns, it is to set off again from elsewhere. From another point of pleasure, or of pain. One would have to listen with another ear, as if hearing *an 'other meaning' always in the process of weaving itself, of embracing itself with words, but also of getting rid of words in order not to become fixed, congealed in them.* For if 'she' says something, it is not, it is already no longer, identical with what she means. What she says is never identical with anything, moreover; rather, it is contiguous. *It touches (upon).* And when it strays too far from that proximity, she breaks off and starts over at 'zero': her body-sex.

[. . .]

However, in order for woman to reach the place where she takes pleasure as woman, a long detour by way of the analysis of the various systems of oppression brought to bear upon her is assuredly necessary. And claiming to fall back on the single solution of pleasure risks making her miss the process of going back through a social practice that *her* enjoyment requires.

For woman is traditionally a use-value for man, an exchange value among men; in other words, a commodity. As such, she remains the guardian of material substance, whose price will be established, in terms of the standard of their work and of their need/desire, by 'subjects': workers, merchants, consumers. Women are marked phallically by their fathers, husbands, procurers. And this branding determines their value in sexual commerce. Woman is never anything but the locus of a more or less competitive exchange between two men, including the competition for the possession of mother earth.

How can this object of transaction claim a right to pleasure without removing her/itself from established commerce? With respect to other merchandise in the marketplace, how could this commodity maintain a relationship other than one of aggressive jealousy? How could material substance enjoy her/itself without provoking the consumer's anxiety over the disappearance of his nurturing ground? How could that exchange – which can in no way be defined in terms 'proper' to woman's desire – appear as anything but a pure mirage, mere foolishness, all too readily obscured by a more sensible discourse and by a system of apparently more tangible values?

A woman's development, however radical it may seek to be, would thus not suffice to liberate woman's desire. And to date no political theory or political practice has resolved, or sufficiently taken into consideration, this historical problem, even though Marxism has proclaimed its importance. But women do not constitute, strictly speaking, a class, and their dispersion among several classes makes their political struggle complex, their demands sometimes contradictory.

[. . .]

But if women are to preserve and expand their autoeroticism, their homo-sexuality, might not the renunciation of heterosexual pleasure correspond once again to that disconnection from power that is traditionally theirs? Would it not involve a new prison, a new cloister, built of their own accord? For women to undertake tactical strikes, to keep themselves apart from men long enough to learn to defend their desire, especially through speech, to discover the love of other women while sheltered from men's imperious choices that put them in the position of rival commodities, to forge for themselves a social status that compels recognition, to earn their living in order to escape from the condition of prostitute . . . these are certainly indispensable stages in the escape from their proletarization on the exchange market. But if their aim were simply to reverse the order of things, even supposing this to be possible, history would repeat itself in the long run, would revert to sameness: to phallocratism. It would leave room neither for women's sexuality, nor for women's imaginary, nor for women's language to take (their) place.

1.8

GENDER DIFFERENCE AND
THE PRODUCTION OF SUBJECTIVITY

Wendy Hollway

Drawing on the work of Michel Foucault, Wendy Hollway suggests that our sexualities derive, in part, from the ways in which we position ourselves within the discourses available to us. She identifies three culturally salient discourses which each offer men and women differing subject positions.

INTRODUCTION

In [what follows] I attempt to analyse the construction of subjectivity in a specific area: heterosexual relations. My framework depends on three conceptual positions [. . .] : the non-rational, non-unitary character of subjectivity; its social and historical production through signification; power relations and the re-production of systematic difference.

I have introduced the term re-production [. . .] since the term reproduction is less than ideal owing to the limitations in its theorization. The dangers are ones for which Althusser has been criticized for failing to avoid. First, the concept stresses mainte-nance rather than change, and second Althusser's notion of economic determination 'in the last instance' avoids recognition of the effectivity of sites such as heterosexual relations [. . .] to re-produce gender difference. My use of the hyphen is intended to signify that every practice is a production. [. . .] Hence recurrent day-to-day practices and the meanings through which they acquire their effectivity may contribute to the maintenance of gender difference reproduction without the hyphen or to its modification (the production of modified meanings of gender leading to changed practices). I am interested in theorizing the practices and meanings which re-produce

From W. Hollway, 'Gender difference and the production of Subjectivity', in J. Henriques, W. Hollway. C. Urwin, C. Venn and V. Walkeraine (eds), *Changing the Subject*, London: Methien, 1984.

gendered subjectivity [. . .] My approach to subjectivity is through the meanings and incorporated values which attach to a person's practices and provide the powers through which he or she can position him- or herself in relation to others. Given the pervasive character of gender difference it is more than likely that all practices signify differently depending on the gender of their subject and object. However, I consider that heterosexual relations are the primary site where gender difference is re-produced. This claim will be substantiated in the detail of the analysis which follows.

[What follows] is organized into [four] parts.

In the first part I explore gender differentiation in discourses by taking the example of women's and men's different positions in discourses concerning sexuality. In the second part I focus on individual women's and men's subjectivity, that is the product of their history of positioning in discourses, and the way this constructs their investments in taking up gender-differentiated positions in heterosexual relations. [. . .] In the third part I consider the multiple meanings, deriving from discourses which produce the practices of heterosexual sex. I demonstrate their connection, expressed or suppressed, with 'desire for the Other' and how this relates to the take-up of gender-differentiated positions with an investment in exercising power. In the fourth part, I consider the recurrent splitting between women and men of gender-specified characteristics.

One way of seeing the different elements of this account is as follows. Gender-differentiated meanings (and thus the positions differentially available in discourse) account for the content of gender difference. The concept of splitting provides an account of how these positions are constantly taken up. Power difference (imaginary as well as real, intimately linked in the psyche with the early desire for the Other) is both the cause and effect of the system of gender difference and provides the motor for its continuous re-production. The concepts of splitting and [. . .] desire draw on psychoanalysis [. . .] . Splitting (in the Kleinian sense) is consistent not only with our stress on the non-unitary and non-rational nature of subjectivity, but also with our emphasis on relations. [. . .] Desire and 'desire for the Other' draw on a Lacanian analysis which theorizes their relation to signification.

[. . .]

GENDER DIFFERENCE IN THREE DISCOURSES CONCERNING SEXUALITY

Foucault's use of the term discourse is historical and this is crucial to the analytical power of the concept. For my purposes the emphasis must be shifted in order to understand how, at a specific moment, several coexisting and potentially contradictory discourses concerning sexuality make available different positions and different powers for men and women. [. . .] Given my objective of theorizing subjectivity as it is re-produced in discourses, it is personal genealogies which are a necessary part of the analysis.

In order to make a reading of the accounts I gathered concerning sexuality, I delineated three discourses: the male sexual drive discourse; the have/hold discourse; and the permissive discourse. I arrived at these three through a combination of my own knowledge and what was suggested by the data. [. . .] Clearly my own assumptions and those of research participants share a largely common historical production. [. . .] Some assumptions are more widespread than others (indeed, some would say that the discourse of male sexual drive was universal and that this supports a claim that it is based on the biological 'fact' of male sexuality). It would be relatively easy to identify more discourses, with different boundaries. For my purposes however, what is more important is the use I make of these three in my analysis of the effects of gender difference in positioning subjects.

The male sexual drive discourse

This needs little introduction because it is so familiar – so hegemonic, or dominant – in the production of meanings concerning sexuality. A man friend of mine captured it succinctly: 'I want to fuck. I *need* to fuck. I've always needed and wanted to fuck. From my teenage years, I've always longed after fucking.' Its key tenet is that men's sexuality is directly produced by a biological drive, the function of which is to ensure reproduction of the species. The discourse is everywhere in common-sense assumptions.

[. . .]

A [. . .] recent example of the discourse being made respectable by experts through recourse to scientific explanations is Glenn Wilson's[1] use of sociobiology to attack feminist accounts of sex differences which are based on social theories of women's oppression. The effect and intention of his argument is to represent women's position as biologically determined and therefore unchangeable.

[. . .]

The have/hold discourse

This has as its focus not sexuality directly, but the Christian ideals associated with monogamy, partnership and family life. The split between wife and mistress, virgin and whore, Mary and Eve, indicates how this and the male sexual drive discourse coexist in constructing men's sexual practices. In some aspects the discourses are consistent; for example both share assumptions about sexuality being linked to reproductivity, and also that sex is heterosexual. Yet the two recommend different and contradictory standards of conduct for men.

This contradiction is resolved for men by visiting it upon women. Either women are divided into two types (as above), or more recently a woman is expected to be both things. In effect we end up with a double standard [. . .] : men's sexuality is understood through the male sexual drive discourse: they are expected to be sexually incontinent and out of control – 'it's only natural'.

The following letter from a man in *Spare Rib* (a British feminist magazine) demonstrates how these discourses can coexist in the beliefs of one person:

> As a mature male, I am in total support of the new 'women against violence against women' campaign, with the proviso that the supporters should realise that the majority of men are decent, of reasonably high principles and respect

women as equal partners, and only a small proportion are grossly anti-social. But man being the animal he is, do you think that the answer to rape is well-ordered government-run brothels to cater for the large section of single, sexually-frustrated men in our society?[2]

The picture is more complicated for women. Underneath the insistence on our asexuality within this discourse is the belief that our sexuality is rabid and dangerous and must be controlled. This is far more explicit in Mediterranean cultures where women are traditionally seen as being in one of two categories: 'fallen' or 'not yet fallen'.[3] The implication is that women's sexuality is inevitable and dangerous. (It is not defined as a lack, as in post-Victorian northern Europe.) The only way to preserve the family honour is thus the total subservience of women to male control. Here men project onto women a rabid and ever-present sexuality, which leads to irrational jealousy.[4] Later I shall approach the question in terms of men's 'desire for the Other' and the reasons for their projections, rather than falling into the assumption that this has something to do with women's sexuality.

According to the have/hold discourse, women's sexuality is seen as a lack, the possibility avoided by the stress on their relationship with husband and children. For example, Eustace Chesser, a liberal sexual reformer in the 1950s, argued that the sex act for women was only a prelude to satisfaction of the 'maternal instinct' and 'finding joy in family life.'[5]

[. . .]

The permissive discourse

The sexual practices of the participants in my study (aged on average around 30 in 1980) cannot be understood without recourse to a third discourse: the 'permissive' discourse. In this, the principle of monogamy is explicitly challenged. [. . .] In assuming that sexuality is entirely natural and therefore should not be repressed, the permissive discourse is the offspring of the male sexual drive discourse. Similarly it takes the individual as the locus of sexuality, rather than looking at it in terms of a relationship.[6] In one important respect it differs from the male sexual drive discourse: it applies the same assumptions to women as to men. In other words it was – in principle at least – gender-blind.

[. . .]

Women could now be subjects of a discourse in a way which meant active initiation of a sexual relationship based on the idea that our natural sexual drives were equal to (or the same as) men's. However, gender difference in sexuality was not suddenly transformed. That this was not the case demonstrates the importance of recognizing the historically specific nature of discourses, their relation to what has gone before and how practices – such as the one-night stands of the permissive era – are not the pure products of a single discourse.

The differences between men's and women's positions in the traditional discourses were never banished in permissive practices. [. . .] In the following extract Jo describes why permissive sex was alienating for her:

Jo: I've fantasized it [the quickie] yes, but it's never functioned like that – even
when that person was a complete stranger. Afterwards I just looked at that
stranger and felt completely alienated from what I'd just done with him. I
mean, really uncomfortable in the extreme. Why did I do it? I think in that
situation I'd almost never come, because I'd just be too guarded. You know,
there was too much, which I'm just not going to let go – with a complete
stranger. . . .

[. . .]

The meanings of sex for Jo are inconsistent with the permissive discourse and
therefore the practice which it promoted felt wrong. [. . .] In contrast to the have/hold
discourse, the permissive discourse did not imply any commitment or responsibility.

[. . .]

However, as I shall argue in the fourth part of this chapter, the meanings of sex are
more contradictory than that.[7]

The practices that a discourse re-produces are not neutral. The liberating effects
of the permissive discourse were particularly contradictory for women. Certainly the
discourse enhanced men's powers (men's 'rights') to a heterosexual practice without
emotional bonds.

[. . .]

BOYS' AND GIRLS' ENTRY INTO MASCULINITY AND FEMININITY

In this part I will try to give an account – albeit schematic – of boys' and girls'
developing relation to sexuality through the available discourses. Any analysis which
focuses on subjective positioning in discourses requires an account of the investment
that a person has in taking up one position rather than another in a different discourse.
Of course some discourses are more hegemonic and thus carry all the weight of social
approval. But successful positioning in these discourses is not automatic, else there
would be no variations. But to assume the mechanical reproduction of discourse
requires asking how it got to be like that in the first place. And that question is in danger
of throwing theory back into answers according to the terms of biological, Oedipal,
or social and economic determinisms.

[. . .]

The point that I [wish] to stress is that discourses coexist and have mutual effects
and that meanings are multiple. This produces choice, though it may not be simple
or conscious. Consequently we have to account for what investments a boy or girl
has in taking up a particular position in discourses by relating in certain ways with the
other. What accounts for the different investments produced historically in people of
the same gender? Clearly other major dimensions of social difference such as class,
race and age intersect with gender to favour or disfavour certain positions. However,
as well as recognizing cultural regularities it is also necessary – without resorting to
essentialism – to account for the uniqueness of individuals. Lacanian theory does
so by stressing the somewhat anarchic character of desire: desire as a motive force
or process is common to all significations (although it is contentious whether it is
universal). Although the significations which it occupies may be quite idiosyncratic,

I try to show that they are not arbitrary. Significations are a product of a person's history, and what is expressed or suppressed in signification is made possible by the availability and hegemony of discourses. Positions available in gender-differentiated discourses confer relative power by enabling the suppression of significations which would be undermining of power.

Growing up properly for a boy

For Jim girls were essential to 'growing up properly':

> *Jim:* I remember very young – before twelve – feeling a pressure to have a girlfriend and not having a clue. I remember hanging around a local cinema thinking that might be how something happened. But it was like an abstract pressure – I just felt that I should in order to show I was growing up properly. It didn't have any connection with the rest of my life, it was just something that I felt I should take on.

What did having a girlfriend mean that it signified 'growing up properly'? It positioned Jim as a 'proper man'; in other words it afforded him a gender-appropriate position:

> *Jim:* I did feel the onus always to actually be pushy, to see how far it was possible to go with somebody, to see how far they were actually *into* me.

> *Wendy:* What did you want?

> *Jim:* Well just an obvious sign of . . . as a way of showing I was into them – well in a way showing I was a proper man.

The sexual (or protosexual) practices he engaged in enabled him to be positioned as subject in the male sexual drive discourse ('being pushy'). He was not the victim of a natural drive (though the girl concerned probably read it that way). His interest was to do with gender not sex. His successful masculine positioning depended on a girl being 'into him' and the proof of this would be that she let him get sexual with her.

'Being attractive' for a girl

The same principle is illustrated in Clare's account of her adolescent feelings about boys. The available positions are different however. Where Jim had to be pushy, Clare had to be attractive. There is a chain of assumptions running through the account: being attractive . . . (means) . . . being attractive to boys . . . (means) . . . engaging in sex (or protosex) with boys . . . (means) . . . having a boyfriend.

> *Clare:* I can see from the photographs that I went from being a child who was quite pretty to an early adolescent who – I felt myself to be fat and ugly, and desperately lacking in confidence. I suspect I lacked confidence because I had had ways of dealing with people, which were to do with being an attractive child. They didn't work any more, because I wasn't one. When I was fourteen or fifteen I went on a diet – and I went down

from being quite big to seven stone. It was an absolutely wonderful thing. It had a lot for me, to do with sexuality. I remember I thought I would be more confident, I thought I would be more attractive to boys.

Wendy: Were you more confident?

Clare: In a way, yes. I was quite good at school, though but certainly – when I lost weight, it seemed like the resolution of a set of contradictions. Having lost weight, I was no longer destined to be the 'ugly, clever type'. It would be alright because I was actually quite attractive as well. The more I dig deep, the more I think of the hurt – there's a hell of a lot of hurt around not being attractive enough and particularly about not having boyfriends. I remember, kind of, going out with anybody who asked me. I was so pleased to be asked, that I would have gone with anybody.

Wendy: When you did go out with them, what did you think of them?

Clare: Not a lot. I thought it was all a bit of a joke. Most of them were fools.

Adolescent girls' sexual practices gain them the reputation of being either slags or drags – a contradiction which is a logical product of women's contradictory positions in the male sexual drive and have/hold discourses. Yet girls do not on the whole feel free to forego relationships with boys, for the reasons that Clare illuminates. Her identity as an attractive girl is at stake. According to McRobbie adolescent girls' main goal is 'to attract and keep a boy'. There are ostensibly few pay-offs and plenty of risks: the danger of being called 'slags', no enjoyment of the kind of sex that boys practise, the experience that the boys are fools anyway. Their investment is in their own identities. Boys are necessary simply because in the only discourse in which being attractive can be understood, being attractive means being attractive to the opposite sex.

Attractiveness and femininity

It is within the practices of gender-differentiated discourses concerning sexuality that girls' and womens' gender identity is re-produced. In the following quote, Clare explores why she felt in a weak position later on when she did get involved in a long-term relationship with a man:

Clare: I mean, with Phil he was very loud and domineering, and I was very quiet and weak. He was strong, and I was weak. I think that was the main thing. And I was more feminine.

Wendy: What did that involve?

Clare: Looking pretty. I think it relates back to when I said that when I was little I was the good, pretty little girl. It's to do with – the fear – being frightened of not being attractive enough.

Wendy: To keep him?

Clare: Mmmm.

Attracting a man is the defining feature of Clare's femininity. Keeping him, according to the male sexual drive discourse, means continuing to be attractive to him. This is the crucial recurrent interest in Clare's take-up of the object position in the male sexual drive discourse. In order to feel herself as gender-appropriate, she thus feels driven to be in a couple relationship with a man. These practices re-produce certain sexual and couple *practices*, and re-produce both gender difference and the inequality of women's position in the dominant discourses concerning sexuality.

I have shown that the practice of heterosexual couple relations (including sexual relations) is a site where different discourses concerning sexuality are available to produce different knowledges or meanings through which practices are mediated. Within this general usage of discourse analysis what is of particular significance is how the gender-differentiated nature of these discourses affects women's and men's powers and therefore the investment they have in taking up gender-appropriate positions and practices. Girls and women actively engage in certain heterosexual practices in order to re-produce their gender identity.

Heterosexual practice and the construction of women's sexuality

However, the investments of those participating in sexual relations are no more unitary than the powers conferred on them through their positions in discourses. In the following extract, Clare indicates that her sexuality was completely subordinated to the need to be attractive:

> *Clare:* I think my understanding of my own sexuality when I was an adolescent was about zero. I mean it felt like doing this thing which meant you had to attract boys – to be attractive to them. There wasn't anything else. But even later, when I began fucking men, it was actually an extension of that.

That this need to be attractive produced her as passive in heterosexual sex is illustrated below. Clare and I discover the similarities in the way that our sexuality and gender was reproduced in the practices which were a product of the male sexual drive. The take-up of a position as object in the discourse of male sexual drive, motivated by the interest in being attractive, constructs the practice of heterosexual sex:

> *Clare:* Well, I don't know, the term 'sexuality' means something quite different now. I don't think I felt I had a sexuality.
>
> *Wendy:* I was never actually aware of having a spontaneous desire, that somehow seemed to be initiated by me, which I could then act out.
>
> *Clare:* Right, yes. That's it.
>
> *Wendy:* . . . Except the desire to attract a man, and follow it through.
>
> *Clare:* Right. It was that which was powerful for me.
>
> *Wendy:* Although, if I was attracted to a boy, and we went out together, or something, I was always – y'know, wanting kisses and cuddles, and fumbles, and . . . I don't know – the kind of things that would signify that it was getting more intense.

Clare: Yes, but I think that was because of what it signified, rather than because I actually liked it.

Wendy: Yes, and even that had a kind of genital goal. Because even though I didn't know at that point what we did, I knew that that was the most risky place.

Clare: Yes – I knew that. But I can't say that I enjoyed it. But then I didn't enjoy screwing very much either. I didn't know that I didn't, even. I feel very ashamed – I feel it's an awful admission. I actually had my first orgasm with Ken. I mean, I was sleeping with men for that long, and I never had one. I mean, I didn't think I was, and I wasn't sure, and for the life of me I wouldn't ask. It took me a long time to realize – well that I had masturbated and reached orgasm. I didn't know it was the same thing. I just thought it was something rather peculiar. I did masturbate when I was younger but I associated it – not one iota – with sex. I suppose later it was a certain kind of confidence which I had, which meant that I was more determined to get what I wanted. Even though I wasn't quite sure what that was. I mean, I think I was probably very passive.

Wendy: That passivity thing – I think is tied up with confidence. Er, with me, in short relationships, where I didn't actually . . . know a man very well, I never trusted the man enough for me to be active. Or, another way of putting it would be – to show myself as someone who had . . . desires.

Clare: I think that's right – for me. I was passive – because I didn't know how to express myself and also because I didn't know what to do. And because I felt judgements were being made of my sexual competence. And I had no idea, whether or not I was doing it right.

Wendy: The criterion that I evolved – of doing it right or not, was . . . um . . . ministering right to a man's needs, to what turned him on. If he seemed to enjoy it. And it was all about his sexuality.

Clare: Yes. Right.

Wendy: . . . I mean, that's how I learned to be sexual.

Clare: . . . Doing things that men liked. Yes.

Wendy: And in that sense I was quite active – I took initiatives.

THE SUPPRESSED IN DISCOURSE AND THE MULTIPLE SIGNIFICATIONS OF SEX

[. . .]

The meaning of sex is no more unitary than the discourses which compete to define the practice of sex. In this section I want to show how suppressed significations coexist with those expressed. Rather than seeing what is suppressed as something which is directly reducible to the Oedipus Complex, or as invisible in the sense that the suppressed meanings have no effects (that is tantamount to the suppressed being non-existent and meaning being unitary), I will show how for men there are continued investments – to do with power – in defining women as subjects of the have/hold discourse, thereby suppressing their own wishes to have and to hold. One participant in my research wrote the following about the man she was in a relationship with:

> If he's saying he has no expectations, no needs, then I can't let him down. If I can't let him down, he has more power. He has the power to hurt me, but I don't have the power to hurt him.

Her observation is a beautifully clear recognition of the relation between knowledge (discourses) and power. As long as she and not he is positioned as the subject of the have/hold discourse, unequal power is the consequence.

[. . .]

[M]en still have needs for the intimacy of a heterosexual relationship. A man writing in *Achilles Heel* (an anti-sexist men's magazine) suggests that this is the only place where men can get these needs met:

> For men (heterosexual) sex works out as a trap because it's the only place where men can really get tenderness and warmth. But they have no skills to evoke these things because there is nothing in the rest of our lives that trains us to do this. So we come into this where we want warmth and intimacy and we don't know how to get it. But it's the only place it exists so there's this tremendous tension for men, getting into bed with women.[8]

This quotation again illustrates that sex can be a cover for men's need for intimacy to be met. The reproduction of women as subjects of a discourse concerning the desire for intimate and secure relationships protects men from the risk associated with their own need (and the consequent power it would give women). Their own simultaneous position as object of the have/hold discourse and subject of the male sexual drive discourse enables them to engage in the practice of sex, and thus get what they want without recognizing those needs or risking exposure. 'Sex' as male drive therefore covers for the suppressed signification of 'sex' as intimacy and closeness. Because the practice itself does not require verbalization, the suppressed signification is not necessarily recognized. These significations (not necessarily conscious) are completely woven in to the practices of sex, suppressed as they are with the aid of the male sexual drive discourse. This is illustrated by Sam's immediate association when asked how a woman makes him feel: 'It's a closeness, isn't it . . . going to sleep, cuddling close. Feeling – I mean, I don't worry about burglars. I think I feel a lot more secure.'

Unlike a reply from within the discourse of male sexual drive, such as 'it turns me on', Sam's response captures significations normally suppressed through projection: closeness and security.

A man's fear of 'getting in deep' requires theorization in its own right. What are the strong feelings that are evoked by women with whom they have – or want – sexual relationships, which are invested in suppressing their own emotions and projecting them on to women?

Desire for the Other, power relations and subjectivity

In the following extract, Martin describes forcefully what happens to him when he feels a little attracted to a woman. The account imposes on my analysis the question of the irrational in couple relations.

> *Martin:* People's needs for others are systematically denied in ordinary relation-
> ships. And in a love relationship you make the most fundamental
> admission about yourself – that you want somebody else. It seems to me
> that that is the greatest need, and the need which, in relationship to its
> power, is most strongly hidden and repressed. Once you've shown the
> other person that you need them, then you've made yourself incredibly
> vulnerable.

[. . .]

Martin's experience of attraction leaves us with a pressing question: what is it that provides us with the irrational charge in sexual attraction? It is the quality of this experience which precipitates Martin's vulnerability and resistance. I call this experi- ence 'desire for the Other', and by the use of this concept, link in to psychoanalytic theory for an explanation: desire for the mother is repressed but never extinguished. It reasserts itself in adult sexual relations.

I want to stress the effects of this subjective experience. Martin's 'desire for the Other' produces a feeling of intense vulnerability which in turn motivates him to exercise whatever powers he can muster in relation to women to whom he feels attracted. Sexist discourses serve this precise function. By reading himself as object of the have/hold discourse he can suppress the recognition of his dependence on a relationship with a woman. As long as he reads the woman as subject of the have/hold discourse he can camouflage his desire. If he succeeds, he can sustain the relationship and meet some of his needs while both remain unaware of them. That this has power effects, even when its suppression is not total, is illustrated in the following account by Martha, the woman with whom Martin has a relationship:

> *Martha:* All these things that we've been talking about hand such power to
> people. Martin and I go up and down like a see-saw. There are days when
> he's in another city, and needing me, and suddenly I'm powerful and
> can dictate terms. We're back here, and I'm wanting a close, reciprocal,
> warm, working-out relationship, and suddenly he's powerful, because
> he doesn't want to give it. It really is dynamite . . . every day of our lives.
> It really is working less and less well. This business of having needs is
> so humiliating, because it makes one vulnerable.

> *Wendy:* And shifts the power.

> *Martha:* And shifts the power – exactly.

Her experience of the effects again bears witness to the way sexist discourse is productive of power – for men.

In the following extract Martha refers to the more general oppressive effects of Martin's resistance to the power he experiences her having in the relationship:

> *Martha:* I put up with it, rather than saying, 'No, this is not the way I want to be treated'. I want to be treated as a complete person, someone who has feelings and ideas and intuitions that are actually worth taking notice of. No room is allowed for me to be myself, fully because it might be too powerful an intrusion on his actions. To be accepted one hundred per cent means that the other person has to be strong enough . . . to keep their own integrity in the face of you being one hundred per cent yourself. It's so hard to find men who might be committed to taking those risks.

Her moving testimony to the effects on her of Martin's power is a specific example of the experience of gender difference: it points to the psychological characteristics which are consistent with – and reproduce – sexist discourses where woman is the inferior 'other'.

Misrecognition of men

When men behave warily and defensively, women do not necessarily read it as stemming from their vulnerability or dependence. This is because women too are subject to the production of meanings through dominant discourses. The available assumptions about men are that they are, for example, powerful, rational, autonomous, in control and self-confident. These features are, by definition, positively valued in sexist discourses. The effect is to foreground men's qualities and conceal their weaknesses and to do the opposite for women. Positioned within such discourses women misread themselves as easily as men. Clare's account of her relationship exemplifies this misrecognition:

> *Clare:* That guy, I didn't even know he was so dependent on me.
>
> *Wendy:* That's so often the way men play it. But it's also so often the way that women read it.
>
> *Clare:* Oh, it's two-way. Precisely. His behaviour was very stereotypical, really. I thought he was a competent person – but he didn't think he was at all. He was outwardly confident – domineering – which actually made me feel incredibly oppressed.
>
> [. . .]

Desire and the signifier 'woman'

Misrecognition of the Other of desire, when it is an opposite-sexed Other, is not explicable simply by the existence of gender-differentiated discourses. I will argue, through analysing Jim's account, that the way in which 'woman' signifies for him has a history going back to his desire for the mother. The argument is an illustration of Lacan's slogan 'the desire for the Other is the desire for the mother'.

[. . .] Jim is aware that he is frightened by strong emotions [. . .] there is an elision between his own and the woman's emotions:

> *Wendy:* And was it that the girls wanted to be more intimate?

> *Jim:* Yeah – I was frightened of making that kind of commitment, that kind of involvement, 'cause I thought I'd be let down, because of what happened the first time, when I was so unreserved about how I felt. I think that really affected my life incredibly, that first time I fell in love.

> *Wendy:* Why was having a relationship with her such a burden?

> *Jim:* She was very strong and very emotional – that's pejorative, but I mean she had strong reactions, so that I didn't actually feel safe that I wasn't going to be knocked out, or sucked in by her.

It transpires that Jim's fear of her strong emotions was a projected fear of his own.[9] He feared them because it felt unsafe to feel so strongly for a woman. As many men experience with their first sexual relationship – particularly if it is with an older woman – their lack of defences leave them painfully hurt when the relationship ends. As I have argued above, this constitutes the investment in reading the woman as the subject of the have/hold discourse.

[. . .]

I have considered in greater detail elsewhere[10] the implications and theorization of this mother/Other link. Here I will give one further instance of the way that seemingly unimportant day-to-day relationships are suffused with meanings which must be explicated in terms of 'desire for the Other' and how the woman of the relationship is linked to the mother. Another woman Jim had a relationship with said:

> I was feeling preoccupied with other things, so I suppose not paying him much attention. Jim got at me twice – about tiny things, in a way that felt antagonistic. When I pointed it out we tried to do some work on it. Blank. Then he came up with the word 'oranges', as if from nowhere. When he thought about it a bit he said it had something to do with his relations with women. If a woman peeled an orange for him, it showed that they cared for him. Then he said that his mother used to do it for him, even when he could do it for himself.

Desire has a history through its occupancy of certain significations – in this case, who peeled oranges. It does not express itself through the rationally accessible layer of meaning – it couldn't be included in the definition of oranges. But when it comes up in the practice of peeling oranges this meaning is there as a presence. For Jim it is part of a wider set of significations around proof of loving and caring through women doing things for him. It is consistent with the common experience of women in relationships with men that men get them to do things for them when they are 'objectively' unnecessary. The suppressed signification is 'I'll do it for you because I love you'. The signifying chain from mother to Other is historically unbroken for men, although, according to Freudian theory, savagely repressed.[11]

Implications for changing gender difference

In this part I have shown that the positions which are available in discourses do not determine people's subjectivity in any unitary way. Whilst gender-differentiated positions do overdetermine the meanings and practices and values which construct an individual's identity, they do not account for the complex, multiple and contradictory meanings which affect and are affected by people's practices. Specifically, men's sexuality is not plausibly accounted for by their positions as subject in the discourse of the male sexual drive and object in the have/hold discourse. 'Sex' signifies in many ways at once. The fact that a man succeeds in reading his sexual practices according to such sexist positions – locating the woman in the complementary positions – only means that the discourse provides the means whereby other significations can be suppressed. Yet 'desire for the Other' is present through the metaphoric axis and affects practices. Thus the knowledge produced by the male sexual drive discourse confers power on men which, in a circular way, motivates them recurrently in taking up that position. This is a specific example of the power-knowledge relation that Foucault theorizes.[12] If the woman is unable to resist her complementary positioning by having access to an alternative discourse and practice, or if her investment in being so positioned is paramount,[13] the couple will reproduce the discourse and thus the existence of gender difference in practices and subjectivity.

What makes this analysis different from one which sees a mechanical circulation of discourses through practices is that there is an investment which, for reasons of an individual's history of positioning in discourses and consequent production of subjectivity, is relatively independent of contemporary positions available. According to my account this is an investment in exercising power on behalf of a subjectivity protecting itself from the vulnerability of desire for the Other. Otherwise power could only be seen as a determined feature of the reproduction of gender-differentiated discourses, which would be left untheorized or reduce to a biological or economic determinism. Instead I have tried to show by concrete example that the interest is specific and part of the history of men and women (in different ways).

I believe that the heterosexual couple relationship (or sexual relationship) is a crucial site for the reproduction of gender difference because of 'desire for the Other'. [. . .] An analysis of race or class difference could follow many of the same principles but it could not rely in quite the same way on the concept of 'desire for the Other'. This issue raises the question of the relation between desire and 'desire for the Other' in psychoanalytic theory.

The analysis is of political importance because it indicates the nature of the problem involved in changing gender difference. It is not only the social division of labour. We have indicated that there are problems with the Oedipus Complex as an explanation. Furthermore, it is not a problem to be addressed at the level of discourses alone, critical as that is. The reproduction of gender-differentiated practices depends on the circulation between subjectivities and discourses which are available. The possibility of interrupting this circle is contained in a grasp of the contradictions between discourses and thus of contradictory subjectivities. While one set of desires may be suppressed, along with their signification, by the dominant sexist discourses, the contradictions are never successfully eliminated. They are the weak points in the stronghold of gender difference: taking up gender-appropriate positions as women and men does not successfully express our multiple subjectivities.

[. . .]

SPLITTING THE DIFFERENCES

The following . . . extract describes splitting between a gender-differentiated pair of characteristics: expressing feelings and giving support. The exclusion, through projection, of one 'side' of this pair is made possible by the way their meaning already contains a specification of what is gender-appropriate. The difference is re-produced in the subjectivities of each member of the heterosexual couple.

> *Jim:* The thing got specialized, as it were polarized, where one person does the feeling. My relationship with Jeanette, who I lived with for many years, developed in such a way that she was responsible for doing the feelings – she was the one that got upset, and I was the one who was coping, providing support, kindness, et cetera. And so what that meant was that I didn't get to express any feelings and she didn't get to express any support. And so what that means is that both sides are completely prevented from experiencing what the other person's 'job' is. Which means that you get a completely shrivelled – a completely incomplete – idea of what's going on.

Two important points emerge from this comment. First – and most obviously – the content of the split is predictable from discourses specifying gender difference: it was the woman whose job it was to do the feeling. Our common-sense experience of this split is through the naturalistic assumption that it is part of women's natural make-up. In consequence, this characteristic of their relationship was not read as a relational dynamic, it was read as aspects of their personalities. Jim said that at the time he firmly believed that he was just not a 'feeling person'. Whereas traditionally this would have been considered a positive characteristic, in the humanist and feminist climate of the post-1960s, he felt that it was a lack. None the less, the effect of the denial, through projection of these feelings, was experienced as part of his 'personality', that is as something fundamental and unchangeable. Clearly then, it is vital to understand the mechanisms whereby gender-differentiated characteristics – such as expressing feelings – are located in one member of a heterosexual couple. By focusing on the mechanisms, I am able to avoid seeing the effect as a once-and-for-all accomplishment of sex-role socialization. Instead I am seeing it as a dynamic which is constantly being re-produced in day-to-day couple relationships. I shall illustrate this in due course.

The second point emerges from the opposition which is implied between expressing feelings and giving support. This is not a logical pair of opposites, but you probably took it for granted when you read it (which illustrates the power of gender-differentiated discourses to construct our assumptions). The value which we are obliged to accept in order to make sense of this opposition is that people, usually women, who express feelings need support because expressing feelings is a weakness.

'Doing the feelings' is equated with 'getting upset'. Conversely the person, usually a man, who gives support is thus obliged to position himself as someone who is strong enough not to have feelings. The logic of the opposition is not contained in the meaning itself, but rather in the judgement attached to it. In our society, the judgement is a sexist one: expressing feelings is weak, feminine and in contradistinction to men's rationality. With the value – which is indeed inextricable from the meaning once it is seen as inserted into the discourse – comes power difference. Men can support women who are subject to the unfortunate bane of feeling and thus men are superior.

[. . .]

[T]his constitutes a substantial investment in taking up such a position recurrently in relations. I have already shown how it can be the fear of their own feelings, signifying weakness, which is concealed by the manoeuvre. Now I shall show how splitting, through projection and introjection, operates as a defence. This accounts for the mechanism whereby gender-differentiated positions in discourses are reproduced.

[. . .]

Many women in heterosexual relations [. . .] feel that they want a man to be stronger than they are. Consistent with their history of positioning they too reproduce themselves as needing support. Their investment, while not so clear cut as for men, is in getting looked after and being required to take little responsibility.[14] Yet because connotations of weakness and inferiority are carried along with their need for support, it contradicts their feelings of effectiveness and their experience of being strong enough to provide support.

The circle of reproduction of gender difference involves two people whose histori-cal positioning, and the investments and powers this has inserted into subjectivity, complement each other. When there remain contradictions in each person's wants of the other, there is ground for an interruption of its reproduction. These contradictions are the products of social changes. It is through the kinds of social changes that I outlined [. . .] that alternative discourses for example feminist ones – can be produced and used by women in the struggle to redefine our positions in gender-differentiated practices, thus challenging sexist discourses still further. Changes don't automatically eradicate what went before – neither in structure nor in the way that practices, powers and meanings have been produced historically. Consciousness-changing is not accomplished by new discourses replacing old ones. It is accomplished as a result of the contradictions in our positionings, desires and practices – and thus in our subjectivities – which result from the coexistence of the old and the new. Every relation and every practice to some extent articulates such contradictions and therefore is a site of potential change as much as it is a site of reproduction.

NOTES

1. G. Wilson, 'The sociobiology of sex differences', *Bulletin of the British Psychology Society*, 32, 1979, pp. 350–53.
2. *Spare Rib*, 104, March 1981.
3. J. Du Boulay, *Portrait of a Greek Mountain Village*, Oxford: Claredon Press, 1974.
4. T. Moi, 'Jealousy and sexual difference', *Feminist Review*, 11, 1984, pp. 53–69.

5. Quoted in B. Campbell, 'A feminist sexual politics: now you see it, now you don't', *Feminist Review*, 5, 1980, pp. 1–18.
6. *Forum* magazine's emphasis on technique reflects this focus. The sexual partner is supposedly necessary 'to take part in reciprocal stimulation that will provide the maximum intensity of voluptuous sensations at coming off' (1971). The individualism of this discourse is characteristic of the epoch generally.
7. *Achilles Heel*, 2, 1979, p. 9.
8. J. Lacan, *Écrits; a Selection*, London: Tavistock, 1977, p. 286.
9. This is not to claim that these feelings weren't the woman's as well. It is the fear of them which indicates his own projection. Another person is a suitable vehicle for a projection precisely when they are subject to the same feelings themselves.
10. W. Hollway, 'Identity and gender difference in adult social relations', unpublished Ph.D. thesis, University of London, 1982.
11. The account of (heterosexual) women's desire for the Other represents a further theoretical problem: how and to what extent does the girl transfer her desire for the Other from the mother, where it is originally located, to father and thence man? In the Freudian account, for the girl unconscious meanings (what Lacan would call the metaphoric axis) slip from wanting to 'be' the penis (that is on identification with the father and continuing desire for the mother) to wanting to 'have' it and give the father a gift of a baby. I cannot enter into a detailed critique here. However, if we see psychoanalytic theory as itself being subject to defence mechanisms operating in its (predominantly male) authors and reproducing sexist discourses, we can hypothesize that this formulation may be a reversal. The valorization of the penis would be a compensation for the power of the mother/woman to give birth and be reproduced through men's investment in this position in discourse. The process is similar to my analysis of Jim's and Sam's accounts who accomplished a reversal through projection.
12. See Julian Henriques, Wendy Hollway, Cathy Urwin, Couze Venn and Valerie Walkerdine (eds), *Changing the Subject*, London: Tavistock, 1984, introduction to section 2, p. 115–18.
13. For a more detailed consideration of women's contradictory investments and powers in sexist discourses see W. Hollway, 'Heterosexual sex: power and desire for the Other', in S. Cartledge and J. Ryan (eds), *Sex and Love: New Thoughts on Old Contradictions*, London: The Women's Press, 1983.
14. This may not be the case in practice, but if the investment has been inserted historically (a history of desire eventually linking back to the mother) it is not simply conditional on a rational view of the outcome. This is one reason why my use of investment in no way slides into a learning-theory explanation.

ANIMALS AND BIOLOGICAL DETERMINISM

Lynda Birke

The final reading in this section brings us back to some of the fundamental issues involved in arguing a case for the social construction of gender and sexuality. Feminists have often approached this through drawing a sharp distinction between animals – seen as part of nature – and human beings – whose culture enables them to transcend nature. Lynda Birke challenges this dichotomy, arguing that it leads to a simplistic understanding of biology and particularly of animal behaviour.

[. . .]

Part of the background to feminist theorizing is the ways in which the social sciences construct ideas about gender, or about humanity. In general, feminists have concurred with much of sociology in being critical of ideas that imply biological determinism. Humans are somehow 'above' mere biology, being located firmly in culture; the realm of the biological – the body, the rest of nature – can thus conveniently be ignored.

BIOLOGICAL DETERMINISM

the grand cause of hysteria . . . that which melts the women of England into powerless babes . . . and shatters their intellect . . . and, by destroying reason, level them with those that chew the cud – this grand traitor and foe to humanity is Polite Education.[1]

Anti-feminist arguments frequently seem to reduce us to the level of mindlessness; in this case, the image invoked is of a bovine mindlessness, chewing the cud. In the

From L. Birke, *Feminism, Animals and Science*, Milton Keynes: Open University Press, 1994.

middle of the nineteenth century, women's biology was held to be limiting; not only would it get in the way of our education, but education itself would damage our biology[2] – thus reducing us to the status of animals. Women's intelligence, like animals, has typically been compared to men's – and found wanting.

Feminists have frequently had to confront arguments rooted in biology. Almost invariably, such arguments seek to justify the status quo. We are all too familiar with the force of claims stating that behavioural differences between women and men are rooted in genetic and/or hormonal differences. As a result, gender becomes immutable, fixed by biology. Typically, parallels are drawn with other animals (usually, but not always, other mammals); for example, the effects of hormones on rats' brains might serve to defend beliefs in fundamental differences between the brains of men and women.[3] The most common reactions to such arguments among feminists are to point to the inadequacies of the underlying science, and to emphasize the extent to which gender is socially constructed.[4]

Politically, this move was important. All too often, women had been told that they should not or could not do something because of (say) their raging hormones, or because they were genetically/evolutionarily preordained to prefer the kitchen sink.[5] The diet of biological forces continues, however, and has even gathered momentum in relation to homosexuality.

Feminist avoidance and rejection of arguments grounded in 'biology' is, politically, in striking contrast to an emerging groundswell of political feelings in the gay community around the question of whether homosexuality has biological bases. In 1991, for example, Simon LeVay, a gay neuroscientist, published a paper in the prestigious journal *Science*, which claimed to show that there were differences in the size of a particular tiny part of the brain (one of the interstitial nuclei of the anterior hypothalamus, or INAH for short) between heterosexual and homosexual men. The INAH in gay men was smaller, LeVay claimed, closer to the size of that of women (or, as he put it in a later book, 'gay men simply don't have the brain cells to be attracted to women'[6]). LeVay's paper came in for criticism by, among others, feminist biologists, for its assumptions and for the quality of its science.

Subsequently further articles appeared, claiming further differences in the brain between straight and gay men[7] and claiming that there were identifiable genes associated with male homosexuality.[8] Whatever the quality of the science (and it is worth remembering that scientific papers can nearly always be subject to critical scrutiny on methodological or rhetorical grounds), what is interesting is the extent to which the gay community seems to have picked up on the biological claims. This seems particularly to be the case in the USA, where religious fundamentalism is rife; the political significance of this is that if gayness is born into you, then you cannot be held morally responsible for it – you cannot thus sin.

The development of these beliefs within the gay community is, perhaps, not surprising, given the power of homophobia. But it should be a cause for concern, partly because it perpetuates the myth that sexuality (or gender) is *either* entirely biologically caused *or* it is the product of social conditioning – or even choice. Partly, too, we should be concerned because there remains a risk that such theories play into the hands of those who seek to 'cure' those of us who are lesbian or gay. The claim that a gene has been found has already led to public suggestions that fetuses carrying that gene could be aborted. Whatever the political responses, debate remains mired in a dichotomy: nature versus nurture, genes versus conditioning. Whichever side is emphasized, there are fundamental problems. Diana Fuss notes, for example, how social constructionism can seem to fail to speak to people's experiences of identity, particularly in the gay community, as it seems to deny shared history through its stress on historical contingency.[9] If everything comes down to social construction/choice, then we have little left in common. That emphasis also fails to address our lived experience as embodied individuals; it is not a social construction when our bodies hurt and bleed.

Indeed, in our rush from biological determinism, feminists have sometimes seemed to deny biology altogether. Several commentators have pointed to ways in which 'the body' is denied; here I am more concerned with the non-human world, but the gap in the theory is there. Humans, in our theorizing, tend to occupy a largely disembodied world of the mind and culture; animals are located in a world of 'nature', of biological determinants, of pure biology.

Biologically determinist arguments about humans typically rely on comparisons with other animals. This may be overt; it may be hidden away in the scientist's mind, but data from other mammals will be lurking somewhere. For example, although Le Vay based his paper on data from human brains (41 to be precise), the hypothesis that there *might* be a biological correlate derived in part from studies using animals. Now it is certainly the case that these studies using animals can be subjected to considerable critique; what a rat does in laboratory studies bears little relationship to human sexual repertoires, for example. But the fundamental assumption that underpins this kind of work goes like this: particular assumptions about human behaviour are made and projected onto animals – for instance, that what constitutes homosexuality is a tendency to behave like one of the opposite sex. Then these findings from animals can be used to 'show' that homosexuality is biological. Then we can speculate that it is similarly caused in humans – and seek a 'cure', perhaps testing that on animals first to show that it works.

All of this relies on assumptions that animals such as rats are an appropriate 'model' for human sexuality. Yet those who argue using biology seem mystified by the strength of opposition, as do those who oppose biological determinism. Part of the problem, as with any controversy, is that the protagonists talk past each other. But another part of the problem here, it seems to me, is the uncertainty (and thus implicit disagreement) about what is meant by the terms. The most obvious source of disagreement is over what 'sexuality' means. To those arguing biological determinism, it seems to mean little more than penis-into-vagina. To critics, human sexuality acquires meanings *in* human culture, and can thus incorporate a wide range of behaviours and responses. Perhaps it does to non-humans too, but biologists' emphasis on reproduction has ensured that animal sex is seen solely in that light.

Not only is sexuality a contested concept in these arguments; so too are terms such as 'biological', 'animal', or even 'human'. For example, in a discussion of what is meant by 'human' (by contrast to animal), Cora Diamond[10] notes the slippage in the way that 'human being' may mean something to do with persons; it may have an existential tone (as in human *being*), or it may be used in the 'biological' sense to represent what is specific to our species. 'Humanity', moreover, means more than just a species; it also represents a quality (we might speak, for example, of the 'humanity' of decisions to help refugees). For various reasons, people are now asking more questions about what that quality represents, and so are beginning to challenge the human/animal boundary more succinctly.

The term 'animal' [. . .] can mean many different things. Opposed to humans, it tends to mean everything we think we are not, or whatever we wish to transcend – the beast within, for example. Colloquially, it can be used synonymously with 'mammal', as in the oft-used (but biologically strange) phrase 'animals and birds'. To biologists, it means any organism that is classified as belonging to the animal kingdom – thus a wide range of creatures, from sponges and seaslugs to eels and monkeys.

'Biology' is also problematic. Obviously, there is one sense in which it means a particular discipline, part of the natural sciences. 'Biology' in this sense connotes the study of living organisms and their processes, but it can also be used synonymously with those processes, as in 'human biology'. It is this that feminist theorizing tends to avoid, although it is not always clear just what it is about our 'biological processes' that is to be avoided.

The meaning of 'the social', of sociality, differs too, in these different discourses, particularly when animal sociality is invoked. In scientific accounts of animal behaviour, 'social behaviour' is held to be what a given species of animal does in groups – communicating, sexual behaviour, aggressive encounters, and so forth. But the 'social' of sociological and political theorists conveys much more than that; it is defined as not including animals. Rather, it is about human culture(s), politics and ideology, and about the conscious design of these.[11]

This is the crux of our belief in our ability as a species to 'transcend' our proximity to other animals. It is this that is uniquely human, we are led to believe, and which separates us from the rest of nature. Or separates some of us; as feminists have been quick to point out, it is not 'humans' who, through their involvement with the social/political domain, are more social than natural. It is men of particular backgrounds – typically white, western and middle-class. Beverley Thiele has pointed out, for instance, that,

> Male nature is independent, active and truly human while female nature, conveniently for the status quo, fits her only for a narrow domestic role . . . his nature is such that he may transcend his animality by escaping into the human political realm of civil society, but only because women, trapped by their biology into remaining in the private sphere, oversee all the animal-like functions of mastication, defecation and copulation.[12]

Small wonder, then, that feminist theory has so often entailed denying proximity to animals/nature, as we seek to escape that world so dominated by 'animal-like functions' (while, paradoxically, many of us share our lives with non-human animals). Despite the sexism of which Thiele complains, the

> notion of a socially constructed subject . . . is . . . absolutely central to feminist theory . . . To view human being [*sic*] as a social product devoid of determining universal characteristics is to view its possibilities as open-ended. This is not to say that human being is not constrained by historical context or by rudimen-tary biological facts but rather that these factors set the outer parameters of possibility only.[13]

Here, then, is the reason for the commitment to social construction within feminist/sociological theorizing; it implies open-ended possibility, by contrast to the constraints set by 'rudimentary biological facts' to which, implicitly, *non*-human organisms are subject.

[. . .]

The assumption in western thought is not only that humans are different from 'other animals', but that what we have/are is superior. [. . .] Now, I would not wish to argue that human cultures have not generated qualities that are different from any other species. Perhaps we have produced many wonderful things (not to mention such appalling things as the capability for global destruction), but this kind of formulation, which sets up particular characteristics as defining humanity's specialness, is asking for trouble.

The biology versus social construction opposition requires that we firmly separate ourselves from other species. Biology is what non-humans have, while we disappear off into realms of virtual (social) reality. That separation runs strongly through the social sciences, and has influenced feminist thought. Thus Chris Shilling[14] outlines the importance of recent sociological thinking about the (human) body, and how we should not relegate it to the realms of the presocial or biological. Yet he retains the biology/culture divide when it comes to animals versus humans, suggesting, for instance, that

> [a]nimals enter the world with highly specialized and firmly directed drives . . . [they] have a species-specific world whose territories and dangers are mapped out from the very beginning of their lives. The bodies of animals are programmed to exist and survive within their environment.[15]

This picture of programmed automata is not a picture that accords with my understanding of many animals.

[. . .]

There are two particular consequences of the animals/nature versus humans/so-ciality dichotomies that I want now to examine. The first concerns their roots in attempts to define what is human by setting up 'others' who are not admitted into the human sphere; the second focuses on the problems of determinism and reductionism for how we see *non*-humans – the kind of reductionism that con-tinues to suppose that other animals are 'programmed' firmly by the dictates of biology.

ANIMALS AND OTHERS

Separating ourselves from less worthy 'others' is, as we have seen, a common trait. Feminists have been critical of this separation, not least because women have so often been other to men. 'Othering' is a trait that links to concepts of global domination, in its reliance on defining what is human against those who are conquered (of whatever species). Rey Chow,[16] for example, points out how the 'efforts to delineate the "human", be it in terms of language, reflection, or subjectivity, took place against a background of looming non-European "others"' who remain part of nature.[17]

The humanist traditions in western thought have tinkered with the boundaries of domination, with what is included or excluded. At various points, different classes of people have shifted from inferior status to claim inclusion in humankind – non-Europeans or women, for example – but none of this shifts the underlying structures and assumptions; all it does is to widen membership of the dominating group.[18] Nature remains firmly outside.

In rejecting biological determinism (however right our arguments may be), while not questioning what that means for and how it depends on particular ideas of animals, we are setting ourselves up as different from/superior to/apart from them; the assumption that our behaviour has very little to do with biology is aligned with one saying that theirs has everything to do with their biology. What we are saying, in effect, is that *we are not like animals*. Why do we want to say this?

Animals in western culture are 'other', objects of scientific enquiry.[19] We have defined ourselves in opposition to a generality of 'animals', irrespective of the qualities of individual species. It seems paradoxical that at a time when much feminist theory is moving beyond simple dualisms of gender (putting great emphasis on differences between women, say), it should do so by implicitly building its analyses on another simple dichotomy – humans versus 'other animals'. A more consistent approach, indeed, might be to extend the emphases on plurality and difference, and to begin to deconstruct the (putative) boundary between us and other species.

DETERMINED ANIMALS?

What we typically do in critiques of biological determinism is, rightly, to object to the way in which simplistic ideas about 'the biological base' are used to justify women's subordination. But what we fail to do is to question sufficiently the premises; we thus do not ask questions about the meaning of the biological body, nor do we ask questions about the behaviour of other animals. What happens, implicitly, in attacks on biological determinism is that the role of biology in bodily functions is not challenged; only its alleged role in our behaviour and capabilities is at fault. So, few would deny that ovaries produce hormones that are involved in the events of menstruation or menopause.

My problem with that is that the body and its internal functions so often seems to become primary and presocial.[20] The critiques of biological determinism, moreover, tend to rest on two dichotomies: mind/body and human/animal. To talk of biological substrates only becomes a problem in these critiques when it applies to humans, and minds. Thus in critiques of biological determinism, the behaviour of animals is rarely seen as problematic; we might, for instance, object to the notion that human gender differences are determined by hormonal effects on the brain while accepting a similar notion from laboratory studies of other species. So, from this perspective, human behaviour is fundamentally different from (discontinuous with) our biology, and human experience is radically different from that of other animals.

One difficulty with assuming human behaviour and abilities to be different from that of other kinds of creatures is that it leaves the lives of all *other* organisms firmly within the jurisdiction of 'biology'. Books on the biology of rats, for instance, are likely to include something about their behaviour and social organization, as well as how ovaries work. This allocation has two problematic effects. First, locating animal, but not human, behaviour within the realms of biology can distort our perception of the behaviour of animals. Second, because the predominant mode of explanation within biology still tends towards reductionism, it is all too easy to see non-human behaviour and social structure as caused by an underlying 'biology' – genes, hormones, or whatever. (This is, however, more obvious in popular accounts. Some areas of biological research have moved away from such simplistic models, towards a recognition that animals do not fit readily into the deterministic picture either. My purpose here is to draw attention to the fact that, if the behaviour of some species is called 'biological', then that behaviour is more easily attributed to 'biological' underlying causes – both in that species and then in humans.)

Biological explanations do tend towards reductionism, a point underscored by feminists often enough. But if reductionism impoverishes our understanding of human behaviour, then surely it must also do so with regard to animal behaviour. I have argued elsewhere[21] how different assumptions underpin questions about gender difference in humans and 'sex differences' (a telling phrase, for it implies fixity) in animals. In animal studies, scientists may note a sex difference in some mode of behaviour; usually this means a difference in the frequency of some kind of behaviour between populations of males and populations of females. Occasionally the frequency in one population is almost zero; more often, the populations differ merely in the relative frequency of that behaviour. For example, male rhesus monkeys may initiate social play more often, on average, than females, but that does not mean that females never engage in social play; nor does it mean that the animal's sex is the only thing that matters – bodily size may be important. Females tend to be smaller among rhesus monkeys. I would certainly hesitate before leaping in play onto a larger male – I imagine that a rhesus monkey would, too!

Now none of these differences are absolute, and they are statements about populations. The next step in reductionist logic is to extrapolate backwards within the developmental histories of individuals, and to look for antecedent causes within those individuals. You start, in other words, with an average abstracted from a population (male rats are more likely to attack strangers than are females, say), and then draw conclusions about the life history of an individual within that population. Because each sex produces different levels of certain sex hormones, those are a popular candidate. So, you might ask whether exposure to particular hormones in infancy makes a male more likely to attack as an adult. Once the hormone has been implicated in laboratory rats, then it is likely that someone, somewhere, jumps to conclusions about people – as indeed has been the case with the tales of hormonal causes of homosexuality.

But why assume that hormones within individuals are the direct and sole cause of any difference between populations? Hormone levels fluctuate in response to social or environmental influences in other mammals just as they do in people. If we can point to variation as a result of social influences in ourselves, then why not in other animals?

[...]

From this perspective we can allow behaviour, even in other animals, to become more than the product of internal 'biology'. We can begin to emphasize the richness of an animal's individual development, and its engagement with its own environment – as well as considering how that engagement could in turn influence the 'biology' itself (hormone levels, say). Acquiring gendered behaviour can then become seen as a more complex and negotiated process – even for non-human animals. We would also then, significantly, be breaking down the logic that locates animal behaviour in a reductionist biology, while retaining human (gender) behaviour in the social domain.

[...]

[I]f we continue to leave the deterministic assumptions about non-humans unchallenged, then biologically determinist arguments about us can easily flourish. For looking to other animals to support such claims lies at its heart. Simplistic accounts of animal societies combine with various normative assumptions derived from our own society to yield a powerful picture of coy submissive females and dominant, pioneering males. We ignore the other side of that picture at our peril. Treating other species as merely puppets of their genes feeds straight back into the biological determinism around human behaviour that feminists so much despise.

REWRITING SUBJECTS

So where does all this leave the 'specialness' of humans, and the assumptions made about that specialness by feminist criticisms of biological determinism? We can certainly argue for human specialness; there may well be features of our social life and culture that no other species at present possesses (just as we may lack certain features that other species possess). But we should not, I have argued, do so by creating an animal mythology. Animals are not automata, subject only to the dictates of biological laws; many species lead complex and rich social lives that cannot be collapsed onto simplistic ideas of biological substrates. Nor are we merely social constructs, beings without a biological body.

If we are effectively to counter biological determinism, we have to examine the various assumptions we make about our relationship to the natural world. We cannot simply escape them by dumping some bits, but not others, into a rubbish bag called 'biology'. To acknowledge a role for our biology – as bodies, or our part in the natural world – has sometimes seemed a dangerous move for feminists. And so it is, if we leave unchallenged the assumptions about what constitutes the biological or about what animals are.

We must, of course, continue to challenge crudely biologically determinist arguments. But we must also remember that determinist arguments do not work even for the 'other animals' that form the implicit counterpoint to our rejection of biological arguments about women. Our understanding of the natural world has, as a result, been impoverished. We must, therefore, insist on seeing (any) other species or individual as a product of complex life histories, in which all kinds of factors interact and play their part. We should strenuously deny that non-humans are 'simply' the product of bits of biology, just as much as we do about women.

[. . .]

Biological determinism relies on picturing animals as crudely driven by biological imperatives; at its worst, these imperatives are simply attributed to humans too. Neither is true. It is not enough for us to rebut only the human version of the story, for that tale relies heavily on an animal fable.

NOTES

1. W. Johnson, 'The morbid emotions of women' (1850), quoted in P. Jalland and J. Hooper (eds), *Women from Birth to Death*, Brighton: Harvester, 1986.
2. C.R. Russet, *Sexual Science*, Cambridge, Mass.: Havard University Press, 1989.
3. See A. Moirand and D. Jessel, *Brain Sex: The Real Difference between Men and Women*, London: Michael Joseph, 1989.
4. For example, L. Birke, and G. Vines, 'Beyond nature versus nuture: process and biology in the development of gender', *Women's Studies International Forum*, 10, 1987, pp. 555–70; R. Hubbard, *The Politics of Women's Biology*, New Brunswick, NJ and London: Rutgers University Press, 1990.
5. For some examples, see L. Birke, *Women, Feminism and Biology: The Feminist Challenge*, Brighton: Wheatsheaf, 1986; Hubbard, *Politics of Women's Biology*.
6. S. LeVay, *The Sexual Brain*, Cambridge, Mass.: MIT Press, 1993, p. 121.
7. L. Allen and R. Gorski, 'Sexual orientation and the size of the anterior commissure of the human brain', *Proceedings of the National Academy of Sciences of the USA*, 89, 1992, pp. 7199–202.
8. D.H. Hamer, S. Hu, V.L. Magnusson, N. Hu and A.H.L. Pattatucci, 'A linkage between DNA markers on the X chromosome and the male sexual orientation', *Science*, 261, 1993, pp. 321–7.
9. Diana Fuss, *Essentially Speaking: Feminism, Nature and Difference*, London: Routledge, 1989, p. 106.
10. Cora Diamond, 'The importance of being human', in D. Cockburn (ed.), *Human Beings*, Cambridge: Cambridge University Press, 1992.
11. R.A. Sydie *Natural Women, Cultured Men: A Feminist Perspective on Sociological Theory*, Milton Keynes: Open University Press, 1987.
12. Beverley Thiele, 'Vanishing acts in social and political thought: tricks of the trade', in C. Pateman and E. Gross (eds), *Feminist Challenges: Social and Political Theory*, Sydney: Allen & Unwin, 1986, p. 37.
13. M. Gatens, 'Feminism, philosophy and riddles without answers', in C. Pateman and E. Gross (eds), *Feminist Challenges: Social and Political Theory*, Sydney: Allen & Unwin, 1986, p. 28.
14. C. Shilling, *The Body and Social Theory*, London: Sage, 1993.
15. *Ibid.*, p. 101.
16. Rey Chow, '"It's you, not me": domination and "othering" in theorizing the "Third World"', in E. Weed (ed.), *Coming to Terms: Feminism, Theory, Politics*, London: Routledge, 1989, p. 158.
17. See also Z.T. Halpin, 'Scientific objectivity and the concept of "the other"', *Women's Studies International Forum*, 12, 1989, pp. 285–94.
18. V. Plumwood, 'Nature, self and gender: feminism, environmental philosophy and the critique of rationalism', *Hypatia*, 6, 1991, pp. 3–27.
19. Halpin, 'Scientific objectivity and the concept of "the other"'.
20. Shilling, *The Body and Social Theory*. This is not to deny that, in some feminist theorizing, the body has been understood as socially contingent. We can understand 'bodies' only through our social and cultural perceptions of them (see S. Hekman, *Gender and Knowledge: Elements of a Postmodern Feminism*, Boston: Northeastern University Press, 1990). But my reading of this kind of theorizing is that it seems to focus on the outer surfaces of the body and the meanings inscribed thereon. This (to me) still leaves the inner processes of bodies (which are the concern of feminist critiques of biological determinism) as relatively untheorized.
21. Birke, *Women, Feminism and Biology*; L. Birke, 'How do gender differences in behaviour develop? A reanalysis of the role of early experience', in P.P.G. Bateson and P.H. Klopfer (eds), *Perspectives in Ethology*. Volume 8 *Whither Ethology?* London: Plenum, 1989.

PART TWO

AFFIRMING AND QUESTIONING SEXUAL CATEGORIES

2.1

THE MYTH OF THE VAGINAL ORGASM

Anne Koedt

This influential article opened up a critique of heterosexuality, in particular the ways in which sex was defined from a male, phallocentric perspective. The arguments advanced here enabled women to think about alternative forms of pleasure, and ultimately about whether men were necessary for women's sexual fulfilment.

Whenever female orgasm and frigidity are discussed, a false distinction is made between the vaginal and the clitoral orgasm. Frigidity has generally been defined by men as the failure of women to have vaginal orgasms. Actually the vagina is not a highly sensitive area and is not constructed to achieve orgasm. It is the clitoris which is the centre of sexual sensitivity and which is the female equivalent of the penis.

I think this explains a great many things: first of all, the fact that the so-called frigidity rate among women is phenomenally high. Rather than tracing female frigidity to the false assumptions about female anatomy, our 'experts' have declared frigidity a psychological problem of women. Those women who complained about it were recommended psychiatrists, so that they might discover their 'problem' – diagnosed generally as a failure to adjust to their role as women.

The facts of female anatomy and sexual response tell a different story. Although there are many areas for sexual arousal, there is only one area for sexual climax; that area is the clitoris. All orgasms are extensions of sensation from this area. Since the clitoris is not necessarily stimulated sufficiently in the conventional sexual positions, we are left 'frigid'.

From A. Koedt, *Radical Feminism*, New York: Quadrangle, 1972.

Aside from physical stimulation, which is the common cause of orgasm for most people, there is also stimulation through primarily mental processes. Some women, for example, may achieve orgasm through sexual fantasies, or through fetishes. However, while the stimulation may be psychological, the orgasm manifests itself physically. Thus, while the cause is psychological, the *effect* is still physical, and the orgasm necessarily takes place in the sexual organ equipped for sexual climax – the clitoris. The orgasm experience may also differ in degree of intensity – some more localized, and some more diffuse and sensitive. But they are all clitoral orgasms.

All this leads to some interesting questions about conventional sex and our role in it. Men have orgasms essentially by friction with the vagina not the clitoral area, which is external and not able to cause friction the way penetration does. Women have thus been defined sexually in terms of what pleases men; our own biology has not been properly analysed. Instead, we are fed the myth of the liberated woman and her vaginal orgasm – an orgasm that in fact does not exist.

What we must do is redefine our sexuality. We must discard the 'normal' concepts of sex and create new guidelines that take into account mutual sexual enjoyment. While the idea of mutual enjoyment is liberally applauded in marriage manuals, it is not followed to its logical conclusions. We must begin to demand that if certain sexual positions now defined as 'standard' are not mutually conducive to orgasm, they no longer be defined as standard. New techniques must be used or devised which transform this particular aspect of our current sexual exploitation.

FREUD – A FATHER OF THE VAGINAL ORGASM

Freud contended that the clitoral orgasm was adolescent and that upon puberty, when women began having intercourse with men, women should transfer the centre of orgasm to the vagina. The vagina, it was assumed, was able to produce a parallel, but more mature, orgasm than the clitoris. Much work was done to elaborate on this theory, but little was done to challenge the basic assumptions.

To appreciate fully this incredible invention, perhaps Freud's general attitude about women should first be recalled. Mary Ellman, in *Thinking About Women*, summed it up this way:

> Everything in Freud's patronizing and fearful attitude toward women follows from their lack of a penis, but it is only in his essay *The Psychology of Women* that Freud makes explicit . . . the deprecations of women which are implicit in his work. He then prescribes for them the abandonment of the life of the mind, which will interfere with their sexual function. When the psychoanalyzed patient is male, the analyst sets himself the task of developing the man's capacities; but with women patients, the job is to resign them to the limits of their sexuality.

[. . .]

It was Freud's feelings about women's secondary and inferior relationship to men that formed the basis for his theories on female sexuality.

Once having laid down the law about the nature of our sexuality, Freud not so strangely discovered a tremendous problem of frigidity in women. His recommended cure for a woman who was frigid was psychiatric care. She was suffering from a failure to adjust mentally to her 'natural' role as a woman.

[. . .]

It is important to emphasize that Freud did not base his theory upon a study of women's anatomy, but rather upon his assumptions of woman as an inferior appendage to man, and her consequent social and psychological role. In their attempts to deal with the ensuing problem of mass frigidity, Freudians embarked on elaborate mental gymnastics. Marie Bonaparte, in *Female Sexuality*, goes so far as to suggest surgery to help women back on their rightful path. Having discovered a strange connection between the non-frigid woman and the location of the clitoris near the vagina,

> it then occurred to me that where, in certain women, this gap was excess-
> ive, the clitoridal fixation obdurate, a clitoridal vaginal reconciliation might
> be effected by surgical means, which would then benefit the normal erotic
> function,[1]

[. . .]

But the severest damage was not in the area of surgery, where Freudians ran around absurdly trying to change female anatomy to fit their basic assumptions. The worst damage was done to the mental health of women, who either suffered silently with self-blame, or flocked to psychologists looking desperately for the hidden and terrible repression that had kept from them their vaginal destiny.

LACK OF EVIDENCE

One may perhaps at first claim that these are unknown and unexplored areas, but upon closer examination this is certainly not true today, nor was it true even in the past. For example, men have known that women suffered from frigidity often during intercourse. So the problem was there. Also, there is much specific evidence. Men knew that the clitoris was and is the essential organ for masturbation, whether in children or adult women. So, obviously women made it clear where *they* thought their sexuality was located. Men also seem suspiciously aware of the clitoral powers during 'foreplay', when they want to arouse women and produce the necessary lubrication for penetration. Foreplay is a concept created for male purposes, but works to the disadvantage of many women, since as soon as the woman is aroused the man changes to vaginal stimulation, leaving her both aroused and unsatisfied.

It has also been known that women need no anaesthesia inside the vagina during surgery, thus pointing to the fact that the vagina is in fact not a highly sensitive area.

Today, with extensive knowledge of anatomy, with Kelly, Kinsey, and Masters and Johnson, to mention just a few sources, there is no ignorance on the subject. There are, however, social reasons why this knowledge has not been popularized. We are living in a male society which has not sought change in women's role.

[. . .]

WOMEN WHO SAY THEY HAVE VAGINAL ORGASMS

Confusion

Because of the lack of knowledge of their own anatomy, some women accept the idea that an orgasm felt during 'normal' intercourse was vaginally caused. This confusion is caused by a combination of two factors. One, failing to locate the centre of the orgasm, and two, by a desire to fit her experience to the male-defined idea of sexual normalcy. Considering that women know little about their anatomy, it is easy to be confused.

Deception

The vast majority of women who pretend vaginal orgasm to their men are faking it to 'get the job'. In a best-selling Danish book, *I Accuse*, Mette Ejlersen specifically deals with this common problem, which she calls the 'sex comedy'. This comedy has many causes. First of all, the man brings a great deal of pressure to bear on the woman, because he considers his ability as a lover at stake. So as not to offend his ego, the woman will comply with the prescribed role and go through simulated ecstasy. In some of the other Danish women mentioned, women who were left frigid were turned off sex and pretended vaginal orgasm to hurry up the sex act. Others admitted that they had faked vaginal orgasm to catch a man. In one case, the woman pretended vaginal orgasm to get him to leave his first wife, who admitted to being vaginally frigid. Later she was forced to continue the deception, since obviously she couldn't tell him to stimulate her clitorally.

Many more women were simply afraid to establish their right to equal enjoyment, seeing the sexual act as being primarily for the man's benefit, and any pleasure that the woman got as an added extra.

Other women, with just enough ego to reject the man's idea that they needed psychiatric care, refused to accept their frigidity. They wouldn't accept self-blame, but they didn't know how to solve the problem, not knowing the physiological facts about themselves. So they were left in a peculiar limbo.

Again, perhaps one of the most infuriating and damaging results of this whole charade has been that women who were perfectly healthy sexually were taught that they were not. So, in addition to being sexually deprived, these women were told to blame themselves when they deserved no blame. Looking for a cure to a problem that has none can lead a woman on an endless path of self-hatred and insecurity. For she is told by her analyst that not even in her one role allowed in a male society – the role of a woman – is she successful. She is put on the defensive, with phoney data as evidence that she'd better try to be even more feminine, think more feminine, and reject her envy of men. That is, shuffle even harder, baby.

WHY MEN MAINTAIN THE MYTH

Sexual penetration is preferred

The best physical stimulant for the penis is the woman's vagina. It supplies the necessary friction and lubrication. From a strictly technical point of view this position offers the best physical conditions, even though the man may try other positions for variation.

The invisible woman

One of the elements of male chauvinism is the refusal or inability to see women as total, separate human beings. Rather, men have chosen to define women only in terms of how they benefited men's lives. Sexually, a woman was not seen as an individual wanting to share equally in the sexual act, any more than she was seen as a person with independent desires when she did anything else in society. Thus, it was easy to make up what was convenient about women; for on top of that, society has been a function of male interests, and women were not organized to form even a vocal opposition to the male experts.

The penis as epitome of masculinity

Men define their lives primarily in terms of masculinity. It is a universal form of ego-boosting. That is, in every society, however homogeneous (i.e. with the absence of racial, ethnic, or major economic differences) there is always a group, women, to oppress.

The essence of male chauvinism is in the psychological superiority men exercise over women. This kind of superior-inferior definition of self, rather than positive definition based upon one's own achievements and development, has of course chained victim and oppressor both. But by far the most brutalized of the two is the victim.

An analogy is racism, where the white racist compensates for his feelings of unworthiness by creating an image of the black man (it is primarily a male struggle) as biologically inferior to him. Because of his position in a white male power structure, the white man can socially enforce this mythical division.

To the extent that men try to rationalize and justify male superiority through physical differentiation, masculinity may be symbolized by being the *most* muscular, the most hairy, having the deepest voice, and the biggest penis. Women, on the other hand, are approved of (i.e. called feminine) if they are weak, petite, shave their legs, have high soft voices.

Since the clitoris is almost identical to the penis, one finds a great deal of evidence of men in various societies trying either to ignore the clitoris and emphasize the vagina (as did Freud) or, as in some places in the Middle East, actually performing clitoridectomy. Freud saw this ancient and still practised custom as a way of further 'feminizing' the female by removing this cardinal vestige of her masculinity. It should be noted also that a big clitoris is considered ugly and masculine. Some cultures engage in the practice of pouring a chemical on the clitoris to make it shrivel up into 'proper' size.

It seems clear to me that men in fact fear the clitoris as a threat to masculinity.

Sexually expendable male

Men fear that they will become sexually expendable if the clitoris is substituted for the vagina as the centre of pleasure for women. Actually this has a great deal of validity if one considers *only* the anatomy. The position of the penis inside the vagina, while perfect for reproduction, does not necessarily stimulate an orgasm in women because the clitoris is located externally and higher up. Women must rely upon indirect stimulation in the 'normal' position.

Lesbian sexuality could make an excellent case, based upon anatomical data, for the irrelevancy of the male organ. Albert Ellis says something to the effect that a man without a penis can make a woman an excellent lover.

Considering that the vagina is very desirable from a man's point of view, purely on physical grounds, one begins to see the dilemma for men. And it forces us as well to discard many 'physical' arguments explaining why women go to bed with men. What is left, it seems to me, are primarily psychological reasons why women select men at the exclusion of women as sexual partners.

Control of women

One reason given to explain the Middle Eastern practice of clitoridectomy is that it will keep the woman from straying. By removing the sexual organ capable of orgasm, it must be assumed that her sexual drive will diminish. Considering how men look upon their women as property, particularly in very backward nations, we should begin to consider a great deal more why it is not in men's interest to have women totally free sexually. The double standard, as practised, for example, in Latin America, is set up to keep the woman as total property of the husband, while he is free to have affairs as he wishes.

Lesbianism and bisexuality

Aside from the strictly anatomical reasons why women might equally seek other women as lovers, there is a fear on men's part that women will seek the company of other women on a full, human basis. The recognition of clitoral orgasm as fact would threaten the heterosexual *institution*. For it would indicate that sexual pleasure was obtainable from either men *or* women, thus making heterosexuality not an absolute, but an option. It would thus open up the whole question of *human* sexual relationships beyond the confines of the present male–female role system.

NOTES

1. Marie Bonaparte, *Female Sexuality*, New York: Grove Press, 1953, p. 148.

2.2

'"DON'T DIE OF IGNORANCE."
I NEARLY DIED OF EMBARRASSMENT'
Condoms in Context

Janet Holland, Caroline Ramazanoglu,
Sue Scott, Sue Sharpe and Rachel Thomson

Based on research carried out almost 20 years after Koedt's paper was published, this piece illustrates the continuing problems which women experience in negotiating sex with men. The authors argue that young women are frequently undermined within gendered power relations which reify male 'needs' at the expense of women's pleasure and safety.

A: If I don't die of ignorance I will die of embarrassment . . . instead.
Q: Do you think that's a real issue?
A: Yes I think it's embarrassment.
Q: Embarrassment about what? Talking about it?
A: Yes, just talking about sex is a very embarrassing thing . . . to do.
(Young woman interviewed in Manchester, 1989)

[. . .]

Our data illustrate the complexity and contradictions of the processes of negotiation over condoms and indicate a range of potential outcomes. We will explore these processes and the relationship between knowledge of risk and safer sex practices through an analysis of our respondents' reported experiences of condom use for contraception and prophylaxis. We make the case that condoms carry symbolic meanings which can differ for each sexual partner and for individuals over time, and that these meanings are illustrative of the gendered nature of responsibility and what is considered 'appropriate' behaviour in contraception and safer sex. These meanings cannot simply be swept away and replaced by public education.

From J. Holland, C. Ramazanoglu, S. Scott, S. Sharpe and R. Thomson, '"Don't Die of Ignorance." I Nearly Died of Embarrassment': Condoms in Context, London: The Tufnell Press, 1990.

ASKING HIM TO USE A CONDOM – THE SOCIAL CONTEXT

The social context of condom use is the gendered relationships within which sexual encounters occur. In feminist social theory, sexual intercourse in western societies has been identified not only as a social relationship, but also as an unequal relationship in which men exercise power over women.[1] Feminist challenges to this male power provoked an immediate popular conception of feminists as personally sexually perverted; as man-hating, unnaturally competing with men or as unattractive, sexually undesirable and frigid. The institutionalisation of heterosexuality[2] means that sexual intercourse is socially located in gendered power relationships. This helps to explain the tensions and embarrassment of condom use and also the risks taken where condoms or other forms of protection are not used. From a feminist perspective, using or not using a condom is not a simple, practical question about dealing rationally with risk, it is the outcome of negotiation between potentially unequal partners. Sexual encounters are sites of struggle between the exercise and acceptance of male power and male definitions of sexuality, and of women's ambivalence and resistance.

The physical intimacy which can lead to orgasm, pregnancy or sexually transmitted disease is potentially an experience of both pleasure and danger,[3] but it is also unknown social territory. Even for the sexually experienced, encounters with new sexual partners are not wholly predictable, yet sexual intercourse entails trusting our bodies, our identities, our self respect to others and, not uncommonly, to strangers. Sexual practice in Western society is heavy with moral meanings but while the English education system may equip pupils with some knowledge of the mechanics of vaginal intercourse, much of the danger, and virtually all the pleasures of sexuality are an embarrassed area of silence.

In many sexual encounters women have little choice about whether or how to engage in sexual activity with men, the options being physical injury or more subtle forms of sanction. The accounts given by the young women in our sample support Liz Kelly's conception of a continuum of sexual violence, from sexism, to mild pressure to have unwanted intercourse, to more overtly coerced sex, child abuse and rape.[4] But women are not simply helpless victims in the face of male control of sexuality. Male power in sexual relationships is both embraced and resisted by young women in the course of negotiating sexual encounters. The same woman can negotiate very different sexual encounters with different men or at different points in her sexual career.

The social context of condom use may or may not be problematic for young women, depending on their priorities in a particular relationship, the degree of trust between partners and other factors which we discuss below, but condom use remains the focus of a number of social tensions. Male sexual power, the privileging of men's sexual pleasure and the dominance of men over women can be challenged by a woman's insistence on her needs for safety being met. Asking him to use a condom is embarrassing when it is a potentially subversive demand. The spontaneity of passion can be undermined by recognition of risk and responsibility. If coming to orgasm means losing control, being taken over by sensation, then condoms symbolise control and a curb on passion and spontaneity. Sexual fulfilment and sexual safety pull against each other when they are defined in terms of men's fulfilment.

[. . .]

We have found that much, if not most, of young women's sexual experience is not particularly pleasurable. Sometimes it seems that what is valued is the social relationship with a partner rather than the sexual activity. Young women are not without the ability to choose and to act for themselves, but they are heavily socially constrained. Young men are much better placed socially to gain sexual pleasure for themselves. When a young woman insists on the use of a condom for her own safety, she is going against the construction of sexual intercourse as men's natural pleasure, and women's natural duty.

[. . .]

POWER, CONTROL AND PLEASURE

General aspects of men's power over women and their control of sexual relationships, emerge from young women's accounts of situations in which they have or have not felt able to ask for, or insist on, condom use. These accounts illustrate the contradictions through which young women often have to negotiate their way. In our data we have found a wide spectrum of behaviour and experience, from the active negotiation of condom use in a situation of trust, to rape. There is an initial problem in discussing these accounts, and that is the question of what constitutes a sexual relationship.

[. . .]

We have taken the young women's own definitions of what constitutes a sexual encounter or relationship, and some of these include events and relationships which did not include sexual intercourse. But, when asked in the interview what sex meant for them, most of the young women accepted the prevailing construction of sex as heterosexual sex with male penetration, whether they are sexually active themselves or not.

    Q: You only count it as a sexual relationship if you actually . . . ?

    A: Having sex I think.

'Sex' was very generally associated with vaginal intercourse:

    A: Yeah, most of the time when I think about sex it is actually sexual intercourse.

    Q: Yeah. And other sorts of things might not be, wouldn't be included, like we've been talking about masturbation and oral sex. I mean, do you think of those as being sex?

    A: It comes in as part of sex, yes, but when I think about sex, those things don't come to my mind.

In general young women saw this association between sex and intercourse as obvious.

    A: When anyone ever said sex before, all I ever thought was sexual intercourse. That's what it is isn't it?

Recent publicity about safe sex had given young women some reason for thinking about the possibilities of 'having sex' without penetration:

> *A:* I know that safe sex can be just touching each other and anything else except for intercourse, but it always seems to me ultimately all sex always leads up to intercourse, so I always just think of safe sex as just using condoms.

But even when they had some knowledge of safer sex, the idea of sex as intercourse seemed to dominate.

> *A:* . . . I think if they say sex they mean going the whole way.
>
> *Q:* So sex actually means penetration –
>
> *A:* I think that's basically what it means now . . . which maybe isn't quite fair because there's lots of other things that go on before you get there, sort of part of the same game as it were, but at the end of the line that's what you're talking about. That's how I would see it anyway.

It was much more uncommon to find young women who had thought of the possibility of sexual pleasure without sexual intercourse.

> *A:* I don't think that, you know, men feel that they have to actually be inside somebody before they can feel as if they've had any pleasure.

It also became clear in the interviews that for many, vaginal intercourse was something they did not particularly enjoy, although they assumed that it was what men wanted. A number said that they never experienced orgasm through penetrative sex and that they much preferred other sexual activities in which they engaged.

[. . .]

Behind this definition of sex as the need to fulfil male sexual desires in a specific way lies the notion of men's uncontrollable sexual drive which cannot be interrupted or diverted. While this idea implies that women must take responsibility for moral standards and contraception, it can also lead to failure to use contraception, particularly condoms where these have connotations of breaking the flow and destroying the passion.

Some women showed a limited sense of the potential for their own sexual pleasure, particularly when this was something which they had not experienced. One young woman [. . .] said [. . .] that sex had been very painful at first but that after the third time it got better. This turned out to mean that intercourse had stopped hurting [. . .] She went on to say that she and her boyfriend didn't talk about sex and she felt unable to tell him what she liked sexually. Even where women had high expectations of sexual pleasure they were often prepared to settle for less:

> *Q:* Have you found the sexual relationship satisfactory, satisfying, pleasurable?
>
> *A:* Yes. Yes.
>
> *Q:* You sound a bit doubtful.

A: Well, I'm not – I've never, in all the sexual relationships I've had I've never – it's never been like it is in the books, I've never, you know – I'm sure it could be a lot better but – yeah, it was okay, yeah.

The meanings associated with a heterosexual encounter, which are accepted or assimilated by young women, help to reinforce male power. These are located in a discourse which positions young men as knowing sexual actors vis-à-vis young women who are constructed as lacking knowledge and expertise in relation to sex. This was sharply illustrated by one young woman who, when discussing her first experience of condom use, explained that her boyfriend had been certain that the condom should be 'blown up' first. She had strongly doubted this but had allowed her views to be overridden on the assumption that men knew better.

There are other more direct modes of the exercise of male power when women accept men's rights or needs to exert control over their sexual behaviour. Men exercise power when they are considered to be the initiators of sex, when they threaten the loss of the relationship if the young woman will not have sex, when they refuse to use a condom even when asked, and when they destroy a young woman's reputation with the epithets such as 'slag' or 'drag'.[5] (The English language has a rich vocabulary of sexually abusive terms for women.[6] It is these behaviours and expectations which constitute a framework of male power within which young women negotiate sexual encounters and relationships. Their sexual understanding and behaviour within this context can demonstrate acceptance of male power, ambivalence towards it or resistance. Variations in these stances means that negotiations around condom use are worked out in a number of different ways.

Where men did agree to use a condom, there was still the problem of how to make the sexual activity pleasurable. Couples need to be relatively sexually experienced to deal with the woman's need for pace and timing. This young woman compared her experience with two different boyfriends:

A: Unless you're quite close it does interrupt things. They [the boyfriends] have got to be quite liberated themselves to use them in a way that's really good. It's frustrating because there isn't an equal amount of knowledge on how you use them. Like with David at the moment. I don't think it would have been a problem with Michael because he's really quite experienced and does it [uses a condom] as a matter of course.

These cases did not necessarily entail much, if any, discussion of condom use, since condoms were either taken to be a precondition for intercourse, or intercourse did not take place. Refusing intercourse without protection was not a trouble-free strategy, however, as women's demands for safe sex illustrate.

WOMEN'S DEMANDS FOR SAFE SEX

Despite a very general perception that men dislike condoms our interviewees did not necessarily see that men's needs must always dominate a sexual encounter. Women are not without agency in protecting themselves when they define sexual safety as a priority. Here again, 'love' can complicate protection.

Q: If you were having a relationship with someone, and they say they don't like using condoms, you know the line, what would you do?

A: I got that last night, I got that line.

Q: So what did you do last night?

A: I made him wear one – we always do if I miss the pill there's no way ... I find it quite interesting, putting it on, it's good fun.

[. . .]

Where women did insist on sex being safe, they were often able to get men's co-operation:

A: Whether I liked them or not, we – we used them. I mean, he doesn't like them, but we – we did use them, because you – you've got to take the responsibility for it.

Sometimes they had to assert themselves quite strongly:

A: He really hates using them, so I used to say to him, 'look, right, look, I have no intention of getting pregnant again and you have no intention to become a father, so you put one of these on'. And he starts whingeing. He goes, 'oh, no, do I have to?' I say, 'look Alan, do it or you know ...' He's all right, he knows how to do it now.

Insistence on this strategy could mean being prepared to give up the relationship:

A: Some boys are just stupid, but if they don't want to wear a condom then tough, you know, go and find someone else. That's it. But most of them don't mind.

A very small number of young women in our sample seemed to be prepared to attempt to negotiate either non-penetrative sex or condom use in a range of different situations. These young women have some characteristics in common. They all seem to have a fairly strong sense of themselves, rather than being highly dependent on having a relationship with a man, and they also talk about sex in terms of pleasure and their own needs. As we have already pointed out, the usual response to the question, 'what do you understand by safe sex?' was, 'condoms', but these women gave more considered responses based on personal experience:

A: Safe sex is as pleasurable an experience as actual penetration. Oral sex, things like touching somebody else's body in a very gentle way, kissing, appreciating one another's bodies.

A more common way for young women to counter young men's rejection of condoms is to assert their fear of pregnancy. There could be considerable embarrassment about telling a new partner that a condom was wanted for protection against possible infection, but it is allowable for women to be concerned with pregnancy.[7]

[. . .]

Fear of pregnancy might well lead young women to feel able to *ask* for condoms to be used but this does not necessarily mean that condoms will be used. Fear of HIV could also be presented as a fear of pregnancy. One young woman had discussed this strategy with a girl friend:

> *A:* Rather than saying, 'Will you wear something, because I don't want to get AIDS?' which sounds really bad, doesn't it, we would say, 'you'll have to wear something because I'm not on the pill'.

A way of using fear of pregnancy to resist unwanted intercourse was to refuse to have sex without a condom, assuming that a young man would rather forgo sex than use a condom. This could be a short term strategy if the young man finally decided to buy a packet, leaving the young woman without an argument.

WOMEN'S OPPOSITION TO CONDOMS

While some young women were refusing or resisting unprotected intercourse, other young women (or the same young women on other occasions) had picked on a range of reasons for not using condoms. While this could be a form of self assertion, it generally seemed to indicate an accommodation to their own relative powerlessness in sexual encounters. While the reasons given varied, they seemed to be a means of incorporating aspects of the ideology of male sexual dominance into women's definitions of sexual encounters. These reasons can be seen as a diversion from, or perhaps a deflection of, women's understanding of their relative powerlessness:

> *A:* Well, it would be nice if it was easier for girls to actually initiate things with men without feeling difficult about it. But I don't really know how it happens.

When it is expected and accepted that what men want from sex is pleasure and penetration, avoidance of practices which limit pleasure is understandable. Where women had accepted this legitimation, they entered into sexual encounters with a general acceptance of the idea that men do not like nor want to use condoms:

> *Q:* What about using a condom?
>
> *A:* No he wouldn't.
>
> *Q:* He wouldn't?
>
> *A:* No, a lot of guys don't really like them.
>
> *A:* I really don't know that many blokes who I think would use a condom or are even concerned about it. I mean they've never been concerned about getting women pregnant have they?

The young women also reported a wide range of negative descriptions of condom use which seemed to reflect male perceptions, for example: 'like picking your nose with a rubber glove', 'going to bed with your wellingtons on', 'washing your feet with your socks on', although these perceptions were not necessarily presented as male:

> *A:* I mean, they're terrible. I mean, the thing is as well, people just won't use

> them because they hate them. It spoils the whole effect of it. It's like – I mean, as most people say, you know, it's like chewing toffee with the wrapper on.

> *Q:* Does it – I mean, do you feel that, that that's the effect, that it is like . . .

> *A:* I can't – I honestly can't abide the things. I really don't like them at all. I mean, we got – we got ones which were sort of special, you know, with the bobbly bits on; but I mean, even them, it just – it just come off, it didn't do a lot for me.

A very different approach to accepting that men would not want to use condoms was for the woman to assume that she would be all right without protection. Some young women felt that they were invulnerable and certainly would not get pregnant:[8]

> *A:* I had this feeling, when I didn't use anything, I had this feeling I'm not going to get pregnant, you know, I was really sure.

Or they did not think about it at all:

> *A:* I can't imagine myself getting pregnant.

At least one reported pregnancy was the result of this attitude. Others employed a method based on 'condoms or cross your fingers', using condoms when they were available or agreed upon, but going ahead anyway when they were not. In this way women justified relinquishing the control they desired.

A further group of reasons for reluctance to use condoms came from the women's fear of upsetting men by asserting their own needs. These reasons were partly to do with the fear of losing a boyfriend and the hope of a more committed or steady relationship, and partly a general unwillingness to hurt the man's feelings:

> *A:* The climax to intercourse is all passion and kissing and I think to actually just stop and he puts a condom on, or me to turn around and say I want you to put this on, it just ruins the whole thing then.

A clear way of avoiding control was to enter into a sexual relationship with no specific expectation that there would be sexual intercourse on this occasion:

> *A:* You meet a lad, and you start kissing, and before you know it, it's happening – and then it's too late [to use a condom].

One young woman described a situation where she had asked a man to use a condom because she was worried about HIV and AIDS, although she could not tell him that. He had no condom, and she did not want to offend him, nor cause an embarrassing social situation by refusing sex. She convinced herself that he must be OK, and went ahead, asking him to withdraw, 'whether he did or not I can't remember'. Another had been having unprotected sex for eighteen months because she did not want to upset her boyfriend: 'yeah, I think that's what it is, you don't want to hurt his feelings'. Another said that, 'if you want the relationship, I didn't want to, like, fuck around with questions', and another, 'I just thought it's all right, I just decided he had to be safe'. These types of explanations were used by young women who feared both pregnancy and HIV infection and occurred in the context of both steady and more casual relationships.

GOING STEADY AND TRUSTING TO LOVE

There is a common sense assumption that negotiations around sex are easier in the context of steady relationships, but this is not necessarily the case. Going steady implies a degree of trust which is lacking in less persistent sexual relationships. Trust then becomes a significant aspect of the context of decision-making about condoms. If love is assumed to be the greatest prophylactic, then trust comes a close second:

> A: If you want to have relationships then you've got to trust them [men]. Otherwise it's no good from the start. Yeah, you have to believe what they tell you. You just hope that they tell you the truth. You can't find out if it's lies or not.

Condoms can be seen as a strategy for occasions when it is not clear whether partners can be trusted. Some young women who were on the pill told new partners that they were not, so that condoms were used as well. But there was a powerful ideological understanding that 'steady' relationships are based on trust. Trust can even develop into a euphemism for monogamy.

A trusting relationship provides a social context in which condom use may be relatively unproblematic. Some of these relationships involved young couples where both lacked sexual experience or where they had been going steady for some time before their first experience of intercourse. Here inexperience provided a basis of trust so that they could discuss the problems of using condoms, and their own embarrassment. Reaching the stage of going to Boots together to buy condoms could become a joint commitment to a deepening relationship. Once the relationship was felt to be well established, the young woman would go on the pill.

This transition from condoms with new partners to the pill with steady partners is laden with symbolic meaning and can be used to signify the seriousness of a relationship, a way of showing someone that they are special. As one of our respondents put it, 'I went on the pill for him'. There is, however, a good deal of pressure to define a relationship as 'serious' in order to justify sex. For the current generation of young women the pill, despite the problems connected with its use, is closely associated with grown up status and grown up sex. This makes the prospect of long term condom use highly problematic, as two of our respondents clearly indicated:

> A: You've got to trust somebody at some time, you can't meet somebody and start, first time say, 'I know, let's use condoms I'm not on the pill' (even if you are), and then a week later still be saying 'let's use condoms', and the week after that still be saying 'let's use condoms' . . .

> Q: You don't think you could do that long term?

> A: You couldn't do that, no.

A: I'd like to think that I would want to use one [condom] but I mean, you start off using one but are you going to carry on using one every single time?

[. . .]

The question of what counts as a steady relationship is clouded by the meanings associated with particular types of relationship, and fears for loss of reputation particularly by the younger women. Most young women are reluctant to describe themselves as having casual sex when the culturally approved objective is to be in a steady, preferably monogamous relationship, supported by the ideologies of romance and love. Conversely they are likely to expect or to express the hope, that relationships of short duration, including one night stands, will in fact last. The positive associations of sex as leisure and pleasure, which have been espoused by the gay movement, tend not to be available to young heterosexual women. The tendency seems to be to expect that relationships will last:

A: If I sleep with anyone I intend it to be a long term relationship – so I don't know, because you don't like to think of the end of a relationship when you start it. So you think it's going to be the right one, but you never know.

Our respondents who described themselves as being in steady relationships tended to think of themselves as not being at risk in relation to HIV and to focus their attention on avoiding pregnancy. This obviously makes some sense when each was the other's first and only sexual partner, but it of course assumes that the relationship will continue to be monogamous.

Another young woman illustrates this tension very clearly:

Q: When you decided to sleep with him did you think it was going to last quite a long time?

A: Yes, I think that was the only reason I did sleep with him really. I think I wanted to do it, but I didn't in a way, but because it was him I did, and I thought it would last a long time really.

This young woman goes on to explain that she was very scared the first time because they used no contraception, but she went on to insist that he used a condom subsequently:

A: I don't know because I couldn't really go on the pill and I couldn't have used a cap or something like that, [she was under 16 at the time] it was easier for him to do it. But before I did it with him I made him put it on. I didn't watch him but I stood there as if to say, 'make sure you put it on', and he did put it on.

She saw condoms as her only option and her fear of pregnancy gave her the strength to insist. It seems clear though that she saw protection as something she would have to fight for, and men as untrustworthy in this respect. She felt it necessary, literally, to stand over him while he did what she wanted.

Often the young women's experience of sexual pressure and physically unpleasant sexual encounters conflicted with their desire for love, romance, caring, closeness and trust. The contradictions of female subordination in loving relationships were expressed in this desire for close, loving relationships without a very positive sexual identity for young women. There was a widespread negative perception of male sexuality. Typical comments being that, 'lads don't care', and 'women want love and men want sex'. One young woman commented, 'I don't trust boys today – I don't trust them at all'. Others insisted that if they did not trust the young man, they would not have sex, or they would not be in a relationship with them. The very fact of being in a steady relationship implied the existence of trust. Where there are social pressures on young women to police sexual encounters and look out for problems, particularly the risk of pregnancy, this mitigates against developing trust even when a steady relationship is wanted. Many women took risks with partners they loved but did not wholly trust.[8]

A small number of the young women clearly stated that they had casual sex or one night stands. Some of these had taken on the idea that it is legitimate for women to be sexually active, to have their own sexual identity, but they were not necessarily any more in control of their encounters. One young woman who was very clear that she wanted to be in control of her life, which included 'choosing' to be sexually active and child-free, was in fact having unprotected sex, including intercourse with partners who were potential health risks. She said that she had come to be interviewed to make her think about what she was doing.

Condom use tends to be associated with one night stands rather than 'steady' relationships,[9] but if young women's relationships are conceived as 'steady' until proved otherwise, this makes condom use rather unpredictable. Where men see sex as a process of attrition, as wearing a girl down until she says yes, there are problems in producing a condom at the right moment:

> A: About two weeks ago I ended up not asking him [to use a condom] and had to go and get the morning after pill.
>
> [. . .]

We found embarrassment about every stage of condom use. When young women put their reputations first, then buying condoms, carrying them, and of course, asking for their use are all embarrassing. Having a condom on one's person indicates a lack of sexual innocence, an unfeminine identity, that of a woman actively seeking sex. The sexual woman, is then, easy, fair game, a slag and generally at men's disposal. Advertising has had to counter this level of meaning by associating condoms with personal responsibility.[10] But the contradictions of sexual safety mean that when the risk of pregnancy or a sexually transmitted disease is a possibility which women feel strongly about, they may be willing to ignore the risk to their reputation:

> Q: Do you think that you'd feel OK asking somebody to use a condom?
>
> A: Definitely, because it would be my embarrassment, or being in danger, and there's no contest if you ask me.

Young men may well be just as embarrassed in sexual encounters as young women, especially when they are inexperienced, but the meanings carried by condoms allow them to hide embarrassment by recourse to a public discourse which legitimates the rejection of condoms. Young men can be fearful of sexual inadequacy and apprehensive about sexual encounters, but as these emotions are not defined as natural aspects of male sexuality, there is no discourse around this issue to which women have access. Condoms are seen to limit male sexual pleasure in situations in which male satisfaction is the main point of the encounter. Dworkin[11] argues that male sexual discourse on the subject of sexual intercourse is the only language available to women. The 'rational' discourse of safer sex promoted as official information can be seen as antithetical to an ideology of femininity which constructs sex as the relinquishment of control in the face of love. Thus young women are constantly working through these contradictions in sexual encounters.

[. . .]

A: But although I really do think about it a lot, I don't know why, it goes straight out the window if I'm – no not straight out the window it doesn't, no, it's always – there's always this nagging at the back of my mind you know, you don't know what you could catch, you could get AIDS, and it's always immediately afterwards I really start panicking. The last two guys, okay, they're probably bastards – whatever, you know – I said something I think, and one of them said, 'oh you're not going to make me wear one of those are you?' And I could have said – I should have said, 'yes', you know; but I wanted sex as much as they did and I didn't want any aggro. I thought straight after, 'you stupid, stupid girl' – and immediately resolved that next time I would, you know.

But this resolution, often expressed by these young women, particularly after frightening or risky sexual experiences, is not so easily realised. One young woman had experienced pregnancy, abortion and a scare about cervical cancer in the most unpleasant circumstances. Together with her current boyfriend she had had an HIV test because she thought that she might have the virus. She felt that she had changed, become more responsible and could and would take control of her own life and sexuality. Or at least this was what she wanted to think she would do. She described her inability to take control of the situation in the past, and inability to voice her wishes:

A: I know I have been in situations where I haven't [used a condom]. I have simply thought to myself, well look, well. When I got pregnant, I thought to myself, 'I'm not using a condom here, I'm not using anything', but I just couldn't say, just couldn't force myself to say, 'look, you know –' and then the consequences were disastrous. But at the time I knew what I was doing, and I knew that I just couldn't say it and I knew that it was wrong.

When she was asked if she felt confident that she could be more assertive (her term) in a future relationship, her ambivalence persisted. She said:

A: I don't know how I would be, because I was telling myself, if this relationship comes to an end, I'm never falling in the same trap as before, that I won't. I'll make sure that I'm sort of thinking that – Oh, God, I bet I will. I don't want to but I don't know whether I am really trying to say look, if all these things happen, you should learn from it. I'm more than fifty per cent confident that it won't, but not a full hundred per cent.

[. . .]

It is these varied patterns of condom use which can alert us to the unpredictable outcomes of situations in which women have to respond to conflicting pressures. To unravel the variability in women's experience of using and not using condoms, we need to develop a theoretical framework which can account for the gendered power relations and the contradictory pressures which constitute the context of sexual risk and safety. If young heterosexuals are to be able to protect themselves against the spread of HIV, we will have to restructure the common sense of sexual relationships. The language of sexuality needs to be challenged, changed and expanded so that women and men can recognise the contradictions of their own experiences, their own responsibilities and their own agency.[12] Women can then develop a positive language which will make public the continuum of sexual pressure, ambivalence and pleasure in sexuality. When women have self-respecting sexual identities which do not depend primarily on being attached to a man, they will be in a stronger position to promote sexual safety. The embarrassment of negotiating condom use with the one you love indicates the current contradictions of female subordination in the close encounters of heterosexual sex.

NOTES

1. A. Shulman, 'Organs and orgasms', in V. Gornick and B.K. Moran (eds), *Woman in a Sexist Society: Studies in Power and Powerlessness*, New York; Mentor Books, 1971; K. Millet, *Sexual Politics*, London: Virago, 1977; A. Dworkin, *Intercourse* London: Arrow Books, 1987; S. Hite, *The Hite Report; Women and Love: A Cultural Revolution in Progress*, London: Penguin, 1989. We have not taken up here the differences between women in terms of age, class, ethnicity, levels of education, etc. These are significant differences and we will include this analysis in subsequent publications.
2. Adrienne Rich, 'Compulsory heterosexuality and lesbian existence', in E. Abel and E.K. Abel (eds), *Women, Gender and Scholarship: The Signs Reader*, Chicago: Chicago University Press, 1983.
3. Carole Vance, 'Pleasure and danger: towards a politics of sexuality', in C.S. Vance (ed.), *Pleasure and Danger: Exploring Female Sexuality*, London: Routledge & Kegan Paul, 1984.
4. Liz Kelly, *Surviving Sexual Violence*, Cambridge: Polity Press, 1988.
5. S. Lees, *Losing Out: Sexuality and Adolescent Girls*, London: Hutchinson, 1986.
6. P. Mahoney, *Schools for Boys? Co-Education Reassessed*, London: Hutchinson/Explorations in Feminism Collective, 1985.
7. D. Cossey, *Teenage Birth Control: The Case for the Condom*, London: Brook Advisory Service, 1979; B. Spencer, 'Young men: their attitudes towards sexuality and birth control', *British Journal of Family Planning*, 10, 1984, pp. 13–19.
8. For this notion in relation to AIDS see D. Abrams, C. Abraham, R. Spears and D. Marks, '"AIDS invulnerability": relationships, sexual behaviour and attitudes among 16–19 year olds', in P. Aggleton, P. Davies and G. Hart (eds), *AIDS: Individual, Cultural and Policy Dimensions*, Basingstoke: Falmer, 1990.
9. See also S. Day, H. Ward and J.R.W. Harris, 'Prostitute women and public health', *British Medical Journal*, 297, 1988, p. 1585; L.M. Nix *et al.*, 'A focus group study of sexually active black male teenagers', *Adolescence*, 23, 91, 1988, pp. 741–3. Research indicates that while women prostitutes in London seem to be prepared to use condoms with clients they rarely use them with their boyfriends (S. Day and H. Ward, 'The Praed Street Project: a cohort of prostitute women in London' in M. Plant (ed.), *AIDS, Drugs and Prostitution*, London: Tavistock/Routledge.
10. See also D. Winn, 'Smart girls carry condoms', *Cosmopolitan*, November 1986.
11. Dworkin, *Intercourse*, p. 159.
12. D. Cameron, *Feminism and Linguistic Theory*, London: Macmillan, 1985.

2.3

COMPULSORY HETEROSEXUALITY AND LESBIAN EXISTENCE

Adrienne Rich

Originally published in 1980, when the relationship between lesbianism and feminism was the focus of much debate, this article questions the assumption that the majority of women are naturally heterosexual. Rich argues that heterosexuality is imposed upon women and reinforced by a variety of social constraints. She also suggests that rather than there being a simple divide between lesbian and heterosexual women, our experience can be located along a lesbian continuum.

I

Biologically men have only one innate orientation – a sexual one that draws them to women, – while women have two innate orientations, sexual toward men and reproductive toward their young.[1]

I was a woman terribly vulnerable, critical, using femaleness as a sort of standard or yardstick to measure and discard men. Yes – something like that. I was an Anna who invited defeat from men without ever being conscious of it. (But I am conscious of it. And being conscious of it means I shall leave it all behind me and become – but what?) I was stuck fast in an emotion common to women of our time, that can turn them bitter, or Lesbian, or solitary[2].

[. . .]

The bias of compulsory heterosexuality, through which lesbian experience is perceived on a scale ranging from deviant to abhorrent or simply rendered invisible, could be illustrated from many texts other than the two just preceding. The assumption made by Rossi, that women are 'innately' sexually oriented only toward men, and that made

---

From A. Rich, *Blood, Bread and Poetry*, London: Virago, 1978.

by Lessing, that the lesbian is simply acting out of her bitterness toward men, are by no means theirs alone; these assumptions are widely current in literature and in the social sciences.

I am concerned here with two other matters as well: first, how and why women's choice of women as passionate comrades, life partners, co-workers, lovers, community has been crushed, invalidated, forced into hiding and disguise; and second, the virtual or total neglect of lesbian existence in a wide range of writings, including feminist scholarship. Obviously there is a connection here. I believe that much feminist theory and criticism is stranded on this shoal.

My organizing impulse is the belief that it is not enough for feminist thought that specifically lesbian texts exist. Any theory or cultural/political creation that treats lesbian existence as a marginal or less 'natural' phenomenon, as mere 'sexual prefer- cnce,' or as the mirror image of either heterosexual or male homosexual relations is profoundly weakened thereby, whatever its other contributions. Feminist theory can no longer afford merely to voice a toleration of 'lesbianism' as an 'alternative life style' or make token allusion to lesbians. A feminist critique of compulsory heterosexual orientation for women is long overdue. In this exploratory paper, I shall try to show why.

[. . .]

II

[. . .]

In her essay 'The Origin of the Family,' Kathleen Gough lists eight characteristics of male power in archaic and contemporary societies which I would like to use as a framework: 'men's ability to deny women sexuality or to force it upon them; to command or exploit their labor to control their produce; to control or rob them of their children; to confine them physically and prevent their movement; to use them as objects in male transactions; to cramp their creativeness; or to withhold from them large areas of the society's knowledge and cultural attainments.'[3] (Gough does not perceive these power characteristics as specifically enforcing heterosexuality, only as producing sexual inequality.) Below, Gough's words appear in italics; the elaboration of each of her categories, in brackets, is my own.

Characteristics of male power include *the power of* men

1. *to deny women* [their own] *sexuality* – [by means of clitoridectomy and in- fibulation; chastity belts; punishment, including death, for female adultery; punishment, including death, for lesbian sexuality; psychoanalytic denial of the clitoris; strictures against masturbation; denial of maternal and postmenopausal sensuality; unnecessary hysterectomy; pseudolesbian images in the media and literature; closing of archives and destruction of documents relating to lesbian existence]

2. *or to force it* [male sexuality] *upon them* – [by means of rape (including marital rape) and wife beating; father–daughter, brother–sister incest; the socializa- tion of women to feel that male sexual 'drive' amounts to a right;[4] idealization of heterosexual romance in art, literature, the media, advertising, etc.; child marriage; arranged marriage; prostitution; the harem; psychoanalytic doc-

trines of frigidity and vaginal orgasm; pornographic depictions of women responding pleasurably to sexual violence and humiliation (a subliminal message being that sadistic heterosexuality is more 'normal' than sensuality between women)]

3. *to command or exploit their labor to control their produce* – [by means of the institutions of marriage and motherhood as unpaid production; the horizontal segregation of women in paid employment; the decoy of the upwardly mobile token woman; male control of abortion, contraception, sterilization, and childbirth; pimping; female infanticide, which robs mothers of daughters and contributes to generalized devaluation of women]

4. *to control or rob them of their children* – [by means of father right and 'legal kidnapping';[5] enforced sterilization; systematized infanticide; seizure of children from lesbian mothers by the courts; the malpractice of male obstetrics; use of the mother as 'token torturer'[6] in genital mutilation or in binding the daughter's feet (or mind) to fit her for marriage]

5. *to confine them physically and prevent their movement* – [by means of rape as terrorism, keeping women off the streets; purdah; foot binding; atrophying of women's athletic capabilities; high heels and 'feminine' dress codes in fashion; the veil; sexual harassment on the streets; horizontal segregation of women in employment; prescriptions for 'full-time' mothering at home; enforced economic dependence of wives]

6. *to use them as objects in male transactions* – [use of women as 'gifts'; bride price; pimping; arranged marriage; use of women as entertainers to facilitate male deals – e.g., wife-hostess, cocktail waitress required to dress for male sexual titillation, call girls, 'bunnies,' geisha, *kisaeng* prostitutes, secretaries]

7. *to cramp their creativeness* – [witch persecutions as campaigns against midwives and female healers, and as pogrom against independent, 'unassimilated' women;[7] definition of male pursuits as more valuable than female within any culture, so that cultural values become the embodiment of male subjectivity; restriction of female self-fulfillment to marriage and motherhood; sexual exploitation of women by male artists and teachers; the social and economic disruption of women's creative aspirations;[8] erasure of female tradition][9]

8. *to withhold from them large areas of the society's knowledge and cultural attainments* – [by means of noneducation of females; the 'Great Silence' regarding women and particularly lesbian existence in history and culture,[10] sex-role tracking which deflects women from science, technology, and other 'masculine' pursuits; male social/professional bonding which excludes women; discrimination against women in the professions]

These are some of the methods by which male power is manifested and maintained. Looking at the schema, what surely impresses itself is the fact that we are confronting not a simple maintenance of inequality and property possession, but a pervasive cluster of forces, ranging from physical brutality to control of consciousness, which suggests that an enormous potential counterforce is having to be restrained.

Some of the forms by which male power manifests itself are more easily recogniz-able as enforcing heterosexuality on women than are others. Yet each one I have listed adds to the cluster of forces within which women have been convinced that marriage and sexual orientation toward men are inevitable – even if unsatisfying or oppressive – components of their lives. The chastity belt; child marriage; erasure of lesbian existence (except as exotic and perverse) in art, literature, film; idealization of heterosexual romance and marriage – these are some fairly obvious forms of compulsion, the first two exemplifying physical force, the second two control of consciousness. While clitoridectomy has been assailed by feminists as a form of woman torture,[11] Kathleen Barry first pointed out that it is not simply a way of turning the young girl into a 'marriageable' woman through brutal surgery. It intends that women in the intimate proximity of polygynous marriage will not form sexual relationships with each other, that – from a male, genital-fetishist perspective – female erotic connections, even in a sex-segregated situation, will be literally excised.[12]

[. . .]

In her brilliant study *Sexual Harassment of Working Women: A Case of Sex Discrimination*, Catharine A.MacKinnon delineates the intersection of compulsory heterosexuality and economics.[13] [. . .] She cites a wealth of material documenting the fact that women are not only segregated in low-paying service jobs (as secretaries, domestics, nurses, typists, telephone operators, child-care workers, waitresses), but that 'sexualization of the woman' is part of the job. Central and intrinsic to the economic realities of women's lives is the requirement that women will 'market sexual attractiveness to men, who tend to hold the economic power and position to enforce their predilections.' And MacKinnon documents that 'sexual harassment perpetuates the interlocked structure by which women have been kept sexually in thrall to men at the bottom of the labor market. Two forces of American society converge: men's control over women's sexu-ality and capital's control over employees' work lives.'[14] Thus, women in the workplace are at the mercy of sex as power in a vicious circle. Economically disadvantaged, women – whether waitresses or professors – endure sexual harassment to keep their jobs and learn to behave in a complaisantly and ingratiatingly heterosexual manner because they discover this is their true qualification for employment, whatever the job description. And, MacKinnon notes, the woman who too decisively resists sexual overtures in the workplace is accused of being 'dried up' and sexless, or lesbian. This raises a specific difference between the experiences of lesbians and homosexual men. A lesbian, closeted on her job because of heterosexist prejudice, is not simply forced into denying the truth of her outside relationships or private life. Her job depends on her pretending to be not merely heterosexual, but a heterosexual *woman* in terms of dressing and playing the feminine, deferential role required of 'real' women.

[. . .]

Given the nature and extent of heterosexual pressures – the daily 'eroticization of women's subordination,' as MacKinnon phrases it[15] – I question the more or less psychoanalytic perspective (suggested by such writers as Karen Horney, H.R. Hayes, Wolfgang Lederer, and, most recently, Dorothy Dinnerstein) that the male need to control women sexually results from some primal male 'fear of women' and of women's sexual insatiability. It seems more probable that men really fear not that they will have women's sexual appetites forced on them or that women want to smother and devour them, but that women could be indifferent to them altogether, that men could be allowed sexual and emotional – therefore economic – access to women *only* on women's terms, otherwise being left on the periphery of the matrix.

The means of assuring male sexual access to women have recently received searching investigation by Kathleen Barry.[16] She documents extensive and appalling evidence for the existence, on a very large scale, of international female slavery, the institution once known as 'white slavery' but which in fact has involved, and at this very moment involves, women of every race and class. In the theoretical analysis derived from her research, Barry makes the connection between all enforced conditions under which women live subject to men: prostitution, marital rape, father-daughter and brother-sister incest, wife beating, pornography, bride price, the selling of daughters, purdah, and genital mutilation. She sees the rape paradigm – where the victim of sexual assault is held responsible for her own victimization – as leading to the rationalization and acceptance of other forms of enslavement where the woman is presumed to have 'chosen' her fate, to embrace it passively, or to have courted it perversely through rash or unchaste behavior. On the contrary, Barry maintains, 'female sexual slavery is present in ALL situations where women or girls cannot change the conditions of their existence; where regardless of how they got into those conditions, e.g., social pressure, economic hardship, misplaced trust or the longing for affection, they cannot get out; and where they are subject to sexual violence and exploitation.'[17]

[. . .]

[P]art of the problem with naming and conceptualizing female sexual slavery is, as Barry clearly sees, compulsory heterosexuality.[18] Compulsory heterosexuality simplifies the task of the procurer and pimp in world-wide prostitution rings and 'eros centers,' while, in the privacy of the home, it leads the daughter to 'accept' incest/rape by her father, the mother to deny that it is happening, the battered wife to stay on with an abusive husband. 'Befriending or love' is a major tactic of the procurer, whose job it is to turn the runaway or the confused young girl over to the pimp for seasoning. The ideology of heterosexual romance, beamed at her from childhood out of fairy tales, television, films, advertising, popular songs, wedding pageantry, is a tool ready to the procurer's hand and one which he does not hesitate to use, as Barry documents. Early female indoctrination in 'love' as an emotion may be largely a Western concept; but a more universal ideology concerns the primacy and uncontrollability of the male sexual drive.

[. . .]

Barry's hypothesis . . . clarifies the diversity of forms in which compulsory heterosexuality presents itself. In the mystique of the overpowering, all-conquering male sex drive, the penis-with-a-life-of-its-own, is rooted the law of male sex right to women, which justifies prostitution as a universal cultural assumption on the one hand, while defending sexual slavery within the family on the basis of 'family privacy and cultural uniqueness' on the other.[19] The adolescent male sex drive, which, as both young women and men are taught, once triggered cannot take responsibility for itself or take no for an answer, becomes, according to Barry, the norm and rationale for adult male sexual behavior. [. . .] Women learn to accept as natural the inevitability of this 'drive' because they receive it as dogma.

[. . .]

[W]hatever its origins, when we look hard and clearly at the extent and elaboration of measures designed to keep women within a male sexual purlieu, it becomes an inescapable question whether the issue feminists have to address is not simple 'gender inequality' nor the domination of culture by males nor mere 'taboos against homosexuality,' but the enforcement of heterosexuality for women as a means of assuring male right of physical, economic, and emotional access.[20] One of many means of enforcement is, of course, the rendering invisible of the lesbian possibility, an engulfed continent which rises fragmentedly into view from time to time only to become submerged again. Feminist research and theory that contribute to lesbian invisibility or marginality are actually working against the liberation and empowerment of women as a group.[21]

The assumption that 'most women are innately heterosexual' stands as a theoretical and political stumbling block for feminism. It remains a tenable assumption partly because lesbian existence has been written out of history or catalogued under disease, partly because it has been treated as exceptional rather than intrinsic, partly because to acknowledge that for women heterosexuality may not be a 'preference' at all but something that has had to be imposed, managed, organized, propagandized, and maintained by force is an immense step to take if you consider yourself freely and 'innately' heterosexual. Yet the failure to examine heterosexuality as an institution is like failing to admit that the economic system called capitalism or the caste system of racism is maintained by a variety of forces, including both physical violence and false consciousness. To take the step of questioning heterosexuality as a 'preference' or 'choice' for women – and to do the intellectual and emotional work that follows – will call for a special quality of courage in heterosexually identified feminists, but I think the rewards will be great: a freeing-up of thinking, the exploring of new paths, the shattering of another great silence, new clarity in personal relationships.

III

I have chosen to use the terms *lesbian existence* and *lesbian continuum* because the word *lesbianism* has a clinical and limiting ring. *Lesbian existence* suggests both the fact of the historical presence of lesbians and our continuing creation of the meaning of that existence. I mean the term *lesbian continuum* to include a range – through each woman's life and throughout history – of woman-identified experience, not simply the fact that a woman has had or consciously desired genital sexual experience with another woman. If we expand it to embrace many more forms of primary intensity between and among women, including the sharing of a rich inner life, the bonding against male tyranny, the giving and receiving of practical and political support, if we can also hear it in such associations as *marriage resistance* and the 'haggard' behavior identified by Mary Daly (obsolete meanings: 'intractable,' 'willful,' 'wanton,' and 'unchaste,' 'a woman reluctant to yield to wooing'),[22] we begin to grasp breadths of female history and psychology which have lain out of reach as a consequence of limited, mostly clinical, definitions of *lesbianism*.

Lesbian existence comprises both the breaking of a taboo and the rejection of a compulsory way of life. It is also a direct or indirect attack on male right of access to women. But it is more than these, although we may first begin to perceive it as a form of naysaying to patriarchy, an act of resistance. It has, of course, included isolation, self-hatred, breakdown, alcoholism, suicide, and intrawoman violence; we romanticize at our peril what it means to love and act against the grain, and under heavy penalties; and lesbian existence has been lived (unlike, say, Jewish or Catholic existence) without access to any knowledge of a tradition, a continuity, a social underpinning. The destruction of records and memorabilia and letters documenting the realities of lesbian existence must be taken very seriously as a means of keeping heterosexuality compulsory for women, since what has been kept from our knowledge is joy, sensuality, courage, and community, as well as guilt, self-betrayal, and pain.[23]

Lesbians have historically been deprived of a political existence through 'inclusion' as female versions of male homosexuality. To equate lesbian existence with male homosexuality because each is stigmatized is to erase female reality once again. Part of the history of lesbian existence is, obviously, to be found where lesbians, lacking a coherent female community, have shared a kind of social life and common cause with homosexual men. But there are differences: women's lack of economic and cultural privilege relative to men; qualitative differences in female and male relationships – for example, the patterns of anonymous sex among male homosexuals, and the pronounced ageism in male homosexual standards of sexual attractiveness. I perceive the lesbian experience as being, like motherhood, a profoundly *female* experience, with particular oppressions, meanings, and potentialities we cannot comprehend as long as we simply bracket it with other sexually stigmatized existences. Just as the term *parenting* serves to conceal the particular and significant reality of being a parent who is actually a mother, the term *gay* may serve the purpose of blurring the very outlines we need to discern, which are of crucial value for feminism and for the freedom of women as a group.[24]

As the term *lesbian* has been held to limiting, clinical associations in its patriarchal definition, female friendship and comradeship have been set apart from the erotic, thus limiting the erotic itself. But as we deepen and broaden the range of what we define as lesbian existence, as we delineate a lesbian continuum, we begin to discover the erotic in female terms: as that which is unconfined to any single part of the body or solely to the body itself; as an energy not only diffuse but, as Audre Lorde has described it, omnipresent in 'the sharing of joy, whether physical, emotional, psychic,' and in the sharing of work; as the empowering joy which 'makes us less willing to accept powerlessness, or those other supplied states of being which are not native to me, such as resignation, despair, self-effacement, depression, self-denial.'[25]

[. . .]

If we consider the possibility that all women [. . .] exist on a lesbian continuum, we can see ourselves as moving in and out of this continuum, whether we identify ourselves as lesbian or not.

We can then connect aspects of woman identification as diverse as the impudent, intimate girl friendships of eight or nine year olds and the banding together of those women of the twelfth and fifteenth centuries known as Beguines who 'shared houses, rented to one another, bequeathed houses to their room-mates . . . in cheap subdivided houses in the artisans' area of town,' who 'practiced Christian virtue on their own, dressing and living simply and not associating with men,' who earned their livings as spinsters, bakers, nurses, or ran schools for young girls, and who managed – until the Church forced them to disperse – to live independent both of marriage and of conventual restrictions.[26] It allows us to connect these women with the more celebrated 'Lesbians' of the women's school around Sappho of the seventh century B.C., with the secret sororities and economic networks reported among African women, and with the Chinese marriage-resistance sisterhoods – communities of women who refused marriage or who, if married, often refused to consummate their marriages and soon left their husbands, the only women in China who were not footbound and who, Agnes Smedley tells us, welcomed the births of daughters and organized successful women's strikes in the silk mills.[27] It allows us to connect and compare disparate individual instances of marriage resistance: for example, the strategies available to Emily Dickinson, a nineteenth-century white woman genius, with the strategies available to Zora Neale Hurston, a twentieth-century Black woman genius. Dickinson never married, had tenuous intellectual friendships with men, lived self-convented in her genteel father's house in Amherst, and wrote a lifetime of passionate letters to her sister-in-law Sue Gilbert and a smaller group of such letters to her friend Kate Scott Anthon. Hurston married twice but soon left each husband, scrambled her way from Florida to Harlem to Columbia University to Haiti and finally back to Florida, moved in and out of white patronage and poverty, professional success, and failure; her survival relationships were all with women, beginning with her mother. Both of these women in their vastly different circumstances were marriage resisters, committed to their own work and selfhood, and were later characterized as 'apolitical.' Both were drawn to men of intellectual quality; for both of them women provided the ongoing fascination and sustenance of life.

If we think of heterosexuality as *the* natural emotional and sensual inclination for women, lives such as these are seen as deviant, as pathological, or as emotionally and sensually deprived. [. . .] But when we turn the lens of vision and consider the degree to which and the methods whereby heterosexual 'preference' has actually been imposed on women, not only can we understand differently the meaning of individual lives, but we can begin to recognize a central fact of women's history: that women have always resisted male tyranny. A feminism of action, often though not always without a theory, has constantly re-emerged in every culture and in every period. We can then begin to study women's struggle against powerlessness, women's radical rebellion, not just in male-defined 'concrete revolutionary situations'[28] but in all the situations male ideologies have not perceived as revolutionary – for example, the refusal of some women to produce children, aided at great risk by other women;[29] the refusal to produce a higher standard of living and leisure for men [. . .] We begin to observe behavior, both in history and in individual biography, that has hitherto been invisible or misnamed, behavior which often constitutes, given the limits of the counterforce exerted in a given time and place, radical rebellion. And we can connect these rebellions and the necessity for them with the physical passion of woman for woman which is central to lesbian existence: the erotic sensuality which has been, precisely, the most violently erased fact of female experience.

Heterosexuality has been both forcibly and subliminally imposed on women. Yet everywhere women have resisted it, often at the cost of physical torture, imprisonment, psychosurgery, social ostracism, and extreme poverty. 'Compulsory heterosexuality' was named as one of the 'crimes against women' by the Brussels International Tribunal on Crimes against Women in 1976. Two pieces of testimony from two very different cultures reflect the degree to which persecution of lesbians is a global practice here and now. A report from Norway relates:

> A lesbian in Oslo was in a heterosexual marriage that didn't work, so she started taking tranquillizers and ended up at the health sanatorium for treatment and rehabilitation. . . . The moment she said in family group therapy that she believed she was a lesbian, the doctor told her she was not. He knew from 'looking into her eyes,' he said. She had the eyes of a woman who wanted sexual intercourse with her husband. So she was subjected to so-called 'couch therapy.' She was put into a comfortably heated room, naked, on a bed, and for an hour her husband was to . . . try to excite her sexually. . . . The idea was that the touching was always to end with sexual intercourse. She felt stronger and stronger aversion. She threw up and sometimes ran out of the room to avoid this 'treatment.' The more strongly she asserted that she was a lesbian, the more violent the forced heterosexual intercourse became. This treatment went on for about six months. She escaped from the hospital, but she was brought back. Again she escaped. She has not been there since. In the end she realized that she had been subjected to forcible rape for six months.

And from Mozambique:

> I am condemned to a life of exile because I will not deny that I am a lesbian, that my primary commitments are, and will always be to other women. In the new Mozambique, lesbianism is considered a left-over from colonialism and decadent Western civilization. Lesbians are sent to rehabilitation camps to learn through self-criticism the correct line about themselves. . . . If I am forced to denounce my own love for women, if I therefore denounce myself, I could go back to Mozambique and join forces in the exciting and hard struggle of rebuilding a nation, including the struggle for the emancipation of Mozambiquan women. As it is, I either risk the rehabilitation camps, or remain in exile.[30]

Nor can it be assumed that women like those in Carroll Smith-Rosenberg's study, who married, stayed married, yet dwelt in a profoundly female emotional and passional world, 'preferred' or 'chose' heterosexuality. Women have married because it was necessary, in order to survive economically, in order to have children who would not suffer economic deprivation or social ostracism, in order to remain respectable, in order to do what was expected of women, because coming out of 'abnormal' childhoods they wanted to feel 'normal' and because heterosexual romance has been represented as the great female adventure, duty, and fulfillment. We may faithfully or ambivalently have obeyed the institution, but our feelings – and our sensuality – have not been tamed or contained within it. There is no statistical documentation of the numbers of lesbians who have remained in heterosexual marriages for most of their lives. But in a letter to the early lesbian publication *The Ladder*, the playwright Lorraine Hansberry had this to say:

> I suspect that the problem of the married woman who would prefer emotional-physical relationships with other women is proportionally much higher than a similar statistic for men. (A statistic surely no one will ever really have.) This because the estate of woman being what it is, how could we ever begin to guess the numbers of women who are not prepared to risk a life alien to what they have been taught all their lives to believe was their 'natural' destiny – AND – their only expectation for ECONOMIC security. It seems to be that this is why the question has an immensity that it does not have for male homosexuals. . . . A woman of strength and honesty may, if she chooses, sever her marriage and marry a new male mate and society will be upset that the divorce rate is rising so – but there are few places in the United States, in any event, where she will be anything remotely akin to an 'outcast.' Obviously this is not true for a woman who would end her marriage to take up life with another woman.[31]

This *double life* – this apparent acquiescence to an institution founded on male interest and prerogative – has been characteristic of female experience: in motherhood and in many kinds of heterosexual behavior, including the rituals of courtship; the pretense of asexuality by the nineteenth-century wife; the simulation of orgasm by the prostitute, the courtesan, the twentieth-century 'sexually liberated' woman.

[. . .]

IV

Woman identification is a source of energy, a potential springhead of female power, curtailed and contained under the institution of heterosexuality. The denial of reality and visibility to women's passion for women, women's choice of women as allies, life companions, and community, the forcing of such relationships into dissimulation and their disintegration under intense pressure have meant an incalculable loss to the power of all women *to change the social relations of the sexes, to liberate ourselves and each other*. The lie of compulsory female heterosexuality today afflicts not just feminist scholarship, but every profession, every reference work, every curriculum, every organizing attempt, every relationship or conversation over which it hovers. It creates, specifically, a profound falseness, hypocrisy, and hysteria in the heterosexual dialogue, for every heterosexual relationship is lived in the queasy strobe light of that lie. However we choose to identify ourselves, however we find ourselves labeled, it flickers across and distorts our lives.[32]

The lie keeps numberless women psychologically trapped, trying to fit mind, spirit, and sexuality into a prescribed script because they cannot look beyond the parameters of the acceptable. It pulls on the energy of such women even as it drains the energy of 'closeted' lesbians – the energy exhausted in the double life. The lesbian trapped in the 'closet,' the woman imprisoned in prescriptive ideas of the 'normal' share the pain of blocked options, broken connections, lost access to self-definition freely and powerfully assumed.

The lie is many-layered. In Western tradition, one layer – the romantic – asserts that women are inevitably, even if rashly and tragically, drawn to men – [. . .] In the tradition of the social sciences it asserts that primary love between the sexes is 'normal'; that women *need* men as social and economic protectors, for adult sexuality, and for psychological completion; that the heterosexually constituted family is the basic social unit; that women who do not attach their primary intensity to men must be, in functional terms, condemned to an even more devastating outsiderhood than their outsiderhood as women. Small wonder that lesbians are reported to be a more hidden population than male homosexuals. The Black lesbian-feminist critic Lorraine Bethel, writing on Zora Neale Hurston, remarks that for a Black woman – already twice an outsider – to choose to assume still another 'hated identity' is problematic indeed. Yet the lesbian continuum has been a life line for Black women both in Africa and the United States.

> Black women have a long tradition of bonding together . . . in a Black/women's community that has been a source of vital survival information, psychic and emotional support for us. We have a distinct Black woman-identified folk culture based on our experiences as Black women in this society; symbols, language and modes of expression that are specific to the realities of our lives . . . Because Black women were rarely among those Blacks and females who gained access to literary and other acknowledged forms of artistic expression, this Black female bonding and Black woman-identification has often been hidden and unrecorded except in the individual lives of Black women through our own memories of our particular Black female tradition.[33]

Another layer of the lie is the frequently encountered implication that women turn to women out of hatred for men. Profound skepticism, caution, and righteous paranoia about men may indeed be part of any healthy woman's response to the misogyny of male-dominated culture, to the forms assumed by 'normal' male sexuality, and to *the failure even of 'sensitive' or 'political' men to perceive or find these troubling*. Lesbian existence is also represented as mere refuge from male abuses, rather than as an electric and empowering charge between women.

[. . .]

[T]here is a *nascent* feminist political content in the act of choosing a woman lover or life partner in the face of institutionalized heterosexuality.[34] But for lesbian existence to realize this political content in an ultimately liberating form, the erotic choice must deepen and expand into conscious woman identification – into lesbian feminism.

The work that lies ahead, of unearthing and describing what I call here 'lesbian existence,' is potentially liberating for all women. It is work that must assuredly move beyond the limits of white and middle-class Western Women's Studies to examine women's lives, work, and groupings within every racial, ethnic, and political structure. There are differences, moreover, between 'lesbian existence' and the 'lesbian continuum,' differences we can discern even in the movement of our own lives. The lesbian continuum, I suggest, needs delineation in light of the 'double life' of women, not only women self-described as heterosexual but also of self-described lesbians. We need a far more exhaustive account of the forms the double life has assumed. Historians need to ask at every point how heterosexuality as institution has been organized and maintained through the female wage scale, the enforcement of middle-class women's 'leisure,' the glamorization of so-called sexual liberation, the withholding of education from women, the imagery of 'high art' and popular culture, the mystification of the 'personal' sphere, and much else. We need an economics which comprehends the institution of heterosexuality, with its doubled workload for women and its sexual divisions of labor, as the most idealized of economic relations.

The question inevitably will arise: Are we then to condemn all heterosexual relationships, including those which are least oppressive? I believe this question, though often heartfelt, is the wrong question here. We have been stalled in a maze of false dichotomies which prevents our apprehending the institution as a whole: 'good' versus 'bad' marriages; 'marriage for love' versus arranged marriage; 'liberated' sex versus prostitution; heterosexual intercourse versus rape; *Liebeschmerz* versus humiliation and dependency. Within the institution exist, of course, qualitative differences of experience; but the absence of choice remains the great unacknowledged reality, and in the absence of choice, women will remain dependent upon the chance or luck of particular relationships and will have no collective power to determine the meaning and place of sexuality in their lives. As we address the institution itself, moreover, we begin to perceive a history of female resistance which has never fully understood itself because it has been so fragmented, miscalled, erased. It will require a courageous grasp of the politics and economics, as well as the cultural propaganda, of heterosexuality to carry us beyond individual cases or diversified group situations into the complex kind of overview needed to undo the power men everywhere wield over women, power which has become a model for every other form of exploitation and illegitimate control.

NOTES

1. Alice Rossi, 'Children and work in the lives of women,' paper delivered at the University of Arizona, Tucson, February 1976.
2. Doris Lessing, *The Golden Notebook* (1962), New York: Bantam, 1977, p. 480.
3. Kathleen Gough, 'The origin of the family,' in Rayna [Rapp] Reiter (ed.), *Toward an Anthropology of Women*, New York: Monthly Review Press, 1975, pp. 69–70.
4. K. Barry, *Female Sexual Slavery*, Englewood Cliffs, NJ: Prentice-Hall, 1979, pp. 216–19.
5. Anna Demeter, *Legal Kidnapping*, Boston: Beacon, 1977, pp. xx, 126–8.
6. M. Daly, *Gyn/Ecology: The Metaethics of Radical Feminism*, Boston: Beacon, 1978, pp. 139–41, 163–5.
7. Barbara Ehrenreich and Deirdre English, *Witches, Midwives and Nurses: A History of Women Healers*, Old Westbury, NY: Feminist Press, 1973; Andrea Dworkin, *Woman Hating*, New York: Dutton, 1974, pp. 118–54; M. Daly, *Beyond God the Father*, Boston: Beacon, 1973, pp. 178–222.
8. See Virginia Woolf, *A Room of One's Own*, London: Hogarth, 1929, and Virginia Woolf, *Three Guineas* (1938), New York: Harcourt Brace, 1966; Tillie Olsen, *Silences*, Boston: Delacorte, 1978; Michelle Cliff, 'The resonance of interruption,' *Chrysalis: A Magazine of Women's Culture*, 8, 1979, pp. 29–37.

9. Daly, *Beyond God the Father*, pp. 347–51; Olsen, *Silences*, pp. 22–46.

10. Daly, *Beyond God the Father*, p. 93.

11. Fran P. Hosken, 'The violence of power: genital mutilation of females,' *Heresies: A Feminist Journal of Art and Politics*, 6, 1979, pp. 28–35; Notes pp. 194–5. [A.R., 1986: See especially 'Circumcision of girls,' in Nawal El Saadawi, *The Hidden Face of Eve: Women in the Arab World*, Boston: Beacon, 1982, pp. 33–43.]

12. Barry, *Female Sexual Slavery*, pp. 163–4.

13. Catharine A. MacKinnon, *Sexual Harassment of Working Women: A Case of Sex Discrimination*, New Haven: Yale University Press, 1979, pp. 15–16.

14. *Ibid.*, p. 174.

15. *Ibid.*, p. 221.

16. Barry, *Female Sexual Slavery*. [A.R., 1986: See also Kathleen Barry, Charlotte Bunch and Shirley Castley (eds), *International Feminism: Networking against Female Sexual Slavery*, New York: International Women's Tribune Center, 1984.]

17. Barry, *Female Sexual Slavery*, p. 30.

18. *Ibid.*, p. 100.

19. *Ibid.*, p. 140.

20. For my perception of heterosexuality as an economic institution I am indebted to Lisa Leghorn and Katherine Parker, who allowed me to read the unpublished manuscript of their book *Woman's Worth: Sexual Economics and the World of Women*, London and Boston: Routledge & Kegan Paul, 1981.

21. I would suggest that lesbian existence has been most recognized and tolerated where it has resembled a 'deviant' version of heterosexuality – e.g., where lesbians have, like Stein and Toklas, played heterosexual roles (or seemed to in public) and have been chiefly identified with male culture. See also Claude E. Schaeffer, 'The kutenai female berdache: courier, guide, prophetess and warrior,' *Ethnohistory* 12(3), Summer 1965, pp. 193–236. (Berdache: 'an individual of a definite physiological sex [m. or f.] who assumes the role and status of the opposite sex and who is viewed by the community as being of one sex physiologically but as having assumed the role and status of the opposite sex' [Schaeffer, 'The kutenai female berdache' p. 231].) Lesbian existence has also been relegated to an upper-class phenomenon, an elite decadence (as in the fascination with Paris salon lesbians such as Renée Vivien and Natalie Clifford Barney), to the obscuring of such 'common women' as Judy Grahn depicts in her *The Work of a Common Woman*, Oakland, CA: Diana Press, 1978, and *True to Life Adventure Stories*, Oakland, CA: Diana Press, 1978.

22. Daly, *Gyn/Ecology*, p. 15.

23. 'In a hostile world in which women are not supposed to survive except in relation with and in service to men, entire communities of women were simply erased. History tends to bury what it seeks to reject' (Blanche W. Cook, '"Women alone stir my imagination" lesbianism and the cultural tradition,' *Signs: Journal of Women in Culture and Society*, 4(4), Summer 1979, pp. 719–20). The Lesbian Herstory Archives in New York City is one attempt to preserve contemporary documents on lesbian existence – a project of enormous value and meaning, working against the continuing censorship and obliteration of relationships, networks, communities in other archives and elsewhere in the culture.

24. [A.R., 1986: The shared historical and spiritual 'crossover' functions of lesbians and gay men in cultures past and present are traced by Judy Grahn in *Another Mother Tongue: Gay Words, Gay Worlds*, Boston: Beacon, 1984. I now think we have much to learn both from the uniquely female aspects of lesbian existence and from the complex 'gay' identity we share with gay men.]

25. Audre Lorde, 'Uses of the erotic: the erotic as power,' in *Sister Outsider*, Trumansburg, NY: Crossing Press, 1984.

26. Gracia Clark, 'The Beguines: a mediaeval women's community,' *Quest: A Feminist Quarterly*, 1(4), 1975, pp. 73–80.

27. See Denise Paulmé (ed.), *Women of Tropical Africa*, Berkeley: University of California Press, 1963, pp. 7, 266–7. Some of these sororities are described as 'a kind of defensive syndicate against the male element,' their aims being 'to offer concerted resistance to an oppressive patriarchate,' 'independence in relation to one's husband and with regard to motherhood, mutual aid, satisfaction of personal revenge.' See also Audre Lorde, 'Scratching the surface: some notes on barriers to women and loving,' in *Sister Outsider*, pp. 45–52; Marjorie Topley, 'Marriage resistance in rural Kwangtung,' in M. Wolf and R. Witke (eds), *Women in Chinese Society*, Stanford, Calif.: Stanford University Press, 1978, pp. 67–89; Agnes Smedley, *Portraits of Chinese Women in Revolution*, ed. J. MacKinnon and S. MacKinnon, Old Westbury, NY: Feminist Press, 1976, pp. 103–10.

28. See Rosalind Petchesky, 'Dissolving the hyphen: a report on Marxist-feminist groups 1–5,' in Zillah Eisenstein (ed.), *Capitalist Patriarchy and the Case for Socialist Feminism*, New York: Monthly Review Press, 1979, p. 387.

29. [A.R., 1986: See Angela Davis, *Women, Race and Class*, New York: Random House, 1981, p. 102; Orlando Patterson, *Slavery and Social Death: A Comparative Study*, Cambridge, Mass.: Harvard University Press, 1982, p. 133.]

30. Russell and van de Ven, *Proceedings*, pp. 42–3, 56–7. Diana Russell and Nicole van den Ven (eds), *Proceedings of the International Tribunal of Crimes against Women*, Millbrae, CA: Les Femmes, 1976.

31. I am indebted to Jonathan Katz's *Gay American History Lesbians and Gay Men in the USA* (New York: Thomas Y. , 1976) for bringing to my attention Hansberry's letters to *The Ladder* and to Barbara·Grier for supplying me with copies of relevant pages from *The Ladder*, quoted here by permission of Barbara Grier. See also the reprinted series of *The Ladder*, ed. Jonathan Katz *et al.*, New York: Arno, 1975, and Deirdre Carmody, 'Letters by Eleanor Roosevelt Detail friendship with Lorena Hickok,' *New York Times*, 21 October 1979.

32. See Russell and van de Ven, *Proceedings*, p. 40: 'Few heterosexual women realize their lack of free choice about their sexuality, and few realize how and why compulsory heterosexuality is also a crime against them.'

33. Lorraine Bethel, '"This infinity of conscious pain": Zora Neale Hurston and the Black female literary tradition,' in Gloria T. Hull. Patricia Bell Scott and Barbara Smith (eds), *All the Women as White, All the Blacks as Men, but Some of us are Brave: Black Women's Studies*, Old Westbury, NY: Feminist Press, 1982.

34. Conversation with Blanche W. Cook, New York City, March 1979.

2.4

THE STRAIGHT MIND

Monique Wittig

In Britain and Europe, as in North America, the idea of lesbianism as a political choice provoked heated argument within the women's movement. This article was central to the development of this debate in France. Monique Wittig argues that the categories 'women' and 'men' are the products of gender hierarchy institutionalised as heterosexuality. Lesbians, living outside the heterosexual contract, are fugitives from patriarchal domination, and are therefore not women.

In recent years in Paris, language as a phenomenon has dominated modern theoretical systems and the social sciences and has entered the political discussions of the lesbian and women's liberation movements.

[. . .]

The science of language has invaded other sciences, such as anthropology through Lévi-Strauss, psychoanalysis through Lacan, and all the disciplines which have developed from the basis of structuralism.

[. . .]

The ensemble of these discourses produces a confusing static for the oppressed, which makes them lose sight of the material cause of their oppression and plunges them into a kind of ahistoric vacuum.

For they produce a scientific reading of the social reality in which human beings are given as invariants, untouched by history and unworked by class conflicts, with identical psyches because genetically programmed. This psyche, equally untouched by history and unworked by class conflicts, provides the specialists, from the beginning of the twentieth century, with a whole arsenal of invariants.

From M. Wittig, *Feminist Issues, Hemel Hempstead: Harvester Wheatsheat, 1992.*

[...]

We are taught that the Unconscious, with perfectly good taste, structures itself upon metaphors, for example, the name-of-the-father, the Oedipus complex, castration, the murder-or-death-of-the-father, the exchange of women, etc. If the Unconscious, however, is easy to control, it is not just by anybody. Similar to mystical revelations, the apparition of symbols in the psyche demands multiple interpretations. Only specialists can accomplish the deciphering of the Unconscious. Only they, the psychoanalysts, are allowed (authorized?) to organize and interpret psychic manifestations which will show the symbol in its full meaning.

[...]

Who gave the psychoanalysts their knowledge? For example, for Lacan, what he calls the 'psychoanalytic discourse,' or the 'analytical experience,' both 'teach' him what he already knows. And each one teaches him what the other one taught him. But can we deny that Lacan scientifically discovered, through the 'analytical experience' (somehow an experiment), the structures of the Unconscious? Will we be irresponsible enough to disregard the discourses of the psychoanalyzed people lying on their couches? In my opinion, there is no doubt that Lacan found in the Unconscious the structures he said he found there, since he had previously put them there.

[...]

   In the analytical experience there is an oppressed person, the psychoanalyzed, whose need for communication is exploited and who (in the same way as the witches could, under torture, only repeat the language that the inquisitors wanted to hear) has no other choice, (if s/he does not want to destroy the implicit contract which allows her/him to communicate and which s/he needs), than to attempt to say what s/he is supposed to say.

[...]

   But can the need to communicate that this contract implies only be satisfied in the psychoanalytical situation, in being cured or 'experimented' with? If we believe recent testimonies[1] by lesbians, feminists, and gay men, this is not the case. All their testimonies emphasize the political significance of the impossibility that lesbians, feminists, and gay men face in the attempt to communicate in heterosexual society, other than with a psychoanalyst. When the general state of things is understood (one is not sick or to be cured, one has an enemy) the result is that the oppressed person breaks the psychoanalytical contract. This is what appears in the testimonies, along with the teaching that the psychoanalytical contract was not a contract of consent but a forced one.

[...]

   The discourses which particularly oppress all of us, lesbians, women, and homo-sexual men, are those which take for granted that what founds society, any society, is heterosexuality.[2] These discourses speak about us and claim to say the truth in an apolitical field, as if anything of that which signifies could escape the political in this moment of history, and as if, in what concerns us, politically insignificant signs could exist. These discourses of heterosexuality oppress us in the sense that they prevent us from speaking unless we speak in their terms. Everything which puts them into question is at once disregarded as elementary. Our refusal of the totalizing interpretation of psychoanalysis makes the theoreticians say that we neglect the symbolic dimension. These discourses deny us every possibility of creating our own categories. But their most ferocious action is the unrelenting tyranny that they exert upon our physical and mental selves.

When we use the overgeneralizing term 'ideology' to designate all the discourses of the dominating group, we relegate these discourses to the domain of Irreal Ideas; we forget the material (physical) violence that they directly do to the oppressed people, a violence produced by the abstract and 'scientific' discourses as well as by the discourses of the mass media. I would like to insist on the material oppression of individuals by discourses.

[. . .]

If the discourse of modern theoretical systems and social science exert a power upon us, it is because it works with concepts which closely touch us. In spite of the historic advent of the lesbian, feminist, and gay liberation movements, whose proceedings have already upset the philosophical and political categories of the discourses of the social sciences, their categories (thus brutally put into question) are nevertheless utilized without examination by contemporary science. They function like primitive concepts in a conglomerate of all kinds of disciplines, theories, and current ideas that I will call the straight mind. (See *The Savage Mind* by Claude Lévi-Strauss.) They concern 'woman,' 'man,' 'sex,' 'difference,' and all of the series of concepts which bear this mark, including such concepts as 'history,' 'culture,' and the 'real.' And although it has been accepted in recent years that there is no such thing as nature, that everything is culture, there remains within that culture a core of nature which resists examination, a relationship excluded from the social in the analysis – a relationship whose characteristic is ineluctability in culture, as well as in nature, and which is the heterosexual relationship. I will call it the obligatory social relationship between 'man' and 'woman.' (Here I refer to Ti-Grace Atkinson and her analysis of sexual intercourse as an institution.[3] With its ineluctability as knowledge, as an obvious principle, as a given prior to any science, the straight mind develops a totalizing interpretation of history, social reality, culture, language, and all the subjective phenomena at the same time. I can only underline the oppressive character that the straight mind is clothed in in its tendency to immediately universalize its production of concepts into general laws which claim to hold true for all societies, all epochs, all individuals. Thus one speaks of *the* exchange of women, *the* difference between the sexes, *the* symbolic order, *the* Unconscious, Desire, *Jouissance*, Culture, History, giving an absolute meaning to these concepts when they are only categories founded upon heterosexuality, or thought which produces the difference between the sexes as a political and philosophical dogma.

The consequence of this tendency toward universality is that the straight mind cannot conceive of a culture, a society where heterosexuality would not order not only all human relationships but also its very production of concepts and all the processes which escape consciousness, as well. Additionally, these unconscious processes are historically more and more imperative in what they teach us about ourselves through the instrumentality of specialists. The rhetoric which expresses them (and whose seduction I do not underestimate) envelops itself in myths, resorts to enigma, proceeds by accumulating metaphors, and its function is to poeticize the obligatory character of the 'you-will-be-straight-or-you-will-not-be.'

In this thought, to reject the obligation of coitus and the institutions that this obligation has produced as necessary for the constitution of a society, is simply an impossibility, since to do this would mean to reject the possibility of the constitution of the other and to reject the 'symbolic order,' to make the constitution of meaning impossible, without which no one can maintain an internal coherence. Thus lesbianism, homosexuality, and the societies that we form cannot be thought of or spoken of, even though they have always existed. Thus, the straight mind continues to affirm that incest, and not homosexuality, represents its major interdiction. Thus, when thought by the straight mind, homosexuality is nothing but heterosexuality.

Yes, straight society is based on the necessity of the different/other at every level. It cannot work economically, symbolically, linguistically, or politically without this concept. This necessity of the different/other is an ontological one for the whole conglomerate of sciences and disciplines that I call the straight mind. But what is the different/other if not the dominated? For heterosexual society is the society which not only oppresses lesbians and gay men, it oppresses many different/others, it oppresses all women and many categories of men, all those who are in the position of the dominated. To constitute a difference and to control it is an 'act of power, since it is essentially a normative act. Everybody tries to show the other as different. But not everybody succeeds in doing so. One has to be socially dominant to succeed in it.'[4]

For example, the concept of difference between the sexes ontologically constitutes women into different/others. Men are not different, whites are not different, nor are the masters. But the blacks, as well as the slaves, are. This ontological characteristic of the difference between the sexes affects all the concepts which are part of the same conglomerate. But for us there is no such thing as being-woman or being-man. 'Man' and 'woman' are political concepts of opposition, and the copula which dialectically unites them is, at the same time, the one which abolishes them.[5] It is the class struggle between women and men which will abolish men and women.[6] The concept of difference has nothing ontological about it. It is only the way that the masters interpret a historical situation of domination. The function of difference is to mask at every level the conflicts of interest, including ideological ones.

In other words, for us, this means there cannot any longer be women and men, and that as classes and categories of thought or language they have to disappear, politically, economically, ideologically. If we, as lesbians and gay men, continue to speak of ourselves and to conceive of ourselves as women and as men, we are instrumental in maintaining heterosexuality. I am sure that an economic and political transformation will not dedramatize these categories of language. Can we redeem *slaves*? Can we redeem *nigger, negress*? How is *woman* different? Will we continue to write *white, master, man*? The transformation of economic relationships will not suffice. We must produce a political transformation of the key concepts, that is of the concepts which are strategic for us. For there is another order of materiality, that of language, and language is worked upon from within by these strategic concepts. It is at the same time tightly connected to the political field, where everything that concerns language, science and thought refers to the person as subjectivity and to her/his relationship to society. And we cannot leave this within the power of the straight mind or the thought of domination.

If among all the productions of the straight mind I especially challenge the models of the Structural Unconscious, it is because: at the moment in history when the domination of social groups can no longer appear as a logical necessity to the dominated, because they revolt, because they question the differences, Lévi-Strauss, Lacan, and their epigones call upon necessities which escape the control of consciousness and therefore the responsibility of individuals.

They call upon unconscious processes, for example, which require the exchange of women as a necessary condition for every society. According to them, that is what the unconscious tells us with authority, and the symbolic order, without which there is no meaning, no language, no society, depends on it. But what does women being exchanged mean if not that they are dominated? No wonder then that there is only one Unconscious, and that it is heterosexual. It is an Unconscious which looks too consciously after the interests of the masters.[7] [...] We must make it brutally apparent that psychoanalysis after Freud and particularly Lacan have rigidly turned their concepts into myths – Difference, Desire, the Name-of-the-father, etc. They have even 'over-mythified' the myths, an operation that was necessary for them in order to systematically heterosexualize that personal dimension which suddenly emerged through the dominated individuals into the historical field, particularly through women, who started their struggle almost two centuries ago.

[...]

This ensemble of heterosexual myths is a system of signs which uses figures of speech, and thus it can be politically studied from within the science of our oppression [...] which introduces the diachronism of history into the fixed discourse of eternal essences. This undertaking should somehow be a political semiology, although with 'this sorrow that we have sorrowed' we work also at the level of language/manifesto, of language/action, that which transforms, that which makes history.

In the meantime, in the systems that seemed so eternal and universal that laws could be extracted from them. [...] This dimension of history belongs to us, since somehow we have been designated, and since, as Lévi-Strauss said, we talk, let us say that we break off the heterosexual contract.

So, this is what lesbians say everywhere in this country and in some others, if not with theories at least through their social practice, whose repercussions upon straight culture and society are still unenvisionable. [...] Meanwhile the straight concepts are undermined. What is woman? Panic, general alarm for an active defense. Frankly, it is a problem that the lesbians do not have because of a change of perspective, and it would be incorrect to say that lesbians associate, make love, live with women, for 'woman' has meaning only in heterosexual systems of thought and heterosexual economic systems. Lesbians are not women.[8]

NOTES

1. For example see Karla Jay and Allen Young (eds.), *Out of the Closets*, New York: Link Books, 1972.
2. Heterosexuality: a word which first appears in the French language in 1911.
3. Ti-Grace Atkinson, *Amazon Odyssey*, New York: Link Books, 1974, pp. 13–23.
4. Claude Faugeron and Phillipe Robert, *La Justice et son public et les représentations sociales du système pénal*, Paris: Masson, 1978.
5. See, for her definition of 'social sex,' Nicole-Claude Mathieu, 'Notes pour une définition sociologique des categories de sexe' ('Notes towards a sociological definition of sex categories'), *Épistemologie sociologique*, 11, 1971. Translated in *Ignored by Some, Denied by Others: The Social Sex Category in Sociology* (pamphlet), Explorations in Feminism 2, London: Women's Research and Resources Centre Publications, 1977, pp. 16–37.
6. In the same way that in every other class struggle the categories of opposition are 'reconciled' by the struggle whose goal is to make them disappear.
7. Are the millions of dollars a year made by psychoanalysts symbolic?
8. This text was first read in New York at the Modern Language Association Convention in 1978 and dedicated to American Lesbians.

2.5

HATING MASCULINITY NOT MEN

Marie-Jo Dhavernas

This article represents the other side of the debate in France. Marie-Jo Dhavernas counters the arguments for political lesbianism advanced by Wittig in the previous reading and elsewhere, challenging both the theoretical and political consequences of separatism.

Among the MLF's [Movement de Libération des Femmes] most important tasks to my mind, is, the attempt to pick up the ways in which we reproduce the models – both theoretical and practical – given to us by patriarchal society (everyone knows that the oppressed have always tended to imitate their masters). This is why I would like first to show how the theory known as 'radical lesbianism' – and which we often call 'separatist' – fits into traditional modes of thought rather than it destroying them, and second, to discuss its paradoxes.

This theory originates with the critique of the ideology of difference, a critique with which we can all agree – except those plunged into the delights of 'neo-femininity' – 'traitors' and 'collaborators'. Unless one is talking in terms of a moral abstraction, the first question we must ask is whether separatism is the best, or the only, way of struggling against the ideology of difference and the patriarchal system it underpins.

We should note first of all that if lesbianism (and more generally homosexuality in both sexes) upsets the notion of *complementarity* of the sexes, it does not do much against the notion of *difference*, which incorporates complementarity but is not reducible to it. Racists see Blacks, Arabs, Asians, etc., as different from whites, but not as particularly

From M.-J. Dhavernas, 'Hating masculinity not men', in C. Duchen (ed.), *French Connections*, London: Unwin Hyman 1987.

complementary to them. This is not without significance – on the contrary – because the myth of complementarity is the specific form that the racist ideology of (natural) difference adopts where relations between the sexes are concerned, at least in our society. It is a myth perpetuated by innumerable dichotomies expressed in terms of sexuality. From this point of view, it is clear that lesbianism is a vital issue, and one that all feminists must confront.

Yet does it necessarily follow that radical lesbianism (not to be confused with simple homosexual practice) is both essential to, and sufficient for, the destruction of patriarchy? Monique Wittig seems to think that it is:

> 'lesbian' is the only concept I know that goes beyond sex categories (woman and man), because the subject (lesbian) is not, in economic, political or ideological terms, a woman. For in fact, what makes a woman is a particular social relationship to a man, which we have called 'servage' – a relationship which implies personal and physical obligations as well as economic obligations. . .a relationship from which lesbians escape by refusing to become or to stay heterosexual.[1]

This quotation reveals clearly both the illusory nature of separatism and the way in which it remains trapped within patriarchal discourse.

The belief that refusing all contact with men is enough to make a woman a 'non-woman', as Wittig says, is not only an illusion but is also in contradiction with the notion of sex-class. As long as there is a system which is founded on two totally distinct 'sex-classes', it will be impossible to step out of the class in which one was born, as society will continue to treat those who see themselves as 'escapees' in exactly the same way as the others. Are lesbians safe from rape? From men's attempts to pick them up? From discrimination at work? From sexist insults? No, of course not. Maybe they are less exposed to them, but as long as they live in a patriarchal society, 'non-women' or not, they will be subjected to the same oppression as all women.

[. . .]

As for the private appropriation described by M. Wittig, you don't have to be a lesbian to escape it. It is true that egalitarian relationships between a woman and a man require constant expenditure of energy, constant vigilance and a never-ending struggle against cultural inertia. It is also true that this struggle is all the harder to engage in, as it has such great emotional investment. This is not, as the radical lesbians think, purely sentimental dependence, but is active, the construction and deconstruction of complex and ambivalent relationships; it does eat up energy – but my energy belongs to me, not to women any more than to men, not even to the movement, to which I have never sworn an oath of allegiance.

[. . .]

The fact that all men, because of their sex, are in the position of oppressor does not mean that all male individuals *are nothing but oppressor* – any more than we are not *nothing but oppressed*. (If this were the case, we wouldn't even be able to fight.) It is because oppression *fails* to make us purely oppressors or purely oppressed that liberation is conceivable: and it is clearly more useful to pick out the system's faults than to inflate its victories.

[. . .]

Radical lesbians seem to forget that the end of oppression implies that either men are exterminated (which is unrealistic, even if it were desirable), or that they change completely. And feminism involves *all* the ways to achieve this goal. Excluding them from our struggle and from our space is one of these ways. It has already begun to show its effectiveness, notably by forcing a certain number of them to admit that it wasn't only the 'system' which was oppressing us, but also them, on a personal level, as agents of this system: and then by teaching them to see things relatively, destroying the base of their complacency.

Ceasing all contact with men is a strategy whose value I don't doubt. But confronting them every day, constantly showing them the ways in which they are oppressive, changing power relations by conquering our freedom not only apart from them but in front of them, forcing them more and more to recognize that women are people and not objects, destroying their interest in maintaining their privileges by making sure that they receive more injuries than advantages from them – this is not 'collaboration', it is a daily struggle, even if this struggle is permeated by emotions (and all struggles are, I think, in a thousand ways). It is the heterosexual, heterosocial form of the feminist struggle. We have the right not to like it. And I still have not seen how, in separatist texts, lesbianism is adequate in itself to uproot the phallocratic mentality without which patriarchy could not be sustained.

[. . .]

Women, says Monique, 'learn how to betray their class for the benefit of others', to 'cut themselves off from the Same, and betray them'.

The Same? What Same? For me, everyone is an other, men and women. Nothing inspires me with more horror than this fusing of female identity, in which, although starting from different premises, radical lesbians and the praisers of 'neo-femininity' come together. If I found all women identical, in what way would they interest me? I don't need to look at myself in a mirror. Excessive similarity is as abhorrent as total 'otherness'. What I like in women, as in men, is the play of similarity and difference, what resembles me and what doesn't. To be identical is to disappear, and women have suffered only too much from this imposed and internalized disappearance of their individuality for the sake of their sexual group. The difference is not between men and women, but between 4000 million human individuals.

Radical lesbians write that patriarchy separates us, that 'heteroppression radically divides women'. But to speak of patriarchy dividing women without saying that it is also patriarchy that unites us, and to say that lesbianism is the 'root' of feminism, supposes an adherence – not necessarily conscious – to the belief that poses a unity between women independently of patriarchy, outside or before it: which, in an oblique way, brings us back to the question of 'difference'. If there is no (natural) difference between the sexes, all we have in common is our oppression and our internalization of this oppression. We are not *the same*, we are only in *the same situation*. As for what divides us – it is not heterosexuality, which in no sense prevents us from struggling together, but is rather the attempt to separate out the 'non-women' from the 'women'.

I don't want to be defined by my 'choice of object' any more than by my biological status. I'm a heterosexual? You're the one who says so. I myself do not see myself in any category and each of my relationships has its own character .

[. . .]

The radical lesbians assert that their homosexuality is a 'political choice'. Unusual idea, which, applied to anything else would seem ludicrous: usually a desire would lead to making a choice. Hard to believe that you just need to be a feminist to reverse cause and effect and have choice arouse desire.

I accept, of course, that desires can change because of ideological changes, which we can call 'choices' out of convenience. But in that case, how can the internalization of patriarchal values be explained? If women have submitted to oppression for so long, it is surely because they haven't really been free.

It is true that there are situations, possibilities and new ideas that can spark new desires or modify them, or reveal those which had been buried under the impossibility of satisfying them. This is why feminism often leads to bisexual or homosexual desire. It is not a decision: it is the lifting of a taboo. [. . .] The 'choice' of lesbianism implies an existent desire, probably unconscious or maybe less strong at that time than an also-present heterosexual desire. The radical lesbians are fully aware of this and talk about the 'repressed homosexuality of heterosexual women' – which presupposes their acceptance of the notion of the unconscious – which in turn has no meaning at all if one claims to be able to 'choose' one's desires.

That many women – maybe all, although at the moment I don't think so (but then I don't know) – have unconscious homosexual desires, I find quite plausible. That these desires are, in most cases, never allowed to come to light because of the dominant heterosexual norm is, I think, equally convincing. However this does not mean that one can *choose* to feel physical desire for women or stop feeling desire for men.

The notion of political choice implies that lesbians could, if they so chose, desire men. To turn desire into a voluntary decision is to remove all meaning from it. To say that all women have, or could have, the same desires is to deny each woman's individuality, her particularity, which comes from an inextricable blend of the dominant culture and her personal history (and it is because this culture evolves, because her history continues and can change direction, that new desires are born). Of course, homosexuality is not a 'different sexuality' – not for the reasons given by separatism, but simply because all sexualities are different. There are as many types of sexuality as there are individuals, and as many different sexual relationships as there are relationships between individuals; there are forms of heterosexuality as there are forms of homosexuality, which is demonstrated, in spite of 'normalizing', 'uniformity-creating' patriarchy, by the diversity of texts on sexuality, homosexual and heterosexual. It is also demonstrated by the fact that radical lesbians do not want to be associated with 'club-going lesbians'. There can be much more in common between one type of homosexual relationship and one kind of heterosexual relationship than between two heterosexual relationships, etc.

If homosexuality is nothing but a bodily practice linked to homosociality, if desire is removed from it, then sexuality dies. If desire is not something you *feel*, which takes you sometimes by surprise, then how do you explain that you feel desire for a *particular person* and not for someone else? If you can choose to desire women rather than men, it should follow that you can choose to desire blondes rather than brunettes, tall women rather than small ones, etc. People become interchangeable: you can desire whom you choose, but you choose not to desire oppressors. This is not what the radical lesbians say, but it is the logical result of their position, and it is a dangerous logic: it ends up the same as patriarchal ideology which is based on lack of distinction, on the idea that there is something called 'woman'.

[. . .]

It is also a ridiculous position, because it implies that one is heterosexual without really wanting to be, but lesbian by choice. What happens to the very notion of choice when there is no alternative?

Resistance, collaborators, kapos – these are the terms that radical lesbians use to talk about this problem. Because they fail to analyse sexual oppression in its complexity and its specificity, radical lesbians are obliged to replace our concrete reality – which doesn't fit into their schemas – by recourse to the imagination, to fit women into the stories of other peoples' oppressions rather than bringing our own history to light. This is why it is important to criticize this theory: stripped of pertinence, it doesn't bring us anything to use in our struggle for our liberation.

On the other hand, it is essential not only to demand the right to be a lesbian, and to have the right to control our own bodies, but to make it possible for women's homosexual desires to come to light. It is in feminists' interests, whoever they are, to sow disorder, in every possible way, in sex categories which serve as legitimation for the oppressive division of individuals.[2]

NOTES

1. This quote is from the original French version of 'One is not born a woman; *Nouvelles questions féministes*, 1980. This is reprinted in M. Wittig, *The Straight Mind and Other Essays*, Hemel Hempstead: Harvester Wheatsheaf, 1990; see p. 20.
2. The orginal title was 'Ah, je ris de me voir si belle en ce miroir' (Ah, I laugh to see my beautiful reflection in the mirror). Dhavernas objects to the notion that all women are identical reflections of each other. Originally published in *La Revue d'en Face*, no. 9/10, 1981.

2.6

LESBIANISM
An Act of Resistance

Cheryl Clarke

Cheryl Clarke, writing as a black lesbian, shows clearly that women's experience of oppression is not homogenous but intersects with other oppressions such as those rooted in racism. Many feminists see lesbianism as a challenge to patriarchal domination; this piece suggests how it might connect with other sites of resistance.

For a woman to be a lesbian in a male-supremacist, capitalist, misogynist, racist, homophobic, imperialist culture, such as that of North America, is an act of resistance. (A resistance that should be championed throughout the world by all the forces struggling for liberation from the same slave master.) No matter how a woman lives out her lesbianism – in the closet, in the state legislature, in the bedroom – she has rebelled against becoming the slave master's concubine, viz. the male-dependent female, the female heterosexual. This rebellion is dangerous business in patriarchy. Men at all levels of privilege, of all classes and colors have the potential to act out legalistically, moralistically, and violently when they cannot colonize women, when they cannot circumscribe our sexual, productive, reproductive, creative prerogatives and energies. And the lesbian – that woman who, as Judy Grahn says, 'has taken a woman lover'[1] – has succeeded in resisting the slave master's imperialism in that one sphere of her life. The lesbian has decolonized her body. She has rejected a life of servitude implicit in Western, heterosexual relationships and has accepted the potential of mutuality in a lesbian relationship – *roles* notwithstanding.

From C. Clarke, 'Lesbianism: an act of resistance', in C. Moraga and G. Anzaldwa (eds), *This Bridge called My Back*, New York. Kitchen Table: Women of Color Press, 1981.

Historically, this culture has come to identify lesbians as women, who over time, engage in a range and variety of sexual-emotional relationships with women. I, for one, identify a woman as a lesbian who says she is. Lesbianism is a recognition, an awakening, a reawakening of our passion for each (woman) other (woman) and for same (woman). This passion will ultimately reverse the heterosexual imperialism of male culture. Women, through the ages, have fought and died rather than deny that passion.

[. . .]

The following analysis is offered as one small cut against [. . .] silence and secrecy. It is not intended to be original or all-inclusive. I dedicate this work to all the women hidden from history whose suffering and triumph have made it possible for me to call my name out loud.[2]

The woman who embraces lesbianism as an ideological, political, and philosophical means of liberation of all women from heterosexual tyranny must also identify with the world-wide struggle of all women to end male-supremacist tyranny at all levels. As far as I am concerned, any woman who calls herself a feminist must commit herself to the liberation of *all* women from *coerced* heterosexuality as it manifests itself in the family, the state, and on Madison Avenue. The lesbian-feminist struggles for the liberation of all people from patriarchal domination through heterosexism and for the transformation of all socio-political structures, systems, and relationships that have been degraded and corrupted under centuries of male domination.

However, there is no one kind of lesbian, no one kind of lesbian behavior, and no one kind of lesbian relationship. Also there is no one kind of response to the pressures that lesbians labor under to survive as lesbians. Not all women who are involved in sexual-emotional relationships with women call themselves lesbians or identify with any particular lesbian community. Many women are only lesbians to a particular community and *pass* as heterosexuals as they traffic among enemies. (This is analogous to being black and passing for white with only one's immediate family knowing one's true origins.) Yet, those who hide in the closet of heterosexual presumption are sooner or later discovered. The 'nigger-in-the-woodpile' story retells itself. Many women are politically active as lesbians, but may fear holding hands with their lovers as they traverse heterosexual turf.

[. . .]

Bisexual is a safer label than lesbian, for it posits the possibility of a relationship with a man, regardless of how infrequent or non-existent the female bisexual's relationships with men might be. And then there is the lesbian who is a lesbian anywhere and everywhere and who is in direct and constant confrontation with heterosexual presumption, privilege, and oppression.

[. . .]

Wherever we, as lesbians, fall along this very generalized political continuum, we must know that the institution of heterosexuality is a die-hard custom through which male-supremacist institutions insure their own perpetuity and control over us. Women are kept, maintained, and contained through terror, violence, and spray of semen. It is profitable for our colonizers to confine our bodies and alienate us from our own life processes as it was profitable for the European to enslave the African and destroy all memory of a prior freedom and self-determination. [. . .] [J]ust as the foundation of Western capitalism depended upon the North Atlantic slave trade, the system of patriarchal domination is buttressed by the subjugation of women through heterosexuality.

[. . .]

As a member of the largest and second most oppressed group of people of color, as a woman whose slave and ex-slave foresisters suffered some of the most brutal racist, male-supremacist imperialism in Western history, the black lesbian has had to survive also the psychic mutilation of heterosexual superiority. The black lesbian is coerced into the experience of institutional racism – like every other nigger in America – and must suffer as well the homophobic sexism of the black political community, some of whom seem to have forgotten so soon the pain of rejection, denial, and repression sanctioned by racist America. While most political black lesbians do not give a damn if white America is negrophobic, it becomes deeply problematic when the contemporary black political community [. . .] rejects us because of our commitment to women and women's liberation. Many black male members of that community seem still not to understand the historic connection between the oppression of African peoples in North America and the universal oppression of women. As the women's rights activist and abolitionist, Elizabeth Cady Stanton, pointed out during the 1850's, racism and sexism have been produced by the same animal, viz. 'the white Saxon man.'

Gender oppression [. . .] originated from the first division of labor, viz. that between women and men, and resulted in the accumulation of private property, patriarchal usurpation of 'mother right' or matrilineage, and the duplicitous, male-supremacist institution of heterosexual monogamy (for women only). Sexual politics, therefore, mirror the exploitative, class-bound relationship between the white slave master and the African slave – and the impact of both relationships (between black and white and woman and man) has been residual beyond emancipation and suffrage. The ruling class white man had a centuries-old model for his day-to-day treatment of the African slave. Before he learned to justify the African's continued enslavement and the ex-slave's continued disfranchisement with arguments of the African's divinely ordained mental and moral inferiority to himself (a smokescreen for his capitalist greed) the white man learned, within the structure of heterosexual monogamy and under the system of patriarchy, to relate to black people — slave or free — as a man *relates* to a woman, viz. as property, as a sexual commodity; as a servant, as a source of free or cheap labor, and as an innately inferior being.

Although counter-revolutionary, Western heterosexuality, which advances male-supremacy, continues to be upheld by many black people, especially black men, as the most desired state of affairs between men and women. This observation is borne out on the pages of our most scholarly black publications to our most commercial black publications, which view the issue of black male and female relationships through the lens of heterosexual bias. But this is to be expected, as historically heterosexuality was one of our only means of power over our condition as slaves and one of two means we had at our disposal to appease the white man.

Now, as ex-slaves, black men have more latitude to oppress black women, because the brothers no longer have to compete directly with the white man for control of black women's bodies. Now, the black man can assume the 'master' role and he can attempt to tyrannize black women. The black man may view the lesbian who cannot be manipulated or seduced sexually by him – in much the same way the white slave master once viewed the black male slave, viz. as some perverse caricature of manhood threatening his position of dominance over the female body. This view, of course, is a 'neurotic illusion' imposed on black men by the dictates of male supremacy, which the black man can never fulfill because he lacks the capital means and racial privilege.

> Historically, the myth in the Black world is that there are only two free people in the United States, the white man and the black woman. The myth was established by the Black man in the long period of his frustration when he longed to be free to have the material and social advantages of his oppressor, the white man. On examination of the myth this so-called freedom was based on the sexual prerogatives taken by the white man on the Black female. It was fantasied by the Black man that she enjoyed it.[3]

While lesbian-feminism does threaten the black man's predatory control of black women, its goal as a political ideology and philosophy is not to take the black man's or any man's position on top.

Black lesbians who do work within 'by-for-about-black-people' groups or organizations either pass as 'straight' or relegate our lesbianism to the so-called 'private' sphere. The more male-dominated or black nationalist bourgeois the organization or group, the more resistant to change, and thus, the more homophobic and anti-feminist. In these sectors, we learn to keep a low profile. [. . .] While the black man may consider racism his primary oppression, he is hard-put to recognize that sexism is inextricably bound up with the racism the black woman must suffer, nor can he see that no women (or men for that matter) will be liberated from the original 'master slave' relationship, viz. that between men and women, until we are all liberated from the false premise of heterosexual superiority.

[. . .]

The tactic many black men use to intimidate black women from embracing feminism is to reduce the conflicts between white women and black women to a 'tug-o'-war' for the black penis. And since the black lesbian, [. . .] is not interested in his penis, she undermines the black man's only source of power over her, viz. his heterosexuality. Black lesbians and all black women involved in the struggle for liberation must resist this manipulation and seduction.

The black dyke, like every dyke in America, is everywhere – in the home, in the street, on the welfare, unemployment and social security rolls, raising children, working in factories, in the armed forces, on television, in the public school system, in all the professions, going to college or graduate school, in middle-management, et. al. The black dyke, like every other non-white and working class and poor woman in America, has not suffered the luxury, privilege or oppression of being dependent on men, even though our male counterparts have been present, have shared our lives, work and struggle, and, in addition have undermined our 'human dignity' along the way like most men in patriarchy, the imperialist family of man. But we could never depend on them 'to take care of us' on their resources alone – and, of course it is another 'neurotic illusion' imposed on our fathers, brothers, lovers, husbands that they are supposed to 'take care of us' because we are women. Translate: 'to take care of us' equals 'to control us'. Our brothers', fathers', lovers', husbands' only power is their manhood. And unless manhood is somehow embellished by white skin and generations of private wealth, it has little currency in racist, capitalist patriarchy. The black man, for example, is accorded native elite or colonial guard or vigilante status over black women in imperialist patriarchy. He is an overseer for the slave master. Because of his maleness he is given access to certain privileges, eg. employment, education, a car, life insurance, a house, some nice vines. He is usually a rabid heterosexual. He is, since emancipation, allowed to raise a 'legitimate' family, allowed to have his piece of turf, viz. his wife and children.

[. . .]

Traditionally, poor black men and women who banded together and stayed together and raised children together did not have the luxury to cultivate dependence among the members of their families. So, the black dyke, like most black women, has been conditioned to be self-sufficient, i.e. not dependent on men. For me personally, the conditioning to be self-sufficient and the predominance of female role models in my life are the roots of my lesbianism. Before I became a lesbian, I often wondered why I was expected to give up, avoid, and trivialize the recognition and encouragement I felt from women in order to pursue the tenuous business of heterosexuality. And I am not unique.

As political lesbians, i.e. lesbians who are resisting the prevailing culture's attempts to keep us invisible and powerless, we must become more visible (particularly black and other lesbians of color) to our sisters hidden in their various closets, locked in prisons of self-hate and ambiguity, afraid to take the ancient act of woman-bonding beyond the sexual, the private, the personal. I am not trying to reify lesbianism or feminism. I am trying to point out that lesbian-feminism has the potential of reversing and transforming a major component in the system of women's oppression, viz. predatory heterosexuality. If radical lesbian-feminism purports an anti-racist, anti-classist, anti-woman-hating vision of bonding as mutual, reciprocal, as infinitely negotiable, as freedom from antiquated gender prescriptions and proscriptions, *then all people struggling to transform the character of relationships in this culture have something to learn from lesbians.*

The woman who takes a woman lover lives dangerously in patriarchy. And woe betide her even more if she chooses as her lover a woman who is not of her race. The silence among lesbian-feminists regarding the issue of lesbian relationships between black and white women in America is caused by none other than the centuries-old taboo and laws in the United States against relationships between people of color and those of the Caucasian race.

[. . .]

The taboo against black and white people relating at any other level than master-slave, superior inferior has been propounded in America to keep black women and men and white women and men, who share a common oppression at the hands of the ruling class white man, from organizing against that common oppression. We, as black lesbians, must vehemently resist being bound by the white man's racist, sexist laws, which have endangered potential intimacy of any kind between whites and blacks.

It cannot be presumed that black lesbians involved in love, work, and social relationships with white lesbians do so out of self-hate and denial of our racial-cultural heritage, identities, and oppression. Why should a woman's commitment to the struggle be questioned or accepted on the basis of her lover's or comrade's skin color? White lesbians engaged likewise with black lesbians or any lesbians of color cannot be assumed to be acting out of some perverse, guilt-ridden racialist desire.

I personally am tired of going to events, conferences, workshops, planning sessions that involve a coming together of black and other lesbians of color for political or even social reasons and listening to black lesbians relegate feminism to white women, castigate black women who propose forming coalitions with predominantly white feminist groups, minimize the white woman's oppression and exaggerate her power, and then finally judge that a black lesbian's commitment to the liberation of black women is dubious because she does not sleep with a black woman. All of us have to accept or reject allies on the basis of politics not on the specious basis of skin color. *Have not black people suffered betrayal from our own people?*

Yes, black women's experiences of misogyny are different from white women's. However, they all add up to how the patriarchal slave master decided to oppress us. We both fought each other for his favor, approval, and protection. Such is the effect of imperialist, heterosexist patriarchy.

[. . .]

Because of her whiteness, the white woman of all classes has been accorded, as the black man has because of his maleness, certain privileges in racist patriarchy, e.g. indentured servitude as opposed to enslavement, exclusive right to public assistance until the 1960's, 'legitimate' offspring and (if married into the middle/upper class) the luxury to live on her husband's income, etc.

The black woman, having neither maleness nor whiteness, has always had her heterosexuality, which white men and black men have manipulated by force and at will. Further, she, like all poor people, has had her labor, which the white capitalist man has also taken and exploited at will. These capabilities have allowed black women minimal access to the crumbs thrown at black men and white women. So, when the black woman and the white woman become lovers, we bring that history and all those questions to the relationship as well as other people's problems with the relationships. The taboo against intimacy between white and black people has been internalized by us and simultaneously defied by us. If we, as lesbian-feminists, defy the taboo, then we begin to transform the history of relationships between black women and white women.

So, all of us would do well to stop fighting each other for our space at the bottom, because there ain't no more room. We have spent so much time hating ourselves. Time to love ourselves. And that, for all lesbians, as lovers, as comrades, as freedom fighters, is the final resistance.

NOTES

1. Judy Grahn, 'The common woman,' *The Work of a Common Woman*, Oakland, Calif. Diana Press, 1978, p. 67.
2. I would like to give particular acknowledgement to the Combahee River Collective's 'A Black Feminist Statement.' Because this document espouses 'struggling against racial, sexual, heterosexual, and class oppression,' it has become a manifesto of radical feminist thought, action and practice.
3. Pat Robinson and Group, 'Poor Black women's study papers by poor black women of Mount Vernon, New York,' in T. Cade (ed.), *The Black Woman: An Anthology*, New York: New American Library, 1970, p. 194.

2.7

IMITATION AND
GENDER INSUBORDINATION

Judith Butler

Since the late 1980s debates on lesbianism have moved in new directions with the development of Queer theory, in which some lesbians have found common cause with gay men. Judith Butler, recognised as one of the key theorists in this area, has developed some of her ideas through reworking Monique Wittig's arguments. She deconstructs not only the categories 'women' and 'men', but also the bipolarity of heterosexuality and homosexuality. Here she suggests that while it may sometimes be strategically necessary to speak as a lesbian, such identities have no absolute existence.

TO THEORIZE AS A LESBIAN?

At first I considered writing a different sort of essay, one with a philosophical tone: the 'being' of being homosexual. The prospect of *being* anything, even for pay, has always produced in me a certain anxiety, for 'to be' gay, 'to be' lesbian seems to be more than a simple injunction to become who or what I already am. And in no way does it settle the anxiety for me to say that this is 'part' of what I am. To write or speak *as a lesbian* appears a paradoxical appearance of this 'I,' one which feels neither true nor false. For it is a production, usually in response to a request, to come out or write in the name of an identity which, once produced, sometimes functions as a politically efficacious phantasm. I'm not at ease with 'lesbian theories, gay theories,' for as I've argued elsewhere,[1] identity categories tend to be instruments of regulatory regimes, whether as the normalizing categories of oppressive structures or as the rallying points for a liberatory contestation of that very oppression. This is not to say that I will not

From J. Butter, 'Imitation and gender insubordination', in D. Fuss (ed.), *Inside Out: Lesbian Theories, Gay Theories*, New York: Routledge Inc., 1991.

appear at political occasions under the sign of lesbian, but that I would like to have it permanently unclear what precisely that sign signifies.

[. . .]

One risk I take is to be recolonized by the sign under which I write, and so it is this risk that I seek to thematize. To propose that the invocation of identity is always a risk does not imply that resistance to it is always or only symptomatic of a self-inflicted homophobia. Indeed, a Foucaultian perspective might argue that the affirmation of 'homosexuality' is itself an extension of a homophobic discourse. And yet 'discourse,' Foucault writes on the same page, 'can be both an instrument and an effect of power, but also a hindrance, a stumbling-block, a point of resistance and a starting point for an opposing strategy.'[2]

So I am skeptical about how the 'I' is determined as it operates under the title of the lesbian sign, and I am no more comfortable with its homophobic determination than with those normative definitions offered by other members of the 'gay or lesbian community.' I'm permanently troubled by identity categories, consider them to be invariable stumbling-blocks, and understand them, even promote them, as sites of necessary trouble. In fact, if the category were to offer no trouble, it would cease to be interesting to me: it is precisely the *pleasure* produced by the instability of those categories which sustains the various erotic practices that make me a candidate for the category to begin with. To install myself within the terms of an identity category would be to turn against the sexuality that the category purports to describe; and this might be true for any identity category which seeks to control the very eroticism that it claims to describe and authorize, much less 'liberate.'

And what's worse, I do not understand the notion of 'theory.'

[. . .]

Is there a pregiven distinction between theory, politics, culture, media? How do those divisions operate to quell a certain intertextual writing that might well generate wholly different epistemic maps? But I am writing here now: is it too late? Can this writing, can any writing, refuse the terms by which it is appropriated even as, to some extent, that very colonizing discourse enables or produces this stumbling block, this resistance? How do I relate the paradoxical situation of this dependency and refusal?

If the political task is to show that theory is never merely *theoria*, in the sense of disengaged contemplation, and to insist that it is fully political (*phronesis* or even *praxis*), then why not simply call this operation *politics*, or some necessary permutation of it?

[. . .]

Is sexuality of any kind even possible without that opacity designated by the unconscious, which means simply that the conscious 'I' who would reveal its sexuality is perhaps the last to know the meaning of what it says?

To claim that this is what I 'am' is to suggest a provisional totalization of this 'I'. But if the I can so determine itself, then that which it excludes in order to make that determination remains constitutive of the determination itself. In other words, such a statement presupposes that the 'I' exceeds its determination, and even produces that very excess in and by the act which seeks to exhaust the semantic field of that 'I'. In the act which would disclose the true and full content of that 'I' a certain radical *concealment* is thereby produced. For it is always finally unclear what is meant by invoking the lesbian-signifier, since its signification is always to some degree out of one's control, but also because its *specificity* can only be demarcated by exclusions that return to disrupt its claim to coherence. What, if anything, can lesbians be said to share? And who will decide this question, and in the name of whom? If I claim to be a lesbian, I 'come out' only to produce a new and different 'closet.' The 'you' to whom I come out now has access to a different region of opacity. Indeed, the locus of opacity has simply shifted: before, you did not know whether I 'am,' but now you do not know what that means, which is to say that the copula is empty, that it cannot be substituted for with a set of descriptions.³ And perhaps that is a situation to be valued.

[. . .]

It is possible to argue that whereas no transparent or full revelation is afforded by 'lesbian' and 'gay,' there remains a political imperative to use these necessary errors or category mistakes, as it were [. . .], to rally and represent an oppressed political constituency. Clearly, I am not legislating against the use of the term. My question is simply: which use will be legislated, and what play will there be between legislation and use such that the instrumental uses of 'identity' do not become regulatory imperatives? If it is already true that 'lesbians' and 'gay men' have been traditionally designated as impossible identities, errors of classification, unnatural disasters within juridico-medical discourses, or, what perhaps amounts to the same, the very paradigm of what calls to be classified, regulated, and controlled, then perhaps these sites of disruption, error, confusion, and trouble can be the very rallying points for a certain resistance to classification and to identity as such.

[. . .]

To argue that there might be a *specificity* to lesbian sexuality has seemed a necessary counterpoint to the claim that lesbian sexuality is just heterosexuality once removed, or that it is derived, or that it does not exist. But perhaps the claim of specificity, on the one hand, and the claim of derivativeness or non-existence, on the other, are not as contradictory as they seem. Is it not possible that lesbian sexuality is a process that reinscribes the power domains that it resists, that it is constituted in part from the very heterosexual matrix that it seeks to displace, and that its specificity is to be established, not *outside* or *beyond* that reinscription or reiteration, but in the very modality and effects of that reinscription. In other words, the negative constructions of lesbianism as a fake or a bad copy can be occupied and reworked to call into question the claims of heterosexual priority. In a sense I hope to make clear in what follows, lesbian sexuality can be understood to redeploy its 'derivativeness' in the service of displacing hegemonic heterosexual norms. Understood in this way, the political problem is not to establish the specificity of lesbian sexuality over and against its derivativeness, but to turn the homophobic construction of the bad copy against the framework that privileges heterosexuality as origin, and so 'derive' the former from the latter. This description requires a reconsideration of imitation, drag, and other forms of sexual crossing that affirm the internal complexity of a lesbian sexuality constituted in part within the very matrix of power that it is compelled both to reiterate and to oppose.

[. . .]

It is important to recognize the ways in which heterosexual norms reappear within gay identities, to affirm that gay and lesbian identities are not only structured in part by dominant heterosexual frames, but that they are *not* for that reason *determined* by them. They are running commentaries on those naturalized positions as well, parodic replays and resignifications of precisely those heterosexual structures that would consign gay life to discursive domains of unreality and unthinkability. But to be constituted or structured in part by the very heterosexual norms by which gay people are oppressed is not, I repeat, to be claimed or determined by those structures. And it is not necessary to think of such heterosexual constructs as the pernicious intrusion of 'the straight mind,' one that must be rooted out in its entirety. In a way, the presence of hetero-sexual constructs and positionalities in whatever form in gay and lesbian identities presupposes that there is a gay and lesbian repetition of straightness, a recapitulation of straightness – which is itself a repetition and recapitulation of its own ideality – within its own terms, a site in which all sorts of resignifying and parodic repetitions become possible. The parodic replication and resignification of heterosexual constructs within non-heterosexual frames brings into relief the utterly constructed status of the so-called original, but it shows that heterosexuality only constitutes itself as the original through a convincing act of repetition. The more that 'act' is expropriated, the more the heterosexual claim to originality is exposed as illusory.

[...]

Sexuality is never fully 'expressed' in a performance or practice; there will be passive and butchy femmes, femmy and aggressive butches, and both of those, and more, will turn out to describe more or less anatomically stable 'males' and 'females.' There are no direct expressive or causal lines between sex, gender, gender presentation, sexual practice, fantasy and sexuality. None of those terms captures or determines the rest. Part of what constitutes sexuality is precisely that which does not appear and that which, to some degree, can never appear. This is perhaps the most fundamental reason why sexuality is to some degree always closeted, especially to the one who would express it through acts of self-disclosure. That which is excluded for a given gender presentation to 'succeed' may be precisely what is played out sexually, that is, an 'inverted' relation, as it were, between gender and gender presentation, and gender presentation and sexuality. On the other hand, both gender presentation and sexual practices may corollate such that it appears that the former 'expresses' the latter, and yet both are jointly constituted by the very sexual possibilities that they exclude.[4]

[...]

NOTES

1. Judith Butler, *Gender Trouble: Feminism and the Subversion of Identity*, New York and London: Routledge, 1990.
2. Michel Foucault, *The History of Sexuality*, vol. 1, trans. John Hurley, New York: Random House, 1980, p. 101.
3. For an example of 'coming out' that is strictly unconfessional and which, finally, offers no content for the category of lesbian, see Barabara Johnson's deftly constructed 'Sula Passing: No Passing', presentation at UCLA, May 1990.
4. Parts of the essay were given as a presentation at the Conference on Homosexuality at Yale University in October 1989.

2.8

QUEER THEORRHEA (AND WHAT IT MIGHT MEAN FOR FEMINISTS)

Catherine Grant

Queer theory has established itself in academic circles and is only tangentially related to Queer politics. The theory often seems abstract and impenetrable to activists, which raises questions about why it has such a following among lesbian and gay intellectuals. Here Catherine Grant offers some explanations.

[. . .] In the present environment, characterised by a flurry of conferences and publications marketed as 'Queer', an atmosphere of veritable 'theorrhea' on this topic exists (a term to describe the end-product of the institutional valorisation and encouragement of 'Theory' in the humanities). Will 'Lesbian Studies', with its 'cumbersome' feminist baggage and/or separatist connotations, be swept away as a rather passé label in this supposed new age of perversity and queerness, along with the broad spectrum of political ideas or commitments which used to be part of it?

How Did We Get Queer?

'Queer', like many umbrella terms, has come to mean different things to different groups. However, as a term applied to theoretical work in Lesbian and Gay Studies it generally denotes the application of poststructuralist and postmodern ideas to interdisciplinary studies of the historical formations of lesbianism and homosexuality, and of the relationship between these formations and those of heterosexuality. It implies a shift from the consideration of lesbianism and homosexuality as discrete identities to one of homosexualities as kinds of discursive construct. 'Queer' theorists also often advocate the disruption or destruction of traditional categories of sex and gender.

[. . .]

Several writers, including Paulina Palmer, have traced in recent accounts how, in the wake of a surge in lesbian and gay political activity, the late 1980s saw the emergence of Lesbian and Gay Studies courses at universities in the USA and Britain. Exactly why this happened has not been so thoroughly explored. The academic state of affairs seems, by default, simply to be the culminating point in all of the political activism. Similarly, the near hegemony of poststructuralist or 'Queer' approaches which has so far characterised lesbian and gay academic theorising in the 1990s has not been convincingly accounted for.

This is, after all, a rather paradoxical, if not totally contradictory development in many ways: 'Queer' theorists have been able to establish their own academic territory, creating their own identity as a group, even as they deconstruct away the notions and categories involved in such a move.

CONSUMING IDENTITIES

Why did this happen? Why did these discursive and institutional spaces open up, and why was it that a particular kind of theory generally filled them up? In Britain, at least, the Thatcherite 1980s with the racist, misogynist and homophobic baiting of the GLC [Greater London Council] and 'Loony Left', and in particular 1988 with the passing of Section 28, saw unprecedented amounts of publicity in all areas of the media on the subjects of homosexuality and lesbianism which were both highly negative and positive. This topicality when taken with the mass mobilisations of lesbians and gay men and their sympathisers against what was originally Clause 28, and the thirst of this temporary community for knowledge, information or 'images' of gay and lesbian identities provided a ready market for publishers, part of which was an academic market. [. . .] Sally Munt [. . .] argues that it was the forging of these social movements in the late 1980s precisely within a *consumerist aesthetic* which paved the way for a mini-boom, for example, in the publication of lesbian-authored texts about lesbian writing. She writes: 'A postmodern culture has seen the development of reading communities with purchasing power, which publishers have rightly perceived as potential micro-markets'.[1] My own memory is that at this time identity politics did indeed fuse with this kind of niche-marketing, so that being lesbian or gay was seen to be partly achieved by buying the right books, wearing the T-shirt (or the 501s) or by dialling the 0898 number. Clearly, neither the causes nor the effects of these developments are only aesthetic; they are part of a wider social, economic and cultural consumerist shift.

This may well answer certain questions about demand, but what of the supply side? Courses, publications or conferences do not just happen without teachers, authors and organisers, and in this case, all with particular identifications. Obviously, there were lesbian and gay-identified academics and theorists before Section 28. Also, many women and men academics and theorists, both during and after this particular struggle, came out or identified as lesbian or gay, or bisexual. Many of the campaign activists have got jobs as academics. Some of them will have been '*self-consciously* moving out of one political location into another, recognising the contextual imperative' (p. xvi), as Sally Munt describes it. In other words they have perhaps been wanting to 'do something' about their identification in their current context, although the pressures on them not to do so would vary according to their job status, gender, class and ethnic background, amongst other factors. Some of this is also true of the earlier development of academic feminism in response to the struggles of the Women's movement, of course. Munt writes that the way in which Lesbian and Gay Studies is being seen in some North American and British universities as now occupying the radical space which was once feminism, is disturbing in that it has displaced feminism as something more academically conventional. On an anecdotal level, we may well agree with her, and some of us, for example, Sheila Jeffreys in her recent article, may suspect that it is all down to dubious alliances with gay men who have not always all been the best friends of feminism.[2] But would we be misplacing our blame?

One of the insights from the work of Michel Foucault, so beloved of certain 'Queer' theorists, is that power has not operated primarily by denying sexual expression but by creating the forms that modern sexuality takes; individuals are categorised and attached to their identities. Similarly, power has not always denied radical political or social expression, for, as John Champagne writes, 'special' fields of knowledge are occasionally created, such as Gay Studies, in attempts by the academy to 'manage diversity', or as Munt puts it, this is the way that the establishment assimilates in order to deradicalise. I would add that it is in this very way that institutions mask the very conflicts which constitute them. Even if, however, the establishment does, once in a while, allow the creation of carefully managed spaces, which it further deradicalises by marginalising them, surely it doesn't always dictate the kind of theory that they must use?

CATCHING THEORRHEA

I feel that a possible key here lies in the term that I mentioned at the beginning of my discussion: 'theorrhea', the current valorisation (and outpouring) of theory. 'Queer Theory', whilst in itself, can hardly be said to have much affected the curriculum in either British or North American universities, has certain antecedents in common with other supposedly radically-oriented theories and practices, such as deconstruction, or with 'Theory' itself, that problematic umbrella term under which are grouped various poststructural and postmodern approaches to particular areas of knowledge. Such perspectives have in certain circles, most notably in academic literary and Cultural Studies, achieved a critical hegemony. Patrick Brantlinger, in his discussion of 'theorrhea' in Cultural Studies, outlines three possible causes for the proliferation of 'Theory' from the 1960s onwards: the existence in the academy of political aspirations thwarted on the 'outside'; authentic, progressive movements of knowledge; and careerist responses to both 'inside' and 'outside' marketing considerations (consumerism at work again?). He sees these causes not as alternatives, but most likely as political, economic and cultural factors that have operated simultaneously. I find this a very convincing argument when discussing not only 'Queer' and Lesbian and Gay Theory, but also some feminist theorising now and in the past.

If 'theorrhea' might link various forms of theorising about sexuality and gender, perhaps now is the time to turn to an examination of some specifically lesbian examples of 'Queer Theory'. [. . .] Interestingly, as I have argued so far, amongst other considerations, the 'outside' of politics has a good deal to do with the 'inside' of theory, Teresa de Lauretis in her introduction to the 1991 'Queer Theory' issue of *differences: a journal of feminist cultural studies* disavows a straightforward connection between 'Queer' activism and theory. De Lauretis argues that 'Queer Theory', based as it is for her on the deconstruction of the binary categories underpinning the formation of gender and sexual subjectivities, is often way too radical for an activism which sometimes just isn't queer enough, frequently recreating, despite its best intentions and efforts, the identity politics it aims to transcend. Judith Butler, in a chapter of her 1993 book, *Bodies that matter*, entitled 'Critically Queer', argues that while in some contexts the term, 'Queer' appeals to a younger generation attempting to resist the reformist politics sometimes signified by 'Lesbian and Gay', this is the same predominantly white movement that 'has not fully addressed the way in which "queer" *plays* – or fails to *play* with non-white communities'[3] (my emphasis; it is interesting to see how Butler portrays racism as such a playful entity, even as she critiques 'Queer' for failing to take it seriously, here). She also argues that there is a similar issue at stake along gender lines: 'whereas in some instances [the term "Queer"] has mobilized a lesbian activism, in others the term represents a false unity of women and men'.[4]

While I note that this account sounds suspiciously like some past phases of lesbian/gay activism, it is interesting that Butler here footnotes Cherry Smyth's book, *Lesbians Talk Queer Notions*, as her example of lesbian activism being mobilised by the term 'Queer'. Smyth's book, which is clearly an artefact of 'Queer Politics' based as it is on fragmented interviews with activists and critics of the movement, is also a self-conscious piece of 'Queer Theory' (in the manner of certain pieces of feminist theory), an attempt at a kind of *écriture queer*. Many (lesbian) feminists would baulk at the assertion of a connection between 'Queer politics' and feminism, with the proliferation of references to an heroic lesbian sexual outlawism pitted against comments about the past 'silencing of anything but "right on" forms of sexual expression',[5] but this is precisely the connection Cherry Smyth invokes when she states in her introduction that '[the book] is situated firmly within feminism and queer politics, while expressing ambivalences towards both'.[6]

For 'ambivalences towards feminism' read code for a feminist ethics set up as the bad, prudish mother in opposition to her renegade, sexual daughters, to paraphrase Arlene Stein's account in her collection of essays edited in the US, *Sisters, Sexperts, Queers: Beyond the Lesbian Nation*. While this current of thought is not an essential component of all 'Queer Theory' it does crop up in many 'Queer' books in some of the old, familiar guises, sometimes, as a romantic attachment to a particular version of 'transgressive' lesbian sexual practice, or as an idealisation of other practices such as lesbian 'butch/femme' role-playing with little or no reference to historical or other contextually specific ways of interpreting these practices.

HIGH (QUEER) THEORY

Judith Butler is an interesting theorist in this regard. Her work, like that of Diana Fuss, falls into what might be described as 'High Queer Theory' (a false binary category, of course . . .), in other words, work heavily informed by feminist philosophy, as well as by many other areas of theory in the humanities. Paulina Palmer, in her survey of contemporary lesbian theory admires the questions which Butler addresses while disliking the 'esoteric tone and elitist attitude'[7] associated with her work. While Butler herself states that she is working within a feminist tradition, the poststructuralist framework of her analyses means that she treats 'woman' and 'lesbian' as very unstable categories indeed, which engenders difficulties for a (lesbian) feminist politics. What happens to your politics when your 'identity' category has been deconstructed out of 'false' existence. Butler discusses this hypothesis in her essay 'Imitation and Gender Insubordination', which opens the 1991 collection of mixed lesbian/gay 'Queer Theory' edited by Diana Fuss, *Inside/Out*. Here, she summarises the above problem:

> It is one thing to be erased by discourse, and yet another to be present within discourse as an abiding falsehood. Hence, there is a political imperative to render lesbianism visible, but how is that to be done outside or through existing regulatory regimes?[8]

Butler resorts in this essay to a defence of these 'necessary errors' or 'category mistakes' of sexual identity categories in the face of the political imperative of fighting homophobia and the oppression of women.

Several things are striking to me about Butler's brand of 'Queer' discourse: it is less confrontational about the whole spectrum of its acknowledged feminist and lesbian antecedents without falling into an apolitical stance. It also tends to stray less than other attempts at 'Queer Theory' into the realm of nostalgia for a mythical, pre-feminist, lesbian past when supposedly we could dress how we liked and do what we wanted within our own outlaw culture. The only time that Butler seems to wander into this area is when she outlines her theories that all gender is performance and that there are no gender 'originals' for which drag performances and lesbian butch/femme 'stylisations' are 'copies'.

[. . .]

In some respects, 'Queer' is posing no new dilemmas for academic, lesbian-feminist theorising, which is still going on in almost all the old spaces, within Women's Studies and Lesbian/Gay/'Queer' studies. This is not to say that it poses no dilemmas at all, it's just that we've met them before. For example, when Cherry Smyth launches an attack in her book on 'misplaced feminist morality' and then another on the sexism of 'Queer' men, she clearly wants to have her cake and eat it too. The old-fashioned kind of 'sex radical' similarly never could jettison completely the 'prudish mother' of feminism, either. This is the paradox that some 'Queer' theorists describe as 'desiring the law', and the precursors of a good deal of lesbian 'Queer' criticism are the earlier attempts at a sex-radical feminism (quite often the theorists involved are one and the same), and both forms of criticism have been afflicted with this anxiety about ethics, or values. It seems that it can never be quite 'queer' (ie. radical) enough just to be lesbian. 'Queer', and publishing in academia, without some larger political, ethical (and institutional?) framework, most usefully provided by feminism.

What has changed in the last seven or eight years is that the proliferation of published academic work on the subject of lesbian/gay/bisexual identities and identifications which has taken place has generally made use of a particular group of poststructuralist theories which have been valorised over and above others by the academy. I have attempted to trace at least a slightly more compelling account of how this 'Queer Theorrhea' came to pass, by arguing that the late 1980s lesbian and gay movements forged their identities almost as much through consumerism as through political activism. After the perceived 'failure' of lesbian and gay movements to effect real political change outside the academy, what were genuine progressive movements of knowledge created by a growing number of lesbian/gay/bisexual-identified academics on the inside were co-opted by difficult-to-avoid careerist responses to both the external and internal marketing considerations. So, while it seems to me that academic lesbian feminism has nothing to fear from the more historically specific accounts of the formations of 'homosexualities' or from the more materialist forms of 'Queer' cultural criticism, the real danger lies not in oppositional theories (which can always be contested) but in the 'theorrhea', in the pressures and demands of careerism and consumerism. While this consumerist version of education and academic publishing is allowed to predominate, we should continue to be aware that the spaces that (lesbian) feminists and other progressive political movements have fought for in academia, from which some of us are able to speak, would not necessarily survive any changes in the 'market' to which we are supposed to respond.

NOTES

1. Sally Munt, (ed.), *New Lesbian Criticism: Literary and Cultural Readings*, Brighton: Harvester, 1992, p. xvii.
2. Sheila Jeffreys, 'The queer disappearance of lesbian sexuality in the academy', *Women's Studies International Forum*, 17(5), 19, pp. 459–72.
3. Judith Butler, *Bodies that Matter*, New York and London: Routledge, 1990, p. 228.
4. *Ibid.*, p. 228.
5. Cherry Smyth, *Lesbians Talk Queer Notions*, London: Scarlet Press, 1992, p. 37.
6. *Ibid.*, p. 12.
7. Pauline Palmer, *Contemporary Lesbian Writings: Dreams, Desire, Difference*, Milton Keynes: Open University Press, 1993, p. 30.
8. Diana Fuss, *Inside/Out: Lesbian Theories, Gay Theories*, New York and London: Routledge, 1991, p. 20.

2.9

SISTERS UNDER THE SKIN:
A POLITICS OF HETEROSEXUALITY

Kadiatu Kanneh

While some feminists are questioning lesbianism as a political identity, others still continue to reaffirm its importance. Recently the debate between lesbian and heterosexual feminists has resurfaced in the pages of Feminism and Psychology. *As part of a special issue of this journal, heterosexual feminists were asked to give an account of the relationship between their sexuality and their politics. This piece was one of the responses. Kadiatu Kanneh argues that maintaining relationships with men might have different meanings for black and for white women. As in Reading 2.4, but from a rather different perspective, our attention is drawn to the intersections between sexual and racial oppression.*

The discussion which has been raging over sexuality and sexual difference in its many political manifestations has centred, in certain feminisms, on the politics of sexual preference. The encoding of sexuality as a political issue becomes strident in the case of strategies of identity, and I use 'strategies' in a deliberate sense. The significance of *placing* oneself within or against a social order can be a choice as well as a coercion. Or, rather, the narrative which inscribes the meaning of that position can be both chosen and necessary.

It seems curious, writing in the times in which I find myself, to discuss the location of a narrative of heterosexuality. How is it possible to inscribe a safe, uncontested identity as a purposeful political stance? I certainly do not wish to write against the painful and triumphant histories of lesbianism, the subversive and positive critiques of the dominant straight and oppressive societies in which we live. I do intend to suggest

From K. *Kanneh, 'Sisters under the Skin: a politics of heterosexuality'*, in S. Wilkinson and C. Kitzinger (eds), *Heterosexuality. A 'Feminism & Psychology' Reader*, London: Sage, 1993.

or intimate a possible reading of heterosexuality which would insist on the value and significance of racial or cultural loyalties within a feminist politics.

Loving women in a world where women are forced into a daily posture of opposition and struggle, is a mode of delight and recognition of the self which I would not dream of letting go. I choose also to listen to another voice of self-recognition which insists on an urgency which I would not wish to equate with an anti-feminist stance.

Having belonged to various feminist theory reading groups, I notice, painfully, that we always come up against the question of racial or cultural identity within or against the boundaries of feminism. How can we articulate a commitment to loving our brothers, our fathers, our vilified and celebratory cultural backgrounds? I find the imperative within my self-understanding as a feminist is to view the politics of anti-imperialism, black struggles, nationalism, within the terms and from the perspective of gender and the feminist movement. In contrast, and to my confusion, I find myself viewing women-identified theories unshakingly from the perspective of my own racial positioning, my own experience of racism, the histories of black people and my own family. These two strategies need not be mutually exclusive, experientially or theoretically, and I will not make the decision to abandon feminism in an either/or dynamic which would unacceptably limit and reduce my life.

Feminism's response to heterosexuality has repeatedly been to dismiss it, to criticize it as a neutral or normalizing area, as a threat to women, as akin to capitalism and male dominance. The other story which remains almost in the guise of feminism's guilty shadow, is that of solidarity with a community, loyalty to a history which still needs, cries out, to be honoured. I think of the black and white lesbians whose emotional suffering rests on their feeling of exile from fathers, brothers, mothers, the warmth of familial acceptance, the joy of staying with ease within the boundaries of home. I am also, necessarily reminded of those women, like myself, who feel caught between two contradictory heritages, coerced alternatively into the context of one or the other, disqualified from forming an identity in harmony with both. The politics of identity do, of course, involve a mass of contradictions, lived as shocks and moments of acute anxiety, invisibility, that sickness of standing at one remove from the body. A mixed-race identity reads as a contradiction in terms. Similarly, but not the same, heterosexuality as a feminist political choice invites an argument.

Can we dream of a feminist movement which could allow women to make different sexual choices within different social categories? Can we dare to suggest a changing pattern of thought where women concentrate the focus of their struggles in different ways? I feel rebellious of a feminist insistence that this movement come first or only, that patriarchy is the first and only key to imperialism, racial domination and capitalism. The feel, the size of the loss I suffer in the face of this call for all my attention, all my love, the anger I am taught to believe is negative, leads me to insist on claiming it all, to recognize, in my own feminist commitment, other locations, other desires which do not necessarily speak the same language.

Feminism can detach itself from the reminiscence of middle-class, white exclusivity, and the strength of anti-racist, socialist or black feminisms is evidence of the flexibility, the recognitions which the feminist movement negotiates. I want to suggest that loving men – as well as women – is not an accident, a problem for feminist identification, but a valid move towards cultural or racial self-determination; another or temporary choice for full self-expression. We need to move beyond locating contradiction as a barrier to political organization. Heterosexuality needs to be recognized as another instance of standing in more than one place at the same time, when race, class, culture, nationality go deeper than the skin.

2.10

HETEROSEXUALITY, POWER AND PLEASURE

Stevi Jackson

This article was a later contribution to the same debate, drawing on earlier analyses of sex classes developed in the French context (see Readings 2.4 and 2.5). It is argued that while feminists need a critical perspective on heterosexuality, we should not reduce the institution to its sexual practice, nor regard sex with men as essentially oppressive. This piece also anticipates some of the issues surrounding pleasure and power which are the focus of the next section.

Since the late 1960s, feminists have been exposing the complexity and ubiquity of power within heterosexual relations. Debates on heterosexuality have, however, often been painful and divisive.

[. . .]

Heterosexuality cannot form the basis of a feminist political identity precisely because it is the institutionalized patriarchal norm. Just as being white in a racist society can only be a political rallying point for the racist right, being heterosexual cannot become a political identity except to preserve heterosexual privilege – as in the construction of the 'heterosexual community' in discourses around AIDS. But heterosexuality can, like whiteness, be problematized by making it visible, challenging its privileged status and struggling to change it in practice.

Since heterosexuality as an institution entails women's subordination to men, it is hardly surprising that heterosexual feminists prefer to be defined in terms of their feminism – their resistance to patriarchy – rather than their heterosexuality, their association with men.[1] Resisting the label heterosexual, however, can imply a refusal to question and challenge both the institution and one's own practice. It can also

From S. Jackson, 'Hetrosexuality, power and pleasure', *Feminism and Psychology*, 5(1), 1995.

serve to invalidate lesbianism as a form of resistance to patriarchy and to deny the specific forms of oppression that lesbians face. It is for this reason that Kitzinger and Wilkinson[2] are critical of those who 'call for the dissolution of the dichotomous categories "lesbian" and "heterosexual"'.[3] Questioning this binary opposition, however, need not be a way of getting heterosexual feminists off the hook: it can represent an honest attempt to problematize heterosexuality. It should also be noted that it is not only heterosexual feminists who are engaged in this deconstructive enterprise, but also lesbian queer theorists.[4] These writers frame their arguments from a postmodernist stance, which does make it difficult to account for the systematic structural bases of any form of oppression and can undercut political identities we forge for ourselves.[5] Nonetheless, treating the categories 'lesbian' and 'heterosexual' as problematic is by no means antithetical to radical feminism: indeed, I would argue that it is essential. In their rejoinder to their critics, Kitzinger and Wilkinson[6] themselves make it clear that they see these categories as socially constructed.

A helpful way of theorizing this is through materialist radical feminism. From this perspective gender and sexual categories are not simply discursive constructs but are rooted in material inequalities. If we take Delphy's[7] argument that 'men' and 'women' are not biologically given entities but social groups defined by the hierarchical and exploitative relationship between them, then the division between hetero and homosexualities is, by extension, also a product of this class relation – the categories heterosexual and lesbian could not exist without our being able to define ourselves and others by gender. To desire the 'other sex' or indeed to desire 'the same sex' presupposes the prior existence of 'men' and 'women' as socially – and erotically – meaningful categories. Desire as currently socially constituted, whether lesbian or heterosexual, is inevitably gendered. What is specific to heterosexual desire, however, is that it is premised on gender *difference*, on the sexual 'otherness' of the desired object. From a materialist feminist perspective this difference is not an anatomical one but a social one: it is the hierarchy of gender which 'transforms an anatomical difference (which is itself devoid of social implications) into a relevant distinction for social practice'.[8] Since it is gender hierarchy which renders these anatomical differences socially and erotically significant, it is hardly surprising heterosexual sex has been culturally constructed around an eroticization of power.

This eroticization of power is not reducible to the mere juxtaposition of certain body parts. There is no absolute reason why desire for someone with a male body needs necessarily to position women as passive or privilege certain sexual acts above others, or even why the act of sexual intercourse has to be thought of as penetration or as something men do to women. The coercive equation of sex = coitus = something men do to women is not an inevitable consequence of an anatomical female relating sexually to an anatomical male, but the product of the social relations under which those bodies meet. Those social relations can be challenged. Even the most trenchant critics of heterosexuality and penetrative sex such as Jeffreys[9] and Dworkin[10] recognize that it is not male and female anatomy nor even, in Dworkin's case, the act of intercourse itself which constitute the problem, but rather the way in which heterosexuality is institutionalized and practised under patriarchy.

Initially feminist analyses of heterosexual sexuality dwelt on its coercive aspects and the lack of pleasure derived from it – and this remains a central issue.[11] Now, however, women's pleasure in heterosexuality has come under fire.[12] While I endorse the need to problematize heterosexual pleasure, there are dangers in simply condemning it unilaterally as eroticized power without taking into account heterosexual feminists' resistance to that power, the ways in which we have contested forms of sexual practice which prioritize male pleasure.[13] We have sought to decentre penetration, to reconceptualize it in ways which do not position us as passive objects, and to change the ways in which we engage in sex with men. Kitzinger and Wilkinson are scathing about such strategies. Attempts to change the meaning of penetration, for example 'obscure the problem of the *institutionalization* of penile penetration under heteropatriarchy'.[14] Those heterosexual contributors to the recent debate who deal with this issue, such as Rowland[15] and Robinson,[16] are in fact very clear about the distinction between the institutionalization of penetration and women's varied experience and practice of it. Wilkinson and Kitzinger, however, see the institution as totally determining practice. The current ordering of gender relations certainly constrains the meaning that can be applied to physical acts and imposes limits on our resistance, but there is some room for manoeuvre within these constraints. To deny this is to deny heterosexual women any agency, to see us as doomed to submit to men's desires whether as unwilling victims or misguided dupes.

It cannot be assumed all women who take pleasure in heterosexual sex are simply wallowing in a masochistic eroticization of our subordination. Some feminists, it is true, endorse the conventional (patriarchal) wisdom that 'new men' are insufficiently masculine to be sexually desirable.[17] I do not think, however, that all heterosexual women, and still less all heterosexual feminists, are looking for domineering, granite jawed romantic heroes.

[. . .]

Kitzinger and Wilkinson[18] imply that we cannot escape the symbolic power of penetration even though some women 'take pleasure in the sensation of a full vagina'. Hollway[19] objects to this phrase on the grounds that it is impersonal and negates women's feelings of intimacy with a male lover. Her traditionally feminine emphasis on the emotional meanings of penetrative sex says no more to me about specifically physical, sensual pleasure than Kitzinger and Wilkinson's description. The coyness of the latter underlines the lack of a public language with which to describe such pleasures – what exists in the public domain is a pornographic discourse of male thrusting activity and female writhing passivity (occasionally reversed). That discussing it publicly at all in feminist circles is distinctly taboo does not help us to develop an alternative language which might enhance our critical understanding of both pleasure and displeasure in heterosex. It also disempowers women struggling to define and assert their right to pleasure.[20]

There are also, as Caroline Ramazanoglu[21] reminds us, very real material constraints on seeking heterosexual pleasure. As she says, we 'need to distinguish between the undoubted possibilities of heterosexual pleasure, and the extremely powerful social forces which constrain these possibilities from being more widely realized.'[22] We academic feminists are relatively privileged compared with most other women – we have access both to economic independence and to feminist ideas and support networks – hence we are better able to dictate the terms under which we enter into heterosexual relations. Many of us have [. . .] managed to effect some changes in our sexual desires and practices even if we have failed to transform ourselves into lesbians. This suggests that heterosexual desire is not fixed and unchanging over the span of our lives, that heterosexual women are not inevitably trapped into a choice between eschewing pleasure or eroticizing our subordination.

I am not suggesting that what heterosexual feminists do in bed constitutes a threat to patriarchy. Conversely, I am not sure that what we do in bed, or who we do it with, is as socially and politically significant as some lesbian feminists imply. Although I have concentrated on sexual pleasure in this article, I do not view heterosexuality as simply a sexual institution. It is founded as much on men's access to women's unpaid work as on their sexual access to our bodies; the home comforts produced by women's domestic labour are at least as important in maintaining patriarchal privilege as the sexual servicing men receive. Sexuality is only one site of women's oppression and needs to be placed in context as such. To give too much weight to sexual desire, practice and identity is to ignore the many other ways in which male domination is colluded with and resisted and the many other means by which women's subordination is perpetuated and challenged.

NOTES

1. See Julia Swindells, 'A straight outing', *Trouble and Strife*, no. 26, 1993, pp. 40–4.
2. Celia Kitzinger and Sue Wilkinson, 'Theorizing heterosexuality', in S. Wilkinson and C. Kitzinger (eds), *Heterosexuality: A Feminism & Psychology Reader*, London: Sage, 1993, p. 7.
3. For example, Alison Young, 'The authority of the name', in S. Wilkinson and C. Kitzinger (eds), *Heterosexuality: A 'Feminism & Psychology' Reader*, London: Sage, 1993; Mary Gergen, 'Unbundling our binaries – genders, sexualities, desires', in S. Wilkinson and C. Kitzinger (eds), *Heterosexuality: A 'Feminism & Psychology' Reader*, London: Sage, 1993.
4. See Diana Fuss, *Inside/Out: Lesbian Theories, Gay Theories*, New York: Routledge, 1991; Judith Butler, *Gender Trouble: Feminism and the Subversion of Identity*, New York: Routledge, 1990.
5. See Stevi Jackson, 'The amazing deconstructing woman: the perils of postmodern feminism', *Trouble and Strife*, 25, 1992, pp. 25–31.
6. Celia Kitzinger and Sue Wilkinson, 'Re-viewing heterosexuality', *Feminism & Psychology*, 4(2), 1994, pp. 320–1.
7. Christine, Delphy, *Close to Home: A Material Analysis of Women's Oppression*, London: Hutchinson, 1984; 'Rethinking sex and gender', *Women's Studies International Forum*, 16(1), 1993, pp. 1–9.
8. Delphy, *Close to Home*, p. 144.
9. Shelia Jeffreys, *Anti-Climax: A Feminist Perspective of the Sexual Revolution*, London: The Women's Press, 1990.
10. Andrea Dworkin, *Intercourse*, London: Secker & Warburg, 1987.
11. See Janet Holland, Caroline Ramazanoglu, Sue Sharpe and Rachel Thomson, 'Power and desire: the embodiment of female sexuality', *Feminist Review*, 46, 1994, pp. 21–38.
12. Jeffreys, *Anti-Climax*; Kitzinger and Wilkinson, 'Theorizing heterosexuality'; Celia Kitzinger, 'Problematizing pleasure: radical feminist deconstructions of sexuality and power', in H.L. Radtke and H.J. Stam (eds), *Power/Gender: Social Relations in Theory and Practice*, London: Sage, 1994.
13. Robyn Rowland, 'Radical feminist heterosexuality: the personal and the political', in S. Wilkinson and C. Kitzinger (eds), *Heterosexuality: A 'Feminism & Psychology' Reader*, London: Sage, 1993; Victoria Robinson, 'Heterosexuality: beginnings and connections', in S. Wilkinson and C. Kitzinger (eds), *Heterosexuality: A 'Feminism & Psychology' Reader*, London: Sage, 1993.
14. Kitzinger and Wilkinson, 'Theorizing heterosexuality', p. 21; emphasis in original.
15. Rowland, 'Radical feminist heterosexuality'.
16. Robinson, 'Heterosexuality'.

17. For example, Naomi Segal, 'Why can't a good man be sexy? Why can't a sexy man be good?', in D. Porter (ed.), *Between Men and Feminism*, London: Routledge, 1992.
18. Kitzinger and Wilkinson, 'Re-viewing heterosexuality', p. 21.
19. Wendy Holloway, 'Theorizing heterosexuality: a response', *Feminism & Psychology*, 3(3), 1993, pp. 412–17.
20. Holland *et al.*, 'Power and desire'.
21. Caroline Ramazanoglu, 'Theorizing heterosexuality: a response to Wendy Holloway', *Feminism & Psychology*, 4(2), 1994, pp. 320–1.
22. *Ibid.*, p. 321.

PART THREE

POWER AND PLEASURE

FEMINISM, MARXISM, METHOD AND THE STATE
An Agenda for Theory

Catharine A. MacKinnon

Catharine MacKinnon is among those feminists who have identified sexual abuse and sexuality more generally as fundamental to women's oppression. In this article she establishes parallels between men's violation of women's sexuality and capital's appropriation of workers' labour. For MacKinnon, then, men's sexual dominance over women is a fundamental feminist issue.

Sexuality is to feminism what work is to marxism: that which is most one's own, yet most taken away. Marxist theory argues that society is fundamentally constructed of the relations people form as they do and make things needed to survive humanly. Work is the social process of shaping and transforming the material and social worlds, creating people as social beings as they create value. It is that activity by which people become who they are. Class is its structure, production its consequence, capital its congealed form, and control its issue.

Implicit in feminist theory is a parallel argument: the molding, direction, and expression of sexuality organizes society into two sexes – women and men – which division underlies the totality of social relations. Sexuality is that social process which creates, organizes, expresses, and directs desire,[1] creating the social beings we know as women and men, as their relations create society. As work is to marxism, sexuality to feminism is socially constructed yet constructing, universal as activity yet historically specific, jointly comprised of matter and mind. As the organized expropriation of the work of some for the benefit of others defines a class – workers – the organized expropriation of the sexuality of some for the use of others defines the sex, woman. Heterosexuality is its structure, gender and family its congealed forms,

From C.A. MacKinnon, 'Feminism, Marxism, method, and the state', *Signs*, 7(3), 1982.

sex roles its qualities generalized to social persona, reproduction a consequence, and control its issue.

Marxism and feminism are theories of power and its distribution: inequality. They provide accounts of how social arrangements of patterned disparity can be internally rational yet unjust. But their specificity is not incidental. In marxism to be deprived of one's work, in feminism of one's sexuality, defines each one's conception of lack of power per se. They do not mean to exist side by side to insure that two separate spheres of social life are not overlooked, the interests of two groups are not obscured, or the contributions of two sets of variables are not ignored. They exist to argue, respectively, that the relations in which many work and few gain, in which some fuck and others get fucked,[2] are the prime moment of politics.

[. . .]

If the literature on sex roles and the investigations of particular issues are read in light of each other, each element of the female *gender* stereotype is revealed as, in fact, *sexual*. Vulnerability means the appearance/reality of easy sexual access; passivity means receptivity and disabled resistance, enforced by trained physical weakness; softness means pregnability by something hard. Incompetence seeks help as vulnerability seeks shelter, inviting the embrace that becomes the invasion, trading exclusive access for protection . . . from the same access. Domesticity nurtures the consequent progeny, proof of potency, and ideally waits at home dressed in saran wrap.[3] Woman's infantilization evokes pedophilia: fixation on dismembered body parts (the breast man, the leg man) evokes fetishism; idolization of vapidity, necrophilia. Narcissism insures that woman identifies with that image of herself that man holds up: 'Hold still, we are going to do your portrait, so that you can begin looking like it right away'.[4] Masochism means that pleasure in violation becomes her sensuality. Lesbians so violate the sexuality implicit in female gender stereotypes as not to be considered women at all.

Socially, femaleness means femininity, which means attractiveness to men, which means sexual attractiveness, which means sexual availability on male terms.[5] What defines woman as such is what turns men on. Good girls are 'attractive,' bad girls 'provocative.' Gender socialization is the process through which women come to identify themselves as sexual beings, as beings that exist for men. It is that process through which women internalize (make their own) a male image of their sexuality *as* their identity as women.[6] It is not just an illusion. Feminist inquiry into women's own experience of sexuality revises prior comprehensions of sexual issues and transforms the concept of sexuality itself – its determinants and its role in society and politics. According to this revision, one 'becomes a woman' – acquires and identifies with the status of the female – not so much through physical maturation or inculcation into appropriate role behavior as through the experience of sexuality: a complex unity of physicality, emotionality, identity, and status affirmation. Sex as gender and sex as sexuality are thus defined in terms of each other, but it is sexuality that determines gender, not the other way around. This, the central but never stated insight of Kate Millett's *Sexual Politics*,[7] resolves the duality in the term 'sex' itself: what women learn in order to 'have sex,' in order to 'become women' – woman as gender – comes through the experience of, and is a condition for 'having sex' – woman as sexual object for man, the use of women's sexuality by men. Indeed, to the extent sexuality is social, women's sexuality *is* its use, just as our femaleness *is* its alterity.

Many issues that appear sexual from this standpoint have not been seen as such, nor have they been seen as defining a politics. Incest, for example, is commonly seen as a question of distinguishing the real evil, a crime against the family, from girlish seductiveness or fantasy. Contraception and abortion have been framed as matters of reproduction and fought out as proper or improper social constraints on nature. Or they are seen as private, minimizing state intervention into intimate relations. Sexual harassment was a nonissue, then became a problem of distinguishing personal relationships or affectionate flirtation from abuse of position. Lesbianism, when visible, has been either a perversion or not, to be tolerated or not. Pornography has been considered a question of freedom to speak and depict the erotic, as against the obscene or violent. Prostitution has been understood either as mutual lust and degradation or an equal exchange of sexual need for economic need. The issue in rape has been whether the intercourse was provoked/mutually desired, or whether it was forced; was it sex or violence? Across and beneath these issues, sexuality itself has been divided into parallel provinces: traditionally, religion or biology; in modern transformation, morality or psychology. Almost never politics.

In a feminist perspective, the formulation of each issue, in the terms just described, expresses ideologically the same interest that the problem it formulates expresses concretely: the interest from the male point of view. Women experience the sexual events these issues codify[8] as a cohesive whole within which each resonates. The defining theme of that whole is the male pursuit of control over women's sexuality – men not as individuals nor as biological beings, but as a gender group characterized by maleness as socially constructed, of which this pursuit is definitive. For example, women who need abortions see contraception as a struggle not only for control over the biological products of sexual expression but over the social rhythms and mores of sexual intercourse. These norms often appear hostile to women's self-protection even when the technology is at hand. As an instance of such norms, women notice that sexual harassment looks a great deal like ordinary heterosexual initiation under conditions of gender inequality. Few women are in a position to refuse unwanted sexual initiatives. That consent rather than nonmutuality is the line between rape and intercourse further exposes the inequality in normal social expectations. So does the substantial amount of male force allowed in the focus on the woman's resistance, which tends to be disabled by socialization to passivity. If sex is ordinarily accepted as something men do *to* women, the better question would be whether consent is a meaningful concept. Penetration (often by a penis) is also substantially more central to both the legal definition of rape and the male definition of sexual intercourse than it is to women's sexual violation or sexual pleasure. Rape in marriage expresses the male sense of entitlement to access to women they annex; incest extends it. Although most women are raped by men they know, the closer the relation, the less women are allowed to claim it was rape. Pornography becomes difficult to distinguish from art and ads once it is clear that what is degrading to women is compelling to the consumer. Prostitutes sell the unilaterality that pornography advertises. That most of these issues codify behavior that is neither countersystemic nor exceptional is supported by women's experience as victims: these behaviors are either not illegal or are effectively permitted on a large scale. As women's experience blurs the lines between deviance and normalcy, it obliterates the distinction between abuses *of* women and the social definition of what a woman *is*.[9]

These investigations reveal rape, incest, sexual harassment, pornography, and prostitution as not primarily abuses of physical force, violence, authority, or economics. They are abuses of sex. They need not and do not rely for their coerciveness upon forms of enforcement other than the sexual; that those forms of enforcement, at least in this context, are themselves sexualized is closer to the truth. They are not the erotization *of* something else: eroticism *itself* exists in their form. Nor are they perversions of art and morality. They *are* art and morality from the male point of view. They are sexual because they express the relations, values, feelings, norms, and behaviors of the culture's sexuality, in which considering things like rape, pornography, incest, or lesbianism deviant, perverse, or blasphemous is part of their excitement potential.

Sexuality, then, is a form of power. Gender, as socially constructed, embodies it, not the reverse. Women and men are divided by gender, made into the sexes as we know them, by the social requirements of heterosexuality, which institutionalizes male sexual dominance and female sexual submission.[10] If this is true, sexuality is the linchpin of gender inequality.

A woman is a being who identifies and is identified as one whose sexuality exists for someone else, who is socially male. Women's sexuality is the capacity to arouse desire in that someone. If what is sexual about a woman is what the male point of view requires for excitement, have male requirements so usurped its terms as to have become them? Considering women's sexuality in this way forces confrontation with whether there is any such thing. Is women's sexuality its absence? If being *for* another is the whole of women's sexual construction, it can be no more escaped by separatism, men's temporary concrete absence, than eliminated or qualified by permissiveness, which, in this context, looks like women emulating male roles. As Susan Sontag said: 'The question is: *what* sexuality are women to be liberated to enjoy? Merely to remove the onus placed upon the sexual expressiveness of women is a hollow victory if the sexuality they become freer to enjoy remains the old one that converts women into objects. . . . This already 'freer' sexuality mostly reflects a spurious idea of freedom: the right of each person, briefly, to exploit and dehumanize someone else. Without a change in the very norms of sexuality, the liberation of women is a meaningless goal. Sex as such is not liberating for women. Neither is more sex.'[11] Does removing or revising gender constraints upon sexual expression change or even challenge its norms?[12] This question ultimately is one of social determination in the broadest sense: its mechanism, permeability, specificity, and totality. If women are socially defined such that female sexuality cannot be lived or spoken or felt or even somatically sensed apart from its enforced definition, so that it *is* its own lack, then there is no such thing as a woman as such, there are only walking embodiments of men's projected needs. For feminism, asking whether there is, socially, a female sexuality is the same as asking whether women exist.

Methodologically, the feminist concept of the personal as political is an attempt to answer this question. Relinquishing all instinctual, natural, transcendental, and divine authority, this concept grounds women's sexuality on purely relational terrain, anchoring women's power and accounting for women's discontent in the same world they stand against. The personal as political is not a simile, not a metaphor, and not an analogy. It does not mean that what occurs in personal life is similar to, or comparable with, what occurs in the public arena. It is not an application of categories from social life to the private world, as when Engels (followed by Bebel) says that in the family the husband is the bourgeois and the wife represents the proletariat.[13] Nor is it an equation of two spheres which remain analytically distinct, as when Reich interprets state behavior in sexual terms,[14] or a one-way infusion of one sphere into the other as when Lasswell interprets political behavior as the displacement of personal problems into public objects.[15] It means that women's distinctive experience as women occurs within that sphere that has been socially lived as the personal – private, emotional, interiorized, particular, individuated, intimate – so that what it is to *know* the *politics* of woman's situation is to know women's personal lives.

The substantive principle governing the authentic politics of women's personal lives is pervasive powerlessness to men, expressed and reconstituted daily *as* sexuality. To say that the personal is political means that gender as a division of power is discoverable and verifiable through women's intimate experience of sexual objectification, which is definitive of and synonymous with women's lives as gender female. Thus, to feminism, the personal is epistemologically the political, and its epistemology is its politics.[16] Feminism, on this level, is the theory of women's point of view. It is the theory of Judy Grahn's 'common woman'[17] speaking Adrienne Rich's 'common language'.[18] Consciousness raising is its quintessential expression. Feminism does not appropriate an existing method – such as scientific method – and apply it to a different sphere of society to reveal its preexisting political aspect. Consciousness raising not only comes to know different things as politics; it necessarily comes to know them in a different way. Women's experience of politics, of life as sex object, gives rise to its own method of appropriating that reality: feminist method.[19] As its own kind of social analysis, within yet outside the male paradigm just as women's lives are, it has a distinctive theory of the *relation* between method and truth, the individual and her social surroundings, the presence and place of the natural and spiritual in culture and society, and social being and causality itself.

Having been objectified as sexual beings while stigmatized as ruled by subjective passions, women reject the distinction between knowing subject and known object – the division between subjective and objective postures – as the means to comprehend social life. Disaffected from objectivity, having been its prey, but excluded from its world through relegation to subjective inwardness, women's interest lies in overthrowing the distinction itself.

[. . .]

Objectification makes sexuality a material reality of women's lives, not just a psychological, attitudinal, or ideological one.[20] It obliterates the mind/matter distinction that such a division is premised upon. Like the value of a commodity, women's sexual desirability is fetishized: it is made to appear a quality of the object itself, spontaneous and inherent, independent of the social relation which creates it, uncontrolled by the force that requires it. It helps if the object cooperates: hence, the vaginal orgasm,[21] hence, faked orgasms altogether.[22] Women's sexualness, like male prowess, is no less real for being mythic. It is embodied. Commodities do have value, but only because value is a social property arising from the totality of the same social relations which, unconscious of their determination, fetishize it. Women's bodies possess no less real desirability – or, probably, desire. Sartre exemplifies the problem on the epistemological level: 'But if I desire a house, or a glass of water, or a woman's body, how could this body, this glass, this piece of property reside in my desire and how can my desire be anything but the consciousness of these objects as desirable?'[23] Indeed. Objectivity is the methodological stance of which objectification is the social process. Sexual objectification is the primary process of the subjection of women. It unites act with word, construction with expression, perception with enforcement, myth with reality. Man fucks woman; subject verb object.

The distinction between objectification and alienation is called into question by this analysis. Objectification in marxist materialism is thought to be the foundation of human freedom, the work process whereby a subject becomes embodied in products and relationships.[24] Alienation is the socially contingent distortion of that process, a reification of products and relations which prevents them from being, and being seen as, dependent on human agency.[25] But from the point of view of the object, objectification *is* alienation. For women, there is no distinction between objectification and alienation because women have not authored objectifications, we have been them. Women have been the nature, the matter, the acted upon, to be subdued by the acting subject seeking to embody himself in the social world. Reification is not just an illusion to the reified: it is also their reality.

[. . .]

Feminism stands in relation to marxism as marxism does to classical political economy: its final conclusion and ultimate critique. Compared with marxism, the place of thought and things in method and reality are reversed in a seizure of power that penetrates subject with object and theory with practice. In a dual motion, feminism turns marxism inside out and on its head.

To answer an old question – how is value created and distributed? – Marx needed to create an entirely new account of the social world. To answer an equally old question, or to question an equally old reality – what explains the inequality of women to men? or, how does desire become domination? or, what is male power? – feminism revolutionizes politics.

NOTES

1. 'Desire' is selected as a term parallel to 'value' in marxist theory to refer to that substance felt to be primordial or aborginal but posited by the theory as social and contingent. The sense in which I mean it is consonant with its development in contemporary French Feminist Theories e.g., in Hélène Cixous, 'The laugh of the Medusa: viewpoint,' trans. Keith Cohen and Paula Cohen, *Signs*, 1(4), Summer 1976, pp. 875–93; and in works of Gauthier, Irigaray, Leclerc, Duras, and Kristeva, in Elaine Marks and Isabelle de Courtivron (eds), *New French Feminisms: An Anthology*, Amherst, Mass.: University of Massachussets

Press, 1980. My use of the term is to be distinguished from that of Gilles Deleuze and Felix Guattari, *Anti-Oedipus: Capitalism and Schizophrenia*, New York: Viking Press, 1977; and Guy Hocquenghem, *Homosexual Desire*, London: Allison & Busby, 1978, for example.

2. I know no nondegraded English verb for the activity of sexual expression that would allow a construction parallel to, for example, 'I am working,' a phrase that could apply to nearly any activity. This fact of language may reflect and contribute to the process of obscuring sexuality's pervasiveness in social life. Nor is there *any* active verb meaning 'to act sexually' that specifically envisions a woman's action. If language constructs as well as expresses the social world, these words support heterosexual values.

3. Marabel Morgan, *The Total Woman*, Old Tappan, NJ: Fleming H. Revell Co., 1973. 'Total Woman' makes blasphemous sexuality into a home art, redomesticating what prostitutes have marketed as forbidden.

4. Cixous, 'The laugh of the Medusa', p. 892.

5. Indications are that this is true not only in Western industrial society; further cross-cultural research is definitely needed.

6. Love justifies this on the emotional level. Shulamith Firestone, *The Dialetic of Sex: The Case For Feminist Revolution*, New York: William Morrow & Co., 1972, see ch. 6.

7. Millett's analysis is pervasively animated by the sense that women's status is sexually determined. It shapes her choice of authors, scenes, and themes and underlies her most pointed criticisms of women's depictions. Her explicit discussion, however, vacillates between clear glimpses of that argument and statements nearly to the contrary.

8. Each of these issues is discussed at length in the second part of this article 'Towards feminist judisprudence,' *Signs*, 8(2) 1983, pp. 635–58.

9. On abortion and contraception, see Kristin Luker, *Taking Chances: Abortion and the Decision Not to Contracept*, Berkeley: University of California Press, 1975. On rape, see Diana E.H. Russell, *Rape: The Victim's Perspective*, New York: Stein & Day, 1977; Andrea Medea and Kathleen Thompson, *Against Rape*, New York: Farrar, Strauss & Giroux, 1974; Lorenne N.G. Clark and Debra Lewis, *Rape: The Price of Coercive Sexuality*, Toronto: Women's Press, 1977; Susan Griffin, *Rape: the Power of Consciousness*, San Francisco: Harper & Row, 1979; Kalamu ya Salaam, 'A radical analysis from the African-American perspective, in his *Our Women Keep Our Skies from Falling*, New Orleans: Nkombo, 1980, pp. 25–40. On incest, see Judith Herman and Lisa Hirschman, 'Father daughter incest,' *Signs*, 2(1), Summer 1977, pp. 735–56. On sexual harassment, see my *Sexual Harassment of Working Women*, New Haven: Yale University Press, 1979. On pornography, see Andrea Dworkin, *Pornography: Men Possessing Women*, New York: G.P. Putnam & Sons, 1981.

10. Ellen Morgan, *The Erotization of Male Dominamce/Female Submission*, Pittsburgh: Know, Inc., 1975; Adrienne Rich, 'Compulsory heterosexuality and lesbian existence,' *Signs*, 5(4), Summer 1980, pp. 631–60.

11. Susan Sontag, 'The Third World of women,' *Partisan Review*, 40(2), 1973, pp. 180–206, esp. p. 188.

12. The same question could be asked of lesbian sadomasochism: when women engage in ritualized sexual dominance and submission, does it express the male structure or subvert it? The answer depends upon whether one has a social or biological definition of gender and sexuality and then upon the content of these definitions. Lesbian sex, simply as sex between women, does not by definition transcend the erotization of dominance and submission and their social equation with masculinity and feminity. Butch/femme as *sexual* (not just gender) role playing, together with parallels in lesbian sadomasochism's 'top' and 'bottom,' suggest to me that sexual conformity extends far beyond gender object mores. For a contrary view see Pat Califia, *Sapphistry: The Book of Lesbian S/M Sexuality Reader*, Berkeley: Samois, 1979, pp. 28–35.

13. F. Engels, *Origin of the Family, Private Property and the State*, New York: International Publishers, 1942; August Bebel, *Women under Socialism*, trans. Daniel DeLeon, New York: New York Labour Press, 1904.

14. Wilhem Reich, *Sex-Pol: Essays, 1929–1934*, New York: Random House, 1972. He examines fascism, for example, as a question of how the masses can be made to desire their own repression. This might be seen as a precursor to the feminist question of how female desire *itself* can become the lust for self-annihilation.

15. Harold Lasswell, *Psychoanalysis and Politics*, Chicago: University of Chicago Press, 1930.

16. The aphorism 'Feminism is the theory; lesbianism is the practice' has been attributed to Ti-Grace Atkinson by Anne Koedt, 'Lesbianism and feminism,' in Anne Koedt, Ellen Levine and Anita Rapone (eds), *Radical Feminism*, New York: New York Times Book Co., 1973, p. 246. See also Radicalesbians, 'The woman identified woman,' *ibid.*, pp. 24–45; Ti-Grace Atkinson, 'Lesbianism & feminism,' *Amazon Odyssey: The First Collection of Writings by the Political Pioneer of the Women's Movement*, New York: Link Books, 1974: 83–8; Jill Johnston, *Lesbian Nation: The Feminist Solution*, New York: Simon & Schuster, 1973, pp. 167, 185, 278. This aphorism accepts a simplistic relationship between theory and practice. Feminism reconceptualizes the connection between being and thinking such that it may be more accurate to say that feminism is the epistemology of which lesbianism is an ontology.

17. Judy Grahn, *The Work of a Common Woman*, New York: St Martin Press, 1978. 'The Common Woman' poems are on pp. 61–73.

18. Adrienne Rich, 'Origins and history of consciousness,' in *The Dream of a Common Language: Poems, 1974–1977*, New York: W.W. Norton & Co., 1978, p. 7. This means that a women's movement exists wherever

women identify collectively to resist/reclaim their determinants as such. This feminist redefinition of consciousness requires a corresponding redefinition of the process of mobilizing it: feminist *organizing*. The transformation from subordinate group to movement parallels Marx's distinction between a class 'in itself' and a class 'for itself.' See Karl Marx, *The Poverty of Philosophy*, New York: International Publishers, 1963, p. 195.

19. In addition to the references in n. 1, see Sandra Lee Bartky, 'Toward a phenomenology of feminist consciousness,' in Mary Vetterling-Braggin *et al.* (eds) *Feminism and Philosophy* Totowa, NJ: Littlefield, Adams & Co., 1977. Susan Griffin reflects/recreates the process: 'We do not rush to speech. We allow ourselves to be moved. We do not attempt objectivity. . . . We said we had experienced this ourselves. I felt so much for her then, she said, with her head cradled in my lap, she said, I knew what to do. We said we were moved to see her go through what we had gone through. We said this gave us some knowledge,' *Woman and Nature: The Roaring Inside Her*, New York: Harper & Row, 1978, p. 197. Assertions such as 'our politics begin with our feelings' have emerged from the practice of consciousness raising. Somewhere between mirror-reflexive determination and transcendence of determinants, 'feelings' are seen as both access to truth – at times a bit phenomenologically transparent – and as artifact of politics. There is both suspicion of feelings and affirmation of their health. They become simultaneously an inner expression of outer lies and less contaminated resource for verification. See San Francisco Redstockings, 'Our politics begin with our feelings,' in Betty Roszak and Theodore Roszak (eds), *Masculine/Feminine: Readings in Sexual Mythology and the Liberation of Women*, New York: Harper & Row, 1969.

20. The critique of sexual objectification first became visible in the American women's movement with the disruption of Miss America Pagent in September 1968. Robin Morgan 'Women disrupt the Miss America Pageant,' *Rat*, September 1978, reprinted in *Going Too Far: The Personal Chronicle of a Feminist*, New York: Random House, 1977, pp. 62–7. The most compelling account of sexual objectification I know is contained in the following description of women's depiction in art and media: 'According to usage and conventions which are at last being questioned but have by no means been overcome, the social presence of woman is different in kind from that of a man. . . . A man's presence suggests what he is capable of doing to you or for you. By contrast, a woman's presence expresses her own attitude to herself, and *defines what can and cannot be done to her*. . . . To be born a woman has been to be born, within an allotted and confined space, into the keeping of men. The social presence of women has developed as a result of ingenuity in living under the tutelage within such a limited space. But this has been at the cost of a woman's self being split into two. A woman must continually watch herself. She is almost continually accompanied by her own image of herself . . . she comes to consider the surveyor and the surveyed within her as the two constituent parts yet always distinct elements of her identity as a woman. She has to survey everything she is and everything she does because how she appears to others, and ultimately how she appears to men, *is of crucial importance for what is normally thought of as the success in her life*. Her own sense of being in herself is supplanted by a sense of being appreciated as herself by another. One might simplify this by saying: men act; woman appear. *Men look at women. Women watch themselves being looked at*. . . . This determines not only most relations between men and women but also the relation of women to themselves. The surveyor of woman in herself is male: the surveyed, female. Thus she turns herself into an object – and most particularly an object of vision: a sight' (John Berger, *Ways of Seeing*, New York: Viking Press, 1972, pp. 46–7; my emphasis). All that is missing here is an explicit recognition that this process embodies a feminist context, aesthetics, including beauty and imagery, become the most political of subjects. See Purple September Staff, 'The normative status of heterosexuality,' in Charlotte Bunch and Nancy Myron (eds), *Lesbianism and the Women's Movement*, Baltimore: Diana Press, 1975, pp. 79–83, esp. pp. 80–1.

Marxist attempts to deal with sexual objectification have not connected the issue with the politics of aesthetics or with subordination: 'She becomes a sexual object only in a relationship, when she allows man to treat her in a certain depersonalizing, degrading way; and vice versa, a woman does not become a sexual subject simply by neglecting her appearance. There is no reason why a women's liberation activist should not try to look pretty and attractive. One universal human aspiration of all times was to raise reality to the level of art . . . Beauty is a value in itself' (Mihailo, Markovic, 'Women's liberation and human emancipation,' in Carol C. Gould and Marx W. Wartofsky (eds), *Women and Philosophy: Toward a Theory of Liberation* New York. G.P. Putnam & Son's, 1976; pp. 165–6. Other attempts come closer, still without achieving a critique, e.g., Power of Women Collective, 'What is a sex object?,' *Socialist Woman: A Journal of the International Marxist Group 1*, no. 1, March/April 1974; p. 7; Dana Densmore, 'On the temptation to be a beautiful object,' in C. Safilios-Rothschild (ed.), *Toward a Sociology of Women*, Lexington, Mass.: Xerox Publication, 1972; Rita Arditti, 'Women as objects: science and sexual politics,' *Science for the People*, 6, 5, September 1974; Charley Shively, 'Cosmetics as an act of revolution,' *Fag Rag* (Boston), reprinted in Pam Mitchell (ed.), *Pink Triangles: Radical Perspectives on Gay Liberation*, Boston: Alyson Publication, 1980. Resentment of white beauty standards is prominent in black Feminism. Beauty standards incapable of achievement by any woman seem to have dual function. They keep women buying products (to the profit of capitalism) and competing for men (to be affirmed by the standard that matters). That is they make women feel ugly and inadequate so we need men and money to defend against rejection/self-revulsion. Black women are further from being able concretely to achieve the standard that no woman can ever achieve, or it would lose its point.

21. Anne Koedt, 'The myth of the vaginal orgasm,' in Koedt *et al.*, *Radical Feminism*, pp. 198–207; Ti-Grace Atkinson, 'Vaginal orgasm as a mass hysterical survival response', op.cit., pp. 5–8.

22. Shere Hite, *The Hite Report: A Nationwide Study of Female Sexuality*, New York: Dell Publishing Co., 1976; pp. 257–66.

23. Jean-Paul Sartre, *Existential Psychoanalysis*, trans. Hazel E. Barnes, Chicago: Henry Regnery Co., 1973, p. 20. A similar treatment of 'desire' occurs in Deleuze and Guattari's description of a man as 'desiring machine,' of a man in relation to the object world: 'Not man as the King of creation, but rather as the being who is in intimate contact with the profound life of all types of beings, who is responsible for even the stars and animal life, and who ceaselessly plugs an organ-machine into an energy-machine, a tree into his body, a breast into his mouth, the sun into his asshole; the eternal custodian of the machines of the universe,' (Deleuze and Guattari, *Anti-Oedipus*, p. 4). Realizing that women, socially, inhabit the object realm transforms this discourse into a quite accurate description of the feminist analysis of women's desirability to man – the breast in the mouth, the energy machine into which he ceaselessly plugs an organ machine. Extending their enquiry into the extent to which this kind of objectification of woman is specific to capitalism (either as a processor in its particular form) does little to redeem the sex-blindness (blind to the sex of its standpoint) of this supposedly general theory. Women are not desiring machines.

24. Peter Berger and Stanley Pullberg, 'Reification and the sociological critique of consciousness,' *New Left Review*, 35, Jan. Feb. 1966; Herbert Marcuse, 'The foundation of historical materialism', in *Studies in Critical Philosophy*, trans. Doris De Bres, Boston: Beacon Press, 1972; Karl Klare, 'Law-Making as Praxis,' *Telos 12 2, Summer 1979, pp. 123–35, esp p. 131.*

25. Istvan Meszaros, *Marx's Theory of Alienation*, London: Merlin Press, 1972; Bertell Ollman, *Alienation: Marx's Conception of Man in Capitalist Society*, London: Cambridge University Press, 1971; H. Marcuse, *Eros and Civilization: A Philosophical Enquiry into Freud*. New York: Random House, 1955, pp. 93–4, 101–2.

3.2

'IT'S EVERYWHERE'
Sexual Violence as a Continuum

Liz Kelly

Sexual violence has been a key focus of concern among feminists, many of whom have made connections between men's sexual abuse of women and routine heterosexual practice. Liz Kelly explicitly employs the idea of a continuum in order to analyse women's accounts of their experience. These accounts were collected from a volunteer sample of sixty British women. The notion of a continuum is not used here to imply that some forms of violence are more extreme than others, but in order to emphasise the regularities underlying diverse forms of abuse and the interconnections between them.

The continuum of sexual violence ranges from extensions of the myriad forms of sexism women encounter everyday through to the all too frequent murder of women and girls by men.

[. . .]

THE THREAT OF VIOLENCE IN PUBLIC, FLASHING AND OBSCENE PHONE CALLS

These three forms of sexual violence arc discussed together as their impact hinges on women's perceptions of what might happen next. Whilst flashing and obscene phone calls are in and of themselves violating, both rely in part for their impact on the explicit or implicit threat of further assault. The link is between the generalized fear that most women experience and forms of visual or verbal violence that accentuate it. All are also unwanted intrusions into women's personal space which transform routine and/or potentially pleasurable activities (for example, a walk in the park, a quiet evening at

From L. Kelly, *Surviving Sexual Violence*, Cambridge. Polity, 1988.

home, a long train journey) into unpleasant, upsetting, disturbing and often threatening experiences.

The continuum of fear and threat extends from being limited to particular times, areas or individuals, through to affecting all aspects of women's daily lives. The extent to which it affects any particular women changes over time; the time frame here can be minute by minute, week by week or longer periods. The wariness of women in the public sphere can be heightened by an awareness of assaults in their local area or, more generally, by media reporting on a national level. Whilst actually in the public sphere, the behaviour of individual or groups of men can affect women's sense of safety. Most women recall an awareness of being watched or possibly followed. It is these perceptions and realities that result in women feeling they have to be constantly aware of their environment, watching and checking the behaviour of men they may encounter, trying to predict their motives and actions. Two feminist researchers refer to this as a 'Geography of fear' that affects all women and which becomes a 'geography of limitation'.[1]

Whilst having been sexually assaulted is likely to make women feel less safe, all the women interviewed were aware of the threat of violence. The women speaking below had not experienced stranger assault in the public sphere.

> 'Rape *is* constantly at the back of my mind when I'm in situations where I feel vulnerable.'

> 'I don't go out at night, I'm a coward, but then it can happen in the daytime. I think we're all very aware these days, through the media, of the very real threat of rape, not just to ourselves but to our own daughters, our friends, our mothers.'

Women who had experienced sexual violence in the home, particularly incest, were more likely to feel that nowhere was safe.

> 'I don't think you stand much chance really, you're no safer whether you're in the house or out of it.'

> [. . .]

The experiences of flashing recorded in the interviews revealed considerable variation in the form of the assault. Flashing may only involve a sudden exposure of male genitals; it may be preceded by being followed or be succeeded by being chased. The abusive man may make verbal remarks, of an apparently innocuous kind to get women's attention, of a sexually provocative nature, or which involve explicit threats of further violence. He may also be masturbating. The context in which incidents took place also varied considerably, ranging from the stereotype of a park or street at night, to daytime exposures on trains or buses, in pubs through to the two young women who were exposed to by relatives in their own homes.

> 'I was abroad and my daughter was having a tantrum and I said "Look I'm going!" and walked off. I turned round to look at her and there was this bloke masturbating *just behind her*. I grabbed her. I almost got violent with her because

she was still carrying on. He just *kept following* us and every time I looked round he was *there*. He followed us until we went into this cafe but that wasn't very nice because the cafe was full of men.'

'It was near my house, and at first I didn't realize what was happening. Then he shouted at me, something about rape – I can't remember exactly – and I saw. I started to run and he chased me right into our garden. I thought afterwards how lucky I was that my house was round the corner.'

[. . .]

'I've wondered whether it was an accident, but he was sitting downstairs playing with himself. He must have heard me coming down the stairs and he didn't stop – so he must have wanted me to see.'

[. . .]

[M]any experiences of flashing took place when the women were children or adolescents. Any explanation of flashing must take account of this fact. Do men who expose themselves deliberately seek out younger, therefore more vulnerable, females? Is part of their motivation to be young women's first encounter with an erect penis? Do they get a 'kick' out of terrorizing/confusing/upsetting young women – using their penis as a hostile threat?

[. . .]

At the time, women did not experience flashing as a 'minor' crime. As children, they were often very frightened; as adult women, they felt personally violated and the uncertainty of what might happen next created fear and tension. When women reflect on their experience with the knowledge that nothing else happened and that flashing is not generally taken seriously, they dismiss or minimize the fear and or distress they felt in order not to appear paranoid or to be over-reacting to a 'trivial' incident.

[. . .]

It is important to remember that although further violence may not be intended women cannot know this until after the event. Indeed, being followed or chased suggests that in some circumstances flashing may be a preliminary to further assault. Evidence from recent studies of sex offenders has shown that many began offending as exposers and moved on to rape, sexual assault and/or sexual abuse.[2] No woman is, therefore, in a position to know at the time of an incident of flashing whether the assault will be limited to exposure. The threat of further violence is, in fact, a very real one.

Obscene phone calls are an example of predominantly verbal violence. Their impact on women is a combination of the invasion of privacy and the explicit or implicit threats of further violence that are made. Whilst abusive callers seldom use the word 'rape' they assume a particularly intrusive form of sexual access to women. It is a form of intrusion which, at least the first time, women cannot anticipate. It is this, alongside the intention to shock, humiliate and frighten women, which makes these calls a form of sexual violence. They are experienced by women both as a specific form of the threat of sexual violence and as violating in themselves. Calls varied over a number of dimensions, some appearing to be random, isolated incidents, others series calls. Some were obviously made by men who knew the woman.

[. . .]

The initial reaction to a call which includes verbal abuse is often one of shock. This rapidly changes into either anger, which allows women to respond in some way, or fear. However they responded, all women felt that their personal space and sense of self had been violated.

[. . .]

It was as much the uncertainty of what the call meant, as the actual content, that concerned women and preoccupied them afterwards. Did the man know them? If their name was used how was it known? Did he know where she lived? If threats were made about other forms of sexual violence, would they be carried out?

'It wasn't the actual fact that he was being obscene to me, it was whether he knew me, or how he got my number. That's the thing that worried me. Whether he actually knew who I was or whether it was at random.'

'I got quite worried about it because I thought he could see me – just because it happened a couple of times just as my husband went out. I thought he was watching from somewhere.'

[. . .]

As with flashing, women often felt that they had over-reacted at the time. It is only in retrospect, however, that women can be sure that no further action will be taken by the man.

[. . .]

SEXUAL HARASSMENT AND SEXUAL ASSAULT

[. . .]

The point at which sexual harassment becomes sexual assault is not clear. There was a considerable area of overlap in the definitions used by the women interviewed. There was one distinction, however: sexual harassment involved a variable combination of visual, verbal and physical forms of abuse; assault always involved physical contact.

Visual forms of harassment include leering, menacing staring and sexual gestures; verbal forms include whistles, use of innuendo and gossip, sexual joking, propositioning and explicitly threatening remarks; physical forms include unwanted proximity, touching, pinching, patting, deliberately brushing close, grabbing. Any incident of sexual harassment may contain visual, verbal and physical elements.

The most common forms of harassment recalled by women took place at work or in the street. Some women, however, gave very clear examples of similar forms of treatment in other situations. All were experienced as intrusive and involved assumptions of intimacy that women felt were inappropriate and/or involved men treating women as sexual objects.

'He sat right next to me, interviewed me and halfway through he grabbed my hands and started fondling my hands, and I had to carry on the interview with him holding my hands! What could I do – I wanted a job – I was *outraged.*'

'They would put their hands up your back and ping your bra, put their hands inside your jumper. You just used to try and ignore it. Well at that point I did, I've perhaps changed my mind now. It seemed to be part of office culture to be mauled by the older male members of staff.'

'Men at work – commenting on the way you dress, the shape of your legs, the size of your bum, your bust, looking up your skirt every opportunity they got.'

'Some would stand really close, breathe down your neck, put their arms round the back of the chair – that sort of thing makes you feel really uncomfortable. They never did it to the other men in the office.'

'I hate it in the local pub, when they look at you as if they are stripping you . . . or men who sit next to you and want to touch you, I can't stand that.'

None of the behaviour listed above would be defined in law, or by the women themselves, as sexual assault. No doubt, many of the men concerned would define their actions as either 'just being friendly' or 'harmless fun'. This was not how women experienced them. By defining harassment as normal, men justify their behaviour and when it is challenged are able to dismiss (read redefine) women's perceptions.

Lin Farley suggests that men use particular forms of sexual harassment to discourage women from entering male preserves in the labour market.[3] Such strategies constitute a refusal to treat women as co-workers. This woman was one of the first women to work on the local buses in the town she lived in.

'When I was working on the buses I was harassed. Everybody in the depot considered any woman who worked there as up for grabs or up for comment.'

[. . .]

The frequency and form of harassment at work depended, to some extent, on how far women's work role was sexualized. Aspects of women's work may be dependent on attractiveness and display: for example, reception and secretarial work. The work situations of women in the sex industry are totally sexualized, and the most extreme examples of harassment at work were experienced by the two women who had worked in the sex industry.

'I wish I had a pound for every time I got called a slag . . . Nine times out of ten you walk onto that stage knowing you're going to be slagged off. The attention that you get is essentially hostile not flattering . . . Whenever groups of men came in, irrespective of their background, they would all behave in a remarkably

similar way . . . Some of the things they would say were *really disgusting*. They'd
do things like grab hold of a girl and try and push a bottle up her.'

The experience of the six women who had worked as barmaids suggests that this
job sits uneasily between display and sexploitation. Each of them felt that sexual
harassment was part of the job. Male customers and co-workers assumed the right to
make sexual remarks and sexual advances.

[. . .]

'Working as a barmaid you get this thing that you are public property, you're the
girl behind the bar. If you look at the bar, most of the people there are men and
there's that whole sexual undertone a lot of the time.'

The extent to which women's work roles are sexualized and the sex ratio in the
workforce affect the forms and frequency of sexual harassment. What men consider
acceptable treatment of strippers would not be acceptable treatment of barmaids, and
what is considered acceptable in the latter case would not be routinely acceptable in
an office. What men are able to get away with in male-dominated environments has
to be moderated in mixed sex and women-dominated work situations.

[. . .]

Street harassment was a common experience for many of the women interviewed.
Through street harassment, men define and treat women as sexual in an aggressive
way. Men who do not know women assume the right of intimacy and/or sexual access.

'I experience a degree of sexual harassment I would say sort of once a week . . .
it varies in intensity, some I remember particularly, others. . . . It depends how
you define it, some of what I mean would be just shouting at you on the street.'

'It's something that happens so much – you just experience it on the street all
the time. It's almost a background of what going out of doors seems to mean.'

'In England they have this favourite thing of 'Cheer up love', which I find very
annoying. It's usually when I'm thinking about something and I find it very
intrusive. Someone I don't know saying pay attention to me. Although it's maybe
a very minor form, it's extremely annoying.'

The final quotation illustrates the continuum of experience very clearly. For women,
sexual harassment ranges from physical assaults through to what, on the surface,
appear to be innocuous remarks. The meaning behind the remark, the fact that through
it men deny women the choice of which individuals to interact and communicate
with and the intrusiveness of the encounter are what defines this, for women, as
harassment. The expectation that women should be paying attention to and gratifying
men, rather than preoccupied with their own thoughts and concerns, underlies this
kind of intrusiveness.

[. . .]

The incidents recorded in the sexual assault category clearly reflect the continuum of
experience ranging from being touched by strangers in the street, which other women
defined as harassment, to attempted rape. One end of the continuum within sexual

assault shades into sexual harassment; the other into rape. What characterized sexual assault for women was physical contact and the intention of the man concerned.

> 'Just *last week* I was cycling along when somebody reached out of his car, grabbed my bottom and tried to shove me off my bike, which is very sexual and aggressive.'

There were a number of examples of men abusing their professional status, including an optician, teachers and driving instructors. Some of these incidents were defined as sexual harassment, others sexual assault. In each case, the woman was temporarily dependent on the man's goodwill. This made responding angrily more difficult, as did the fact that the assault was always totally unexpected.

[. . .]

The majority of attempted rapes by known men involved acquaintances rather than friends or lovers and just under half occurred on holiday.

> 'It was one of those situations on holiday with friends when everybody pairs off and disappears. I was left with this bloke waiting for the others to come back. I spent the rest of the evening with him. He started to cuddle me and then he pushed and he pushed and he pushed and was trying to have intercourse with me. I spent at least half an hour having to keep him off me. I had a lot of flashbacks to it afterwards when I went back to school, feeling *absolutely petrified.*'

[. . .]

A disproportionate number of women's recollections of flashing, sexual harassment and sexual assault occurred whilst they were on holiday. Indeed, a considerable number took place abroad and some women explicitly referred to the conflicts and contradictions that had arisen for them concerning cultural differences. A few women made overtly racist remarks, suggesting that particular groups of men of Colour were, by nature, more sexually aggressive. These remarks are a variant of a more common tendency to define 'types' of men as potentially violent. In a racist culture, race is easily transformed into a 'type'. In attempting to explain the disproportionate incidence of assaults whilst on holiday, three possibilities occurred to me. The figures may be an artifact in so far as women may be more likely to remember incidents which take place outside of their daily routines and in a context in which they expected to relax and enjoy themselves. Alternatively, women may, in fact, be more vulnerable in situations where they either relax or are unable to refer to and use their routine precautionary strategies. Finally, men may, across cultures, share a construction of foreign women as more vulnerable and/or more 'available'. This suggests that foreign women in the UK would experience British men as more sexually aggressive than men from their country of origin.

PRESSURIZED SEX, COERCIVE SEX AND RAPE

A number of feminist writers have argued that one of the key problems in 'proving' rape in a court of law is that forced or coerced sex are common experiences for women.[4] This analysis challenges the assumption that all sexual intercourse which is not defined as rape is, therefore, consensual sex. Pauline Bart has developed a continuum which begins from consensual sex and moves through altrusitic sex (women do it because they feel sorry for the man or guilty about saying no), to compliant sex (the consequences for women of not doing it are worse than the consequences of doing it), to rape.[5] I have deliberately separated out consensual heterosexual sex from my continuum – it is a continuum of non-consensual sex. It is both conceptually and politically important to retain the possibility, at least, of consensual heterosexual sex. The categories of altruistic and compliant sex are covered by my category of pressurized sex. The category of coercive sex was introduced to cover experiences women described as being 'like rape'.

Paul Willis and Sue Lees have both documented the still existing double standard for young men and women in relation to heterosexual sex.[6] Willis describes boys' attitudes to girls as: 'exploitative and hypocritical. Girls are pursued, sometimes roughly, for their sexual favours, often dropped and labelled "loose" when they give in.'[7] Over three-quarters of the women interviewed recalled being on the receiving end of this exploitative male sexuality during their adolescence.

> 'He was never violent or anything – but he – it depends what you call violence – pushy in the sense of, you know, when you are a teenager, when you're with your boyfriend there's this constant pressure to go further sexually . . . There's this constant thing about boys needing sex and confusion about how you feel about it.'

> 'I didn't actually want to stop seeing him but I ended up having to because I couldn't see him and not have sex . . . I can remember quite early on him not taking no for an answer, and then him being very shocked when he saw that I did mean no, I wasn't just so called "messing about".'

> 'Most boys pressurized girls for sex. I don't think they wanted deep relationships. They wanted a score on their card.'

> 'Always there was pressure, well most of the time. It was like you had to do something to satisfy them.'

Pressure continued into adult life, as did this sense of obligation to meet men's sexual 'needs'. Specific obligations were incurred for which payment was assumed to be sex when men spent money on women. The situations range from the proverbial dinner for two, to a holiday or paying the rent. Pauline Bart's altruistic sex fits some of these experiences but does not include the sense of responsibility women internalize for satisfying men's desire for sex.

> 'I used to feel terrible. It's like women feel responsible for men's erections. You're conditioned into feeling that. But I don't anymore, I can say "It'll go down in a minute, don't worry".' (laughs)

'I went on holiday with this man and I *knew* that it was expected of me but I didn't want it. So I just gritted my teeth and did it because it was expected and I couldn't really say no.'

'When I was living with Mark, I'd come home from work and I'd be shattered. I'd just want to go to bed and sleep. He'd start cuddling up and touching me and I'd think "oh here we go again". It was like a *duty*, that was sort of paying the rent. I had a roof over my head and that was what I was expected to pay.'

A further form of obligation existed for women in marriage or long-term relationships.

'There are even occasions in my relationship now when I don't particularly want to. ... I tend to acquiesce more often than not. ... I think that's a problem that women have. We find it difficult to say no, particularly if you feel you've been agreeing, that there's some kind of tacit understanding that you are withdrawing from.'

These tacit agreements and obligations are seldom made specific, which partly accounts for why they are so difficult to challenge. Women often felt unable to assert their interpretations or needs in the face of male assumptions.

[...]

Within relationships, many women recalled times when having sex was a price they had to pay to improve the situation, receive affection, and/or prevent their partner behaving in particular ways that upset them.

'I wanted the cuddles, the touching, but the intercourse was the thing you had to do for that.'

'I had a number of relationships in which I seemed to be under *pressure* and that wasn't what I wanted, but I did want the affection.'

'Generally in relationships I've felt that I've had to do it to save myself the trouble of persuading him not to want it. I would do it because it was easier than spending a whole day with him sulking about it.'

'I knew that if he didn't have an orgasm he would actually be *terribly* bad tempered. He was an emotionally violent sort of person, I knew if I wanted a quiet morning it would be best just to let him. . . . My god, I'm glad I got out of that relationship.'

[...]

Pressurized sex involved women assessing the costs of refusing sex. Past experience with a man or other men resulted in the feeling that to say no always had negative consequences. Women frequently had sex for men's pleasure rather than their own. Once a sexual relationship was established, the majority of men assumed sexual access; it was not something which involved negotiation and women's right to say no was seldom openly discussed, let alone accepted.

The general socialization of women to place the needs of others before their own and naturalistic models of sexuality where needs (usually male) are given the status of biological urges or drives result in many women internalizing a sense of responsibility for men's sexual pleasure. Hence, women find it difficult to say no to sex. Moreover, they realistically fear the consequences of saying no. In addition, it was obvious that many men assumed the right of sexual access within heterosexual relationships. They clearly also wanted to control when sex took place and what forms of sexual practice it was to consist of. Many women expressed considerable anger when discussing men's hypocritical refusal to respond to women's desire for sex if it was not what they, the men, wanted at the time.

Whilst many of women's discussions of pressurized sex referred to a general experience within one or a number of relationships, incidents of coercive sex were specific events: experiences of forced sex that women did not define as rape at the time of the interview. Men ignored women's physical or verbal resistance; explicit pressure, often including the threat of or actual physical force, was used. The majority of the men were known to the women and much of the difficulty women felt about naming these experiences rape was linked to this fact, particularly if the relationship had included consensual sex in the past.

[. . .]

'Where do you define rape? The pressure to have sex was so overwhelming . . . I was made to feel guilty. It isn't rape, but *incredible* emotional pressure was put on and I wanted that man out of my room as soon as possible.'

'I didn't say no, I didn't dare to . . . you know you don't want to, but you are still doing it. That's why in my eyes now it's rape with consent. It's rape because it's pressurized, but you do it because you don't feel you can say no.'

'I couldn't call that rape . . . I mean there was that one bad case of it. He'd forced sex on me a number of times, that's what I would call taking a woman for granted.'

'The early time that I would say was – ohh – bordering on rape was a friend of – a married friend in my first marriage. He used to come round and pester me a hell of a lot and I didn't know what to do about it. Basically because my husband was violent to me and I knew he'd *kill* me, he'd blame me as well as the friend when he found out. I was dead scared of the neighbours seeing the car. I didn't have the strength to say fuck off in those days and in the end used to make love just to get rid of him.'

What distinguished some incidents of coercive sex from rape for the women was that they did not resist after a certain point.

'No not rape . . . not in the (sighs) . . . not actually physically forced to have sex, only . . . coerced I think, yes.'

She added later in the interview:

'I remember an occasion where he wouldn't let me get up, and he was very strong. He pulled my arms over my head. I didn't put up much of a *struggle*. I mean I wouldn't have seen that as rape because I associated rape with strangers, night and struggle. I didn't put up much of a struggle, but I *didn't want to*, so in a sense that was rape, yes.'

Three other women who lived with violent men were coerced into sex by one of their partner's friends and lived in fear of him finding out. In each case, the woman eventually told her partner and in each case she was held responsible. This woman is describing what happened after she told her ex-cohabitee:

'We got to the flat and he dragged me into the bedroom and – ohh I just wanted him to go, I just wanted him to get out. Then he forced me into bed, made me have sex with him and he scratched all my back open. Then he got a tin of deodorant and sprayed it into every scratch (sighing and upset) then he started laughing and said "Go and show that to your boyfriend".'

[. . .]

The assaults that women defined as rape took place in a range of contexts and the rapists were in a range of relationships to the women. A minority of the rapes were what have been called 'blitz rapes', where strangers took advantage of the fact that women were alone. A far greater number took place in the context of day-to-day interactions with husbands, lovers, boyfriends and fathers. Others were more obviously planned. One man pretended to arrange a modelling session. Another took a woman's purse and ran off with it knowing she would follow him. One woman's ex-boyfriend went out to make a phone call while she was visiting his flat; when she left, his friends were waiting outside and she was gang raped. The two quotations below illustrate two other situations in which women were raped by men they knew. The first woman was staying with a married couple, both her friends, and had been drinking with them during the evening.

'You know that feeling when you're just *out*, I was completely unconscious. The next thing I knew I woke up – I was in bed with *my baby son* – and he was actually raping me *then*. . . . I can remember saying to him "What are you doing!" and he went "Sssh" – great! (ironic laugh). And he got out of the bed and left.'

'I'd just split up with this boyfriend who had been hitting me and I was feeling quite hurt about it. This friend started paying attention to me and in a way it was a bit of an ego boost. He came round to my house. We were watching tv. Suddenly he was undressing me. I tried to stop him, I was pushing him away . . . in the end I thought "I'll just go dead".'

In both cases male 'friends' took advantage of situations in which women had absolutely no reason, at the time, to suspect what was later to happen.

The assaults by strangers took place either outside or as the result of accepting a lift. Every woman was aware that accepting a lift from a man was a risk but felt safe due to specific circumstances or because the alternatives involved greater risk. For example, a young woman and her friend had missed their last bus home. It was raining and a man offered them a lift. They felt safe as there were two of them.

'He dropped my friend off first and before I could even *think* he'd driven off to this deserted heath.'

Another woman was hitching on the continent with a male friend. The man giving them a lift drove off leaving her friend at a garage.

The forms of sexual practice the rapists forced on women and their use of physical violence also varied. Of the rapes 85 per cent involved forced sexual intercourse, 31 per cent forced oral sex and one woman was raped anally. In eight rapes, considerable physical violence was used by the man. In a further eight, threats of violence were made. In 13 cases the women were held down and one was tied up. Only two rapes involved weapons, in both cases a knife. In two cases, brutal sadistic violence was used. The majority of women became fearful of physical injury when their initial resistance failed to deter their attacker and they stopped struggling making further violence unnecessary. The fear women experienced, particularly when raped by strangers, was fear for their lives although no specific threat may have been made.

[. . .]

This section has demonstrated that many women experience non-consensual sex on a recurring basis. It is a minority of such experiences that are defined by women as rape. The number would be even smaller if I had applied current British legal definitions of rape to the interview data, and smaller still if we only took into account those rapes which were reported to the police and recorded in official statistics. It is not possible to make clear and precise distinctions between pressurized sex, coercive sex and rape, but the concept of the continuum both validates the abuse women feel and the shifting boundaries between these categories as their own understandings and definitions change over time.

[. . .]

SEXUAL ABUSE OF GIRLS AND INCEST

The connections between child sexual abuse and incest are in one sense obvious. Many researchers have defined incest as a specific form of child sexual abuse. Within this general linkage, there are also more specific ones. Both may involve a single assault or repeated assaults by the same abuser. In both, the nature of the assaults ranges through forms of unwelcome intimate contact, as discussed in the section on sexual harassment, to flashing, to getting a girl to undress, to touching her body and or genitals and/or getting her to touch the abuser's body, to masturbation and rape. The girl may be gently encouraged, bribed, tricked, pressured, coerced or forced to take part. Whilst in incest the abuser is always known to the girl, many of the examples of child sexual abuse also involved known men. In both cases the abuser may be a peer or an adult, one or two generations older.

[. . .]

Sexual aggression experienced in childhood and adolescence included abuse by adult strangers, acquaintances and relatives. There were also a number of incidents which involved male peers and slightly older boys.

> 'I was about 7 and a 12-year-old boy from down the road used to terrorize me. First it was pull up your dress and I wouldn't because I knew what was coming next. It was like a battle of wills for about 15 minutes and I was absolutely terrified . . . My sister and I lived in fear. We came out of school and looked to make sure he wasn't there.'

Many children have memories of being bullied. What makes this situation, and the many similar ones girls experience, sexual assault is the combination of sex and aggression.

[. . .]

> 'I remember uncles coming over and me just feeling uncomfortable about them. Now I know they were rubbing themselves up against me and things like that. I knew it was dirty and horrible and it used to make me shudder – now I know why.'

> 'When I was around 10 or 11 my aunt's fiancé was always touching me up. I just didn't like it. I told him off about it. I know he did it to my niece as well who was younger than me.'

> 'I was molested when I was about 12 by my godfather. . . . I *adored* him, he was a father figure. He'd invite my sister and I to stay in a posh hotel along with his son who was a couple of years older. He would start embracing you, but then get very rough, put his arms right round – I adored this affection. *But then* he started putting his hand under my sweater and holding onto my breast and taking my bra off. I wouldn't get into the lift alone with him *because I didn't want to be molested*. I wasn't terrified but *I didn't* enjoy it. My sister told me recently that he used to come in from his bath either naked or in his pyjamas with his *prick hanging out* (anger and disgust) and he would stand over my sleeping sister and she would open her eyes and be staring straight into this man's penis.'

These women's experiences are similar in some respect to those defined by women as incest in that the abuse involved an extension of affection. There were also a number of incidents involving strangers that women recalled as being very frightening and disturbing.

> 'We'd built this tree house and this guy chased me into it. He didn't do anything to me but he was shouting that he was going to pull my knickers down and stuff. I remember vividly that it quite frightened me at the time.'

> 'I've just remembered an experience when I was 12 which *really* disturbed me for about two years. It was only in my twenties that I could even

talk about it. I was molested on the underground and the reason it was horrible was because I was at that age where I was old enough to understand and yet I was still a child. This man was sitting opposite me playing with a camera, just started being friendly and talking to me. Being a nice, friendly polite child I responded. He started holding my hand, I thought uhh uhh this is a bit off, but I was *too polite* to snatch it away. It was politeness that made me acquiesce, because he was an adult. He made me feel him up.

[. . .]

Considerable numbers of women feared violence and/or picked up sexual messages from male family members. Many women had experienced similar paternal controls to those recalled by incest survivors, but were not themselves incestuously abused. Where the control and sexual messages interlinked women were aware of the connection to incest but did not define their experiences as incest. Judith Herman defines this form of father–daughter interaction as 'seductive' and she found it had as damaging effects on women as more overt abuse.[8]

> 'He very obviously started seeing me as a sexual being . . . I think I was more nervous of him because of the sexual vibes he was . . . I mean, I think he was the central person I was afraid of when I was going through all that terror. I've often thought about what it was he actually did . . . Apart from the initial things, like coming up beside me and putting his arm around my waist, slapping me on the bum. . . . When I think about it now there was something very creepy about him. . . .

Other women's feelings were often less clearly connected to overt behaviour but, none the less, they felt uncomfortable. Most of these women resisted attributing incestuous motives to their fathers.

> 'I don't say he had incestuous feelings. If he did, I don't think he would *ever* have translated it into action. I think some of it was *over-strong* paternal feelings, but I do think there's a sexual undercurrent to that with a girl.'

> 'It was more of a feeling of something that I shied away from. When he was tickling us or something like that there was some feeling in my mind that this wasn't what it should be.'

> 'I don't think I ever experienced physical pressure from my father, yet I had similar reactions to those I've read incest survivors have. I don't know where they come from really. Does it just come from that sort of social conditioning of it's a possibility?'

Many women recalled their father ignoring them or being very controlling, critical or verbally and/or physically abusive. Some fathers, whether or not they were sexually abusive, called their daughters whores or sluts. Many women recalled relationships with fathers worsening in adolescence. Much of the conflict concerned girls challenging their father's authority. Many of the incest survivors recalled similar attitudes and forms of control to those common in the lives of women who had not experienced incest.

[. . .]

The majority of women were frightened of their fathers. Some had good reason to be. In the case of others, the reasons why they felt fearful were less clear. Many abusive aspects of relationships with fathers emerged during the interviews; father-daughter incest was the extreme end of a continuum of father/daughter relationships. Where incestuous abuse was by adult relatives other than biological fathers, these men were always in some form of 'social father' relation to the girl: step-father, mother's boyfriend or the adult male in the household.

[. . .]

The majority of the experiences women defined as incest involved men who were their biological or social fathers. One woman was abused by an older male cousin over a period of about a year, one by her grandfather when she was living with her grandparents temporarily and one woman by a combination of uncles and lodgers. In the first two cases abuse took place over the relatively short period of time that the girl and abuser lived in the same household and in the latter case there was a succession of abusers, rather than abuse over a long period by the same man. There were no examples of brother-sister incest in the interviews, but this form of incest may well be of longer duration as siblings, in most circumstances, live in the same household until they leave home as adults.

None of the women had any idea about the possibility of abuse before it happened to them and ten picked up no signs before the abuse began.

[. . .]

[W]omen [. . .] defined aspects of the abuse as rape and another three as attempted rape. For several women, the interview was the first time that they had named their experience in this way. Not every woman could remember how long the abuse lasted for. It tended to last longer if it began in early childhood. For two women, it was a single experience of rape, although the threat that it might be repeated remained until they left home. Only the woman who was first approached when she was 15 knew that the abuse was against the law at the time although five other women felt it was wrong from the beginning. For the other women, the abuse began as an extension of affection and it was when either the aspects of the abuse changed or they were older that they too defined what was happening as wrong. When abuse began as an extension of affection women recalled confused and ambivalent feelings. This was either because they wanted affection from the man or because they experienced pleasurable physical sensations.

> 'I remember my father teaching me how to masturbate when I was four. He said "I'll show you something nice", and it was.'

Unlike the popular stereotype that incest involves treating a child as special and that it is an extension of a close, affectionate relationship, the majority of these women felt that they had virtually no relationship with the abuser or a predominantly negative one before the abuse began.

'He totally ignored me until 11. When I started my periods, he started to sort of take notice. In fact, he took me out for a meal, started to buy me presents. I was quite pleased 'cos he was actually taking an interest in me. Then after that it started.'

Four women did recall at some point feeling, or being treated as, 'special' within the family. For all of them, however, this became a form of bribery and involved aspects of control, such as not being able to choose their own clothes. For one woman, what were seen by other members of the family as treats consisted of her father taking her out for day-trips during which he took photographs of her which he threatened to send away to pornography magazines or pretended that she was a prostitute and he her pimp.

[. . .]

The majority of women had been explicitly told to keep the abuse secret. Two fathers told their daughters that their behaviour was normal. The pledge to secrecy that most abusers demanded was usually underlined either by threats of violence or threats that telling someone would upset their mother and/or cause the family to break up. [. . .] The fear of family break-up or of 'abandonment', which many researchers have presented as some sort of unconscious defensive mechanism in families where incest is happening [. . .], was, for this group of women, the result of internalizing explicit threats from the abuser. It is not surprising, therefore, that none of these women told anyone about the abuse whilst it was happening. The reasons women gave for not telling anyone were similar to those women discussed in relation to other forms of sexual violence. They feared being disbelieved or blamed and/or the reaction of the abuser. Several women stressed that they did not know how to tell anyone as they had no words to describe what was happening [. . .]. For five women, either the threats about upsetting their mothers or an awareness that their mothers were unhappy and that if they knew they would feel guilty and responsible silenced them. [. . .] The sense of responsibility and blame that many abusers instilled in girls was reinforced by the general silence that surrounds incest.

NOTES

1. K. Schepple and P. Bart, 'Through women's eyes: defining danger in the wake of sexual assault', *Journal of Social Issues*, 39(2), 1983, p. 44.
2. See, for example, S. Levine and J. Koenig, *Why Men Rape: Interviews With Convicted Rapists*, Toronto: Macmillan, 1980.
3. L. Farley, *Sexual Shakedown*, London: Melbourne House, 1978.
4. See, for example, L. Clark and D. Lewis, *Rape: The Price of Coercive Sexuality*, Toronto: Women's Press, 1977; A. Dworkin, *Right-Wing Women: The Politics of Domesticated Females*, London: Women's Press, 1983; C. MacKinnon, 'Violence against women – a perspective', *Aegis*, 33, 1982; pp. 51–7.
5. P. Bart, 'Women of the right: trading for safety, rules and love', *The New Women's Times Feminist Review*, Nov.–Dec., 1983, pp. 1–2, 9–11.
6. S. Lees, *Learning to Lose*, London: Hutchinson, 1987; P. Willis, *Learning to Labour: How Working-Class Kids get Working Class Jobs*, Fairnborough: Saxon House, 1977.
7. Willis, *Learning to Labour*, p. 67.
8. J. Herman, *Father–Daughter Incest*, Cambridge, Mass.: Harvard University Press, 1981.

3.3

THE MURDERER AS MISOGYNIST?

Deborah Cameron and Elizabeth Frazer

This piece is taken from the concluding chapter of a study of sexual murder in Western societies since the nineteenth century. Where many other feminists have argued that sexual violence, including murder, are expressions of male dominance, Deborah Cameron and Elizabeth Frazer take a different view. They argue that there is more to sexual murder than men's hatred of and power over women, that this form of killing is a relatively recent phenomenon, and should be understood as a quest for transcendence which is rooted in the specific cultural conditions of modernity.

[. . .]

[T]here are two kinds of discourses about the sexual murderer. There is a 'cultural' discourse in which he is a hero, at the centre of literary and philosophical celebration; and there is a 'scientific' discourse in which he is a deviant. There is a flaw in both these accounts, however: they overlook the highly salient issue of how sexual murder is structured by gender. Sexual murderers are, as it turns out, men who murder the objects of their desire. [. . .]

To a feminist, by contrast, the maleness of sex killers is immediately visible and highly significant. The last two decades of feminist activity have made available a conceptual framework in which this maleness seems almost inevitable. Its central notion is that of 'male violence' or 'violence against women'.

SEXUAL MURDER AS VIOLENCE AGAINST WOMEN

Male violence against women is defined broadly by feminists to include not just the most obvious abuses — rape, wife-battering and incest for instance — but also and

From D. Cameron and E. Frazer, *The Lust to Kill: A Feminist Investigation of Sexual Murder*, Cambridge: Polity, 1987.

importantly, a range of male behaviours that have often been dismissed as mere routine minor nuisances, like flashing, stealing underwear and making obscene phone-calls. Feminist analysis puts these various things together for two reasons.

First, they all enact very similar assumptions about male sexuality and women's relation to it. They say that men need and feel entitled to have, unrestricted sexual access to women, even – sometimes especially – against women's will. They say that men's sexuality is aggressive and predatory. Superficially, flashing is quite different from rape, yet from the point of view of their function they are surprisingly similar: both are acts which men do in order to reassure themselves of their power and potency; both include, as a crucial factor in that reassurance, the fear and humiliation of the female victims.

Secondly, the myriad manifestations of male violence collectively function as a threat to women's autonomy. They undermine our self-esteem and limit our freedom of action – not only must we all live with the fear of sexual violence, society makes it our own responsibility to prevent it. If the worst does happen we may be blamed, not protected; our suffering will be trivialized, questioned or ignored. Thus a powerful incentive exists for us to police our own behaviour and acquiesce in the idea that men's sexuality is 'naturally' predatory, only to be contained by female circumspection.

These facts have led feminists to locate male violence against women in the realm of the *political*. It expresses not purely individual anger and frustration but a collective, culturally sanctioned misogyny which is important in maintaining the collective power of men. We can extend to all forms of male violence the phrase that is often used specifically about rape: 'an act of sexual terrorism'.

Is sex murder also a form of sexual terrorism? Certainly, we believe it can be given a partial analysis in those terms. It is relatively easy to see killing as male violence taken to its logical extreme, where humiliation becomes annihilation. Death is the ultimate negation of autonomy, and the kind of death inflicted by many sexual killers – the ripped breasts and genitals, the wombs torn out – is the ultimate violation of the female sex and body.

'Sexual terrorism', moreover, is a very apt description of the effect of sexual murder on the female population. A generalized fear of the lurking sex beast is instilled in women from their early years; it is death we fear, just as much as rape, and sadistic killers haunt our very worst nightmares. When a multiple killer is at large in our communities, we often end up living in a state of siege.

[. . .]

Terrorism: the rule of fear. Violence against women: the law of misogyny. No account of sexual murder could possibly be adequate which did not point out how perfectly the lust to kill exemplifies both.

Yet it is equally true that no account of sex murder could possibly be adequate if it ended there. There is more to sexual killing than misogyny and terror; and if this seems like a rather unorthodox conclusion, we can only reply that in the course of our research we were forced, despite initial resistance, to draw it.

SEXUAL MURDER AS MASCULINE TRANSCENDENCE

Feminists have written little specifically about sexual murder and what they have written tends to focus on specific cases; as far as we know, there is no other feminist study of sexual killing as a general phenomenon. And this is probably an important reason why feminists tend to identify sex murder as another, extreme form of violence against women, motivated (like rape, only more so) by misogyny. We have already explained that we agree with this view – but only up to a point. It can only be a partial, incomplete account, for if one examines sexual killers *as a group*, it is evident misogyny is not their only motive and indeed that not all are engaged in violence *against women*. Let us take these two points one at a time.

To begin with, the point that many sexual killers have desires and motivations that cannot be analysed as merely or exclusively misogynistic [. . .] takes us [. . .] to the quest for transcendence and the way in which murder has been used as an act of self-affirmation. To be sure, this may be mixed up with hatred for the victim, but often 'transcendence' is the dominant theme.

[. . .]

Some [Sexual murders] [. . .] moreover, are not easily analysed as expressions of misogyny at all, for the simple reason that their victims were not women. From the start of our research we have had to take seriously the existence of killers whose victims are *men*. We did initially consider the possibility that such killers were a totally different breed, but this idea did not stand up to scrutiny, since we found that men who murdered other men or boys were quite strikingly similar to those who murdered women. Furthermore, they fitted neatly into our definition of sex-killers as men who murder their objects of desire – the only difference being that their desires were homosexual ones.

Does homosexual murder present special problems for our thesis? Certainly, it does not challenge the generalization that sex-killers are male (like other women, lesbians have killed for motives of jealousy and revenge, but there has never been a lesbian Nilsen or Cooper [Sexual mass murderers]). But it does challenge any simple equation of sex murder with violence against women.

If in this last remark we seem to be stating the obvious, it must be borne in mind that for many psychoanalytically oriented writers, homosexual sex murder *is* directed against a woman. Like all sexual murder, it is really an act of revenge against the mother and male victims must therefore be analysed as symbolic woman-substitutes. We find this line of argument less than compelling, deriving as it does from an unquestioned assumption that homosexuality is nothing more than a distorted or pathological heterosexuality and that all sexual objects are by definition 'female'.

We can surely accommodate the striking resemblance between heterosexual and homosexual sex-murderers without pretending they are one and the same. Rather, what we need is a 'common denominator' which connects sexual killings of women and of men. Instead of focusing on the gender of the victim, we must look at what does not vary – the gender of the *killer*. The common denominator is not misogyny, it is a shared construction of masculine sexuality, or even more broadly, masculinity in general. It is under the banner of masculinity that all the main themes of sexual killing come together: misogyny, transcendence, sadistic sexuality, the basic ingredients of the lust to kill.

What is it, then, about masculinity that permits the emergence of these fatal themes? We believe the answer lies in the combination of two factors: first, the way that men have historically been defined as social and sexual subjects, and secondly, the particular notion of subjectivity that has been developed in Western culture. Let us take each of these factors in turn.

That Western thought has defined men as Subjects is often asserted, but it needs to be explained. After all, a philosophically-minded sceptic might enquire, are not all human beings by definition subjects? Is this not the measure of what being human *is*? If so, surely women too possess subjectivity; it cannot be part of masculinity *per se*. In one sense the sceptic would be perfectly correct, for women like men are conscious actors in the world. Nevertheless, gender does make a difference. Although both men and women may be subjects in virtue of their shared humanity, culturally it is men who stand at the centre of the universe. As Andrea Dworkin observes, the male subject is 'protected in laws and customs, proclaimed in art and in literature, documented in history, upheld in the distribution of wealth . . . when the subjective sense of self falters, institutions devoted to its maintenance buoy it up'.[1] Lacking these supports in social institutions and representations, women's subjectivity can easily slip away. Furthermore, in order to protect the centrality of the male subject, the not-male, the female, are defined by the culture as Other, objects. Thus subjectivity is at the heart of men's existence, whereas women's subject status is constantly being negated. Being treated as an object is a threat to male being in a way it can never be a threat to female.

Andrea Dworkin also points out that the importance of male self is part of male power. It is hard to challenge what she refers to as 'an *I am* that exists a priori, absolute', inscribed in every corner, every aspect of the culture.[2]

If the subject of Western culture is male, how has this male subjectivity been defined? In [. . .] constructions of male subjectivity in philosophy and literature from the eighteenth century onward [. . . one] theme [has been . . .] man's *transcendence*, the struggle to free oneself, by a conscious act of will, from the material constraints which normally determine human destiny.

In fact, this theme has always been important in the Western philosophical tradition. 'Man' has been seen as a subject engaged in a struggle to master and subdue his object, nature, to know and act upon it (upon *her*, of course, in traditional parlance). This view is reflected in many ancient myths: the story of Prometheus who stole fire from the gods, of Faust and Satan, the overreachers, of quest narratives like the romance of the Holy Grail. Interestingly, myths about female seekers after knowledge, such as Eve and Pandora, have a different significance. Rather than being admired as tragic heroes and admitted to the category of transcendent subjects, these women are depicted as wicked or stupid, their feminine curiosity bringing nothing but trouble.

In the eighteenth century, however – the age of 'enlightenment' – Western philosophy came to understand man himself as an object, a part of nature and a proper object for scientific study. But this recognition of man's objectivity brought into sharper focus his striving for subjectivity. Many philosophers grappled with the problem of subjectivity. David Hume, the empiricist and sceptic, concluded that the 'self' was only an illusion.[3] Immanuel Kant insistently wrote the self back in, arguing that we cannot have objectivity without subjectivity and vice versa.[4] With Hegel and Nietzsche, transcendence of the body and bodily consciousness becomes a matter of overcoming the other – the overcoming of objectivity and the attainment of freedom and power. But one thing all these thinkers have in common is their conflation of the Subject with the masculine subject, 'Man'. Transcendence has therefore come to be seen both as the project of the masculine and the sign of masculinity.[5]

Since sexuality does not stand apart from the rest of culture, these themes have been echoed in erotic practice and in the definition of masculine sexuality. The motifs of that sexuality are *performance, penetration, conquest.* In the writings of Sade and his later admirers, the quest for transcendence is explicitly eroticized. Sexual acts and desires that transgress social or religious norms are redefined as inherently forms of transcendence, thus becoming the source of both power and pleasure, and paving the way for that male sexual sadism which becomes, at its most extreme, the lust to kill.

According to this argument, the lust to kill arose as part of a particular historical process, a transformation of sexual desire. In the remainder of this [. . .] chapter, we want to focus on the possibilities for further transformation of our culture's sexual practice. [. . .] How can feminists intervene effectively in the cause of a different, less destructive desire? Should this, in fact, be a goal of feminism?

[. . .]

FEMINISM, THE SUBJECT AND SEXUALITY

[. . .] [O]ne of modern feminism's crucial assertions is that women under patriarchy are denied their subjectivity. Men are the subjects, women the objects. Simone de Beauvoir, in her ground-breaking *The Second Sex*, declared that for women to become fully human we would need to attain the transcendent subjectivity which has been the historical prerogative of men.[6] Her analysis is echoed by feminists today, especially the influential Lacanian tendency. Many of these theorists argue that transcendence and subjecthood are not inherently masculine characteristics: it is language and culture that lead us to think so, but this error of 'essentialism' must be 'deconstructed'. Then, we can aspire to the transcendent subjectivity which makes us men's equals as full human beings.

The struggle to be subject is played out in many fields, but [. . .] one key site of struggle is the field of sexuality. Sexuality has been a major issue for the Women's Liberation Movement since its inception and has recently assumed a new importance and urgency. [. . .] [T]he feminist critique of male sexual violence [. . .] has not gone uncontested by feminists. Against the contention that heterosexual practice is abusive and misogynist, certain feminists have posed the awkward question, 'Yes, but what about the pleasure we get from it? What about our desire for sexual expression?' This question implicitly raises the whole issue of women's aspirations to sexual subjecthood.

Various writers, lesbian as well as heterosexual, have pointed out that women's desires are not automatically for egalitarian 'caring' sexual relationships: female fantasies are not all sexual sweetness and light. Recently, women have begun to speak out frankly about the connection many make between 'pleasure and danger' (which is, incidentally, the title of an anthology from a conference on sexuality at Barnard University in 1982).[7] Among the topics debated and polemicized are pornography, sado-masochism (especially lesbian S/M), butch/femme roles among lesbians and adult child sex. Willingness to support and engage in these practices is sometimes referred to as being 'pro-pleasure' and we will use that term for a particular current in present-day feminism (despite our own resistance to the obvious implication that those who disagree are in some sense 'anti-pleasure').

'Pro-pleasure' feminists argue that women have been denied their 'right' to an autonomous sexuality. We must stress again that this idea is by no means peculiar to them, it is pretty much an axiom of the modern Women's Liberation Movement and the right to express one's sexuality freely was one of the British movement's seven demands. [. . .] Rather than being autonomous *subjects*, women have been defined and treated as sexual *objects*; insofar as our desires were given any attention they were constructed essentially as masochistic and passive. One of feminism's projects, there-fore, is to reclaim for women an *active* sexuality, defined autonomously by women's own desires and making women into sexual subjects. In our culture, one outcome is the emergence of female *sadists* and this requires us to pursue the 'pro-pleasure' argument further.

Sexual subjecthood and freedom for women is usually taken by 'pro-pleasure' feminists as involving not the construction of *new* desires, but the exploration of desires that are already there and have merely been suppressed by patriarchal imperatives, or moulded into acceptable forms (such as masochism and passivity). This gives an extra dimension to the argument that things like pornography and sado-masochism are valid: not only do they tend to the attainment of transcendence, they are in the final analysis, *natural*.

In the writings of the more thoughtful 'pro-pleasure' theorists the rationale for this naturalness claim is often couched in psychoanalytic terms. A much-cited example is Jessica Benjamin's article 'Master and slave: The Fantasy of Erotic Domination',[8] an analysis of the pornographic fiction *The Story of O*. Benjamin believes that this fiction is erotic for both sexes because it resonates with sado-masochistic fantasies that develop in infancy and are common to all of us. We all have an erotic relationship with our first love-object, the mother. [. . .] [T]he child both rages against the mother, fantasizes about destroying her and desires to be controlled by the mother, to the point where the child's own identity is destroyed. The adult reflexes of these fantasies, acted out in sexual practice, are sadism and masochism. Men, through pornography and other practices, are able to explore both these elements in their psyche; women are permitted to explore only their masochism, but if female sexuality is 'given its head', sadistic tendencies will also emerge – and when explored in a 'consensual' sexual scenario, these will surely be a force for the liberation of women.

[. . .]

So far, then, we have two connected propositions, both increasingly important in feminist debate: that women should pursue an autonomous sexual subjectivity as part of our liberation and secondly, that this entails the acknowledgement and exploration of the suppressed sado-masochism which is present in us all.

We shall have more to say about each of these arguments, since it seems to us that they are seriously flawed in their refusal to consider in sufficient depth the culturally constructed aspects of sexual desire and practice. But before we move on to a critique of the 'pro-pleasure' position, we want to point out that it converges neatly with another very influential discourse of our time. We mean the discourse of 'sexual liberation', spearheaded by libertarian and (mostly male) gay liberation activists and recently gathered under the banner of the 'New Pluralism'. This 'pluralism' is a celebration of all the possibilities for the individual pursuit of pleasure and like 'pro-pleasure' feminism, it believes sexual desire and the pursuit of unfettered transcendence to be natural and liberating. Its adherents have referred to the mushrooming of sexual subcultures as 'a refusal to refuse the body any more', which implies that the body has unchanging desires which however have long clamoured in vain to be heard.

The convergence of these currents, 'pro-pleasure' feminism and sexual liberationist 'pluralism' has produced a formidable lobby on sexuality. Yet we insist that its twin motifs of pluralism and transcendence and the project of sexual liberation it has developed, are highly problematic because they appeal to 'desire' as a bottom line – the analysis begins with existing desires and thereby takes them to be 'natural', immutable and ultimately valid. For feminists, especially, this is a very strange position to take – no feminist would *dream* of saying that women's desire for heterosexual romantic love was natural and valid. On the contrary, feminism takes the individual's sexual and other desires to be constructed socially, and thus susceptible to social revolution.

In modern Western culture sexual desire and practice are socially constructed according to the imperatives of what feminists have called *compulsory heterosexuality*. Radical feminists have two connected lines of attack on the institution of heterosexuality. First, we criticize the ways in which it is enforced: the rewards accruing to the heterosexual – cornucopias of money, jobs, status, public celebrations and religious festivals, and perhaps above all, the knowledge that one is 'normal'. The sanctions preventing lesbianism and homosexuality, on the other hand, are draconian – a lack of all the above, plus physical violence, legal punishment and even death. Secondly, radical feminists point to the ways in which heterosexuality structures a particular sort of society, based on the sexual division of labour, which benefits men as a class far more than it benefits women. The difficulty of breaking out of the heterosexist norm can be seen in the fact that homosexual subcultures do so often feature 'masculine' and 'feminine' role-play, that is, there are pressures for all forms of sexuality to be parasitic upon heterosexist forms.

It is true, as we have observed, that psychoanalysis strongly suggests that certain sorts of desires (sadistic and masochistic ones, the desire to destroy and be destroyed) *are* fundamental to the human condition. Theorists like Jessica Benjamin [. . .] point to the tension set up in the human baby's psyche as she rages at the mother for being absent, and, at the same time feels overwhelming dependence on, and love for, the mother. [. . .] They take this fact about human infancy to constitute an explanation of sado-masochism, and a sufficient account of the pervasive presence of sadistic and masochistic images in pornography, and the way pornography 'speaks to' both men and women, touching them deeply.

However, there seem to us to be two serious flaws in this analysis. The first concerns the blatant unnaturalness of all adult sexual practice. 'Sadism' and 'masochism' are categories of our *language*: like all linguistic signs, they cannot be taken as unproblematic reflections of experience, and especially not of the chaotic emotions of infancy, before language is acquired. A massive work of cultural transformation is needed before these emotions can be labelled 'love', 'hate', 'rage' and so on, let alone translated into the clear symbolic artifice of sado-masochistic paraphernalia (leather, bondage, rubber fetishism, etc.). [. . .] The naturalness and inevitability of sado-masochism is one of those truisms which does not stand up to closer scrutiny: in a different kind of culture the inchoate experience of infants might well be moulded into something quite different.

This leads us to our second objection. Psychoanalysis notoriously overlooks the extent to which childrearing practices themselves are culturally and historically specific. Infant psychic states – not to mention the interpretation society makes of them – might be very different in a culture with different arrangements (for instance, if more than one person fed and tended the baby).

Feminists must concur with the Freudian notion of the plasticity of the sex drive, even while we criticize Freud for his failure to follow through the social implications of this. But if desires for 'transcendence' and 'pluralism' are not natural and inevitable, we need to ask the question, in what sense might they be *desirable*? Against the sexual liberationists we would answer this question very firmly, 'in *no* sense', for two reasons.

First, transcendent sexuality intrinsically requires unequal relationships. The subject needs an object, the Self needs an Other, the Master needs a Slave. It could, of course, be argued (and is, interminably), that these are merely roles which could be taken on at will by partners in a consensual, erotic situation. But this argument overlooks a second difficulty. Given that we live in a power structure where men are dominant and women are subordinate, which has produced two-thousand years' worth of representations in which this point is hammered home, it hardly seems as if the choice of roles will be freely made by equal partners. On the contrary, who will do what to whom under the new pluralism is depressingly predictable. Many of those involved in current S/M scenes lament the great shortage of female sadists; according to a classic article by Paul Gebhart such women are 'highly prized' in S/M culture.[9] We do not think this is just a coincidence! Without major changes in the power structure, and new possibilities encoded in the culture, 'pluralism' can only mean more of the same.

To pluralists and would-be transcendents who say 'I have discovered these desires in myself – you cannot ask me to repress them' we reply, therefore, 'not repress, but question'. Elizabeth Carola, a member of Lesbians Against Sado-Masochism, insists that all of us must challenge and question our own sado-masochism.[10] She does not pretend, as some of the 'pro-pleasure' lobby have misrepresented feminist opponents of pornography and sado-masochism as pretending, that there are some 'right-on' feminists who are *untouched* by either sadistic or masochistic desires. But, she does insist that we look at the social consequences of acting out such desires.

We insist that there can be a vision of the future in which desire will be reconstructed totally. This involves being critical of our sado-masochistic tendencies. We must be suspicious of 'pluralisms' which leave masochism and sadism untransformed; above all, we must be critical of the whole project of transcendence and the subject-object, self-other dichotomies it entails. It also involves, as we have already hinted, a struggle to once and for all overthrow the structures of male power and masculinity, on which transcendence has always in fact been based. In other words, the struggle must go on, but we must add to it an imaginative concern with the future of women and men in our culture. We must aspire to an equal and feminist future in which murder is no longer a metaphor for freedom, in which transcendence is not the only possible self-affirmation and in which the lust to kill has no place.

NOTES

1. Andrea, Dworkin, *Pornography*, London: Women's Press, 1981; pp. 13–14.
2. *Ibid.*, p. 13.
3. D. Hume, *A Treatise on Human Nature*, ed. D.C. McNabb, London: William Collins, 1962, Book 1, section 6.
4. I. Kant, *Critique of Pure Reason*, trans. N. Kemp Smith, New York. St Martin's Press, 1965.
5. See G. Lloyd, *The Man of Reason*, London: Meuthen, 1984.
6. Simone de Beauvoir, *The Second Sex*, trans. H.M. Parshley, London: Jonathan Cape, 1953.
7. Carole Vance ed., *Pleasure and Danger*, London: Routledge & Kegan Paul, 1984.
8. J. Benjamin, 'Master and slave: the fantasy of erotic domination', in A. Snitow, C. Stansell and S. Thompson, (eds), *Desire: The Politics of Sexuality*, London: Virago, 1984.
9. P. Gebhart, 'Sadomasochism and fetishism', in his *Dynamics of Deviant Sexuality*, New York: Grune & Stratton, 1969.
10. See N. Griffith, *et al.*, 'Agreeing to differ? Lesbian sadomasochism', *Spare Rib*, September 1986.

3.4

CONTINUED DEVALUATION OF BLACK WOMANHOOD

bell hooks

The issue of sexual violence becomes particularly problematic in the context of a history of racist violence and exploitation. bell hooks is critical of white feminists who see the rape of women slaves as merely another instance of sexual violence and as of purely historical significance. She argues that the abuse of black women continues — alongside exaggerated fears of the rape of white women by black men and consequent false accusations. In both cases this is bound up with an overly sexualised image of black women and men and with ideas about interethnic sexual relations in which racist and sexist ideologies intersect.

Scholars who write about mass sexual exploitation of black women during slavery rarely discuss its political and social impact on the status of black women. In her important feminist analysis of rape, *Against Our Will*, Susan Brownmiller[1] neglects this issue in the section on slavery. She comments:

> Rape in slavery was more than a chance tool of violence. It was an institution-alized crime, part and parcel of the white man's subjugation of a people for economic and psychological gain.

Brownmiller seemingly acknowledges the importance of discussing the rape of black women during slavery by including such a section in her book, she effectively dismisses it by emphasizing that this was history, past, over with. Her chapter is titled, 'Two Studies in American Experience.' And she begins with the statement:

From b. hooks, *Ain't I a Woman*, London. Pluto Press, 1982.

> The American experience of the slave South, which spanned two centuries, is a perfect study of rape in all its complexities for the black woman's sexual integrity was deliberately crushed in order that slavery might profitably endure.

While Brownmiller successfully impresses upon readers the fact that white men brutally assaulted black women during slavery, she minimizes the impact that oppression has had on all black women in America by placing it solely in the limited historical context of an 'institutionalized crime' during slavery. In so doing she fails to see that the significance of the rape of enslaved black women was not simply that it 'deliberately crushed' their sexual integrity for economic ends but that it led to a devaluation of black womanhood that permeated the psyches of all Americans and shaped the social status of all black women once slavery ended. One has only to look at American television twenty-four hours a day for an entire week to learn the way in which black women are perceived in American society – the predominant image is that of the 'fallen' woman, the whore, the slut, the prostitute.

The success of sexist-racist conditioning of American people to regard black women as creatures of little worth or value is evident when politically conscious white feminists minimize sexist oppression of black women, as Brownmiller does. She does not inform readers that white men continued to sexually assault black women long after slavery ended and that such rapes were socially sanctioned. She does not make the point that a primary reason rape of black women has never received what little attention rape of white women receives is because black women have always been seen by the white public as sexually permissive, as available and eager for the sexual assaults of any man, black or white. The designation of all black women as sexually depraved, immoral, and loose had its roots in the slave system. White women and men justified the sexual exploitation of enslaved black women by arguing that they were the initiators of sexual relationships with men. From such thinking emerged the stereotype of black women as sexual savages, and in sexist terms a sexual savage, a non-human, an animal cannot be raped. It is difficult to believe that Brownmiller is ignorant of these realities; I can only assume she deems them unimportant.

As far back as slavery, white people established a social hierarchy based on race and sex that ranked white men first, white women second, though sometimes equal to black men, who are ranked third, and black women last. What this means in terms of the sexual politics of rape is that if one white woman is raped by a black man, it is seen as more important, more significant than if thousands of black women are raped by one white man. Most Americans, and that includes black people, acknowledge and accept this hierarchy; they have internalized it either consciously or unconsciously. And for this reason, all through American history, black male rape of white women has attracted much more attention and is seen as much more significant than rape of black women by either white or black men. Brownmiller further perpetuates the belief that the real danger to women of interracial sexual exploitation in American society is black male rape of white females. One of the longest chapters in her book is on this subject. It is significant that she titles her discussion of the rape of Native American women and black women by white men 'A Study in American History' but titles her section of black male rape of white women 'A Question of Race.' In the opening paragraph to this section she writes, 'Racism and sexism and the fight against both converge at the point of interracial rape, the baffling crossroads of an authentic, peculiarly American dilemma.' Brownmiller fails to mention terms like 'interracial rape' or 'sexism' in her chapters dealing with the rape of non-white women.

A devaluation of black womanhood occurred as a result of the sexual exploitation of black women during slavery that has not altered in the course of hundreds of years. I have previously mentioned that while many concerned citizens sympathized with the sexual exploitation of black women both during slavery and afterwards, like all rape victims in patriarchal society they were seen as having lost value and worth as a result of the humiliation they endured. Annals of slavery reveal that the same abolitionist public that condemned the rape of black women regarded them as accomplices rather than victims. In her diary, the southern white woman Mary Boykin Chesnut recorded:

> (March 14, 1861.) Under slavery, we live surrounded by prostitutes, yet an abandoned woman is sent out of any decent house. Who thinks any worse of a Negro or mulatto woman for being a thing we can't name? God, forgive us, but ours is a monstrous system, a wrong and an inequity! Like the patriarchs of old, our men live all in one house with their wives and their concubines; and the mulattoes one sees in every family partly resemble the white children. Any lady is ready to tell you who is the father of all the mulatto children in everybody's household but her own. Those, she seems to think, drop from the clouds. My disgust sometimes is boiling over. Thank God for my country women, but alas for the men! They are probably no worse than men everywhere, but the lower the mistress, the more degraded they must be.

> (April 20, 1861.) Bad books are not allowed house room except in the library under lock and key, the key is in the Master's pocket; but bad women, if they are not white and serve in a menial capacity, may swarm the house unmolested. The ostrich game is thought a Christian act. These women are no more regarded as a dangerous contingent than canary birds would be.

> (Aug. 22, 1861.) I hate slavery. You say there are no more fallen women on a plantation than in London, in proportion to numbers; but what do you say to this? A magnate who runs a hideous black harem with its consequences under the same roof with his lovely white wife and his beautiful and accomplished daughters?

These diary entries indicate that Chesnut held enslaved black women responsible for their fate. Her wrath and anger is aimed at them and not at white men. Although stereotypical images of black womanhood during slavery were based on the myth that all black women were immoral and sexually loose, slave narratives and diaries of the 19th century present no evidence that they were in any way more sexually 'liberated' than white women. The great majority of enslaved black women accepted the dominant culture's sexual morality and adapted it to their circumstances. Black slave girls were taught, like their white counterparts, that virtue was woman's ideal spiritual nature and virginity her ideal physical state, but knowledge of the acceptable sexual morality did not alter the reality that no social order existed to protect them from sexual exploitation.

When slavery ended, black women and men welcomed their newly acquired freedom to express their sexuality. Like the early white colonizers, newly manumitted black folks were without any social order to govern and restrain their sexual behavior and indulged themselves with proper abandon. It must have been a good feeling for the manumitted slaves to suddenly have the freedom to choose a sexual partner and to behave in whatever manner they so desired. Some manumitted black women exercised their new found sexual freedom by engaging freely in sexual relationships with black men. Whites saw the sexual activity of the manumitted female slave as further evidence to support their claim that black women were sexually loose and innately morally depraved. They chose to ignore the fact that the great majority of black women and men attempted to adapt the values and behavior patterns deemed acceptable by whites.

[. . .]

Sexual exploitation of black women undermined the morale of newly manumitted black people. For it seemed to them that if they could not change negative images of black womanhood they would never be able to uplift the race as a whole. Married or single, child or woman, the black female was a likely target for white male rapists. Young black girls were admonished by concerned parents to avoid walking down isolated streets and to avoid contact with white men whenever possible. While these practices curtailed sexual exploitation, it was not eliminated because most sexual assaults occurred on jobs. A young, newly married black woman employed as cook for a white female reported that only a short period of time lapsed before she was accosted by the white husband:

> I remember very well the first and last work place from which I was dismissed. I lost my place because I refused to let the madam's husband kiss me. He must have been accustomed to undue familiarity with his servants, or else he took it as a matter of course, because without any lovemaking at all, soon after I was installed as a cook, he walked up to me, threw his arms around me, and was in the act of kissing me, when I demanded to know what he meant, and shoved him away. I was young then, and newly married, and didn't know then what has been a burden to my mind and heart ever since, that a colored woman's virtue in this part of the country has no protection. I at once went home, and told my husband about it. When my husband went to the man who had insulted me, the man cursed him, and slapped him, and – had him arrested! The police judge fined my husband $25. I was present at the hearing and testified on oath to the insult offered me. The white man, of course, denied the charge. The old judge looked up and said, 'This court will never take the word of a nigger against the word of a white man.'

Black women were often coerced into sexual liaisons with white employers who would threaten to fire them unless they capitulated to sexual demands.

[. . .]

The sexual assault of black women was so prevalent in both the North and the South after slavery ended that outraged black women and men wrote articles in newspapers and magazines pleading with the American public to take action against white and black male offenders who assaulted black women. An article published in the January 1912 issue of the *Independent* written by a black nurse pleaded for an end to sexual abuse:

> We poor colored women wage-earners in the South are fighting a terrible battle . . . On the one hand, we are assailed by white men, and, on the other hand, we are assailed by black men, who should be our natural protectors; and whether in the cook kitchen, at the washtub, over the sewing machine, behind the baby carriage, or at the ironing board, we are but little more than pack horses, beasts of burden, slaves! In the distant future, it may be, centuries and centuries hence, a monument of brass or stone will be erected to the Old Black Mammies of the South, but what we need is present help, present sympathy, better wages, better hours, more protection, and a chance to breathe for once while alive as free women.

When black people urged the white public to aid them in their struggles to protect black womanhood, their appeals fell on deaf ears. So pervasive was the tendency of whites to regard all black women as sexually loose and unworthy of respect that their achievements were ignored. Even if an individual black female became a lawyer, doctor, or teacher, she was likely to be labeled a whore or prostitute by whites. All black women, irrespective of their circumstances, were lumped into the category of available sex objects.

[. . .]

Systematic devaluation of black womanhood was not simply a direct consequence of race hatred, it was a calculated method of social control. During the reconstruction years, manumitted black people had demonstrated that given the same opportunities as whites they could excel in all areas. Their accomplishments were a direct challenge to racist notions about the inherent inferiority of dark races. In those glorious years, it seemed that black people would quickly and successfully assimilate and amalgamate into the mainstream of American culture. White people reacted to the progress of black people by attempting to return to the old social order. To maintain white supremacy they established a new social order based on apartheid.

[. . .]

In the case of black women and white men, inter-racial sex was both encouraged and condoned as long as it did not lead to marriage. By perpetuating the myth that all black women were incapable of fidelity and sexually loose, whites hoped to so devalue them that no white man would marry a black woman. After manumission, white men who treated black women with respect or sought to integrate a black female into respectable white society were persecuted and ostracized. During slavery, it had been a common occurrence for an upper class or middle class white man to take a black woman mistress and live openly with her without incurring much public disapproval.

[. . .]

Marriages between black women and white men could be tolerated during slavery because they were so few in number and represented no threat to the white supremacist regime. After manumission they were no longer tolerated. In the state of Kentucky, the Supreme Court was asked to judge insane a white man who desired to marry a female slave he had once owned. Once slavery ended and whites declared that no black woman regardless of her class status or skin color could ever be a 'lady,' it was no longer socially acceptable for a white man to have a black mistress. Instead, the institutionalized devaluation of black womanhood encouraged all white men to regard black females as whores or prostitutes. Lower class white men, who had had little sexual contact with black women during slavery, were encouraged to believe they were entitled to access to the bodies of black women. In large cities their lust for black female sex objects led to the formation of numerous houses of prostitution which supplied black bodies to meet the growing demands of white men.

[. . .]

White Americans have legally relinquished the apartheid structure that once characterized race relations but they have not given up white rule. Given that power in capitalist-patriarchal America is in the hands of white men, the present obvious threat to white solidarity is inter-marriage between white men and non-white women, and in particular black women. As whites have been much more voyeuristically, phobically interested in sexual relationships between white women and black men, the existence of rigid social taboos prohibiting white male marriage to black females is often totally ignored, yet such taboos may prove to have far greater impact on our society than taboos against black male-white female mating.

[. . .]

Taboos against white women mating with black men were maintained by white men because they were interested in limiting the sexual freedom of white women and insuring that their female 'property' was not trespassed on by black men. Now that improved male-invented contraceptive devices have diminished the emphasis on female sexual purity and provided all men greater access to women's bodies, white men have shown less interest in overseeing the sexual activities of white women. In contemporary times, marriages between black men and white women are more readily accepted and occur in ever increasing numbers. Explanations as to why marriages between white women and black men are more readily accepted than marriages between white men and black women can be found in patriarchal sexual politics. Since white women represent a powerless group when not allied with powerful white men, their marriage to black men is no great threat to existing white patriarchal rule. In our patriarchal society if a wealthy white woman marries a black man she legally adopts his status. Accordingly a black woman who marries a white man adopts his status; she takes his name and their children are his heirs. Consequently, if a large majority of that small group of white men who dominate decision-making bodies in American society were to marry black women, the foundation of white rule would be threatened.

A complex system of negative myths and stereotypes daily socializes white men to regard black women as unsuitable marriage partners. In American history, white men

have never sought to marry black women in as great numbers as black men have sought
to marry white women.

[. . .]

Negative images of black women in television and film are not simply impressed
upon the psyches of white males, they affect all Americans. Black mothers and fathers
constantly complain that television lowers the self-confidence and self-esteem of black
girls. Even on television commercials the black female child is rarely visible – largely
because sexist-racist Americans tend to see the black male as the representative of
the black race. So commercials and advertisements in magazines may portray a white
female and male but feel that it is enough to have a black male to represent black
people. The same logic occurs in regular television programs. On many shows there
are single black male figures or single black female figures but rarely are a black woman
and man together.

[. . .]

Whites who control media exclude black women so as to emphasize their undesirability either as friends or sexual partners. This also promotes divisiveness between black
men and black women, for white people are saying via their manipulation of black roles
that they accept black men but not black women. And black women are not accepted
because they are seen as a threat to the existing race-sex hierarchy.

While negative images of black womanhood are used to impress upon white men
their undesirability as marriage partners, the belief that all white men desire from black
women is illicit sex prevents black women from seeking such unions. Just as whites
have not been interested in myths and stereotypes black people perpetuate about them,
there is little discussion of the fact that the idea that all white men are eager to rape
black women continues to be a widespread belief in black communities. Of course this
belief was once based on the actual fact that for many years large numbers of white
men could and did sexually exploit black women. The fact that this may no longer
be the case has not caused black people (and in particular black men) to change their
attitudes, largely because many black people are just as committed to racial solidarity
as white people and they believe it can best be maintained by discouraging legalized
union between white men and black women.

Black men have a vested interest in maintaining existing barriers which discourage
black female white male marriage, for it eliminates sexual competition. Just as sexist
white folks used the idea that all black men were rapists to limit the sexual freedom
of white women, black people employ the same tactic to control black female sexual
behavior. For many years, black people warned black females to beware involvement
with white men for fear such relationships would lead to exploitation and degradation
of black womanhood. While there is no need to deny the historical fact that white
men have sexually exploited black women, this knowledge is used by the white and
black public as a psychological weapon to limit and restrain the freedom of black
females. Black females who have been socialized by parents to feel threatened or
even terrorized by contact with white men often have difficulty relating to white male
employers, teachers, doctors, etc. There are many black women who have as phobic a
fear about white male sexuality as the fear white women have traditionally felt towards

black men. Phobic fear is not a solution to the problem of sexual exploitation or rape. It is a symptom. While an awareness of male power to rape women with impunity in a patriarchal society is necessary for woman's survival, it is even more important that women realize that they can prevent such assaults and protect themselves should they occur.

[. . .]

The emphasis on the white male as sexual exploiter in black communities often deflects attention away from black male sexual exploitation of black women. Many black parents who warned their daughters against the sexual overtures of white men did not warn them about black male exploiters. Since black men were seen as possible marriage candidates, it was more acceptable for them to cajole and seduce black women into potentially sexually exploitative relationships. While black parents admonished daughters not to submit to sexual assaults by white men, they were not encouraging them to reject similar approaches from black men. This is just another indication of the way in which the pervasive concern black people have about racism allows them to conveniently ignore the reality of sexist oppression. They have not been willing to acknowledge that while racism caused white men to make black women targets, it was and is sexism that causes all men to think that they can verbally or physically assault women sexually with impunity. In the final analysis, in the case of white male sexual exploitation of black women, it is the sexism motivating these assaults that is important and not just the racial background of the men who initiate them. It was common during the sixties' black power movement for black men to overemphasize white male sexual exploitation of black womanhood as a way to explain their disapproval of inter-racial relationships involving the two groups. Often they were merely interested in controlling black females sexually.

[. . .]

Another tactic many black men employ to explain their acceptance of inter racial relationships with white women and their condemnation of black female-white male relations is to assert that they are exploiting white women like white men exploited black women. They evoke a false sense of avenging themselves against racism to mask their sexist exploitative feelings about white women and finally all women. The collective effort on the part of white and black people to curtail marriage and even friendship between black women and white men serves to help maintain white patriarchal rule and to support continued devaluation of black womanhood.

NOTE

1. Susan Brownmiller, *Against Our Will: Men, Women and Rape*, London: Secker & Warburg, 1975.

3.5

DESIRE FOR THE FUTURE
Radical Hope in Passion and Pleasure

Amber Hollibaugh

Amber Hollibaugh acknowledges the dangers that sexuality has often posed for women, but argues that we should give equal attention to pleasure. More controversially she suggests that there is a need to develop a feminist language of sexual pleasure that recognises that power in sex can be a source of pleasure.

[. . .]

Women in this culture live with sexual fear like an extra skin. Each of us wears it differently depending on our race, class, sexual preference and community, but from birth we have all been taught our lessons well.

Sexuality is dangerous. It is frightening, unexplored, and threatening. The ways that women enter a discussion of sexuality are different from each other. The histories and experiences are different; the ways we express those differences (and define them politically) are extremely varied.

Many of us became feminists because of our feelings about sex: because we were dykes or we weren't; because we wanted to do it or we didn't; because we were afraid we liked sex too much or that we didn't enjoy it enough; because we had never been told that desire was something for ourselves before it was an enticement for a partner; because defining our own sexual direction as women was a radical notion.

But in all our talking about sex, we have continuously focused on that part of our sexuality where we were victims. Our rage, which had given us the courage to examine the terrible penalties attached to being female in this culture, had now trapped us into

From A. Hollibaugh, 'Desire for the future: radical hope in passion and pleasure', in C.S. Vance (ed.), *Pleasure and Danger: Exploring Female Sexuality*, Hammersmith: HarperCollins Publishers Ltd, 1989.

a singularly victimized perspective. Our horror of what had happened to us made it impossible to acknowledge any response other than fury at the images and acts of sexuality surrounding us.

It is painful to admit that the main focus of our feminist sexual theory has been aimed primarily at pornography, as easy to justify as it is deeply feminine. 'Good' women have always been incensed at smut. Our reaction went far beyond disgust at pornography's misogyny or racism; we were also shocked at the very idea of explicit sexual imagery. At heart, our horror at pornography is often horror at sex itself and reflects a lesson all women carry from their earliest childhoods: sex is filthy.

But looking at the danger and damage done us is only a part of coming to terms with sex. We should also begin to look a sexuality itself and at what we mean by words like desire, passion, craving and need.

Do we think that sex is socially constructed? Is there any element of biology influencing or defining aspects of desire? If we think of sexuality as a combination of language, consciousness, symbolism, pleasure and motion, then how does that fit with our real lives as sexual women? What do we share in common; why are we each sexually different from one another? Should we attempt to wipe the sexual slate clean and begin again? Could we if we wished to? Do we desire what is forbidden? If the forbidden is connected to taboo, how can we resist oppression without destroying our means to excitement? What is the connection between the erotic and danger, the erotic and comfort? What creates the need to 'fuse' temporarily with a partner during sex? What are the options created by imagining a separation between sex and gender; what are the dangers? Is there 'feminist' sex? Should there be?

It is important to keep in mind that we're not discussing sexual abstraction, but creating the atmosphere and opportunities for ourselves in bed. Our theories affect the way we *feel* sex today and shape what we consider talking about with each other as well as what we will go home and try. This discussion will change the sensation of our orgasms as well as the way that women in the future will experience their own sexual feelings. The way each of us was raised lies close to the surface of sexual desires and the explanations we explore today will have the same effect on the women who follow us.

We will never open up women's futures if we censor the dangerous material of this debate before we have begun. We are in grave peril if we edit out of our analysis all women whose sexual histories do not correspond to a 'correct' notion of feminist sex. At this moment, we have gone further than just removed experiences and people who don't fit comfortably within our picture of the sexual universe; we have also attempted to slander and quiet those women whose intellectual ideas disagree or challenge the prevailing attitudes in the women's movement about sex.

[. . .]

Who are all the women who don't come gently and don't want to; don't know yet what they like but intend to find out; are the lovers of butch or femme women; who like fucking with men; practice consensual s/m; feel more like faggots than dykes; love dildoes, penetration, costumes; like to sweat, talk dirty, see expressions of need sweep across their lovers' faces; are confused and need to experiment with their own tentative ideas of passion; think gay male porn is hot; are into power? Are we creating a political movement that we can no longer belong to if we don't feel our desires fit a model of proper feminist sex?

Feminism has always had trouble expressing the radically different ways that oppressions bear on women, just as it has a terrible time facing the idea of sexual differences among women, straight or gay, working-class, Jewish, third world, young, old or physically different. It is easy, for example, to speak of the double or triple oppression of working-class and/or women of color but another to reckon with the actual realities of working life. It may make much more sense to spend eight hours stripping than working in a dry cleaning plant, or as an LPN (Licensed Practical Nurse) or office worker. [. . .] Sex industry work may offer a woman not only more money but a greater sense of power. Contrary to popular middle-class beliefs, working in a peep show is not the end of the world. The sex industry and its surrounding communities are often more socially and economically desirable than the jobs or groups of people that form the alternative.

I have always been more ashamed of having been a dancer in night clubs when I've talked about it in feminist circles than I ever felt in my hometown, working-class community. There are many assumptions at work behind feminist expressions of surprise and horror: I must be stupid or I could have done something better than that; I must have been forced against my will or I was just too young to know better; I have prefeminist consciousness; I had a terrible family life; I must have hated it; I was trash and this proved it; and finally, wasn't I glad I'd been saved?

I hear these sentiments endlessly in the feminist movement, distinctions which confuse the reasons for making different choices and what they mean in women's lives. Sex is not the same for all of us, and a movement that is primarily white and middle-class (or includes women who aspire to middle-class values) cannot afford to decide who or how women are made victims in a sexual system built on class and race mythologies equally as damaging and vicious as sexist ones. 'The Man' has many different faces, some of them female and white, and our alliances are not automatic or clear-cut.

Unfortunately, the idea that sexual variation, that *difference*, could be the key to analyzing sexuality and desire, a way of untying the stubborn knots of a bitterly heterosexist culture, has yet to appear distinctly enough in our theorizing about sexuality. As simple an action as patting somebody's ass may have wildly different meanings depending on family, culture, time, race and expectations. When a woman looks at a picture of a man and a woman fucking, doesn't it matter if she is straight or gay, likes cocks or thinks they're awful, was raised a Catholic in a small town in Minnesota or was the only gypsy child in her community? Doesn't that have a deep and radical impact on what a woman considers pornographic and what she considers sexy? Or are we to believe that there is a 'natural' reaction which all women have to sexually explicit images which warns us immediately if and when those images cross the line to lewd?

People fuck differently, feel differently when they do it (or don't) and want sex differently when they feel passion. We live out our class, race, and sex preferences within our desire and map out our unique passions through our varied histories. These are the differences that move the skin, that explode the need inside a cunt and make sex possible.

Women are always made to pay on either side of the sexual dialectic. We live terrified of harassment or attack on the street and in our homes and we live terrified that other people will discover our secret sexual desires. Much is forbidden even to women's imaginations. We are deprived of the most elementary right to create our images of sex. It is a hard truth that far too many women come up blank when they are asked what their sexual fantasies look like. Sexual fantasies are the rightful property of men, romance the solid female terrain. Yet most of our ability to act on our desires rests in the possibility of imagining the feel and smell of the sex we want.

When I was younger, I tried to control my imagination more strictly than my sex life; my mind scared me much more than the actual things I was doing in bed. No one had ever told me that I could explore fantasy without ever going further than dreaming. I really believed that if an image rested at the corners of my mind, giving it center stage would inevitably lead to doing it. So, every time I dreamed of fucking fur, not flesh, I was horrified. I worried I might still dream of fucking a man, that I would betray both lesbianism and feminism by dreams of penetration, power, and of being overwhelmed.

[. . .]

I spent too many years struggling against what I was afraid would surface if I let myself go. It was a deeper closet than the one I had been in before I had come out as a lesbian.

It is a bitter irony to me that I was in my mid-thirties before someone explained to me that I was not what I dreamed, that fantasies had a reality of their own and did not necessarily lead anywhere but back to themselves. I had never understood that I might be deeply fascinated by an idea but not enjoy it at all if I actually tried it, that fantasy could give me a way to picture different aspects of my own growing sexual consciousness (or explore my lover's) without going any further. It would also allow me a freedom unhindered by the limits of my body or the boundaries of my conscience. In my life I need monogamy, but I am free to experiment with an army of lovers in my fantasy. In reality I am limited to a certain number of orgasms done in a particular sequence, but in my mind I am capable of infinite climaxes and paths to satisfaction.

I am often shocked by my own sexual world. It is much denser and more forbidden than I knew. But it is also richer and has helped me find the beginnings of the words that might make sex of the body as complex and satisfying as my dreams of it. It has begun to give me back sensation in my body that had been lost for years.

[. . .]

Every time we have been afraid of our own desires, we have robbed ourselves of the ability to act. Our collective fear of the dangers of sexuality has forced us into a position where we have created a theory from the body of damage done us. We have marked out a smaller and smaller space for feminists to be sexual in and fewer actual ways for physical feelings to be considered 'correct.' By recognizing the dangers of our circumstances, we have said, 'There is no way to be a woman in this culture and be sexual too. I will live first with the anger and then hope we can change enough about the world that the woman after me may be safe enough to fuck. For now, it will have to be enough.' But this isn't enough, and we know it. We have settled for an easy way out of the terrible problem we face. We have accepted a diminished set of alternatives and become paralyzed by the fear.

But there is another way, a way that's more difficult and demands we take a riskier stance to define and act on our desires. We can begin to reclaim our rights to fight, to experiment, to demand knowledge and education about sex. We can begin in another spot, saying that there is too much we don't know yet to close any doors that a woman enters to try and capture her sexual feelings. We can say that our sexuality is more complex than the things that have been done to us and that we gain power through our refusal to accept less than we deserve. We can dare to create outrageous visions.

The borders are shrinking and fewer women feel that they can reconcile their sexual desires with their political beliefs. We must live with the danger of our real desires, give them credit and airing. We must demand better contraception, self-defense classes, decent, non-judgmental sex education, the right to control our bodies and set new boundaries of female experimentation and self-knowledge. Feminism should be seen as a critical edge in the struggle to allow women more room to confront the dangers of desire, not less. By selecting our truths, we have censored the roots of our own future as sexual people. Every history of desire that we have refused to acknowledge has removed us a step in an attempt to unravel and reclaim the daring of our sexual selves. Each judgment has scaled down our own ability to fuck, and our desperate need to explore why we feel the desires we each call our own.

The truth is that our current state of feminist affairs has demanded that women live outside power in sex. We seem to have decided that power in sex is male, because it leads to dominance and submission, which are in turn defined as exclusively masculine. Much of our theorizing has suggested that any arousal from power felt by women is simply false consciousness. In real life this forces many feminists to give up sex as they enjoy it, and forces an even larger group to go underground with their dreams. For many women who have no idea what they might eventually want, it means silencing and fearing the unknown aspects of their passions as they begin surfacing. Silence, hiding, fear, shame – these have always been imposed on women so that we would have no knowledge, let alone control, of what we want. Will we now impose these on ourselves?

[. . .]

No matter how sex is played out or with what gender, power is the heart, not just the beast, of all sexual inquiry.

It is the undertow of desire between my lover and myself that propels me through all the 'good' reasons I can invent to stop myself from wanting sex. It is erotic tension that ignites the wildness of my imagination and the daring to figure out how to make my desires feel against the skin as I imagined them beforehand. With these, I let go, finally, to another woman's direction and sexual need for me, and find ways to crack through my lover's defenses and push her further. [. . .] I want to let go, to compel my desires into an experience of my body that awakens me, satisfies me, finally, and doesn't leave me angry and bitter that yet another woman was too afraid of her own passion to push against mine and see how far we could have gone.

Sometimes I want to play, resist, fight against another woman sexually; sometimes I want to surrender. I can't imagine sex without this. In the end, I don't want to do away with power in sex like a part of the feminist movement; I want to redistribute that power and knowledge so I can use it (and use it better) for myself and my partner. I think there is a way to confront the sexism and racism within sex without erasing the sources and intensity of our pleasures. Doing it side by side doesn't guarantee that sex is free of any fantasy of power, and refusing to experiment with elements of our desires leaves us all the more terrified of our right to sex and satisfaction.

We must say we want sex and set our own terms. We must build a movement that validates the right for a woman to say yes instead of no; a movement that thinks we haven't heard enough about sex rather than too much, and which reclaims an eroticism not defined by a simple political perspective or narrow vision which insists on excluding women to sustain its standards. We are searching for ways to examine sexuality, consent and power. We want to expand what we understand about sexuality so that more of us can live the desires we envision. We must start from where we are right now, from the real bodies we live in, the real desires we feel.

[. . .]

Feminists must enter the fight again, angrily, passionately. Feminism cannot be the new voice of morality and virtue, leaving behind everyone whose class, race, and desires never fit comfortably into a straight, white, male (or female) world. We cannot afford to build a political movement that engraves the sexual reactions of nineteenth-century bourgeois women onto a twentieth-century struggle.

Instead of pushing our movement further to the right, we should be attempting to create a viable sexual future and a movement powerful enough to defend us simultaneously against sexual abuse. We must demand that our pleasure and need for sexual exploration not be pitted against our need for safety. Feminism is a liberation movement; it needs to fight with that recognition at its center. We cannot build a movement that silences women or attempts to fight sexual abuse isolated from every other aspect of our oppression. And we can never afford to build a movement in which a woman can 'lose her reputation.' Feminism must be an angry, uncompromising movement that is just as insistent about our right to fuck, our right to the beauty of our individual female desires, as it is concerned with the images and structures that distort it. This goal is not an end in itself but a means which will ultimately determine the future and direction of our desires. As feminists, we should seek to create a society limited only by those desires themselves.

3.6

FEMINISM AND SADOMASOCHISM

Pat Califia

This classic defence of sadomasochism made a crucial contribution to what have come to be known as the feminist 'sex wars'. In justifying her own position and practices, and insisting on their congruence with feminism, Pat Califia is critical of what she sees as the desexualisation of lesbianism within much feminist discourse.

Three years ago, I decided to stop ignoring my sexual fantasies. Since the age of two, I had been constructing a private world of dominance, submission, punishment, and pain. Abstinence, consciousness-raising, and therapy had not blighted the charm of these frightful reveries. I could not tolerate any more guilt, anxiety, or frustration, so I cautiously began to experiment with real sadomasochism. I did not lose my soul in the process. But in those three years, I lost a lover, several friends, a publisher, my apartment, and my good name because of the hostility and fear evoked by my openness about my true sexuality.

Writing this article is painful because it brings back the outrage and hurt I felt at being ostracized from the lesbian feminist community. I've been a feminist since I was 13 and a lesbian since I was 17. I didn't lose just a ghetto or a subculture – lesbian feminism was the matrix I used to become an adult. Fortunately for my sanity and happiness, I managed to construct a new social network. My friends and lovers are bisexual women (some of whom do S/M professionally), gay and bisexual men, and other outlaw lesbians. If I were isolated, I would not be strong enough to speak out about something that makes me this vulnerable.

From P. Califia, 'Feminism and Sadomasochism', *Heresies*, 12, 1981.

I describe my feelings about this issue because sadomasochism is usually dealt with in an abstract, self-righteous way by feminist theorists who believe it is the epitome of misogyny, sexism, and violence. In this article I shall examine sadomasochism in a theoretical way, and attempt a rapprochement between feminism and S/M. But I am motivated by my concern for the people who are frightened or ashamed of their erotic response to sadomasochistic fantasies. I don't want to hear any more tragic stories from women who have repressed their own sexuality because they think that's the only politically acceptable way to deal with a yearning for helplessness or sexual control. I don't believe that any more than I believe homosexuals should be celibate so they can continue to be good Catholics. The women's movement has become a moralistic force, and it can contribute to the self-loathing and misery experienced by sexual minorities. Because sexual dissenters are already being trampled on by monolithic, prudish institutions, I think it is time the women's movement started taking more radical positions on sexual issues.

It is difficult to discuss sadomasochism in feminist terms because some of the slang S/M people use to talk about our sexuality has been appropriated by feminist propagandists. Terms like 'roles,' 'masochism,' 'bondage,' 'dominance,' and 'submission' have become buzzwords. Their meanings in a feminist context differ sharply from their significance to S/M people. The discussion is rendered even more difficult because feminist theorists do not do their homework on human sexuality before pronouncing judgment on a sexual variation. Like Victorian missionaries in Polynesia, they insist on interpreting the sexual behavior of other people according to their own value systems. A perfect example of this is the 'debate' over transsexuality. In its present form, feminism is not necessarily the best theoretical framework for understanding sexual deviation, just as unmodified Marxism is an inadequate system for analyzing the oppression of women.

Since the label 'feminist' has become debased coinage, let me explain why I call myself a feminist. I believe that the society I live in is a patriarchy, with power concentrated in the hands of men, and that this patriarchy actively prevents women from becoming complete and independent human beings. Women are oppressed by being denied access to economic resources, political power, and control over their own reproduction. This oppression is managed by several institutions, chiefly the family, religion, and the state. An essential part of the oppression of women is control over sexual ideology, mythology, and behavior. This social control affects the sexual nonconformist as well as the conformist. Because our training in conventional sexuality begins the minute we are born and because the penalties for rebellion are so high, no individual or group is completely free from erotic tyranny.

[. . .]

The term 'sadomasochism' has also been debased, primarily by the mass media, clinical psychology, and the anti-pornography movement. After all, homophobia is not the only form of sexual prejudice. Every minority sexual behavior has been mythologized and distorted. There is a paucity of accurate, explicit, nonjudgmental information about sex in modern America. This is one way sexual behavior is controlled. If people don't know a particular technique or lifestyle exists, they aren't likely to try it. If the only images they have of a certain sexual act are ugly, disgusting, or threatening, they will either not engage in that act or be furtive about enjoying it.

Since there is so much confusion about what S/M is, I want to describe my own sexual specialties and the sadomasochistic subculture. I am basically a sadist. About 10% of the time, I take the other role (bottom, slave, masochist). This makes me atypical, since the majority of women and men involved in S/M prefer to play bottom. I enjoy leathersex, bondage, various forms of erotic torture, flagellation (whipping), verbal humiliation, fist-fucking, and watersports (playing with enemas and piss). I do not enjoy oral sex unless I am receiving it as a form of sexual service, which means my partner must be on her knees, on her back, or at least in a collar. I have non-S/M sex rarely, mostly for old times' sake, with vanilla friends[1] I want to stay close to. My primary relationship is with a woman who enjoys being my slave. We enjoy tricking with other people and telling each other the best parts afterward.

Because sadomasochism is usually portrayed as a violent, dangerous activity, most people do not think there is a great deal of difference between a rapist and a bondage enthusiast. Sadomasochism is not a form of sexual assault. It is a consensual activity that involves polarized roles and intense sensations. An S/M scene is always preceded by a negotiation in which the top and bottom decide whether or not they will play, what activities are likely to occur, what activities will not occur, and about how long the scene will last. The bottom is usually given a 'safe word' or 'code action' she can use to stop the scene. This safe word allows the bottom to enjoy a fantasy that the scene is not consensual, and to protest verbally or resist physically without halting stimulation.

The key word to understanding S/M is *fantasy*. The roles, dialogue, fetish costumes, and sexual activity are part of a drama or ritual. The participants are enhancing their sexual pleasure, not damaging or imprisoning one another. A sadomasochist is well aware that a role adopted during a scene is not appropriate during other interactions and that a fantasy role is not the sum total of her being.

S/M relationships are usually egalitarian. Very few bottoms want a full-time mistress. In fact, the stubbornness and aggressiveness of the masochist is a byword in the S/M community. Tops often make nervous jokes about being slaves to the whims of their bottoms. After all, the top's pleasure is dependent on the bottom's willingness to play. This gives most sadists a mild-to-severe case of performance anxiety.

The S/M subculture is a theater in which sexual dramas can be acted out and appreciated. It also serves as a vehicle for passing on new fantasies, new equipment, warnings about police harassment, introductions to potential sex partners and friends, and safety information. Safety is a major concern of sadomasochists. A major part of the sadist's turn-on consists of deliberately altering the emotional or physical state of the bottom. Even a minor accident like a rope burn can upset the top enough to mar the scene. And, of course, a bottom can't relax and enjoy the sex if she doesn't completely trust her top. The S/M community makes some attempt to regulate itself by warning newcomers away from individuals who are inconsiderate, insensitive, prone to playing when they are intoxicated, or unsafe for other reasons. The suppression of S/M isolates novice sadists and masochists from this body of information, which can make playing more rewarding and minimize danger.

For some people, the fact that S/M is consensual makes it acceptable. They may not understand why people enjoy it, but they begin to see that S/M people are not inhuman monsters. For other people, including many feminists, the fact that it is consensual makes it even more appalling. A woman who deliberately seeks out a sexual situation in which she can be helpless is a traitor in their eyes. Hasn't the women's movement been trying to persuade people for years that women are not naturally masochistic?

Originally, this slogan meant that women do not create their own second-class status, do not enjoy it, and are the victims of socially constructed discrimination, not biology. A sexual masochist probably doesn't want to be raped, battered, discriminated against on her job, or kept down by the system. Her desire to act out a specific sexual fantasy is very different from the pseudopsychiatric dictum that a woman's world is bound by housework, intercourse, and childbirth.

Some feminists object to the description of S/M as consensual. They believe that our society has conditioned all of us to accept inequities in power and hierarchical relationships.

[. . .]

It is true, as I stated before, that society shapes sexuality. We can make any decision about our sexual behavior we like, but our imagination and ability to carry out those decisions are limited by the surrounding culture. But I do not believe that sadomasochism is the result of institutionalized injustice to a greater extent than heterosexual marriage, lesbian bars, or gay male bathhouses. The system is unjust because it assigns privileges based on race, gender, and social class. During an S/M encounter, the participants select a particular role because it best expresses their sexual needs, how they feel about a particular partner, or which outfit is clean and ready to wear. The most significant reward for being a top or a bottom is sexual pleasure. If you don't like being a top or a bottom, you switch your keys. Try doing that with your biological sex or your race or your socioeconomic status. The S/M subculture is affected by sexism, racism, and other fallout from the system, but the dynamic between a top and a bottom is quite different from the dynamic between men and women, whites and Blacks, or upper- and working-class people. The roles are acquired and used in very different ways.

Some feminists still find S/M roles disturbing, because they believe they are derived from genuinely oppressive situations. They accuse sadomasochism of being fascistic because of the symbolism employed to create an S/M ambiance. And some S/M people do enjoy fantasies that are more elaborate than a simple structure of top versus bottom. An S/M scene can be played out using the personae of guard and prisoner, cop and suspect, Nazi and Jew, white and Black, straight man and queer, parent and child, priest and penitent, teacher and student, whore and client, etc.

However, no symbol has a single meaning. Its meaning is derived from the context in which it is used. Not everyone who wears a swastika is a Nazi, not everyone who has a pair of handcuffs on his belt is a cop, and not everyone who wears a nun's habit is a Catholic. S/M is more a parody of the hidden sexual nature of facism than it is a worship of or acquiescence to it. How many real Nazis, cops, priests, or teachers would be involved in a kinky sexual scene? It is also a mistake to assume that the historical oppressor is always the top in an S/M encounter. The child may be chastising the parent, the prisoner may have turned the tables on the cop, and the queer may be forcing the straight man to confront his sexual response to other men. The dialogue in some S/M scenes may sound sexist or homophobic from the outside, but its real meaning is probably neither. A top can call his bottom a cocksucker to give him an instruction (i.e., indicate that the top wants oral stimulation), encourage him to lose his inhibitions and perform an act he may be afraid of, or simply acknowledge shame and guilt and use it to enhance the sex act rather than prevent it.

S/M eroticism focuses on whatever feelings or actions are forbidden, and searches for a way to obtain pleasure from the forbidden. It is the quintessence of nonreproductive sex. Those feminists who accuse sadomasochists of mocking the oppressed by playing with dominance and submission forget that *we* are oppressed. We suffer police harassment, violence in the street, discrimination in housing and in employment. We are not treated the way our system treats its collaborators and supporters.

The issue of pain is probably as difficult for feminists to understand as polarized roles. We tend to associate pain with illness or self-destruction. First of all, S/M does not necessarily involve pain. The exchange of power is more essential to S/M than intense sensation, punishment, or discipline. Second, pain is a subjective experience. Depending on the context, a certain sensation may frighten you, make you angry, urge you on, or get you hot. People choose to endure pain or discomfort if the goal they are striving for makes it worthwhile. Long-distance runners are not generally thought of as sex perverts, nor is St Theresa. The fact that masochism is disapproved of when stressful athletic activity and religious martyrdom are not is an interesting example of the way sex is made a special case in our society. We seem to be incapable of using the same reason and compassion we apply to nonsexual issues to formulate our positions on sexual issues.

S/M violates a taboo that preserves the mysticism of romantic sex. Any pain involved is deliberate. Aroused human beings do not see, smell, hear, taste, or perceive pain as acutely as the nonaroused individual. Lots of people find bruises or scratches the morning after an exhilarating session of lovemaking and can't remember exactly how or when they got them. The sensations involved in S/M are not that different. But we're supposed to fall into bed and do it with our eyes closed. Good, enthusiastic sex is supposed to happen automatically between people who love each other. If the sex is less than stunning, we tend to blame the quality of our partner's feelings for us. Planning a sexual encounter and using toys or equipment to produce specific feelings seems antithetical to romance.

What looks painful to an observer is probably being perceived as pleasure, heat, pressure, or a mixture of all these by the masochist. A good top builds sensation slowly, alternates pain with pleasure, rewards endurance with more pleasure, and teaches the bottom to transcend her own limits. With enough preparation, care, and encouragement, people are capable of doing wonderful things. There is a special pride which results from doing something unique and extraordinary for your lover. The sadomasochist has a passion for making use of the entire body, every nerve fiber, and every wayward thought.

Recently, I have heard feminists use the term 'fetishistic' as an epithet and a synonym for 'objectifying.' Sadomasochists are often accused of substituting things for people, of loving the leather or rubber or spike heels more than the person who is wearing them. Objectification originally referred to the use of images of stereotypically feminine women to sell products like automobiles and cigarettes. It also referred to the sexual harassment of women and the notion that we should be available to provide men with sexual gratification without receiving pleasure in return and without the right to refuse to engage in sex. A concept which was originally used to attack the marketing campaigns of international corporations and the sexual repression of women is now being used to attack a sexual minority.

Fetish costumes are worn privately or at S/M gatherings. They are as unacceptable to employers and advertising executives as a woman wearing overalls and smoking a cigar. Rather than being part of the sexual repression of women, fetish costumes can provide the women who wear them with sexual pleasure and power. Even when a fetish costume exaggerates the masculine or feminine attributes of the wearer, it cannot properly be called sexist. Our society strives to make masculinity in men and femininity in women appear natural and biologically determined. Fetish costumes violate this rule by being too theatrical and deliberate. Since fetish costumes may also be used to transform the gender of the wearer, they are a further violation of sexist standards for sex-specific dress and conduct.

The world is not divided into people who have sexual fetishes and people who don't. There is a continuum of response to certain objects, substances, and parts of the body. Very few people are able to enjoy sex with anyone, regardless of their appearance. Much fetishism probably passes as 'normal' sexuality because the required cues are so common and easy to obtain that no one notices how necessary they are.

[. . .]

S/M relationships vary from no relationship at all (the S/M is experienced during fantasy or masturbation) to casual sex with many partners to monogamous couples, and include all shades in between. There are many different ways to express affection or sexual interest. Vanilla people send flowers, poetry, or candy, or they exchange rings. S/M people do all that, and may also lick boots, wear a locked collar, or build their loved one a rack in the basement. There is little objective difference between a feminist who is offended by the fact that my lover kneels to me in public and suburbanites calling the cops because the gay boys next door are sunbathing in the nude. My sexual semiotics differ from the mainstream. So what? I didn't join the feminist movement to live inside a Hallmark greeting card.

Is there a single controversial sexual issue that the women's movement has not reacted to with a conservative, feminine horror of the outrageous and the rebellious? A movement that started out saying biology is *not* destiny is trashing transsexuals and celebrating women's 'natural' connection to the earth and living things. A movement that spawned children's liberation is trashing boy-lovers and supporting the passage of draconian sex laws that assign heavier sentences for having sex with a minor than you'd get for armed robbery. A movement that developed an analysis of housework as unpaid labor and acknowledged that women usually trade sex for what they want because that's all they've got is joining the vice squad to get prostitutes off the street. A movement whose early literature was often called obscene and banned from circulation is campaigning to get rid of pornography. The only sex perverts this movement stands behind are lesbian mothers, and I suspect that's because of the current propaganda about women being the nurturing, healing force that will save the world from destructive male energy.

Lesbianism is being desexualized as fast as movement dykes can apply the white-wash. We are no longer demanding that feminist organizations acknowledge their lesbian membership. We are pretending that the words 'feminist' and 'woman' are synonyms for 'lesbian.'

The anti-pornography movement is the best of the worst of the women's movement, and it must take responsibility for much of the bigotry circulating in the feminist community. [. . .] It has encouraged violence against sexual minorities, especially sadomasochists, by slandering sexual deviation as violence against women. Their view of S/M is derived from one genre of commercial pornography (male-dominant and female-submissive). [. . .] S/M pornography can be divided into several types, each designed for a different segment of the S/M subculture. Most of it represents women dominating and disciplining men, since the largest market for S/M porn is heterosexual submissive males. Very little S/M porn shows any actual physical damage or even implies that damage is occurring. Most of it depicts bondage, or tops dressed in fetish costumes and assuming threatening poses.

Very little S/M porn is well produced or informative. But eliminating it will have the effect of further impoverishing S/M culture and isolating sadomasochists from one another, since many of us make contact via personal ads carried in pornographic magazines. The excuse for banning 'violent' porn is that this will end violence against women. The causal connection is dubious. It is indisputably true that very few people who consume pornography ever assault or rape another person. When a rape or assault is committed, it usually occurs after some forethought and planning. But legally, a free-society must distinguish between the fantasy or thought of committing a crime and the actual crime. It is not a felony to fantasize committing an illegal act, and it should not be, unless we want our morals regulated by the Brain Police. Banning S/M porn is the equivalent of making fantasy a criminal act. Violence against women will not be reduced by increasing sexual repression. People desperately need better information about sex; more humanistic and attractive erotica; more readily available birth control, abortion, and sex therapy; and more models for nontraditional, nonexploitative relationships.

I am often asked if sadomasochism will survive the revolution. I think all the labels and categories we currently use to describe ourselves will change dramatically in the next 100 years, even if the revolution does not occur. My fantasy is that kinkiness and sexual variation will multiply, not disappear, if terrible penalties are no longer meted out for being sexually adventurous.

There is an assumption behind the question that bothers me. The assumption that sadomasochists are part of the system rather than part of the rebellion has already been dealt with in this article. But there is another assumption – that we must enjoy being oppressed and mistreated. We like to wear uniforms? Then we must get off on having cops bust up our bars. We like to play with whips and nipple clamps and hot wax? Then it must turn us on when gangs of kids hunt us down, harass and beat us. We're not really human. We're just a bunch of leather jackets and spike heels, a bunch of post office boxes at the bottom of sex ads.

> *We make you uncomfortable, partly because we're different, partly because we're sexual, and partly because we're not so different. I'd like to know when you're going to quit blaming us, the victims of sexual repression, for the oppression of women. I'd like to know when you're going to quit objectifying us.*

NOTE

1. Vanilla is to S/M what straight is to gay. I don't use the term as a pejorative, but because I believe sexual pretences are more like flavor preferences than like moral political alliances.

3.7

SADOMASOCHISM

Sheila Jeffreys

From the other side of the debate, Sheila Jeffreys is highly critical of sadomasochism. She sees it as deriving from masculine, and particularly gay male, sexual practices. As a celebration of masculine power and violence it is antithetical to feminism and cannot have the same meanings for lesbians as it has for gay men. Her critique derives from a perspective which argues that feminists should problematise pleasure and avoid any eroticisation of power and inequality.

Sadomasochists are [one] of the 'sexual minorities' espoused by gay male libertarian theory. Jeffrey Weeks quotes lesbian rather than male gay theorists of sadomasochism and mentions only lesbian sadomasochism in his book, *Sexuality and its Discontents*.[1] In the 1980s some lesbians have set up promotional groups and written promotional literature on S/M, but S/M as a practice and an idea was well embedded in male gay culture long before. Gay men have not produced much theory about S/M. They have simply practised it and taken it for granted. Lesbians were impelled to theory by their uncomfortable feeling that S/M ideology is in contradiction to the most cherished precepts of feminism. This sense of contradiction forced them into print and justification, which has been convenient for gay men who support or practise S/M, who can hide from the flak of feminist criticism behind the barricade of 'lesbian' sadomasochism. Lesbian practitioners and theorists are quoted by gay men in every argument so that they do not have to take feminist challenges seriously or state their own position.

But such gay men are not at all neutral on the issue. The only 'feminist' theorists quoted with real enthusiasm throughout Weeks' book are the two best-known American lesbian proponents of S/M, Pat Califia and Gayle Rubin. Those radical feminists

From S. Jeffreys, *Anti-Climax: A Feminist Perspective of the Sexual Revolution*, London: The Women's Press, 1990.

who oppose S/M politics are pilloried throughout. On occasion his political sympathies for S/M are expressed more straightforwardly. In the tenth anniversary issue of the old *Gay News* in 1982, Weeks asserts that there are two approaches to sexuality among feminists and gays: 'one is working towards redefining the nature of sexual relations; the other towards defending the importance of sexual choice'.[2] It is not immediately clear why there should be any conflict since both seem to be unimpeachable aims. Then when Weeks describes those who are so bold as to suggest redefinition his prejudice becomes clear. These are lesbian separatists, 'some of whom are very hostile to gay male lifestyles', and 'paradoxically . . . the more purist male survivors of early gay liberation'.

[. . .]

For a sexual radical such as Weeks, change is anathema. Feminists are a problem because they insist on demanding change. 'Choice' has become the new grail for sexual radicals. [. . .] He describes the feminist position as a 'new absolutism' and the pro-S/M position as 'radical pluralism'.

[. . .]

Weeks concludes with warnings against the danger that feminists will [. . .] 'ally with the old absolutism of evangelical Christian morality'.

[. . .]

Weeks' hostility to feminism because of its threat to the sacred absolutes of the male gay sexual agenda is profound.

Sadomasochism is described by one exponent, Ian Young, as 'sex involving pain, either physical (such as slapping or spanking) or symbolic (such as enacted domination or restraint of one partner by another)'.[3] More generally, S/M has come to mean such practices as those designated as 'unusual sexual activities' in the Spada report, a survey of gay male sexuality compiled from 1,000 questionnaires and published in 1979. Spada includes in this category 'fistfucking (active or passive), sadism and masochism, bondage and discipline, humiliation, watersports (sex involving urination), scat (sex involving defecation)'.[4] All these activities are routinely included beneath the generic umbrella of S/M in contemporary lesbian S/M literature. It turns out that these practices were not all that unusual among Spada's respondents, who covered a wide cross-section of the gay community. Nearly 30 per cent of respondents engaged in one or more of the activities.

It would be wrong to see S/M as a bizarre practice quite unconnected with everyday sex. An examination of routine male gay practice shows that dominance and submission and gender role playing are fundamental to male gay eroticism. The Spada report is very useful in forming a picture of standard gay male sexual practice. The questionnaires were open-ended and respondents were encouraged to express their feelings and motivations towards a range of everyday practices at length.

Anal intercourse was enjoyed by 76 per cent and disliked by 12 per cent and is therefore a standard sexual practice. There is no reason to assume that anal intercourse is inherently linked with sadomasochism any more than other sexual practices might be. What is clear from the Spada respondents is that they invest the practice with emotional loadings of eroticised dominance and submission. One question asked: 'During anal intercourse, are you usually "top" or "bottom" man? If both, what determines which it will be – your partner, your mood, or what?' The language is revealing. 'Top' and 'bottom' are the words used for the active and passive roles in S/M. Many of the respondents quoted were unequivocal that anal intercourse is about dominance and submission. As a Spada respondent points out, 'the combination of emotional domination-submission and the closeness it provides between the two people, mixed with the animal sensations and orgasm, are almost inseparable'.

[. . .]

Many of the respondents go so far as to describe anal intercourse as a grotesque parody of what they imagine vaginal intercourse to be like. One man described himself as feeling when 'on top' like 'the all-penetrating male! I am the man'. His role he describes as being to 'gently impale his partner'. He treats his partner 'as I would a woman when he is in that vulnerable position' and sees himself when being penetrated as being in the same position, 'When I am on my back with my legs thrown over the shoulders of my partner', as 'the vulnerable woman'.[5] Another respondent saw anal intercourse as 'a great way to express the masculine and feminine parts of your personality'.[6] The top role represented the 'traditional male role' and vice versa.

Clearly a decade of gay liberation had not had much impact on gay men's conflation of effeminacy with homosexuality, or on their concept of the 'real man'. One respondent spoke of the advantages of the practice in bolstering the masculinity and heterosexuality of his partner.

[. . .]

In the Spada report 59 per cent of men said they didn't get aroused by uniforms and leather but 25 per cent found uniforms sexually exciting and 18 per cent found leather so. Spada comments: 'Most of the men who find these things arousing do so because they heighten masculinity and sexuality.'

[. . .]

The achievement or imitation of masculinity is so important to gay men and to their sexual practice that it is worth looking at responses to the Spada report question, 'How would you define masculinity?' One respondent defined masculinity as 'virility, courage, strength, muscles, a prick and balls', another as 'Males boot-tough and wolf-mean'.[7] One defined masculinity simply as 'Leather'.[8] One described masculinity as 'being straight'.

For feminists these definitions are chilling in their implications. The respondents were not asked to define femininity but it is not difficult to work out what the opposite of the above would entail. Male gay theorists tend to be indulgent towards the worship of masculinity by gay men. It is explained as being a reaction to the fact that gay men have always been defined and looked down on as effeminate. They are thus getting their own back. It is not easy to be so indulgent as women and lesbians. The worship of masculinity and the attempt to construct a sexuality and a culture which reflects this is a direct threat to the possibility of women's liberation. Spada remarked upon the connection his respondents made between masculinity and performance with the penis so that sex in general between two men 'is the epitome of masculinity'.[9]

Even the most radical and politicised of gay men fall prey to the worship of masculinity and seem unwilling to change. Martin Humphries writes in a collection on *The Sexuality of Men* by writers from the British anti-sexist men's magazine *Achilles' Heel*. He describes the impact of the shift to masculinity which has overwhelmed the early gay liberation aim to break down 'the social distinctions between femininity and masculinity', in order to create 'an androgynous world . . . within which gender would no longer be relevant'.[10] These politics succumbed to a cult of machismo.

[. . .]

Humphries says he is implicated in this climate. He has fantasies focused on men who conform to 'current images of masculinity' and looks for 'butch-looking' men when cruising. Humphries, not surprisingly, does not wish to eliminate such role playing but merely seeks ways of 'widening the realms of desire in such a way that we are not trapped into rigid and highly delineated patterns of behaviour suggested by these images'. He wants roles to 'become only a part of sex' and not a 'straitjacket'.[11] Roles would enable gay men to act out masculinity or to worship it according to their mood. Roles, then, would remain, but gay men would seek to swap roles more routinely. He does not question the very construction of desire around the heterosexual S/M romance, nor believe that 'roles' can be eliminated.

The S/M scenario that many gay men are able to make of their whole sexual practice, based upon fetishised masculinity and femininity, should make clear, supposing any doubt remains, that the traditional heterosexual system is an S/M romance. Through the exaggeration of the characteristics of gender roles, the naked, eroticised power dynamic which fuels heterosexuality is laid bare.

[. . .]

Since most gay men in the Spada survey interpreted a routine gay sexual practice such as anal intercourse to constitute dominance and submission, expressed in the form of parodied male female heterosexual gender roles, we should not be surprised to discover that 30 per cent of gay male respondents engaged in S/M-related practices. It could be argued that not all the practices labelled 'unusual' in the report involve S/M. Some men, for instance, reported that watersports, i.e. urinating into each other's mouths and over other parts of the body, were engaged in simply for sensual delight. But practices like fistfucking and scat are fairly clearly about power and humiliation and therefore deserve to fall under the umbrella of S/M. Fistfucking is not a rare activity. Of the Spada respondents 14.5 per cent had engaged in active fistfucking and 8.2 per cent in passive fistfucking.

In practice . . . the whole of the active partner's forearm is inserted *per anum* into the passive partner's body. [. . .]

Gay men have produced very little theory about why S/M exists. S/M proponents perceive questions about motivation as hostile. For those who see S/M as natural, inevitable and good there is no need for explanation. Explanation, they argue, is only required for practices which are disapproved of, and which hostile interrogators would like to bring to an end. As an example they cite homophobes who seek to explain homosexuality and see heterosexuality as 'natural'. For libertarian gay male theorists all forms of male sexuality are valid, natural and inevitable. Paedophilia and transsexualism require no more explanation than S/M. They direct their energies to justifying the practices, explaining why they are positive and why all progressive, radical people should support and defend them.

The Lavender Culture's *Forum on Sadomasochism* consists of written replies by two gay men and two lesbians to ten questions on sadomasochism. The questions force the respondents to apply themselves to explanation. Ian Young, who is pro-S/M, offers the argument that S/M is natural.

> Everyone has erotic fantasies. People into S&M are simply more aware of their erotic imaginations in this respect and have found ways to externalise their fantasies in agreeable ways, to act on them. As far as the dominance-submission aspect of S&M goes, and this is what is most upsetting to outsiders – we all have a need for aggression and a need for submission in our lives . . . [12]

Young also argues that S/M is a superior form of sexual practice to non-S/M sex. Only 'creative and highly imaginative' people, he says, have the capacity for S/M because S/M 'is a pretty sophisticated and complex mode of behaviour'.[13] He concludes that S/M is 'a more evolved form of sexuality, *higher on the human evolutionary ladder*' than reproductive sex.

[. . .]

Young goes on to congratulate himself further by stating that S/Mers are anarchists and libertarians devoted to ending oppression. S/M, he argues, enables practitioners to understand, through ritualised dominance and submission, how power and powerlessness really work in the world beyond the bedroom.

[. . .]

John Rechy is no libertarian and [. . .] states unequivocal condemnation of S/M, asserting that the 'proliferation of sadomasochism is the major threat to gay freedom'.[14] Rechy sees the self-hatred of male gays as the main reason for S/M. He describes the oppression that anyone gay experiences from the straight world as they grow up. The ritual of S/M, he says, follows from this and 'embraces the straight world's judgement, debasement, hatred, and contempt of and for the homosexual'.[15] The male homosexual grows up ashamed of his love for other men, according to this analysis, and only feels able to practise sex with men when forced to do so in S/M ritual, or while receiving punishment for 'desiring homosexual sex acts'.[15] The 'S' is included in this explanation. Rechy explains that 'he is transferring his feelings of self-contempt for his own homosexuality on to the cowering "M", who turns himself willingly into what gayhaters have called him'.[17] The result is that the 'S' says, 'You are the queer now, not me, and I'll punish you for it, just as I was punished for it . . .'[18] According to Rechy, 'Gay S&M is the straight world's most despicable legacy'.[19]

This is a persuasive argument. It really seems to explain the attack made, in S/M practice, upon the flesh, the apparent hatred of sexuality. [. . .] This explanation [. . .] doubtless helps to explain gay male S/M, but one vital ingredient is missing. It doesn't explain the differences between male gay and lesbian sexual practice. Where there are differences related to gender it is necessary to look for a feminist explanation. Rechy has no understanding of gender politics. He makes this clear in *The Sexual*

Outlaw partly through the great incongruity of his ability to condemn S/M so fiercely in the context of what looks to be a paean of praise to S/M practice. Half of the book, described as a 'documentary', details the cruising adventures of the hero Jim on beaches, in alleyways, and in abandoned buildings. [. . .] The whole 'sex-hunt' is described in terms of conquest and defeat. It is about dominance and submission and the assertion of masculinity. [. . .] Yet the gay men who do this macho posturing, this terrifying and brutal battle in which silent men, seeking to look like thugs, struggle to immolate themselves in masochistic tribute to a 'masculine' body or to win victories by being constantly worshipped in the act of fellatio, are called by Rechy the 'shock troops of the sexual revolution'.[20] Rechy seeks to make a clear and absolute distinction between this activity he sees as so positive and S/M, which he sees as such a threat. It is difficult to know where the line could be drawn. Rechy is not prepared to do less than eulogise about cruising. To be consistent he should see male gay S/M as simply the tip of an iceberg. When mainstream male gay sexual practice eroticises dominance and submission then male gay S/M has to be explained in the context of the construction of male sexuality.

John Stoltenberg sees S/M as the inevitable result of a 'social structure of male-over female sexual domination'. 'For the genital male,' he explains, 'eroticised violence against women results in male sexual identity reification.'[21] How can this work between two men? Stoltenberg sees the top as embodying 'the cultural norm of male sexuality' and identifying with 'male-supremacist values and behaviours'. The bottom shores up his male sexual identity, his masculinity, by absorbing into himself either the body fluids of the real man or his violence.

> For this partner, gratification consists in the fact that he ingests the sadist's semen and/or absorbs the sadist's violence. These mythic residues of the sadist's virile presence stay in his body, and he assimilates potency like a battery getting charge.[22]

Spada respondents bear out Stoltenberg's insights into the ingestion of masculinity by bottoms in sexual encounters. Their comments on fellatio are particularly relevant. One fellater remarked: 'I always feel I am draining a bit of male power from my partner's body to mine.'[23] On the swallowing of ejaculate one man commented: 'It makes me feel like I have the seed of superman if my partner is a real turn-on.'[24] Others described semen as 'mysterious, potent . . . the beginning of life and creation', and 'the most vital part of his [the partner's] manhood'.[25]

The difference between male gay S/M and lesbian S/M is clarified by such statements. Lesbians cannot ingest ruling-class power by serving as bottoms since no women have that power. Stoltenberg explains that the urge to S/M practice is quite different in men and women 'because the male homosexual drive to incorporate manliness functions as a means of dissociating himself from the inferior status of the female, while the masochism of a woman functions to fix her in that state'.[26] It may be that to understand the importance of S/M in male gay culture we need to combine explanations based on gay oppression with explanations based on gender oppression. Sexual acting out is crucial to male sexual identity and a main source of ego enhancement. For gay men this is complicated by self-hatred and the fact that the object of their desire is the male ruling class. The worship of the masculinity principle can be carried out in either active or passive roles in S/M.

NOTES

1. Jeffrey Weeks, *Sexuality and its Discussions*, London: Routledge, 1985.
2. *Gay News*, Tenth Anniversary Issue, June 1982, no. 243.
3. *Ibid.*, p. 94.
4. James Spada, *The Spada Report*, New York: Signet, New American Library, 1979, p. 26.
5. *Ibid.*, p. 103.
6. *Ibid.*, p. 94.
7. *Ibid.*, p. 157.
8. *Ibid.*, p. 158.
9. *Ibid.*, p. 160.
10. Andy Metcalfe and Martin Humphries, *The Sexuality of Men*, London: Pluto Press, 1985, p. 71.
11. *Ibid.*, p. 83.
12. K. Jay and A. Young (eds), *Lavender Culture*, New York: Harcourt Brace Jovanovich, 1978, p. 90.
13. *Ibid.*, p. 95.
14. J. Rechy, *The Sexual Outlaw*, London: Futura, 1979, p. 253.
15. *Ibid.*, p. 257.
16. *Ibid.*, p. 259.
17. *Ibid.*, p. 261.
18. *Ibid.*
19. *Ibid.*, p. 262.
20. *Ibid.*, p. 298.
21. Jay and Young, *Lavender Culture*, p. 92.
22. *Ibid.*, p. 93.
23. *Ibid.*
24. *Ibid.*, p. 86.
25. *Ibid.*
26. *Ibid.*, p. 87.

3.8

SEX AFTER AIDS

Rosalind Coward

Anxiety about AIDS and HIV infection has created an imperative for safer sex. Rosalind Coward argues that for heterosexual women safer sex, which de-privileges penetrative sex, enhances rather than restricts the potential for sexual pleasure and more egalitarian heterosexual relations.

'Safer sex' is the cry on the lips of all concerned with preventing the spread of AIDS. Avoiding certain kinds of sexual practices and indulging in others is widely held to be one of the few ways in which a major health disaster could be minimised. Yet if the call for safer sex were to be taken seriously by the population, this would mean a drastic change.

Such changes are not easy to make and for many, the concept of safer sex looks like just another attempt to infringe recent hardwon sexual freedoms. Virtually all discussion of the subject has been in these terms, revolving around the problems of the freedom of the individual versus interference or limitations on personal behaviour. It is curious that there has been virtually no acknowledgement that we live in a sexually unequal society and that sexual practices are the place where this inequality is often expressed.

In most talk about AIDS, what feminists have to say about sexual relations has been almost completely ignored. It is as if feminists have never criticised existing sexual practices between men and women as usually dreary, often oppressive and occasionally downright dangerous. Suddenly everyone is yearning nostalgically for the pre-AIDS era when choice and spontaneity were the names of the game. But it's clear to me at least that men and women have different interests at stake in any possible sexual revolution

From R. Coward, 'Sex after AIDS', *New Internationalist*, March 1987.

and that the crisis produced by AIDS may well have different implications for men and women. It is just possible that there may be things women can gain from the current situation – distressing as it may be.

For men, safer sex is seen as a curtailment. It means, at least at first sight, an almost compulsory use of condoms and a strong suggestion that penetration of the vagina or anus ought to wait until you feel pretty sure of your partner.

For women, safer sex has different resonances. Heterosexuality has never been safe for women, nor particularly spontaneous. The pill allowed women an unprecedented degree of spontaneity but it could hardly be described as unpremeditated or unrisky. In going on the pill, women make a definite decision – one that entails putting themselves at risk medically. It is too well-documented to ignore that women on the pill are in higher-risk categories for thrombosis and breast cancer. The choice to have an Intra-Uterine Device (IUD) fitted is also known to involve medical risks.

As far as statistics are available, it's apparent that women have been bearing the brunt of making sex safe for men in the past. It's been our problem because it's women who get pregnant, and women who have abortions; and unless a heterosexual partner is especially pro-feminist he's unlikely to have had sufficient motivation to use condoms. But now, suddenly, it's a matter of life and death to *men* that they abandon their historical privilege of spontaneous sex and assume personal responsibility for their actions.

Nor is it just a question of the gains to be had in heterosexual, penetrative sex. The crisis around AIDS demands we find sexual alternatives to penetration of the vagina and anus, or oral sex where semen is swallowed. Again, it seems to me that feminists have had quite a lot to say about the limited amount of pleasure which these activities bring women.

Feminists over the last 15 years have mounted a full-scale attack on men's obsession with penetration and ejaculation which has often denied to women any genuine sexual pleasure. Most women describe themselves as enjoying other forms of stimulation especially to the clitoris, at least as much, if not more, than penetration. This is particularly so if an obsessive focus on penetration and ejaculation minimises other pleasures. The endless tale told at sex therapy clinics is of women seeking other stimulation, verbal and physical, and of looking for other forms of physical closeness which do not inevitably lead to penetration. It has been described over and over again how women can become physically rejecting because they don't want all physical encounters to end in penetration.

A common form of advice given to heterosexual couples who have run into this problem is to put a temporary taboo on penetrative sex. It's a period where individuals are encouraged actually to learn about each other's pleasures, to find out about each other's bodies without the inevitable goal of penetration. Perhaps AIDS could be seen as a social version of this therapeutic taboo, a pause used for people to find out about each other, less obvious pleasures, and a moment where sexuality could be redefined as something other than male discharge into any kind of receptacle. In this new context where penetration might literally spell death, there is a chance for a massive relearning about sexuality.

It is an important aspect of this crisis that organisations like the Terrence Higgins Trust in London and the San Francisco AIDS Foundation[1] have set the terms of the debate in explicit language about the kinds of practices which would be safe and the need to 'decentralise' penetration. In capturing the initiative, albeit often directed at the most vulnerable group – male homosexuals – such propaganda has become sufficiently widespread to make it difficult for governments to turn their backs on the need for sex education.

When I saw the literature of the Terrence Higgins Trust I was overwhelmed with regret that such explicit talk about what happened in sexual relations had not been available to me as a girl. Part of female oppression has been lived out through the ignorance in which women are kept about their bodies and sexuality. Indeed[. . .]there is *still* a fight on about how much women are entitled to know and choose in childbirth. And as various feminist commentators make clear in that case, knowledge is power. The more women know about what is likely to happen to them, the more likely they are to be able to take control of what is happening to them. The same clearly applies to sexual relations. The more women know about their own bodies and their responses, the more likely they are to be partners in sex who are not to be used just as repositories for male sexual urges and fantasies.

The question of knowledge about sexuality is one very pressing reason why 'sexual liberation' was not wholly a bad thing for women – in spite of the fact that it was men who mainly benefited from this freedom since they never had to bear the consequences of sex. The increased sexual freedom and possibility of choice and experimentation did give *some* women the possibility of knowing more and taking more control of their own sexuality. The new need to communicate about sexual habits and practices is something which could greatly benefit girls since it would extend the information which they have about sex. It seems to me that what is really at stake in the AIDS crisis is not whether we can preserve our existing freedoms but whether we can use the crisis to transform the balance of power between the sexes. This, of course, will not happen if we leave AIDS to governments and the 'experts' who have already demonstrated themselves more sympathetic to calls for sexual monogamy and a morality based on the nuclear family. This right-wing vision holds nothing for women. Traditional family life with its fixed sexual roles for men and women is probably far more disastrous for women than the heady days of sexual freedom. Within the traditional family lies the complete exploitation of women who are not only financially dependent on men but also deprived of personal and sexual equality.

[. . .]

If AIDS does indeed develop in the ways predicted then it will, whether we like it or not, transform the terrain on which sexual relations and sexual politics are played out. It would be foolish and defeatist if feminists did not engage in discussions about what to do about AIDS, or failed to recognise that this is an issue which concerns us politically.

3.9

PRESSURED PLEASURE
Young Women and the Negotiation
of Sexual Boundaries

Janet Holland, Caroline Ramazanoglu,
Sue Sharpe and Rachel Thomson

This research on young women's sexuality counters the earlier optimism of feminists who hoped that safer sex might mean better sex for heterosexual women. This piece draws on data from the Women, Risk and AIDS Project, identifying some of the difficulties young women face in attempting to negotiate with male sexual partners. In particular it shows that the lack of a language of sexual pleasure limits young women's understanding of the possibilities, leaving them without a position from which to assert their own desires.

Problems of how to explain the nature and legitimation of men's power over women lie at the heart of feminist sociology. While much has been done to identify the mechanisms through which such power is exercised, relatively little is known about the sexual politics of sex at the level of heterosexual practices. Feminists have tended to have been more concerned with the sexual politics of heterosexuality and lesbianism[1] than with how women can experience safer and more positive sexual relations with men.[2] The tragedy of the AIDS epidemic has now given urgency to questions about the ways in which sexual encounters are constituted as gendered social relationships; how female and male sexual identities are constructed and what an empowered femininity could mean in bodily encounters.

[. . .]

Young women who assert their own needs, however, have to negotiate sexual relationships with men which resist the commonsense of masculine and feminine sexuality. In this paper, we consider two aspects of sexual politics: the pressures to which even

From J. Holland, C. Ramazanoglu, S. Sharpe and R. Thomson, *Pressured Pleasure: Young Women and the Negotiation of Sexual Boundaries*, London. The Tufnell Press, 1992.

assertive young women are exposed in the negotiation of heterosexual encounters, and the ways in which we can begin to think about the empowerment of women in heterosexual relationships.

[...]

We argue that a young woman can only assert sexual needs in terms of her own bodily pleasure if she can negotiate sexual boundaries with her partner. She may have to stand up to, if not go against, the boundaries of femininity in sexual relationships, since a positive femininity is a challenge to dominant masculinities.

When young women, often under the age of consent, begin to engage in sexual relationships and to test out their sexual identities, they do not initially have direct personal experience to draw on and much that they need to know is hidden from them. They have to make sense of information from different sources – childhood experiences, schools, parents and siblings, peers, the mass media – while often receiving contradictory messages from these sources. They may have well-established ideas on how sexual relationships ought to be; how a one night stand compares with going steady; how a good night kiss compares with letting him touch you 'there', or going 'all the way'; they know that sex is risky, at least for girls. They usually have information about the mechanics of heterosexual intercourse and the existence of contraception. They will have ideas about romance, femininity and their bodies, but they may have little emotional or practical information that they can use to define the boundaries of their own pleasure or their own safety.[3] There is little conception of how male and female desires, risks and pleasures may be related, or how to raise questions about pleasure and safety on the way to sexual intercourse.[4]

PRESSURE FROM MEN IN SEXUAL ENCOUNTERS

We have classified the pressures that young women experience in sexual encounters in terms of personal pressure, social pressure, and pressures coming directly from men. Personal pressures are incorporated into the individual's conception of self and way of organising and understanding her own sexuality. Social pressures emanate from the variety of cultural and institutional contexts in which the person is located; family, peer group, school, workplace, religion, mass media, culture, sub-culture. It is the different messages from these different sources that oblige young women to live with, and make sense of, contradictions in the social construction of feminine sexuality. The pressures, however, are not all treated as equally important. Running through the various sources are pressures which are experienced in terms of their expectations of and pressures from men, and it is these pressures that we have concentrate on in this paper.

One of the most successful areas of feminist knowledge has been the feminist study of male violence. It has reconstructed women's supposedly private failures as victims, as the widespread abuse of patriarchal power by men.[5] This is the main area in which arguments for the generality of women's subordination by men can be supported.[6]

Some physical expressions of violence are very obvious, but other social pressures for controlling women's sexuality are harder to identify, as the ways in which gender ideologies are embedded in social and economic processes can be complex.[7] The sexual pressures which women experience are, in part, enmeshed in loving and caring relationships, and the ideology of male control of sexuality is part of the social constitution of masculinity and femininity. Feminism's contribution here has been to show that violence can be conceived as a range of mechanisms which are linked to the exercise of power. It is this exercise of power which constitutes a set of interrelated constraints on the empowerment of young women.

[. . .]

Liz Kelly[8] has developed the notion of a continuum of sexual violence and argues that all forms of sexual violence are serious in terms of their impact on women's lives, but the impact at the time, and women's subsequent reactions are complex matters. Kelly uses the notion of a continuum of sexual violence to express both the common features of different experiences in which men control or subordinate women, and also the range of more or less violent behaviour which cannot be easily identified as discrete categories of men's behaviour.

Men's ability to exercise power over women in individual sexual encounters, or attempted encounters, can also be conceptualised in terms of a continuum of men's sexual behaviour towards women.[9] At one end of this continuum men's behaviour can be sexually non-aggressive, using persuasion, seeking consensual sex; intermediate pressures could be regarded as sexually coercive, using social or emotional coercion, or verbally expressed demands for sex; at the other end, men's behaviour can be sexually aggressive and impelling, where they obtain sexual intercourse through threats, or the use of force.[10] Men are not necessarily always located at one point on the continuum; they can behave differently with different partners, at different points in their sexual careers or in different types of relationship. This descriptive continuum of men's behaviour differs from Kelly's continuum of sexual violence as conceptualised by women,[11] and our categorisation of men's behaviour is developed in terms of women's accounts of their experiences.

We do not intend to imply that men's sexual behaviour is always violent nor that women are never violent. [. . .]

Feminist knowledge of male violence requires a redefinition of public and private boundaries. The control which men exert over women in the private sphere cannot be separated from the legitimation of male dominance, the greater value of men and the dominance of patriarchal political and economic institutions in the public sphere. As violence and sexuality are very closely linked in the social construction of western scxualities, it was to be expected that young women's accounts of their negotiations of the boundaries of sexual practices, would include accounts of sexual pressures exercised by men. These varied from accounts of reluctant consent to sexual intercourse which they did not want, to an account of a prolonged and violent experience of gang rape.

CONCEPTUALISING THE EMPOWERMENT OF YOUNG WOMEN

Feminists have conceived the notion of women's empowerment in different ways. These have enabled us to think of women as resisting the pressures of patriarchal societies; as having collective power which gives them agency rather than being the individual victims of patriarchy. The problem with thinking about empowerment in sexual encounters is that these encounters are defined as private.

[. . .]

It is easy to talk of how to empower young women so as to make sex safer or more pleasurable; but it is more difficult to specify what exactly is meant by empowerment in sexual relations when women are subordinate to men.

[. . .]

There is no language or model of positive female sexuality for young women. Feminine sexualities as socially constituted in western cultures are generally disempowering in that they are constructed in subordination to dominant masculine sexualities. As Janeway[12] has put it, this is the myth of female power: 'her submission makes him a man'. Any exercise of women's power in sexual relations is not only unfeminine, but also threatening to men.

Envisaging empowerment for young women means defining the power relations which *could* be changed and defining strategies for transforming relationships. In the context of sexual encounters, empowering women need not mean women exerting power over men, or behaving like men. We have conceptualised this as a 'male model empowerment' and have categorised it as a form of disempowerment for women.[13] Whereas the exercise of male power means the subordination and control of women by men, we do not take women's empowerment to be the subordination of men. Empowerment is both contested, and a process, in which women struggle to negotiate *with* men to increase control over their own sexuality. Effective empowerment could mean any of the following: not engaging in sexual activity; not engaging in sexual activity without informed consent; getting men to consent to safer practices; negotiating sexual practices which are pleasurable to women as well as to men.

YOUNG WOMEN'S RESPONSES TO MALE SEXUAL PRESSURE

The dominance of male sexuality, men's needs and women's compliance, constitutes a social context within which the young women we spoke to negotiate their sexual experience. The possibility of empowerment for young women then entails critical consideration of how women can respond to the pressures on them to treat sexual encounters as primarily for fulfilling men's sexual needs. The lack of a positive model of female sexuality means that women have to undertake a great deal of critical reflection on their experience in order to gain control of their responses to men.

[. . .]

It is difficult to disentangle in practice the range of pressures to which women are subject, and where women have experienced the more violent and coercive forms of sexual pressure, such as child abuse, rape, assault or threats, these experiences can shape their expectations of men's behaviour in subsequent sexual encounters. In the section which follows we have selected some categories . . . to indicate the complexity of the issue, and the extent to which both male pressure and women's empowerment need to be understood as contested processes rather than as stable categories of young women's experience.

Verbal sexual pressure: persuasion

In some cases women had effectively consented to sex, or to unsafe sex, which they did not want, because of what they felt to be social pressures, or the importance to them of their relationship or potential relationship with a man. Men did not need to take any decisive action in these cases to exert pressure for women to feel that they should submit.

> *A:* I was really like used to blokes treating me really bad. Like I don't think I'd ever really had a bloke as a friend. Like they were all sort of sexually orientated, and not much between us in the way of friendship.
>
> [...]

One young woman reflecting on her first sexual experience when she was fourteen was ambivalent about pressure. The man concerned was seventeen, and uncertain of his own sexual identity.

> *Q:* And were you pressured into it?
>
> *A:* Looking back on it now, I would say, yeah, I was a bit. Yeah a little bit. But I don't actually remember having any memory of saying to myself 'this is what I want to do' I just remember doing it and thinking 'it's not much of a big deal' . . . It just happened. I just accepted it.
>
> [...]

The interaction of personal social and male pressures could be difficult for women to disentangle when they looked back at their initial experiences of sex. Later knowledge and experience puts previous experiences in a different light.

> *A:* I liked him at the start, but I didn't like him enough to have sex with him, I don't think. I need to really like someone to have sex with them. I know that now, but at the time I was quite immature and I just wanted to have sex basically.
>
> *Q:* Whose idea was it?
>
> *A:* I think it was his, but I let him. He didn't rape me or anything.

Looking back on their sexual experiences the young women were generally reluctant to describe men's behaviour as violent, or as rape, unless overt force had been used. They usually saw themselves as contributing to the pressure because they had not stopped it.

Verbal sexual pressure: coercion

Verbal persuasion from men could be experienced as coercive not directly because of the man's behaviour, but because of the woman's beliefs about the meanings of men's behaviour and what would happen if intercourse was denied.

A: I was also a little bit worried, but I just tried to brush it off a little bit. But it was obvious that he wasn't going to take no for an answer. I suppose in a way I was scared of what he would do if I said 'No' any more. Because he was really like pushing me. Not pushing me physically, but pushing me in the sense of – 'Oh, come on' – you know. I thought, – Oh God I felt guilty, because I thought – 'you've led him on – led him on.'

Here the fears of what the man might do were compounded by the woman's conception of male sexuality which made her feel responsible for his state of arousal and its resolution. In another case, the young women had much more explicit fears about what might happen, based both on expectations in this relationship and on earlier experiences of violence.

A: I was very young – I didn't know what was – well I did know what was happening, but he was about five years older than me, and he was very very persuasive and very pushy, and I was so frightened of him at the time that you don't want to say no. If you think – if you say no then they won't want to see you again.

Her account starts with pressure coming from the man in terms of his age, and his persuasion, but the salient issue for her is her belief that sexual intercourse is the price of a continued relationship. The lack of any pleasure from intercourse makes her realise that this price was not worth it, but she is then caught by her own expectations of men's behaviour:

A: . . . At the time, you know – awfully painful – and just kind of lying there and wishing that it'd go away: and that went on for about – I suppose that was about seven or eight times we had sex and I – every time cringing and not – not enjoying it. It – it seems silly – at the time you think, 'well, why can't you say no?'

[. . .]

The reason that she could not say no was obviously difficult for her to articulate in the interview:

A: . . . But, as – because I – every – I was very afraid of men at the time because my Dad used to hit me all the time when I was – didn't do something he wanted I'd get hit and I was, like for a long – for three years afterwards I thought that any man would hit me if – if I didn't do what he says, that you – you know, that you have to do. If you say 'no' to somebody then they're going to hit you.

Physical sexual pressure: intimidation

Physical pressure could be associated with situations where men interpreted a social relationship as entitling them to sex. A young woman whose first experience of sex was in an arranged marriage discussed her fear and dislike of sex. Her husband had tried to discuss sex with her, had explained that intercourse was supposed to be a pleasure, had arranged for her to go on the pill and had bought her a book on sex, but he did not know how to deal with her fears of sex nor how to make intercourse pleasurable for her. She had no information on, nor sense of, women's pleasure which she could bring to the encounter. As they did not have a home of their own, she lived with her parents and he visited her two or three times as week.

> A: He told me, 'whatever I do, don't say no, just say yes', and – I don't know – and he says, 'you have to say yes, you have to listen to me'. And then he goes to do that thing.
>
> Q: But did you know what he was going to do?
>
> A: Yes, I did know what he was going to do, but I didn't know the feeling I was going to get, so I was scared . . . I tried to push him off the bed. But everytime I pushed him he pulled my hair. He said, 'if you don't let me, I'm going to pull your hair' . . .
>
> Q: Do you think you will ever grow to like it?
>
> A: No, I don't think so.

The only way in which she could preserve some agency was in a negative way by refusing sex as often as possible. Since she had found that stopping him at the bedroom door was too late, she had to state at the front door 'I am not doing it today'.

Physical sexual pressure: sex when drunk

Where women had been drunk at the time of unwanted sexual intercourse, they were particularly unwilling to describe themselves as having been raped or physically forced into sex. They felt that they must take some responsibility because they had not been in a state effectively to choose not to have sex.

> A: I'd had something to drink, and I started to sober up, very drunk and I started to sober up. And somebody, a friend of this person who was having a party . . . We'd had this party, and we'd come back to this person's flat . . . just like a friend of a friend. I mean I can't say that I was forced into it or whatever, but I was in that position where I thought, 'God, I don't want to do this, I don't want to do this,' and I sobered up a little bit, and I was still slightly tipsy anyway. I thought, 'Oh God, you know, what am I going to say?' Because it was obvious what he was expecting. And really when I was quite drunk I went along with this, not really making the decision to do that . . . So I didn't really have a conscious decision to make, but it was obvious, because I had let myself.

For other women though, an experience of having unwanted sexual intercourse could make them more assertive in relation to the man.

> A: So, on the second day of me going out with him, I got drunk and he had sex with me and I really regretted it. Like the next day I hated it and I didn't like

him. And it seemed that after that, after he'd actually got his sex, it seemed like he thought he could treat me like dirt. He just started speaking to me rudely, just being stupid, you know? So on the fourth day I just told him, I don't want to know. Because he thought because he got it once, he thought he was going to get it every day and I said to him it was a big mistake I made. I really regretted it. I think it was from that point that it made me realise I'm not going to do that again, no way.

Physical sexual pressure: child abuse

Sexual abuse as a child was profoundly disempowering, but the experiences of those who recognised that they had been abused show links between the processes of pressure and empowerment as young women coming to terms with their sexuality as adults try to understand the impact of their previous experiences.

A: Well, when I was very young I was sexually abused by my uncle. He also abused my two sisters and when it actually happened to me I told my Mum and Dad. It was all hush hush then. It was the time when it was never spoken about and they wouldn't believe me. So since then I decided, 'don't trust anybody, forget all about it', and then somehow I made myself forget. I don't know how I did it, I just made myself forget. And then I started getting close to this lad when I was about fourteen and then it just started coming back, sort of in little bits.

Child abuse became a possible source of empowerment when women could look back on their experiences (usually as a result of counselling some years after the abuse), give a name to what had happened, and connect subsequent negative sexual experiences (usually an absence of any enjoyment of sex even in a close relationship) with the abuse. That is, they had to be able to recognise the experience as an abuse of power and to reflect on its impact on them. One young woman (who had been recommended to see a counsellor, but had refused because she felt she would break down when recalling the abuse) discussed her first subsequent sexual experience in the following terms. At the time she was sixteen and was coming under pressure to have sex with her boyfriend who was a year older and had been her friend since she was thirteen.

A: And my boyfriend – I was frightened of losing him really, at the time. Now when I think back it wasn't worth having that.

Q: So he put you under quite a lot of pressure, is that what you are saying, that you felt you were under pressure?

A: Yes.

Q: And what about when it actually happened, how did you feel about that?

A: I felt awful. I remember crying and saying, 'I just can't do it'. It was the worst thing, it was awful.

She had reflected a good deal since then on her experience and also got other women to discuss the quality of their sexual experiences with her so that she could compare her own. With later boyfriends she had sex with them because it was what they wanted, but in a longer relationship she felt some pressure from the quality of the relationship itself.

> *A:* It sounds as if I have been used as an innocent victim here. No, I wasn't an innocent victim, I went along with it [sexual intercourse] because I had been going out with him for a long time and I couldn't see us finishing in the future and it wasn't a fling. He wanted it and I wanted to make him happy.

At the time of her interview she was nineteen and in a much more equal relationship, but the abuse in her childhood still constrained the possibility of her finding sexual pleasure.

> *A:* He's twenty three. It's the best relationship I have ever had . . . he doesn't pressurise me into doing anything that I don't want to. If something is the matter, he will ask me and make sure that I tell him, and if he has any problems he will tell me. He's fun and he's relaxed, but he is also caring. He cares about what I want to do, not just what he wants to do.

> *Q:* So it's something you talk about. Is sex something that you feel better about now or is it something that you still see as not being a very positive part of your life?

> *A:* I don't really enjoy it at all.

> *Q:* Does he know you don't really enjoy it?

> *A:* I think he thinks I am not bothered about it, because I wouldn't like to deprive him. I think a lot about him and I am not repulsed by sex, I don't think, 'oh God'. I will have sex but I don't think, 'oh brilliant' when its finished, and 'really great'. I would rather get up and make a cup of tea or something.

> *Q:* To be blunt, do you have orgasms?

> *A:* No.

> *Q:* Do you think that's an issue?

> *A:* From what I have heard and read, women don't have orgasms a lot, like every time and things like that, so I would like to have an orgasm I suppose, but if I don't it doesn't bother me . . . I think it's what has happened in the past really. I would like to enjoy sex.

While this may not seem a very positive example, this young woman has developed some sense of her own needs, has transformed the way in which she relates to a sexual partner, and perceives the possibility of a positive sexuality for women, even if she does not yet know how to achieve it.

Physical sexual pressure: the use of force or the threat of force

Women were sometimes unwilling to use the term rape when they felt they might somehow have been able to prevent or avoid the situation, or that this was what sex was like.

> *Q:* Did you want to do it at the time?
>
> *A:* Not really, I think. No it wasn't, because I was like 13, he was 27. He was, know what I mean? He knew that I really liked him. He just sort of like – I didn't want to. He didn't rape me, but I didn't want to, but he just, you know – it's like, 'Oh, come on, come on' – know what I mean? Then it wasn't anything romantic with no clothes on or anything like that. It was just sort of skirt up, know what I mean, and then by the time he did it, it was all over and done with.

In other cases women were clear that they had been raped. In the following quotation, the definition of rape was clear to the young woman even though she found it difficult not to blame herself for what had happened and she already had a relationship with the man concerned.

> *A:* . . . I only went out with him for two weeks.
>
> *Q:* Is he the one that hit you?
>
> *A:* Yes, but he did rape me as well . . . it was a very important thing in my life. It's changed me.
>
> *Q:* Did you feel guilty about it? Did you feel responsible?
>
> *A:* Yes I did. I did feel it was my fault, and I still do in a way, but I know it wasn't. I feel angry that I feel that way.
>
> *Q:* Why did you feel it was your fault?
>
> *A:* Well, I was there.

Women's attitudes to rape or forced intercourse by a man they knew were complicated by their feelings of responsibility for being part of the relationship. They did not have a vocabulary of 'date rape' and felt that it was their responsibility either to keep male ardour under control, or to give way to it if they did not exercise such control.

Even where women are empowered to the extent that they recognise that they are being violently treated, they do not always have the power to end a violent relationship decisively.

> *Q:* Is it when he became violent that you finished with him?
>
> *A:* Yeah. Well, it wasn't exactly straight away. I'd been out with him a year after that. He'd been hitting me for a year.

She states that her first experience of sexual intercourse was when she was fifteen and her boy friend was twenty four. He got her drunk at a party so that she did not know what she was doing. However, she did not experience this as forced sex as she had felt she had enjoyed it. The man had hit her twice with an iron bar in the first year of their subsequent relationship:

Q: Were you scared of him?

A: It wasn't there all the time. The first year it was OK; I enjoyed the relationship, but I was frightened then because in the second year it was either have sex or get battered. It was – it was like every night of the week. Even if I was on my period, he had to have it.

These experiences, however, should not be taken as simply negative. The experience of pressured sex was one which contradicted young women's expectations of loving, fulfilling and romantic relationships, and could make them determined not to be used, dominated or controlled in the same way again.

[. . .]

While young women cannot always put their positive intentions into practice in every situation, making sense of the pressures in sexual encounters can be one level of empowerment for them.

PRESSURED PLEASURE: YOUNG WOMEN AND EMPOWERMENT

The problems that women face in negotiating sexual encounters can be clarified by distinguishing between two levels of empowerment. The experience of pressured sex is one possible source of a process of *empowerment at an intellectual level* where young women reflect critically on their knowledge and experience and make decisions about future sexual strategies. They will ask him to use a condom, not let him hit them, not have intercourse just because he is aroused, ensure that they are not at risk of pregnancy, STDs or HIV, make their own sexual needs known. This level of empowerment can be a powerful force in transforming women's consciousness and leading them to work out more positive models of female sexuality. Empowerment at the intellectual level, however, does not mean that young women can achieve empowerment in subsequent sexual encounters.

[. . .]

If they are to control their own sexuality and to negotiate a positive balance of sexual power with men, young women need to be *empowered at an experiential level.* This level of empowerment means achieving in practice a shift in the male domination of sexual encounters. But this level of practice can be extremely unstable. A young woman may be safe with one man, but not with others, assert her needs in one relationship, but not in subsequent relationships. Effective empowerment then needs the *integration* of the intellectual and experiential levels, so that the critical consciousness of a positive female sexuality can be negotiated in practice in more than one situation.[14]

While we can classify women's experiences by the types of pressure to which they have been subject, their responses to these pressures are variable, and depend on how they make sense of their experiences. Categories of pressure are not then a static classification, but rather expressions of processes of negotiation in sexual encounters. While some women become more assertive as the result of their experiences of pressured sex, others will settle for unrewarding sexual relationships as adequately fulfilling their expectations. One young woman illustrated in the course of her interview something of the process of moving from intellectual to intellectual/experiential empowerment. She first discussed how she moved from acceptance of a violent relationship to rejection of it.

> *A:* I went out with someone for six months and it was a really bad relationship, as in he was treating me badly. He was a very spoilt only child. And then for a long while I just accepted it. I was really downtrodden and that sort of thing, and then suddenly I just realised he treated me like rubbish, 'I'm not staying with you, you know, this is no good, this is not a good relationship. You've done a lot of things to upset me.' It was – I read a book called *Women Who Love Too Much* and it was typical relationship that I read in that; you know, you would do everything to try and please him, and then it doesn't work and you – something wrong with yourself. And I suddenly thought it's not, it's not me, and I got out of it.

Later in the interview she commented on how her expectations at the time of this relationship did not work out in practice.

> *A:* I remember thinking if you had sex with someone you could control him.
>
> *Q:* You could?
>
> *A:* Mm. You know, you had that control over them. Because it was something so personal and so special to me, it must be to them, so I could then, you knew – if they'd said to me, do this, so I could do it back. But then, you know – you can't, you can't at all.

Empowerment in this young woman's account then comes to mean not her exercising control over men, but being able to exercise control over herself in the negotiation of sexual boundaries. [. . .]

Although she wanted a relationship with a man and saw mutually pleasurable sex as important part of any such relationship, she also saw being empowered not to have sex as an important part of her development.

> *A:* . . . this bloke Dave decided that he really had the hots for me and he wanted to go out with me. And a couple of years ago I would have probably done it, because I wouldn't have wanted to upset him.

Now she feels able to turn Dave down and to take his anger and insults when she disappoints him. This decision to avoid unwanted sex illustrates her integration of intellectual and experiential empowerment, and is dependent on her having a positive conception of female sexuality which included the possibility of female sexual pleasure.

Sexual pleasure

It was unusual for young women to discuss sex in terms of their own pleasure, rather than men's needs, or their feelings for a man or a relationship. Sexual pleasure was seen as dependent on the quality of the relationship with a man. Where they were intellectually empowered to the extent of being conscious of women's pleasure then they realised that they needed to be able to communicate with men.

[. . .]

Sometimes women only discovered sexual pleasure through meeting men who showed them what could be done. One young women had only experienced intercourse with two men, but these had been very different experiences. The first had been with a man several years older than herself. He had first had sex with her when she was drunk, and afterwards had been violent towards her. She had gained no pleasure from their sexual relationship. Her current relationship with Michael was of a very different quality.

> *A:* Yeah. It's a lot closer. A lot closer. Like, it took me a year to get used to he's not going to hit me. Every time he moved, I was ducking and things, but – he's dead nice Michael, he's alright. [. . .]
> . . . He gets enjoyment out of making me enjoy it.
>
> *Q:* Did you know about that before?
>
> *A:* No, I didn't realise.
>
> *Q:* How did you think about sex with this older guy?
>
> *A:* I just thought it was like a few different positions, he had his fun, and that was it, sort of thing.

Where women had a notion of their own pleasure to which men would consent, they could negotiate the boundaries of safer sex in ways which were acceptable to men, but also satisfying and effective for women.

> *Q:* Do you see safe sex as meaning using a sheath or are there other sorts of ways of . . .
>
> *A:* I suppose you . . .
>
> *Q:* having sex or . . .
>
> *A:* Yeah. You don't necessarily have to have intercourse you know. You can just sort of sleep – I don't know – kiss someone or whatever, you know. You don't necessarily have to penetrate, I suppose. Penetrative sex, I don't – yeah, I mean, that – you know, just it's all right just to be with someone isn't it, you know. You don't necessarily have to sleep with them in the full extent, just enjoy being with them. I suppose that's a form of safe sex, not indulging yourself to the full extent.

The rarity of this empowered stance in relation to non-penetrative sex indicates how far there is to go in empowering young women more generally.

CONCLUSION: THE NEGOTIATION OF SEXUAL BOUNDARIES

If women are to be able to negotiate the boundaries of sexual encounters so as to ensure both their safety and their satisfaction, the way in which both men and women are constituted as sexual subjects must change. Fine[15] argues that 'the missing discourse of desire' which is silenced in . . . school sex education effectively treats women as victims of men's sexuality, rather than as female sexual subjects who can negotiate with men . . . [A]nalysis of our data shows that we cannot simply classify women according to men's behaviour towards them as passive victims of pressured sex. The categories of pressure which we have illustrated indicate something of the complexities of the social context of women's sexual empowerment, and the contradictions of the processes involved.

1. We have considered empowerment as a process at the level of knowledge and ideas. Achieving intellectual empowerment requires a model of a positive female sexuality which offers women a way of reflecting critically on their experiences of pressured sex. Women are only victims to the extent that their experiences of pressured sex appear to them as isolated personal experiences for which they are responsible, and which they cannot prevent in future. Intellectual empowerment is an uneven process of moving away from this position to a more collective sense of women's relationships to men.

2. Intellectual empowerment, however confident, is insufficient to ensure that women can act effectively on their positive conceptions. Empowerment is also a process of putting into practice ways of negotiating safe and pleasurable sex with men. This experiential level is contested and unstable and to be effective must be integrated with a process of intellectual empowerment. In our analysis we have illustrated some of the many constraints on this level of intellectual/experiential empowerment which come from men's continuing power over women, and women's acceptance of this power.

The concept of empowerment as a contradictory and contested process is intended as a starting point for considering practical strategies for transforming pressured sexual relationships between women and men.

Empowerment is complicated by the divisions between women such as those of class, race, ethnicity, culture and religion. Women's accounts of their experiences remain a primary source of understanding how these contradictions are dealt with in practice. From their accounts of their experiences, knowledge of a positive female sexuality can be created which perhaps can be developed in ways which can be put into practice by those who need the knowledge.

NOTES

1. B. Campbell, 'A feminist sexual politics: now you see it now you don't', *Feminist Review*, 5, 1980, pp. 1–18; A. Rich, 'Compulsory heterosexuality and lesbian existence', in E. Abel and E. Abel (eds), *Women, Gender and Scholarship: the SIGNS reader*, Chicago: University of Chicago Press, 1983; L. Coveney, M. Jackson, S.

Jeffreys, L. Kaye and P. Mahonan, *The Sexuality Papers: Male Sexuality and the Control of Women*, London: Hutchinson, 1984; C. Kitzinger, *The Social Construction of Lesbianism*, London: Sage, 1987.

2. S. Hite, *The Hite Report*, London: Pandora, 1976; S. Thompson, 'Searching for tomorrow: on feminism and the reconstruction of teen romance', in Carole S. Vance (ed.) *Pleasure and Danger: Exploring Female Sexuality*, London: Routledge & Kegan Paul, 1984.

3. Thompson, 'Searching for tomorrow'; R. Thomson, and S. Scott, *Researching Sexuality in the Light of AIDS: Historical and Methodological Issues*, WRAP Paper 5, London: The Tufnell Press, 1990; D. Stears and S. Clift, *A Survey of AIDS Education in Secondary Schools*, Horsham: AVERT, 1990).

4. V. Kent, M. Davies, K. Devesell and S. Gottesman, 'Social interaction routines involved in heterosexual encounters: prelude to first intercourse', Paper presented at the *Fourth Conference on the Social Aspects of AIDS*, London, 1990.

5. E. Wilson *What is to be Done about Violence against Women?*, Harmondsworth: Penguin, 1983; J Hammer and S. Saunders, *Well-Founded Fear: A Community Study of Violence to Women*, London: Hutchinson, 1984; J. Hammer and M. Maynard, *Women, Violence and Social Control*, London: Macmillan, 1987; D. Rhodes and S. McNeil, *Women against Violence against Women*, London: Onlywomen Press, 1985; E. Stanko, *Intimate Intrusions: Women's Experience of Male Violence*, London: Routledge & Kegan Paul, 1985; L. Kelly, *Surviving Sexual Violence*, Cambridge: Polity, 1988.

6. Where male violence towards women is general it is to be expected that there will also be male violence towards other men and children.

7. L. Stanley and S. Wise, *Georgie Porgie: Sexual Harassment in Everyday Life*, London: Pandora, 1987.

8. Kelly, *Surviving Sexual Violence*.

9. M.P. Koss, C.A. Gidyez and N. Wisniewski, 'The scope of rape: incidence and prevalence of sexual aggression and victimization in a national sample of students in higher education', *Journal of Consulting and Clinical Psychology*, 55, 1987, pp. 162–70.

10. These are points on a scale of male aggression adapted from M.P. Koss and K.E. Leonard, 'Sexually aggressive menoempirical findings and theoretical implications', in N. Malmuth and E. Donnerstein (eds), *Pornography and Sexual Aggression*, New York: Academic Press, 1984, who describe four categories of degrees of aggression used by men to accomplish sexual intercourse.

11. Kelly, *Surviving Sexual Violence*.

12. E. Janeway, *Man's World, Women's Place*, Harmondsworth: Penguin, 1977, p. 54.

13. J. Holland, C. Ramazanaglu, S. Scott and R. Thomson, *Pressure, Resistance, Empowerment: Young Women and the Negotiation of Safer Sex*, WRAP Paper 6, London: The Tufnell Press, 1991.

14. Holland, *et al., ibid.*

15. M., Fine, 'Sexuality, schooling and adolescent females: the missing discourse of desire', *Harvard Educational Review*, 58(1), 1988, pp. 29–53.

3.10

BODIES–PLEASURES–POWERS

Linda Singer

In this piece Linda Singer argues that polarising the debate about sexuality in terms of liberation versus regulation makes little sense. What is required in an age of anxiety about sexual epidemics – and epidemic sex – is a new sexual politics. Drawing on the work of Michel Foucault she argues that we should locate the sexual at the intersection of the multiplicity of discourses relating to pleasure, power and the body. She makes a claim for the analysis of specific sites of intersection in order to understand both the local and the global implications of sex.

Although the 1960s are the decade usually credited with making sex a political issue and the subject of popular and scholarly discourse, the 1980s have been a time when sexual political issues have become both targets of major social agenda, and ubiquitous elements of popular culture. It is also a time when sexual politics is not very sexy.

[. . .]

Most contemporary sexual discourse is not very sexy, because it operates within a logic and language of 'sexual epidemic.' Central to the emergence of epidemic as a historically specific hegemony has been a concern with the rise in sexually transmitted diseases, most notably AIDS, but also the herpes virus which, though not fatal like AIDS, is a chronic condition which has been in wide circulation for some time.

[. . .]

The threat and fear of contagion have transformed the economy of sexual exchange, reconfiguring the relationship between prospective profit and loss, benefit and risk, for both individuals and the so-called 'social body.' When one of the possible

From L. Singer, 'Bodies – pleasures – powers', J. Butler and M. Macgrogan (eds), *Erotic Welfare*, New York: Routledge, Inc., 1992.

consequences of sexual activity is the contraction of a debilitating fatal disease or one which is likely to remain and recur, the logic and strategies of judgment and decision are irrevocably altered, even for those who try to avoid such considerations.

Hence it is neither deniable nor surprising that the emergence of the hegemony of epidemic is affecting personal sexual practice, a change with existential and political implications. The anxieties unleashed by the current epidemic are not limited to concerns about disease transmission. The recognition of this unhappy connection between sex and death has also prompted renewed concern about the production of life itself, about reproduction, fertility, and the family, which are also seen as threatened by current conditions. At a time when so-called sexual adventurism is under attack as unsafe, there is a felt need to construct a new, more prudential sexual aesthetic, in terms of which desires and behaviors are stylized, valorized, and eroticized.

[. . .]

While gay men find their situation made problematic by a revived and newly legitimated climate of homophobia, women are also being subjected to a new set of gender-specific regulatory strategies designed to maximize their social utility as breeders while minimizing the social costs attached to sexual exchanges. Such strategies include, but are not limited to, rapid developments in fertility technology which allow, in surrogacy situations, reproduction without exposing men to the risks entailed in the exchange of bodily fluids. It is not surprising that, at a time when there is a need to reinvent sexuality or reorganize the erotic economy, a disproportionate weight is falling on the bodies of women.

[. . .]

Common to all discussions of sexual liberation was an awareness of the political dynamics of dominance and hierarchy that structured and were reproduced in sexual exchange. Under attack was a hegemonic formation that privileged heterosexism over homosexuality and lesbian experience, phallocentricity over gynocentricity, reproductive over non-reproductive sex. Following this logic, the regime of repression could be challenged on political grounds namely, that its operations constituted unauthorized, arbitrary, or unjustified restrictions on the lives of bodies and the forms of exchange in which they privately chose to engage. Hence sexual revolution necessitated confrontation with and transgression of forms of sexual authority which constituted barriers to better sex. Conspicuous proliferative sexuality, which violated and exposed the repressive regime, consequently took on the value of liberatory strategies of subversion, critique, and rebellion, especially for those groups which had been most disadvantaged or marginalized by the operative sexual economy. For many women and members of the gay community, a climate of proliferative sexuality offered occasions both for self-affirmation and for enfranchising their needs and desires in a way that connected them with larger movements of resistance to these same systems of privilege.

In this sense, sexual political struggles over the past two decades have not just been struggles over sexual activities as such, but have also been concerned with contesting the order of privilege and visibility defined by the operative political organization of sexual differences. For gays, especially gay men, the urgency to make those differences visible by getting out of the closet and into the street was compatible with and facilitated by a proliferative aesthetic which functioned as a promissory alternative. For many heterosexual women, a proliferative sexuality provided a potent weapon against the double standard, while allowing them to explore a gynocentric economy that had been marginalized by the phallocentrism that dominated social life.

[. . .]

EPIDEMICS AND SEXUAL POLITICS

With the rise of the hegemony of sexual epidemic, the optimism implied by this proliferative logic reaches a certain kind of dead end. Consequently, a variety of strategic and tactical shifts have emerged which contribute [. . .] a 'recessionary erotic economy.' The ethos of an ecstatic carnival is progressively being displaced by a more sober and reserved aesthetic of 'sexual prudence' and 'body management.' The language of 'better sex' is being replaced by that of 'safe sex' and the promotion of a 'new sobriety.' These historically specific changes are most visible and pressing at this point for gay men but will not remain so for long as the AIDS virus spreads to other segments of the population. Given the current state of medical research, epidemic conditions are likely to persist for some time and hence continue to structure the context for sexual-political discourse, particularly in the absence of some counter-hegemonic discourse of resistance.

The age of sexual epidemic demands a new sexual politics, and therefore, a rethinking of the relationship between bodies, pleasures, and powers beyond the call for liberation from repression. That is because, as Michel Foucault pointed out with a certain prescience, the power deployed in the construction and circulation of an epidemic, especially a sexual epidemic, functions primarily as a force of production and proliferation rather than as a movement of repression. The determination that a situation is epidemic is always, according to Foucault, a political determination[1]. Epidemics differ from diseases not in kind but in quantity. Hence the epidemic determination is in part a mathematical one, made by those with access to information and the authority to make and circulate such determinations.

[. . .]

An epidemic emerges as a product of a socially authoritative discourse in light of which bodies will be mobilized, resources will be dispensed, and tactics of surveillance and regulation will appear to be justified. Foucault argues that a medicine of epidemic could only exist with supplementation by the police.[2] In this view, the construction of an epidemic situation has a strategic value in determining the configurations of what Foucault calls 'bio-power,' since the epidemic provides an occasion and a rationale for multiplying points of intervention into the lives of bodies and populations. For this reason, epidemics are always historically specific in a way that diseases are not, since the strategic imperatives motivating particular ways of coping with an epidemic always emerge as tactical responses to local utilities and circumstances. The construction of a sexual epidemic, as Foucault argues, provides an optimum site of intersection between individual bodies and populations. Hence sexual epidemic provides access to bodies and a series of codes for inscribing them, as well as providing a discourse of justification. When any phenomenon is represented as 'epidemic,' it has, by definition, reached a threshold that is quantitatively unacceptable. It is the capacity to make and circulate this determination, and to mobilize people in light of it, that constitutes the real political force of the discourse of sexual epidemic.[3] With respect to our current situation, it is important to emphasize that the response to AIDS has been quite different from that given to other sexually transmitted diseases before remedies for them were found. This is not because venereal diseases did not have dire consequences for those who contracted them. Rather, the differences can be attributed, at least in part, to the belief that Victorian social structures could limit transmission by restricting the access of bodies to one another, especially given the dominance of particular institutions and ideologies. The AIDS epidemic is different, in part, because it comes on the heels of a period of explicit advocacy for proliferative sexuality, and because this epidemic first surfaced in a community that was already regarded as marginal, and to some, as morally suspect.

[. . .]

The establishment of a connection between epidemic and transgression has allowed for the rapid transmission of the former to phenomena that are outside the sphere of disease. We are thus warned of the 'epidemics' of teenage pregnancies, child molestation, abortion, pornography, and divorce. The use of this language marks all of these phenomena as targets for intervention because they have been designated as unacceptable, while at the same time reproducing the power that authorizes and justifies their deployment. According to this discourse, it is existing authority that is to be protected from the plague of transgressions.

Part of what is useful about the conservative polemic is that it provides some insight into the anxiety and malaise that permeate sexual discourse, even amongst those populations, like monogamous heterosexual Christians, who are least at risk of contracting a sexually transmitted disease. By using the occasion of a health crisis to revivify authority, the New Right makes clear that, as another theorist of plague, Albert Camus, points out, plagues are never just medical problematics. They are also world-transforming moments of ontological crisis which pervade the entire logic and fabric of a community's existence by calling it into question in a fundamental way, i.e., within the currency of life and death.[4] A plague, according to Camus, always marks a radically anxious point of rupture with respect to the economy of the everyday and its system of stabilized and sedimented significations. A plague is always 'unusual, out of place'.[5] One can no longer simply go on with business as usual. One is forced to call one's habits, values, and pleasures into question, precisely because the world in which they have a place is in the process of slipping away. Just what one calls into question and just what is lost will depend on one's position within the operative configuration of differences.

[. . .]

Camus's analysis helps to explain the malaise and despair that seems to have permeated much of the sexual political arena, a mood that marks a radical break with the optimism induced by the politics of ecstasy. The threat posed by the new sexual epidemic is the problematization of sexual hegemonies in a direction of diminishing returns and reduced expectations, especially for those who came of age during the sexual revolution. But the sexual epidemic has also helped to induce a reversal in the direction of social policy. In the 1960s and 1970s, legislative and policy initiatives reflected traditional liberal concerns for civil rights, individual freedom, right to privacy, and the principles of equality and equity. The liberal initiative helped establish legalized abortion and civil rights for homosexuals, enfranchise the principles of affirmative action and compensatory legislation, as well as contributed a climate of tolerance for sexual pluralism. What is disturbing about the current state of sexual political debate, particularly in the sphere of social policy, is the apparent failure of traditional liberalism to provide an adequate alternative to a conservative authoritarian social logic which advocates increased surveillance and regulation of bodies in ways that support and reproduce hegemonic relationships of dominance.

[. . .]

The limits of existing political discourse, as well as the urgency of the current situation, call for new forms of sexual political discourse, currency, and struggle. In this context, Foucault's work is especially helpful since his analysis of the proliferative operation of power supplements the limits of the repressive hypothesis, and offers the option of a strategic analysis which allows us to consider not only what is lost but also what is produced by the current organization of the sexual field which is itself a product of previous power deployments. This means that, counter to a logic which opposes erotic urgency and social utility or ghettoizes the sexual as some stable and invariable set of imperatives, Foucault's analysis demonstrates how the construction of each is dependent upon and made in light of the others, often, as in our age, with dire results which place our existence as a species in question. Part of the agenda for a sexual politics of epidemic will have to be a reconsideration of this 'Faustian bargain,' along with the generation of alternatives capable of mobilizing bodies sufficiently so as not to paralyze them in an economy of deprivation.[6]

With respect to the techniques of embodiment operative in this particular sexual epidemic, we should expect to find that these techniques will reflect and inscribe a system of utilities and pleasures compatible with other demands made on bodies in late patriarchal capitalism. Foucault's insights provide conceptual machinery for making sense of some of what is at stake in the new sexual technology, which operates not through threat of death and pain, but instead establishes dominion over life through a currency of historically specific pleasures and powers. According to Foucault, the consequence of much of contemporary body techniques is that modern man has become 'an animal whose politics places his existence as a living being in question'.[7] The implication of Foucault's analysis is the need to reconsider strategies in light of historical specificities.

EPIDEMIC STRATEGIES

In an effort to concretize and extend Foucault's analysis, which in some sense was cut short by the sexual epidemic, I will examine some of the modes of embodiment that have emerged as responses to current conditions. I will begin by discussing the discourses of 'safe sex' and 'the new sobriety' as two tactical responses to the hegemony of epidemic. I will then focus on some contemporary techniques of 'body management' and will conclude with a discussion of some contemporary technologies aimed at intervening in human reproduction as strategies for exercising power over the lives of bodies and populations.

[. . .]

The discourses and techniques known as 'safe sex' and 'the new sobriety' [. . .] represent exercises in theory and practice which emerged from discussions within the gay community, at once the initial source and the audience for them. But as AIDS begins to infect other segments of the population, these techniques are being far more widely promulgated and circulated through mainstream channels of communication. [. . .] As opposed to the absolutist logic employed by the New Right, these secular strategies employ a cost-benefit logic drawn from the discourses of finance; management, and to some extent, preventive medicine. Both strategies assume that sexual proliferation, like nuclear proliferation and the national debt, is not something one can hope to eliminate. The goal instead is to try to manage it strategically so as to minimize the risks of sexual contact without resorting to abstinence, which for many is clearly an untenable option.

In 'safe sex,' one minimizes the risks of sexual contact by developing an erotics which privileges prudential judgment over spontaneity, and prioritizes selectivity over variety. Minimally, safe sex entails the prophylactic use of condoms and avoidance of what are termed 'high risk activities,' like anal sex, and 'high risk groups,' like IV users. Making this prudential logic operational will demand changes in the economy of genital gestures and erotic choreography. It will also necessitate a reorganization of pleasure, a reconstruction of the erotic body, and an alteration in the terms and expectations of sexual exchanges.

Part of the change proffered by epidemic conditions is a shift in the relationship between knowledge and desire as they function in erotic situations. Specifically, knowledge of one's partners' physical condition and sexual history now becomes a prime object of concern. The erotic gaze is thus infected to some degree by the medical gaze which must learn to see sickness. The prudential aesthetic which characterizes the new sobriety creates specific forms of desire, like dating agencies which promise matches with prescreened AIDS-free partners.

Failing such elaborate screening procedures, and given the limits of their reliability, the ideology of safe sex encourages a reorganization of the body away from the erotic priorities with which it has already been inscribed. Specifically, safe sex advocates indulgence in numerous forms of non-genital contact and the reengagement of parts of the body marginalized by an economy of genital primacy. It also entails a reconfiguration of bodies and their pleasures away from an ejaculatory teleology toward a more polymorphous decentered exchange, reviving and concretizing the critique of genital condensation begun over twenty years ago by sexual theorists like Marcuse and Firestone.

The underlying assumptions about the relationships among bodies, pleasures, and powers which make safe sex possible depend, at least indirectly, on Foucault's analysis and its destabilizing consequences. Safe sex presumes that pleasure and practice can be reorganized in response to overriding utilities and presumes, as well, the capacity of regimentary procedures to construct a body capable of taking pleasure in this new form of discipline. Unless bodies and pleasures are politically determined, they cannot be redetermined, even in cases where that is what rational prudence would demand. The success of this strategy will thus depend not only on promulgating these techniques, but also on circulating a discourse that allows individuals to reconsider their bodies in a more liberatory and strategic way. What is new about the new sobriety is that its aesthetic of restraint is not represented in terms of a monastic economy of self-denial or obedience to some authoritative imperative, but is instead presented as a gesture of primary narcissism, a way of caring for and about oneself. Liberation, in this context, is relocated in an economy of intensification of control over one's body and one's position in sexual exchanges.

[. . .]

The connection of the discourse of 'body management' with primary narcissism creates a complex of strategies and disciplines which extend beyond the sphere of sexual practices to include other bodily techniques like nutrition, fitness, hygiene, cosmetics, diets, and what is referred to as 'body building.' I want to focus on the phenomenon of body building, partly because it is undergoing an historically unprecedented popularity, especially among women, and partly because body building, as both theory and practice, reveals how bodies are constructed within the new disciplinary regime, and what utilities, pleasures, and powers are being pursued in this reconstruction.

The very language of 'body building' already targets a body that is assumed to be rebuildable. The disciplinary regimen, and its accompanying aesthetic, mobilizes the body as a divisible collection of parts which can be individually fine-tuned or standardized according either to some aesthetic ideal, or to the demands of the labor process. Such a regimen often involves the use of mechanical apparatuses like the Nautilus machine which isolate, target, and differentially work specific muscle groups. The fine-tuning of the body is often supplemented by far more interventionist procedures like plastic surgery, skin grafting, hair coloring and transplants, and the tanning booth to further control and refine the finished product, which is regarded as in need of perpetual maintenance and surveillance. The popularity of these techniques can be attributed to the proliferative effects of the slippage between energies organized according to a predetermined pattern of behavior, and the mobilizations of those energies as activities of self-love and personal development. Rather than depending on a regime of repression, the new discipline operates through a strategy of control by stimulation, which mobilizes energies through anonymous channels of regulation which can also be represented as activities of individuation.

When reproductive imperatives are added to the utilities to be mobilized by the discourse of body management, women's bodies become targets for gender-specific strategies and tactics. If, as Foucault suggests, the deployments of modern power seek to intervene at a place where individual bodies intersect with the body of the social, it is not surprising that reproduction is being restructured by a series of technologies designed to make that process, and the bodies who accomplish it, more malleable and responsive to fluctuations in demographic utilities.

Given women's subordinate position within a patriarchal social order, discipline has always been a technique used to marshall women's energies and bodies in pursuit of utilities not of their own making. Given that women's place is often constructed as one of self-effacing service, it is not surprising that female disciplinary strategies often take the form of radical self-denial, as in the case of body practices such as anorexia and bulimia. But the well-managed female body of the '80s is constructed so as to be even more multifunctional than its predecessors. It is a body that can be used for wage labor, sex, reproduction, mothering, spectacle, exercise, or even invisibility, as the situation demands. It is also a body that is constructed to accommodate the variable whims of fashion, and a postmodern aesthetic which demands the capacity to project a multiplicity of looks and attitudes with apparent effortlessness.

Most important, however, and what is historically specific about this construct is that this body's reproductive potential is managed and disciplined so as to be capable of conceiving and producing children on demand, as well as deferring that process until the time is right. Most of the innovations in reproductive ideology and technology have sought to render women's bodies more easily mobilizable in response to shifting utilities, most notably the production and coordination of populations. In order to address the different sorts of intervention that produce the contemporary ideologies of motherhood, I will begin by examining the differential strategies by which motherhood is being marketed to particular segments of the female population. I will then analyze the strategic value of the new reproductive technology and will conclude with a discussion of one recent and conspicuous case of fallout from this technology, the Baby M case. [. . .] The necessity to market motherhood appears to have been motivated, at least in part, by the development of contraceptive technologies which give women some measure of control over their fertility and its consequences. Current marketing strategies have also emerged as responses to what can be read as a demographic gap in the birth rate amongst white middle-class educated women who, beginning in the early '70s, began in larger numbers to defer motherhood or to avoid it altogether. This mobilization of women's energies was facilitated by a feminist discourse which explicitly challenged the reproductive imperative[8] and in some cases made women's liberation dependent upon refusing such imperatives. During approximately the same period of time, however, there was also a statistically significant rise in pregnancies amongst teenagers, especially poor women of color, who were more likely than their older counterparts to have their babies delivered, and in some cases supported, at state expense. In a white-male-dominated culture this was perceived as a situation that called for adjustment.

Hence we start to find images of attractive successful women [. . .] as well as media feminists [. . .] proudly posing on magazine covers and bus shelters advocating the pleasures of motherhood. Never mind that these women mother under conditions that are likely to be radically different from those of the women addressed in the ads. The strategy of these campaigns was to inscribe motherhood within a series of elements the sum of which was represented as 'having it all' in the proper sequence, which is the mark of any 'superwoman.'

[. . .]

Contemporaneous with these images is an ad campaign in which Planned Parenthood addresses potential teenage mothers. The poster series consists of several versions of the same basic format varied by racial type, in which a young woman holding a baby stares dead-pan at the viewer in what is clearly depicted as dismal surroundings. The accompanying boldface copy reads, 'It's like being grounded for eighteen years.'[9]

The tactics employed in these cases are obvious at the first and are intended to work in precisely opposite ways, discouraging younger women of color from reproducing by emphasizing the burdens of motherhood, while effacing those burdens when addressing women whose reproductive services are regarded as useful, either from the standpoint of maintaining race and class dominance, or as a strategy for inducing women's voluntary defection from more competitive segments of the labor market. Certainly, if motherhood demobilizes women, it does so regardless of the mother's age, though class, race, and educational differences determine the forms such demobilization will take. But for a variety of reasons it is strategically desirable to circulate a discourse of differences, and to abridge recognition of the continuities in women's experience that emerge as a consequence of the gender caste system, which links all women by their subordination to phallocentric utilities. In any case, given the complexities of race and class differences, along with the degree of specificity attempted, we should not be surprised when some of these messages get crossed in transmission and arrive at destinations for which they were not intended, since within any dominant strategic deployments sites of opposition and resistance are also created. The political challenge is to develop strategies for organizing and coordinating those positions in a way that mobilizes their counter-hegemonic potential.

At the level of reproductive technology and technique, the radical disparity between the development rates of fertility, as opposed to contraceptive, technology [. . .] helps mark both a strategy and a dominant set of utilities. While fertility technology becomes more sophisticated and widely available, contraceptive technology and distribution, along with public debate, seem in many respects to be moving in the opposite direction. New fertility clinics and surrogate mothering agencies open while abortion clinics are being bombed.

The current fertility technology has been strategically designed for maximum flexibility in its capabilities for deployment. It can be used, or has the potential to be used, either to intervene so as to enlist more women in the reproductive brigades, or to render women biologically extraneous. Developments in fetal medicine and eugenics offer the prospects of regulating the product as well as the process of reproduction and normalizing intervention into the lives of persons by beginning even before they have that status. Each of these techniques touches the core of the bio-power system, the control over production of life, in a way that thus far has worked primarily to solidify and support a hegemony of white male heterosexist dominance. The question remains as to whether such techniques also offer more liberatory possibilities. Any response to this challenge will be dependent upon recognizing the complex intersections between bio-power and other systems of deployment which produce both the discourse and the terms of sexual struggle.

Nowhere do the complexities of this multi-layered apparatus become more visible in their contradictions than in what has probably been the hottest and most widely circulated sexual political issue of the '80s, save AIDS, namely the Baby M case. Its import is immediately felt at the level of language, where it introduced the neologism 'surrogate motherhood' into popular parlance. But as one might expect, it also began a new logic and politics of parental privilege.

The use of the term 'surrogate mother' to apply to Mary Beth Whitehead already reflects a bias in favor of paternal prerogative and a privileging of contractual relations regulating commodities over issues of biology and maternal desire. Given the way the issues were framed, i.e., as a choice between legally authorized paternity and biological maternity, and the context presumed by legal discourse, i.e., a class-stratified male-dominated hegemony, it is not surprising that the ruling granted custody of the child to the more affluent father. But what is really at stake in this case is less a contest between paternal and maternal claims than a question of maternal prerogative. The strategic value of the Baby M case, and its resolution, lies more with the way it manages the contest between two competing claims of motherhood, the one legal and contractual, the other biological and genetic, which in this case was resolved in terms of a legal discourse structured by and facilitating class stratification and male dominance. The consequence in this case was the determination of Whitehead as the surrogate mother, and most significantly, the granting of immediate legal motherhood to Mrs Stern. But apart from a contractual discourse which defines Whitehead as surrogate, Whitehead is in every other sense the mother of the child. She is the female progenitor and genetic contributor, and hence, at the very least the child's birth mother. She has the connection with the child regardless of her relationship to the male progenitor. In the context of the case, Mrs Stern's claim to maternity is entirely dependent upon and has status only in terms of her husband's desire to claim paternity. Had Mr Stern for some reason chosen not to exercise his paternal claim, the question of Mrs Stern's maternity would never have come up.

But the claims made on behalf of Mrs Whitehead and the language of organized feminist support which focused on Whitehead's rights as a 'natural mother' are equally problematic, and in some sense they reproduce the ideological framework in terms of which Mr Stern's claim proved to be more legally persuasive. Specifically, the appeals to 'natural motherhood' overlook an extensive feminist discourse which documents how the discourse of motherhood has been strategically deployed historically to exert control over women's bodies while devaluing and effacing maternal labor, effort, and commitment which are therein reduced to the status of a natural aptitude. These contradictions point toward the strategic value of the discourse of surrogate motherhood, part of which is to pit women against women, largely on the basis of class, and then to reinstitute male prerogative and class privilege[10] as the legal basis for resolving competing claims.

The arguments made on behalf of Mr Stern's property rights reveal the intersections between the sexual reproduction system and the logic regulating the commodity market. Mr Stern's attorney argued that he was entitled to the child not because he had paid for her as such, but because he had paid for the use of Whitehead's body for breeding purposes. Retreating to a neo-Aristotelian biology, Stern's attorney redescribed Mary Beth Whitehead as a vessel rented by the client for the express purpose of gestating and delivering the product of his seed. As such, it is argued, he is entitled to get what he paid for, while Whitehead's consent to the contract invalidates any of her further claims.

These arguments clearly place surrogate motherhood on a continuum with other institutional forms of commodifying women's bodies, including prostitution and 'mail-order brides.' Surrogate motherhood is a technological extension of the wet-nurse, where some women are in the position of using their bodies to support other more privileged women's offspring. In some sense, the decision in this case is compatible with the logic which produces laws that protect the consumers rather than the providers of women's sexual services and that use women's position as sellers to limit their rights and prerogatives. In the case of prostitution, the woman's position as seller of sexual service is regarded as making her unfit for inclusion under laws that protect providers in most other industries. In the case of surrogate motherhood, the judge determined that Whitehead's decision to sell her body for breeding purposes is an indication of her unfitness to mother.[11]

The figuring of the issue of maternal fitness in the Baby M case also reveals the strategic considerations already invested in the discourse of surrogate motherhood. In this case, the question of Whitehead's fitness to mother emerged only as a consequence of Mr Stern's desire for custody. In cases where paternity is unacknowledged or refused, custody falls *de facto* to the mother, independent of any discourse of maternal fitness. Under ordinary circumstances, questions of parental fitness are displaced to the private sphere of familial autonomy. They arise in this case only as a consequence of paternal and class prerogatives. In this case 'fitness' is determined to mean fitness to produce potential consumers rather than potential providers of surrogate services. Hence not only custody but also contractual prerogatives are distributed along hegemonic lines of class and gender privilege.

The way the Baby M case both raises and settles questions about the social and political organization of parenthood and about the meaning and power attached to the positions of paternity and maternity is part of its historically specific strategic value. What makes the Baby M case possible is a confluence of social forces which divide the body and body functions into separable units, linking them with a commodity system that proliferates sites and forms for these exchanges, a legal system that regulates and authorizes such transactions, and a system of sexual and class differences according to which functions and prerogatives are differentially distributed. It was against this background that a drama represented in the language of desire was played out, pitting Mr Stern's desire to father a child to which he had a genetic connection against Mrs Whitehead's desire to remain in touch with the child which had emerged from her body. What was being asked of the court in this case, and what is likely to be demanded in the future, was the production of a discursive grid in terms of which the claims established within different disciplinary codes could be mapped, ordered, and ultimately resolved. The Baby M case is the beginning of the attempt to construct the differential calculus. But because the resolution is likely to be challenged, and because this case raises as many questions as it answers, maximum flexibility in deployment is maintained which in turn allows for adjustments in the organization of reproduction according and in relation to other variable utilities and imperatives.

I have chosen to conclude my discussion of sexual politics in the age of epidemic with a discussion of the Baby M case because I think it points toward the kind of sexual political issues that are likely to confront us in the future, and because it functions as the opposing pole to those issues emerging from the logic of sexual disease. Given the proliferative possibilities of both reproductive technology and commodity culture, it is likely that more cases of contested parenthood will arise. It is clear that in the case of surrogate mothering, as in the case of prostitution, a regime of repression, even if one could find grounds for endorsing it, would prove inadequate as a response. In instances of surrogacy, perhaps the best solution will be to treat problems as cases of breached contract, and to let prospective fathers know that there are risks in making such an arrangement.

In a larger context, issues surrounding reproductive technology and organization constitute another series of challenges that confront us in the age of sexual epidemic. Conflicts which entail bodies, pleasures, and the production of life will continue to play out against the background of the struggle against death. Both kinds of struggle will be transacted, at least in part, at the level of cultural currency identified as sexuality, in forms that are likely to reflect and reproduce sexuality's proliferative dynamics, and with an intensity which speaks to the levels of cultural investment in this discourse.

If sexuality, now more than ever, constitutes the turf and terms in which struggles of life and death will be transacted, questions of sexual politics, i.e., of the construction and distribution of bodies, pleasures, and powers, will no longer simply be sites of elective engagement. Because sexuality functions as a force of production and proliferation as well as a currency of valuation, conflicts, as they arise, will continue to force reconsideration of our assumptions about and investment in these hegemonic formations, with the recognition of how much is at stake in the decisions we make. One way to begin is to relocate the sexual not outside but at the intersection of the multiplicity of discourses by which bodies, pleasures, and powers are circulated and exchanged. We ought to do so strategically with attention paid to the specificity of local conditions. We must also remember that in saying yes to sex we are not saying no to power. If sexuality in our age has become, at least for some people, worth the exchange of life itself, it behooves us to reconsider the situation in which we find and risk losing ourselves. The real sexual epidemic may very well turn out to be a politics which places our very existence in question. We therefore need to ask ourselves, with renewed urgency, whether sex is worth dying for, how it is we got to this place, and where we can go from here.

NOTES

1. M. Foucault, *The Birth of the Clinic: An Archaeology of Medical Perception*, New York: Pantheon, 1973, p. 15.
2. *Ibid.*
3. Cindy, Patton, *Sex and Germs: The Politics of AIDS*, Boston: South End Press, 1985, pp. 51–66.
4. M. Foucault, *The History of Sexuality*, vol. 1, *An Introduction*, trans. Robert Hurley, New York: Vintage, 1980, p. 145.
5. Albert Camus, *The Plague*, trans. Stuart Gilbert, New York: Vintage-Random, 1972, p. 3.

6. Simon Watney, *Policing Desire: Pornography, AIDS and the Media*, Minneapolis: University of Minnesota Press, 1987, pp. 123–35.
7. Foucault, *History of Sexuality*, p. 141.
8. Jeffner, Allen, 'Motherhood: the annihilation of women,' in Marilyn Pearsall (ed.), *Women Values: Readings in Recent Feminist Philosophy*, New York: Wadsworth, 1985, pp. 91–101.
9. This ad campaign was placed in subway stations in New York during the summer of 1987.
10. This argument has prompted legislation in several states to outlaw paid surrogacy contracts.
11. This judgment was also reversed on appeal.

3.11

CONSTRUCTING LESBIAN SEXUALITIES

Diane Richardson

Diane Richardson raises questions about what counts as lesbian sex, surveying the changes which have occurred in representations of lesbian eroticism over the last few decades and the diversity of lesbian sexual practices in the 1990s. She locates these trends in the context of political and theoretical debates about lesbian practices and identities.

[. . .]

Why as lesbians do we rarely talk about sex?[1] One explanation is that this is an understandable reaction, given that it is the sexual aspects of being a lesbian that have tended to dominate how others see us. Another limit on how easy we find it to talk about sex, even among ourselves, is the knowledge that sex between women is often interpreted as a 'turn on' for men, as the pornography industry can easily testify. One other possible constraint is the history of anti-lesbianism within the feminist movement[2] which, especially in the early days, resulted in some lesbians experiencing a pressure to downplay their sexuality to avoid giving 'feminism a bad name' or scaring off heterosexual women. We can proclaim our identity and our politics, but to be publicly passionate is a different matter!

[. . .]

One of the consequences of not discussing our sex lives is that we often have to struggle alone, or with lovers, in dealing with our sexual difficulties and worries. Breaking down the silence around lesbian sex is also important so that we can realistically assess what health risks, if any, we are taking sexually.

From D. Richardson, 'Constructing lesbian sexualities', in K. Plummer (ed.), *Modern Homosexualities*, London: Routledge, 1993.

On a theoretical level, there are questions which need to be addressed about the relationship between sexual conduct and sexual identity: between being a lesbian and desiring and having sex with women. How vital is sex to lesbian identity and what kinds of sex at that? What do you have to do, sexually speaking, to be a 'real' lesbian? Do you have to *do* anything? Sexual activity *is* often seen as proof of our lesbianism; when we are first coming out being sexually involved may make us feel like we are 'one of the girls'. The relationship between sex and identity is also an important area of political debate within lesbian feminism, in particular discussions about political lesbianism. These are some of the issues which will be addressed in this chapter, but first I want to consider the question, What is lesbian sex?[3]

One way of answering this question is to ask it another way: What is a sexual partner? Or, how do you know you've had sex with a woman? Is it sex only if you have an orgasm? What if she comes and you don't? Is she a sexual partner or were you just giving a helping hand? What if you are both fully dressed and during a close embrace pressed up against her you 'accidentally' come without her realizing? What if what you did wasn't genital, say you stroked each other and kissed and caressed, would you later say you'd had sex with that woman? And would she say the same?

The answer, of course, is that it depends; it would depend on how you and she interpreted what happened. Sex cannot be defined simply in terms of what we do; it is the meaning we give to situations and behaviours which defines them as sexual – or not.[4] From this perspective, the important question is where do these meanings come from? What are the ideas and beliefs from which we construct our experience of lesbian sex?

Two interrelated sources can be identified: views of sexuality and views of female sexuality and lesbianism.

WHAT IS 'SEX'?

Prevalent ideologies concerning sexuality, such as those coming from religious, legal, medical, psychiatric, and psychological discourses, influence common-sense ideas about what is both 'normal' and 'appropriate' sexual behaviour. For example, it is commonly felt that it is 'normal' to be heterosexual but 'abnormal' to be lesbian or gay; or that it is 'normal' for men to be more interested in sex than are women. Similarly, some sexual practices are regarded as inherently better (normal, natural, more satisfying) than others, with vaginal intercourse privileged as the 'Real Thing'. Such beliefs, influenced by views about sex as ultimately a reproductive function, continue to be perpetuated through discourses on sex despite a number of important contradictions. The existence of enormous sexual variation as documented by Kinsey[5] and others, the fact that in the majority of cases the aim in heterosexual sex is not to reproduce, the evidence that it is a majority of women who say they do not have orgasms during vaginal penetration, all these challenge dominant definitions of sex as intercourse. For instance, *The Hite Report* found that two-thirds of the women who were interviewed did not have orgasm during vaginal intercourse although they came easily in other ways.[6] Other studies echo this finding that most women 'have a problem' having orgasms through vaginal intercourse.[7] Sociologically speaking this tells us something about the power relations at play in defining good sex. If over 50 per cent of men didn't regularly achieve orgasm during intercourse would penetration be still seen as so important? Similarly would we still be talking about women 'having a problem'? (For whom exactly is not coming during intercourse a problem?) Is it a problem if you accept the many ways women have of reaching orgasm as part of what we call 'sex' and consider these to be as important and exciting as the activities which lead to male orgasms?[8]

While sexual surveys may have raised some difficult questions for sexology, it was the 'discovery' of the clitoral rather than the vaginal orgasm by Masters and Johnson that appeared really to set the cat among the pigeons.[9] Feminist writers on the whole greeted Masters and Johnson's work enthusiastically. [. . .] With the advantage of hindsight however we might want to ask whether such enthusiasm was misguided.[10] Even if it is now acknowledged that the female orgasm always starts in the clitoris, vaginal intercourse is still seen as normal, necessary, and desirable within heterosexual relationships. After all, the necessity of penetration for male orgasm was not being questioned! It is clear from their writings that this is what Masters and Johnson themselves believed. Although the vagina may have been ascribed a subsidiary role in the experience of female orgasm, women were still told that the clitoris could be stimulated through vaginal thrusting.

The social construction of 'sex' as vaginal intercourse affects how other forms of sexual activity are evaluated as sexually satisfying or arousing; in some cases whether an activity is seen as a sexual act at all. For example, unless a woman has been penetrated by a man's penis she is still technically a virgin even if she has had lots of sexual experience. If you've not had intercourse, you've not really had sex. The perception of sex as vaginal intercourse is also enshrined in the law as well as in religious teachings. For example, the legal definition of rape in most countries is unlawful sexual intercourse which means the penis must penetrate the vagina. Other forms of sexual violence towards women such as forced oral sex or anal intercourse, or the insertion of other objects into the vagina, constitute the 'less serious' crime of sexual assault.

This view of sex as penis in vagina, as something done to a woman by a man, implies that lesbians don't really have sex they have 'foreplay'. (The fact that we don't talk about afterplay also says something about the dominance of a goal-orientated view of sex rather than sex as a process.) Lesbian sex has often been conceptualized as immature, not as satisfying as intercourse, second-best sex. Many psychoanalytic theorists, for example, would argue that mutual masturbation produces a less satisfying form of orgasm than vaginal penetration. Even if lesbian sex does involve penetration it is still not seen as an authentic and autonomous form of female sexuality; rather it is understood as an imitation of what all women are supposed to want, a man's penis inside them. This is exemplified by referring to objects which a woman may use to penetrate herself or another woman as 'phallic objects' or 'penis-substitutes'. From a different point of view we could define a penis as a finger/vibrator/dildo substitute.

Language is important in shaping sexual behaviour, not only in what it categorizes and labels as erotic but also through what it does not articulate. Do we, for instance, have a language which adequately expresses female sexual experience in general and lesbian sex in particular?

Sex is defined largely in terms of male experience. The vocabulary of sex is much more concerned with describing what happens to a man's body during sexual arousal than a woman's. Similarly, there are very few words for women's genitals, whereas there are a great many other terms for the penis. In many ways language is either silent about women's bodies and sexuality or, where it does exist, ridicules and insults them.[11]

The language of sex also reflects and reinforces the idea that sex equals intercourse. There are a wide range of words for intercourse, but very few for other ways of making love such as body rubbing or cunnilingus. For instance, take the term 'mutual mastur-bation'. One of the problems with this phrase, in addition to the fact that it suggests that what you are doing is an imitation of masturbation with yourself, is its vagueness. It might include you and your partner taking it in turns to touch each other, touching your partner at the same time as she is touching you, touching her while touching yourself, touching yourself while she touches you or watching each other masturbate. One phrase to describe many different ways of having sex with another woman.

This is not however to suggest that just because some activities or parts of the body are not defined as specifically sexual they will not be part of a woman's sex life. On the contrary you might want to argue that opportunities for sex between women are restricted by labelling certain behaviours as sexual. Or, to put it another way, that defining some things and not others as sexual can serve to restrict opportunities for sexual pleasure, whereas the absence of labels can increase erotic potential.

For instance, Lillian Faderman, commenting on sexual relationships between women during the eighteenth century, claims that 'a narrower interpretation of what constitutes eroticism permitted a broader expression of erotic behaviour since it was not considered inconsistent with virtue'.[12]

In other words the phallocentric view of sex as penis in vagina meant sex between women was less easy to categorize as sexual and that therefore there was less pressure to restrict erotic interests in the same sex. It rendered sex between women as more invisible, but also more harmless.

[. . .]

WHAT'S A WOMAN SUPPOSED TO DO?

Fundamental to the social meaning of lesbian sexual practice are the views about fe-male sexuality and lesbianism which emanate from the 'scientific' discourse about sex and sexuality. Two main stereotypes of lesbians emerge, apparently in contradiction with each other.

Sexualized

Despite conceptualizing male and female sexuality as different (but complementary), a comparison has been drawn between women's and men's same-sex relationships. The application of theories of homosexuality, which were primarily concerned with men, to lesbians contributed to sex and sexual desire being seen as central to definitions of lesbianism, despite prevailing views of female sexuality as sexually responsive rather than active.

This construction of lesbians (and, even more so, gay men) as essentially *sexual*, a social group defined by its sexuality, is made particularly apparent in the kind of concerns expressed about the relationships lesbians have with children, for instance, in the case of the employment of lesbians who work with children or, alternatively, of children living with lesbian mothers. In such cases the traditional perception of women as maternal is overshadowed by the notion of lesbians, either directly or indirectly, posing some sort of sexual threat to children.

As I have already suggested, the view of lesbians as highly sexed would seem to contradict dominant discourses of sex, in particular the view of female sexuality as 'passive', responsive, primarily concerned with meeting a man's needs and 'sex' as synonymous with intercourse. This might help to explain why some people apparently find it hard to imagine what lesbians can possibly do in bed (or wherever): hence that all too familiar question 'But what do you do?' which, translated, means without a penis what can you do! The allocation of sexual agency to lesbians is, however, congruent with the view of the lesbian as unlike real women in her interests and desires and, to varying extents, more like a man, where men's interest in sex largely goes unquestioned.

The portrayal of the lesbian as a pseudo-man has also been influential in the way sex between women, when it is acknowledged, has often been interpreted as a mimicry of vaginal intercourse. It is often assumed that sex between women usually involves dildos or 'penile substitutes' – the stereotype of the 'dildo-wielding dyke'. In addition, lesbians have been described as suffering from feelings of 'virile inferiority' and wanting a penis of their own. Some studies in the past have gone so far as to suggest that lesbians are not only psychologically 'masculine' but are biologically like men. For instance, earlier this century Lang put forward the hypothesis that female homosexuals were genetically male, albeit having 'lost all morphological sex characteristics except their chromosome formula'.[13]

[. . .]

The notion that lesbian sex necessarily involves 'role playing', that one woman plays the part of the 'man' and the other the part of the 'woman', is also widely believed by some people, including some lesbians.[14] Thus, while the idea of a 'feminine' lesbian is potentially more challenging than that of the 'masculine' lesbian, it is contained by the assumption that such women are attracted to and form relationships with butch women and are not in any case 'real lesbians'. (The concept of two 'femmes' or two 'butches' having sex is much more challenging to these assumptions.)

At an individual level, such stereotyping can create anxieties in some lesbians about imitating heterosexuality. This may discourage them from engaging in certain kinds of sex: for example, lying on top of a woman and gaining sexual pleasure by rubbing against her body, or putting fingers or an object into the vagina of another woman, or having that done to themselves. As one woman said, 'If I want that I might as well go with a man'.

Others would argue that we need to construct alternative images which articulate the experience of certain kinds of sex between women as other than an imitation of heterosexuality. For instance, some women may very much enjoy the feeling of having their vaginas touched during sex precisely because they have rejected the way in which the potential pleasures of penetration have previously been defined, almost exclusively, in heterosexual terms and have reappropriated the vagina as part of lesbian love-making. However, there is still the question of language. Do we murmur to our partner that, as *The Joy of Lesbian Sex* puts it, we want to be fingerfucked? Or is this use of language one that harks back to the idea that what we are doing is heterosexual mimicry?

Desexualized

Other portrayals of lesbians have also been influential in the construction of lesbian sexuality, in particular the view, heavily influenced by psychoanalytic accounts, of the lesbian as 'mother-fixated', seeking, through her relationships with other women, to be mothered. Such a view within theoretical accounts of homosexuality in the past encouraged a tendency to see lesbian relationships as primarily emotional rather than sexual.[15] In part this can be understood in terms of the way women's sexuality has traditionally been seen as 'passive', needing to be brought to sexual fulfilment and orgasm by a man. But it can also be understood in terms of dominant definitions of sex. For if to the predominantly male 'experts' what lesbians do isn't real sex, then it's perhaps not altogether surprising that studies of lesbian relationships have often focused on emotional attachment rather than sexual behaviour.[16]

Some studies of lesbian history have also been seen as desexualizing lesbianism. For instance, Lillian Faderman's[17] definition of lesbianism does not necessarily include genital contact. In rejecting what she sees as a male definition of lesbianism (and 'sex') as defined by genital contact, she describes women who had passionate friendships with other women as lesbians, where sexual contact may or may not have been part of their relationship. Critics of such a definition, such as Ruehl,[18] accuse Faderman of 'watering down lesbianism by playing down the sexual content'.[19]

Others have appealed to social conditioning in describing lesbians as having a relatively low interest in sex. Lesbians, by virtue of their socialization as women, are likely to act 'just like other women'[20] [. . .] for whom sex is primarily a way of expressing love. Some lesbian writers echo this view in claiming that lesbians, as women, are sexually inhibited and repressed. For example, Margaret Nichols states that: 'Two women together, each primed to respond sexually only to a request from another, may rarely even experience desire, much less engage in sexual activity'.[21]

While Nichols is right to suggest that as lesbians we have to engage with the expectations of a heterosexual upbringing, her suggestion that we 'obediently comply' is highly questionable. As Annabel Faraday[22] has pointed out, such a functionalist approach fails to take sufficient account of how we, as lesbians, question those definitions and negotiate new meanings. It is this process I want to consider next.

'WOMAN-IDENTIFIED WOMAN' TO LUSTFUL LESBIAN

[. . .] Over the last twenty years lesbians have challenged what others have said about them, most obviously that lesbianism is a disease or mental illness. The question we next need to consider therefore is: how have lesbians defined lesbian sex for themselves? We might also ask how far the meanings derived from lesbian culture have challenged the heterosexual values incorporated in traditional medical and psychiatric definitions of sex.

For some lesbians, and indeed for some feminists, lesbianism is regarded as a sexual preference/practice; as being about who we desire and have sex with. However during the 1970s there was decreasing emphasis placed on lesbianism as a sexual and erotic experience, arguably partly as a reaction to the way psychiatry and medicine had previously defined lesbianism largely in terms of sexual orientation and sexual acts. Instead, there was greater emphasis on understanding lesbianism and indeed heterosexuality, in political terms. Lesbian feminists asserted that lesbianism is not simply a sexual practice but a way of life and political struggle – a challenge to the institution of heterosexuality. As Ti-Grace Atkinson put it, 'Feminism was the theory, lesbianism the practice.'

This analysis of lesbianism as more than a sexual preference, as a political choice, implied a critique of heterosexuality as an institution. It was a form of resistance to what Adrienne Rich[23] later termed 'compulsory heterosexuality', the process whereby heterosexuality is instituted and maintained under conditions of male supremacy. In the United States the classic 'Woman-identified woman' paper by Radicalesbians, written in 1970, was one of the first attempts at defining lesbianism in political terms. It asserted that 'woman-identified lesbianism' was the political strategy necessary for women's liberation and the end to male supremacy. The implication for heterosexual feminists was that they should give up relationships with men and put their commitment, love, and emotional support into relationships with women. This included an acknowledgement of a sexual element in lesbianism:

> Until women see in each other the possibility of a primal commitment which includes sexual love, they will be denying themselves the love and value they readily accord men, thus affirming their second-class status.[24]

In Britain this idea that feminists should withdraw from sexual relationships with men and become political lesbians as a strategy to challenge women's oppression was put forward in a now famous paper, first published in 1979, by the Leeds Revolutionary Feminist Group, The paper, 'Political lesbianism: the case against heterosexuality'[25] defined a political lesbian as a 'woman-identified woman who does not fuck men'. It was primarily concerned with not having sex with men rather than with lesbian sexual practice; the main issue was *identifying* as a political lesbian.

At the same time as many lesbian feminists, in the early 1970s, were defining lesbianism as political rather than sexual practice, lesbian and gay liberation movements were also engaged in redefining 'homosexuality'. In their emphasis on the importance of the development of a sense of lesbian/gay pride and the public affirmation of the validity of lesbianism/gay relationships through coming out they too were primarily concerned with identity rather than sexual behaviour, with being rather than doing.

Some lesbians responded angrily to the arguments for political lesbianism on the grounds that it desexualized lesbianism.[26] Their concern was that lesbianism was becoming associated with a critique/rejection of heterosexuality and feelings of sisterhood for other women, rather than a positive and sexual attraction to women. Lesbianism stripped of its sexual element was better described as political celibacy.

Another common response to lesbian feminist critiques of heterosexuality is that they encouraged a view of lesbian sex as the only politically acceptable sexual practice; lesbianism was the model for describing good sex for women. This evoked a particular representation of lesbian sex. It was sex that was reciprocal, non-oppressive, equal, less goal-orientated, not penetrative or genitally focused. The term used by some writers[27] is 'politically correct lesbian sex', an expression that is generally used negatively to imply a curtailment of lesbian desires and sexual practices and provides a context for understanding critiques of 'vanilla sex'.

In recent years a concern with resexualizing lesbianism has become more evident. Never mind politicizing sex, let's put sex back into politics has been the rallying cry. In 1984 Susie Bright, editor of *On Our Backs*, the first American porn magazine for lesbians, declared that it was the Year of the Lustful Lesbian. Similarly, co-editor Debi Sundahl believes that a political and social revolution has begun as a result of lesbians producing erotica and pornography for other lesbians, not to mention live strip shows, sex toys, and so on.[28] The association of sexual liberation and the political liberation of women has been subject to serious criticism, particularly in recent analyses of the so-called sexual revolution of the 1960s.[29] Nevertheless, to disagree with the sentiments expressed by Sundahl and her contemporaries is to risk being characterized by some as a political dinosaur who is anti-sex or, even worse, anti-lesbian.

The libertarian stance urging us to celebrate sex can be seen not only as a reaction to the desexualization of lesbianism which many felt had occurred during the 1970s, but also partly as a response to the emphasis on the dangers of sexuality for women within feminist discourses, in particular debates around sexual violence and pornography. This is nothing new of course. Earlier this century feminists were divided over the emphasis placed on sex as danger/sex as pleasure, which inevitably led to differences in feminist campaigning around sexual and reproductive issues.[30]

Another factor in the emergence of discussions of lesbian sexual practice has been AIDS and the debates about safer sex it has generated.[31] AIDS has created a context in which we are allowed to talk about sex. Indeed, telling each other what we do sexually has suddenly become not only permissible but a social requirement, a necessary and important part of lesbian health concerns. AIDS has, then, provided a 'legitimate' focus for lesbians to talk about sex generally, with safer sex as the starting point.

It is in this context of insisting that lesbianism *is* about sex that we have witnessed the emergence of lesbian sex-manuals such as *The Joy of Lesbian Sex*, *Sapphistry*, and *Lesbian Sex*,[32] but more especially pornography and erotic fiction for lesbians by lesbians. This includes the production of magazines such as, in the United States, *On Our Backs* and *Bad Attitude*, in Britain, *Quim* and (with gay men) *Square Peg* and, in

Australia, *Wicked Women*. [. . .] Lesbianism as sex has been politicized, and often in the name of feminism, but we need to ask, what as? What kind of lesbian sex is being represented? – especially as writers such as Bright[32] and Califra[33] are claiming the new sexual agenda to be revolutionary, a challenge to the heterosexual norms of the past.

A close examination of recent lesbian porn and erotica reveals that the dominant forms of sex represented are penetrative and/or sado-masochistic (S/M) activities. Dildos or, as they are often referred to, 'cocks' appear with great regularity, as do chains, manacles, studs, leather straps, and whips. Stories about 'playing with power', of bondage and dominance, of S/M sex are what we have come to expect. Representations of lesbian desire as desire for a full vagina or, to a lesser extent, a full anus are the norm and include 'fist-fucking' as well as penetration with objects. Byron[34] describes this as 'the renaissance of vaginal sex amongst lesbians', which she sees as borrowed from gay male porn and its emphasis on penetrative sex. There are some strange ironies here, not least that the celebration of the pleasures of penetration in lesbian porn has occurred at a time when, because of AIDS, penetrative sex has been challenged.

These developments have provoked discussion, debate, and, in some cases, outrage among many lesbians. The question I want to address here however is how far does this so-called resexualization of lesbianism reproduce, rather than challenge, traditional sexual values by placing a primacy on penetration and associating lesbian desire with eroticized power difference?

One answer to the question is that acts which may be regarded as oppressive/harmful/unsatisfying to women in heterosexual relationships will in a different context (i.e. between two women) have different meaning. At one level this is obviously true. The experience, both psychologically and physically, of a man's penis in your vagina is not the same as the experience of a woman's fingers inside you, not to mention bananas, vibrators, or dildos. It's also the case that a lot of lesbians enjoy touching themselves, being touched, and touching their lovers in their vaginas. Some lesbians also like to be touched in their anuses and rectums. Having said that, the concern is that in representing lesbian sex as primarily penetrative there becomes a pressure that lesbians should want to be touched or put objects in their vaginas – an expectation that passion means penetration.

Similarly, the focus in lesbian porn on sado-masochism challenges a sexual desire and practice which eroticizes mutuality and equality. Despite the appeals to sexual liberation, some lesbian porn writers clearly feel that sexual diversification has its limits: all things are not equal; it is not simply a case of whatever turns you on. It is implied that lesbians who don't like or desire a full vagina, who don't want to play with sex toys, who don't turn on to power are somehow conservative, prudish, immature, or boring sexually. They are 'bambis' or vanilla dykes, where vanilla is certainly not flavour of the month! Indeed, one might ask will it mean in future that you've not gone all the way with a woman, not really had sex, are not a 'real lesbian', unless you've, say, fist-fucked or tried bondage and dominance? Consider, for instance, Pat Califia's response to lesbians who don't like, for whatever reasons, what lesbian porn has to offer: 'If you don't like to read about pussy maybe you don't like pussy and you should be lickin' something else'.[35] This is doubly ironic when one considers another trend in lesbian porn, the portrayal of lesbians becoming aroused through heterosexual and gay male sex.

A central question has to be whether lesbian porn is liberating or constricting for lesbians. Quite clearly some believe it is the former and it is certainly the case that recent lesbian porn has challenged the soft-focus, romantic imagery of lesbianism which, from a feminist perspective, can be regarded as oppressive. It's also true that lesbian porn differs in certain respects from heterosexual porn, for instance while the penis is often the only focus of genital satisfaction in heterosexual porn the emphasis in lesbian porn is on the woman's desire and pleasure; it's she who comes, not the dildo, vibrator, or finger. Despite this, I want to argue that this so-called radical, liberatory discourse is in fact more of the same, colluding with rather than challenging dominant discourses of sex which are fundamentally oppressive to women. Thus we could see the recent emergence of lesbian porn and erotica, with its privileging of certain kinds of activities, as a pressure to accept as the norm for lesbian sex sexual values which have previously been associated with heterosexuality.[36] The experience of a full vagina is represented in ways that replicate the language, values, and imagery of heterosexual sex; [. . .] 'fucking' ends in 'ejaculation'.

[. . .]

Whatever we think about these developments what we are witnessing, in the absence of a diversity of cultural representations of lesbian sex, is a redefinition of what lesbian sex is. As I stated at the beginning of the chapter, the answer to the question 'What is lesbian sex?' will depend on the meanings available to us from social discourses about sex. As those meanings change then so may our desires and our practices. Different parts of the body may become more or less sexualized. I have already indicated how in recent lesbian porn the anus and the vagina have been more privileged than either the clitoris or breasts. Similarly, different activities may become eroticized as lesbian sex; 'fist-fucking' and bondage are part of lesbian consciousness in the 1990s in a way they never were in the 1950s and 1960s. We've come a long way since then, when lesbian sex was represented by one long smouldering kiss and then. . . . Or have we?

NOTES

1. The use of the word 'sex' to describe lesbian desire and sexual pleasure is not unproblematic (see M. Frye, 'Lesbian "sex"', in J. Allen (ed.), *Lesbian Philosophies and Cultures*, New York: State University of New York Press, 1990; and S.L. Hoagland, *Lesbian Ethics. Towards New Values*, Palo Alto, Califo. Institute of Lesbian Studies, 1988). In choosing to use it I am conscious of the difficulties it presents.
2. This is not to imply that all feminists were anti-lesbian.
3. While it makes more sense in terms of transmission of HIV and sexually transmitted diseases to talk about sex between women, in terms of the social and political aspects of lesbianism it makes more sense to talk about lesbian sex. As Campbell (B. Campbell, 'A feminist sexual politics: now you see it, now you don't', *Feminist Review*, 5, 1980, pp. 1–18) and others have pointed out, lesbianism is a specific sexual practice between women with its own history, it is not the same thing as sex between women.
4. What is highlighted here is the need to distinguish same-sex sexual attraction and relationships from the historically specific sexual categorizations and identities which provide the meanings and conditions in which individuals experience the former. It is these socially constructed meanings that are the basis for the experience of sexual desire: who does what to whom with what and in what order.
5. A.C. Kinsey, W.B. Pomeroy and C.E. Martin, *Sexual Behaviour in the Human Male*, Philadelphia: Saunders, 1948; and A.C. Kinsey, W.B. Pomeroy, C.E. Martin and P.H. Gebhard, *Sexual Behaviour in the Human Female*, 1953.

6. S. Hite, *The Hite Report*, New York: Macmillan, 1976.
7. M. Hunt, *Sexual Behaviour in the 1970s*, New York: Dell, 1975.
8. S. Hite, *Women and Love*, New York: Alfred A. Knopf, 1987.
9. W.H. Masters and V.E. Johnson, *Human Sexual Response*, Boston: Little, Brown & Co., 1966.
10. L. Coveney, M. Jackson, S. Jeffreys, L. Kaye and P. Mahonan, *The Sexuality Papers*, London: Hutchinson, 1984.
11. D. Richardson, *Safer Sex*, London: Pandora, 1990.
12. L. Faderman, *Surpassing the Love of Men: Romantic Friendships between Women from the Renaissance to the Present*, London: Junctions Books, 1981, p. 33.
13. T. Lang, 'Studies on the genetic determination of homosexuality', *Journal of Nervous and Mental Disorder*, 92, 1940, pp. 55–64.
14. S. Kitzinger, *Woman's Experience of Sex*, Marmondsworth. Penguin, 1985.
15. See for example, C.W. Socarides, 'The psychoanalytic Theory of homosexuality with special reference to therapy', in I. Rosen (ed.), *Sexual Deviations*, 2nd edn, Oxford: Oxford University Press, 1979; A. Stoss, *Sexual Deviation*, London: Penguin, 1964.
16. In both of these stereotypes of the lesbian – as sexualized and desexualized – an autonomous female sexuality is denied: in the former case by seeing a woman's interest in sex as 'pseudo-male' behaviour; in the latter by representing lesbianism as the mother-child dynamic,
17. Faderman, *Surpassing the Love of Men*.
18. S. Ruehl, 'Sexual theory and practice: another double standard', in S. Cartledge and J. Ryan (eds), *Sex and Love*, London: The Women's Press, 1983.
19. Sheila Jeffreys, 'Does it matter if they did?', *Trouble and Strife*, no. 3, 1984, pp. 25–9.
20. J.H. Gagnon and W.S. Simon, *Sexual Conduct: The Social Sources of Human Sexuality*, Chicago: Aldine, 1973.
21. 'Lesbian sexuality: issues and developing theory', in Boston Lesbian Psychologies Collective (eds), *Lesbian Psychologies*, Chicago, University of Illinois Press, 1987, p. 103. Nichols goes on to argue that if sexual desire requires a 'barrier', some kind of tension, difference, power discrepancy, this is a problem for lesbian sexuality. She suggests that we need to find ways of introducing 'barriers' into our relationships to enhance sexuality and sexual desire. For instance, 'through the use of sex toys and props, through costume, through S/M (which maximizes differences between partners), by developing sexual rituals with our partners, and by introducing tricking into our relationships' (*ibid.*, p. 108).
22. A. Faraday, 'Liberating lesbian research', in K. Plummer (ed.), *The Making of the Modern Homosexual*, London: Hutchinson, 1981.
23. Adrienne Rich, 'Complusory heterosexuality and lesbian existence', *Signs*, 5(4) Summer 1980, pp. 631–60; reprinted in A. Snitow, C. Stansall and S. Thompson (eds), *Desire: The Politics of Sexuality*, London: Virago, 1984.
24. Radicalesbians, 'The woman-identified woman', in A. Koedt, E. Levine and A. Rapone (eds), *Radical Feminism*, New York: Quadrangle Books, 1973; p. 243.
25. Leeds Revolutionary Feminist Group, 'Political Lesbianism: the case against heterosexuality', in Onlywomen Press (eds), *Love Your Enemy*, London: Onlywomen Press, 1981.
26. See B. Campbell, 'A feminist sexual politics: now you see it, now you don't', *Feminist Review*, 5, 1980, pp. 30–4; P. Califia, 'Feminism and sadomasochism', *Heresies*, 12, 1981, pp. 30–4; Onlywomen Press, *Love Your Enemy*. Heterosexual feminists also criticized the notion of political lesbianism, arguing for the 'right to choose' relationships with men S. Jeffreys, *Anti-climax: A Feminist Perspective on the Sexual Revolution*, London: The Women's Press, 1990.
27. For example, Nichols, 'Lesbian sexuality'.
28. D. Sundahl, 'Lesbian sex – part 11', *The Advocate*, October 1985.
29. See B. Ehrenrich, E. Hess and G. Jacobs, *Remaking Love: The Feminization of Sex*, London: Fontana, 1987 Jeffreys, *Anti-climax*.
30. L. Gordon and E. Dubois, 'Seeking ecstasy on the battlefield: danger and pleasure in nineteenth-century feminist thought', in C.S. Vance (ed.) *Pleasure and Danger*, London: Routledge & Kegan Paul, 1984.
31. D. Richardson, *Women and AIDS Crisis*, 2nd edition, London: Pandora, 1989.
32. P. Califia, *Sapphistry: The Book of Lesbian Sexuality*, 3rd edition, Florida: Naiad, 1988; J. Loulan, *Lesbian Sex*, San Francisco: Spinsters Ink, 1984.
33. S. Bright (ed.), *Herotica*, California: Down There Press, 1988; Califia, *Sapphistry*.
34. P. Byron, 'What we talk about when we talk about dildos', *The Voice*, 5 March 1985.
35. Califia, *Sapphistry*, p. x.
36. Another concern expressed over the recent emergence of lesbian porn and erotica is what effect this will have on how lesbians are regarded and socially controlled.

PART FOUR

COMMERCIAL SEX

4.1

THE POLITICS OF PROSTITUTION

Judith Walkowitz

Feminist concern about commercial sex has a history which stretches back to the nineteenth century. Judith Walkowitz draws parallels between early feminist campaigns against vice and prostitution and more recent campaigns against pornography. Her analysis suggests that there are dangers in feminists allying themselves with right-wing moral crusaders whose goal is the regulation of sexuality rather than the liberation of women.

In this essay, I shall outline some historical precedents for the current feminist attack on commercial sex, as represented by the Women against Pornography campaign.[1] The radical feminist attack on commercial sex has its roots in earlier feminist campaigns against male vice and the double standard. Past generations of feminists attacked prostitution, pornography, white slavery, and homosexuality as manifestations of undifferentiated male lust. Their campaigns were brilliant organizing drives that successfully aroused female anger, stimulated grass-roots organizations, and mobilized women not previously brought into the political arena. The vitality of the women's suffrage movement of the late nineteenth and early twentieth centuries cannot be understood without reference to the revivalistic quality of these antivice crusades, which often ran in tandem with the struggle for the vote.

Nonetheless, these earlier moral campaigns were in many ways self-defeating. Frequently, they failed to achieve their goals; feminists started a discourse on sex and mobilized an offensive against male vice, but they lost control of the movement as it diversified. In part, this loss resulted from contradictions in their attitudes; in part, it reflected feminists' impotence to reshape the world according to their own image.

From J. Walkowitz, 'The politics of prostitution', *Signs*, 1980.

Four recent works illuminate this process in Great Britain and the United States. Deborah Gorham's 'The Maiden Tribute of Modern Babylon Re-examined' and Edward Bristow's *Vice and Vigilance*[2] explore the unhappy alliance between British feminists and repressive moralists in the agitation against white slavery during the social purity crusade of 1870–1918. The public discourse on prostitution is also the subject of Mark Connelly's *The Response to Prostitution in the Progressive Era*, while *The Maimie Papers*,[3] an edited collection of letters by a former prostitute, sheds light on the lives and self-perceptions of prostitutes themselves. These studies tell us how feminists and others mobilized over prostitution and how their campaigns helped to define and construct sexuality in the late nineteenth century; they also delineate the relationship between public intervention and definitions of deviance.

In both Britain and America, feminist moral crusades against male vice began with a struggle against the state regulation of prostitution.

[. . .]

Although capable of enunciating a radical critique of prostitution, middle-class feminists still felt ambivalent about prostitutes and the right of working-class women to control their own sexuality. By and large, these anxieties remained submerged during the libertarian struggle against state regulation, but they soon surfaced in the more repressive campaign against white slavery. After the suspension of the Contagious Diseases Acts in 1883, Butler and her circle turned to the agitation against the foreign 'traffic in women' and the entrapment of children into prostitution in London. When Parliament refused to pass a bill that would raise the age of consent and punish traffickers in vice, Butler and Catherine Booth of the Salvation Army approached W.T. Stead of the *Pall Mall Gazette* for assistance. The result was the 'Maiden Tribute of Modern Babylon,' published in the summer of 1885.

The 'Maiden Tribute' was one of the most successful pieces of scandal journalism published in Britain during the nineteenth century. In prurient detail, it documented the sale of 'five pound' virgins to aristocratic old rakes, graphically describing the way, according to Gorham, the 'daughters of the people' had been 'snared, trapped and outraged either when under the influence of drugs or after prolonged struggle in a locked room.'[4] The series had an electrifying effect on public opinion. A public demonstration (estimated at 250,000) was held in Hyde Park to demand the passage of legislation raising the age of consent for girls from thirteen to sixteen. For one brief moment, feminists and personal rights advocates joined with Anglican bishops and socialists to protest the aristocratic corruption of young innocents.

In their examination of the 'Maiden Tribute' episode, both Gorham and Bristow part company with most historians, who, as Gorham notes, have traditionally 'accepted the definition of the problem that the reformers themselves offered.'[5] Other commentators have accepted as a fact the existence of widespread involuntary prostitution among British girls at home or abroad; they have also assumed that in pressing for age-of-consent legislation, moral reformers were motivated by a simple desire to protect innocent victims from sexual violence.

Gorham and Bristow delineate the vast discrepancy between the reformers' view and the reality of prostitution. Both observe that the evidence of widespread involuntary prostitution of British girls in London and abroad is slim. During the 1870s and 1880s, officials and reformers were able to uncover a small traffic in women between Britain and the continent, although the women enticed into licensed brothels in Antwerp and Brussels were by no means the young innocents depicted in the sensational stories. Similarly, there undoubtedly were some child prostitutes on the streets of London, Liverpool, and elsewhere; most of these young girls were not victims of false entrapment, as the vignettes in the 'Maiden Tribute' would suggest.

Why, then, did feminist reformers endorse this crusade and ally with repressive moralists and antisuffragists who were as anxious to clear the streets of prostitutes as to protect young girls from vicious aristocrats? Gorham brilliantly untangles the complex motives of feminists and others in taking up the question of involuntary and child prostitution. Her study is a model of cultural analysis, which examines middle-class views of childhood, gender, and sexuality in the context of ongoing political struggles and social divisions within Victorian society. Although sensitive to the distinct political agenda of feminists in the campaign, Gorham shows how their professed solidarity with working-class women was undermined by their allegiance to hierarchical notions of authority that divided women along class and generational lines.

[. . .]

By portraying young prostitutes as sexually innocent and passive victims of individual evil men, the reformers were able to assuage middle-class guilt without implicating members of their own class in the sexual oppression of working-class women and girls. 'Had they allowed themselves,' suggests Gorham, 'to see that many young girls engaged in prostitution not as passive, sexually innocent victims, but because their choices were so limited, the reformers would have been forced to recognize that the causes of juvenile prostitution were to be found in an exploitative economic structure.'[6]

According to Gorham, feminists tended to share the same feelings of anxiety over youthful female sexuality as other members of the middle class. Although they felt obliged to redress the sexual wrongs done to working-class girls by men of a superior class, they registered the same repugnance toward incorrigible girls as they had earlier toward unrepentant prostitutes. For them, as well as for more repressive moralists, the desire to protect young girls thinly masked coercive impulses to control their voluntary sexual responses and to impose a social code on them in keeping with the middle-class view of female adolescent dependency.

Bristow considers the legal and institutional legacy of the 'Maiden Tribute' in *Vice and Vigilance*. Although he traces the history of antivice crusades back to the Society for the Reformation of Manners of the 1960s, he concedes that the 'heart' of his study lies in the period 1880 and altered the climate of opinion about sex. *Vice and Vigilance* is witty, informative, and well researched, but it does not offer a rigorous interpretation of modern sexuality, nor does it fully explore the meaning and timing of these antivice crusades. Caught between a popular narrative and a scholarly project, Bristow is at his best when describing the infrastructure of purity organizations and their political maneuverings at the national and municipal level.

The public furor over the 'Maiden Tribute' forced the passage of the Criminal Law Amendment Act of 1885, a pernicious piece of omnibus legislation which raised the age of consent for girls from thirteen to sixteen but also gave police far greater summary jurisdiction over poor working-class women and children, a trend that Butler and her circle had always opposed. Finally, it contained a clause making indecent acts between consenting male adults a crime, thus forming the basis of legal prosecutions of male homosexuals in Britain until 1967.

Despite the public outcry against corrupt aristocrats and international traffickers, the new bill was mainly enforced against the working-class women, not their social betters or foreigners. Under pressure from local vigilance associations, police officials cracked down on streetwalkers and brothel keepers. The prosecution of brothels increased fourteenfold, and similar drives against solicitation were instituted in the capital and major provincial cities.

Bristow simply reports these developments, but does not suggest how legal repression affected the structure and organization of prostitution. Although we still await a detailed study of late-Victorian prostitution, some preliminary generalizations are possible. By providing for easy, summary proceedings against brothel keepers, the 1885 act helped to drive a wedge between prostitutes and the poor working-class community. Prostitutes were uprooted from their neighborhoods and had to find lodgings in other areas of the city and in the periphery. Their activity had become more covert. Cut off from other sustaining relationships, increasingly they were forced to rely on pimps for emotional security and for protection against legal authorities. Indeed, the wide prevalence of pimps in the early twentieth century meant that prostitution had shifted from a female- to a male-dominated trade, and there existed a greater number of third parties with an interest in prolonging women's stay on the streets.[7]

In the wake of Stead's 'shocking revelations,' the National Vigilance Association (NVA) was formed. First organized to ensure the local enforcement of the Criminal Law Amendment Act, the NVA soon turned its attention to burning obscene books and to attacking music halls, theaters, and nude painting. It condemned the works of Balzac, Zola, and Rabelais and successfully prosecuted their British distributors; it attacked birth-control literature and advertisements for 'female pills' (abortifacient drugs) on the same grounds. To these moral crusaders, 'pornographic literature,' broadly defined, was a vile expression of the same 'undifferentiated male lust'[8] that ultimately led to homosexuality and prostitution. As Bristow observes, the fact that pornography was now available in cheap editions heightened middle-class concern. They visualized the masses, whose political loyalty they doubted, perusing works that might further weaken their allegiance to the dominant moral order.

While the social purity movement served middle-class interests, it is a common error among historians to assume, as Gorham does, that working-class support for social purity was 'ephemeral' or that both 'before and after the summer of 1885 [social purity] remained almost exclusively a middle-class movement.'[9] Middle-class evangelicals may have predominated in the National Vigilance Association, but Bristow presents suggestive evidence that the values of social purity were internalized among some portions of the working class in the late nineteenth century.

[. . .]

Edwardian working-class parents were notable for their strict schedules, puritanical treatment of masturbation, and for the severe restrictions they placed on their teenage daughters' social and sexual behavior. Although the late-Victorian and Edwardian years represented a 'germination' period for the 'new sexuality,' the available 'facts' about adult sexuality in this period, the general decline in both venereal disease and prostitution, the high age of marriage and low illegitimacy rates, and the apparently limited use of contraceptives among the working classes would seem to support Bristow's hypothesis that 'sexual restraint' was indeed 'spreading down through society.'[10] As we shall see in the American case, certain countervailing tendencies were perceptible as well.

Why was social purity so attractive to respectable workingmen? As Bristow notes, it provided an avenue of social mobility for some men, like William Coote, a former compositor who became the national secretary of the National Vigilance Association. Sexual respectability became a hallmark of the labor aristocrat, anxious to distance himself from the 'bestiality' of the casual laboring poor, as increased pressure was placed on the respectable working class to break their ties with 'outcast' groups. Other structural factors were at work as well, although Bristow does not elaborate on them. Changing employment patterns seem to have reinforced patriarchal tendencies among skilled sectors of the working class by the end of the century, as the proportion of married women working outside the home declined and the family wage for male workers became a demand of trade unions. Seen in this context, social purity, which called upon men to protect and control their women, served as the ideological corollary of the family wage, morally legitimating the prerogatives of patriarchy inside and outside the family. Thus, social purity served to undermine working-class solidarity, while tightening definitions of gender among respectable workingmen and working women.

What was the subsequent relationship between feminism and social purity? Initially, feminists filled many committee positions of the National Vigilance Association, but this connection was short-lived for Butler and her circle, who resigned when the repressive direction of the NVA became apparent. Throughout the late eighties and nineties, Butlerites warned their workers to 'beware' of the repressive methods of the social purity societies, but their warnings were too late. The new social purity movement had passed them by, while absorbing a goodly number of the Ladies National Association rank and file.

Conservative suffragists like Millicent Fawcett and Elizabeth Blackwell still remained within the ranks of social purity, but they never controlled the direction of the movement. On the other hand, social purity permanently left its imprint on the women's movement; its theme of the sexual wrongs perpetrated against women by men permeated later feminist consciousness. After the 1880s, the 'women's revolt' became 'Puritan and not Bohemian. It is uprising against the tyranny of organized intemperance, impurity, mammonism, and selfish motives.'[11]

These, then, are the historical links between feminism and repressive crusades against prostitution, pornography, and homosexuality. Begun as a libertarian struggle against the state sanction of male vice, the repeal campaign helped to spawn a hydra-headed assault against sexual deviation of all kinds. The struggle against state regulation evolved into a movement that used the instruments of the state for repressive purposes. It may be misleading to interpret these later crusades as 'blind' repressive attacks on sexuality, as Bristow suggests; rather, they extended the meaning of sexuality. According to Michel Foucault, this discourse on sex was a strategy for exercising power in society.[12] By ferreting out new areas of illicit sexual activity and defining them into existence, a new 'technology of power' was created that facilitated control over an ever-widening circle of human activity. However, power is not immanent in society; it is deployed by specific human agencies. During the repeal campaign, feminist leaders were able to control and shape the public discourse on sex; but, according to Bristow, they 'rapidly lost control of a spreading and diversifying movement and social purity had begun to lose sight of [Butler's] ideal of the "supremacy of conscience" with its non-repressionist implications. Purity reform came to mean the harassing of prostitutes and systematic blind repression in the arts and entertainment.'[13]

The story is much the same in America.[14] In the 1860s and 1870s, American feminists and other moral reformers were able to forestall the introduction of regulation for prostitutes in U.S. cities. [. . .]

Mark Connelly's *The Response to Prostitution in the Progressive Era* is less concerned with feminist participation in purity work than with the widespread phenomenon of 'anti-prostitution.' The book has the virtues, and some of the vices, of traditional cultural history. Connelly astutely dissects literary genres associated with discourse on prostitution during the progressive era: white-slave narratives, vice commission reports, medical literature on venereal disease, even the clauses of the Mann Act. His discussion of that 'rare exotic literary genre,' the white-slave tract, is superb. These narratives served as 'spicy cultural counterpart to the stuffy vice commission reports'; they were 'vicarious "tour guides" ' to the red-light districts for individuals who would not go there in person.' Like the exposés of child prostitution in the 'Maiden Tribute,' the child-woman figure of the white-slave tract 'reflected an inability to confront prostitution as a manifestation of *adult* sexuality totally outside the prescription of civilized morality. Childish victims were perhaps easier to deal with psychologically than libidinous men and women.'[15] Connelly also provides a judicious guide to the more 'scientific' vice commission reports. As social documents, these reports can not be read 'straight'; but if properly decoded, they can yield a wealth of information about the social profile of prostitutes, their material culture, and community life. By focusing exclusively on the documents as texts, however, Connelly fails to use them to construct a rounded description of prostitutes and their response to the crisis precipitated by the police crackdowns.

Whereas Bristow presents a breezy narrative of the personages and events of British social purity, Connelly is committed to the task of uncovering the larger cultural meaning of the public discourse on American prostitution. In trying to do so,

Connelly homogenizes the progressives, whose specific identities are rarely discussed, who all seem to be last-ditch defenders of Victorian morality, riddled by the same psychological blind spots. They may have employed different literary tableaux, but fundamentally they spoke with one voice. When he considers why the theory that women resorted to the streets because of inadequate wages enjoyed such currency among progressives, Connelly concludes that 'anxiety seems as strongly provoked by the fact that women were working in industrial jobs at all as by the low wages they received.' 'This is not to dismiss,' he hastens to add, 'the very genuine concern over the economic plight of working women expressed by many who addressed the wages-and-sin issues.'[16] Yet he never tells us who in fact held these varying positions, under what conditions these differences were expressed, and why one opinion prevailed over another. The discourse on prostitution represented a power struggle among distinct social constituencies, inside and outside the bourgeoisie. As the British case demonstrates, that conflict reflected both class and gender divisions. Connelly's generalized discussion of cultural anxiety posits a bourgeois hegemony, but ignores Raymond Williams' critical reminder that the 'reality of any hegemony . . . is that while by definition it is always dominant, it is never either total or exclusive.'[17] The struggle between cultures is a dynamic historical process; unfortunately, Connelly's well-crafted book tends to obscure that process.

This problem aside, Connelly's book illuminates many aspects of prostitution that interest feminist scholars. His discussion of clandestine prostitution is particularly insightful. The obsession with 'clandestines' or 'amateurs,' Connelly argues, was a reaction to changing sexual and social mores. Even before the First World War, traditional moralists were shocked by the perceptible increase in 'flappers,' female adolescents in open rebellion against rigid Victorian sexual standards. The free and easy sexual habits of this small vanguard were symptomatic of the more widespread departure of women from traditional social and economic roles.

[. . .]

The desire of young working women to lead lives different from those of their mothers may have constituted an unprecedented change in popular female conscious-ness. This partial break with traditional gender roles took many forms. In the early twentieth century, a new leadership cadre of trade-union organizers, suffragists, and radical agitators was recruited from the ranks of working-class women. But can one equate the sexual rebellion of flappers with these more self-conscious, focused, and politicized acts of emancipation?

Let us consider the case of Maimie Pinzer, a former prostitute and author of the letters collected in the *Maimie Papers*. Maimie's letters to Fanny Howe, a Boston pa-trician and philanthropist, constitute a brilliant autobiography of a survivor struggling to maintain her independence and self-respect against terrible odds. Written between 1910 and 1922, they reveal little of Maimie's experience in prostitution (she was never a streetwalker but seems to have carried on a discreet trade with gentlemen in the afternoon). The letters do, however, tell us a great deal about her subsequent working life outside prostitution, and about the circumstances that might have impelled 'self-respecting errant girls' like herself to move into prostitution.

As Ruth Rosen notes in her sensitive introduction, Maimie's social background closely paralleled that of other working-class girls in the progressive era. A crisis in the family economy, caused by the death of her father; an estranged relationship with her mother; early sexual experiences with men of her own class – all forced Maimie and thousands of her contemporaries to leave their families and strike out on their own in their late teens. Many of these young working women eventually drifted into prostitution as a temporary solution to uneasy circumstances. Their move into prostitution, Rosen reminds us, was still a choice, because prostitutes were not simply 'passive victims of impersonal economic and social forces,'[18] but active historical agents, women who made their own history, albeit under restrictive conditions.

Judging from Maimie's experience, however, one should not underestimate the practical impediments to female self-sufficiency. Maimie tried all the options available to women at the time: marriage, prostitution, female employment within the tertiary sector, from office work to rescue work.

[. . .]

Ironically, her most satisfying venture turned out to be rescue work. In 1913, with financial backing from middle-class benefactors, she opened a mission in Montreal for 'self-respecting errant girls'. [. . .] For Maimie, sexual expression represented a form of female rebellion. Although she evinced little interest in politics and feminism, she had this much in common with the female political activists of her generation: Maimie, like Rose Schneiderman of the Women's Trade Union League (WTUL) or Annie Kenney of the Women's Social and Political Union (WSPU), struggled personally against the fatalism and acquiescence of her class and gender.

By 1922, when the correspondence ends, Maimie had closed the mission and settled into a monogamous, privatized relationship with her second husband, Ira Benjamin. Her life continued to parallel larger historical developments, for the postwar years witnessed the disappearance of segregated red-light districts and the demise of a self-conscious women's culture that had earlier energized the women's rights movement and antivice crusades. In the 1920s, women were told that they had achieved emancipation and that happiness lay in working out a close, intimate relationship with a man. Concern over prostitution, Connelly tells us, 'dissipated almost as rapidly as it had emerged two decades earlier.' It remains to be seen, however, whether the 1920s truly marked the end of an era. Although the market for prostitution may have altered since the prewar period, the same modes of class and gender domination organize social relations today. As the Women against Pornography campaign demonstrates, commercial sex can still arouse female anger and mobilize women into symbolic crusades against male vice.

Yet, if there is any moral lesson to be learned from these moral crusaders, it is that commercial sex is a hot and dangerous issue for feminists. In their defense of prostitutes and concern to protect women from male sexual aggression, earlier generations of feminists were still limited by their own class bias and by their continued adherence to a 'separate sphere' ideology that stressed women's purity, moral supremacy, and domestic virtues. Moreover, feminists lacked the cultural and political power to reshape the world according to their own image. Although they tried to set the standards of sexual conduct, they did not control the instruments of state that would ultimately enforce these norms. There were times, particularly during the antiregulationist campaign, when feminists were able to dominate and structure the public discourse on sex and arouse popular female anger at male sexual license. Yet this anger was easily diverted into repressive campaigns against male vice and sexual variation, controlled by men and corporate interests whose goals were antithetical to the values and ideals of feminism.

NOTES

1. Of course, the Women against Pornography campaign protests against sexual violence as well as commercial sex. However, earlier feminist crusaders also protested against sexual violence, although their efforts often victimized the women they were seeking to protect.
2. Deborah Gorham, "'The maiden tribute of modern Babylon" re-examined: child prostitution and the idea of childhood in late-Victorian England,' *Victorian Studies*, 21, 1978, Spring, pp. 353–79; Edward Bristow, *Vice and Vigilance: Purity Movement in Britain since 1700*, Dublin: Gill and Macmillan, 1977.
3. Mark Connelly, *The Response to Prostitution in the Progressive Era*, Chapel Hill NC: University of North Carolina Press, 1980; *The Maimie Papers*, ed. Ruth Rosen and Sue Davidson, Old Westbury, NY: Feminist Press, 1977.
4. Gorham, 'Maiden tribute'; p. 353.
5. Ibid., p. 362.
6. Ibid., p. 355.
7. See Abraham Flexner, *Prostitution in Europe*, New York: Century Co., 1914.
8. Jeffrey Weeks, *Coming out: Homosexual Politics in Britain, from the Nineteenth Century to the Present*, London: Quartet Books, 1977, p. 18.
9. Gorham, 'Maiden Tribute,' p. 378.
10. Bristow, *Vice and Vigilance*, p. 125.
11. 'The new woman', *Woman's Signal*, 29 November 1894.
12. Michel Foucault, *The History of Sexuality*, vol. 1, *An Introduction*, trans. Robert Hurley, New York Pantheon Books, 1978.
13. Bristow, *Vice and Vigilance*, p. 77.
14. For an interpretation of the American social purity movement, see David Pivar, *Purity Crusaders: Sexual Morality and Social Control*, Westport, Conn.: Greenwood Press, 1976.
15. Connelly, *Response to Prostitution*, p. 127.
16. Ibid., p. 35.
17. Raymond and Williams, *Marxism and Literature*, Oxford: Oxford University Press, 1977, p. 113.
18. Rosen and Davidson, *The Maimie Papers*, p. xxv.

4.2

PORNOGRAPHY

Andrea Dworkin

In defining pornography, Andrea Dworkin makes explicit the connections with prostitution which are intrinsic to the etymology of the term. In this powerful polemic she asserts the aptness of the term pornography since it effectively transforms women into whores, into objects to be used by men.

[. . .]

The word *pornography*, derived from the ancient Greek *pornē* and *graphos*, means 'writing about whores.' *Pornē* means 'whore,' specifically and exclusively the lowest class of whore, which in ancient Greece was the brothel slut available to all male citizens.

The *pornē* was the cheapest (in the literal sense), least regarded, least protected of all women, including slaves. She was, simply and clearly and absolutely, a sexual slave. *Graphos* means 'writing, etching, or drawing.'

The word *pornography* does not mean 'writing about sex' or 'depictions of the erotic' or 'depictions of sexual acts' or 'depictions of nude bodies' or 'sexual representations' or any other such euphemism. It means the graphic depiction of women as vile whores. In ancient Greece, not all prostitutes were considered vile: only the *porneia*.

Contemporary pornography strictly and literally conforms to the word's root meaning: the graphic depiction of vile whores, or, in our language, sluts, cows (as in: sexual cattle, sexual chattel), cunts. The word has not changed its meaning and the genre is not misnamed. The only change in the meaning of the word is with respect to its second part, *graphos*: now there are cameras – there is still photography, film, video. The methods of graphic depiction have increased in number and in kind: the content is the same; the meaning is the same; the purpose is the same; the status of the women

From A. Dworkin, *Pornography: Men Possessing Women*, London: The Women's Press, 1981.

depicted is the same; the sexuality of the women depicted is the same; the value of the women depicted is the same. With the technologically advanced methods of graphic depiction, real women are required for the depiction as such to exist.

The word *pornography* does not have any other meaning than the one cited here, the graphic depiction of the lowest whores. Whores exist to serve men sexually. Whores exist only within a framework of male sexual domination. Indeed, outside that framework the notion of whores would be absurd and the usage of women as whores would be impossible. The word *whore* is incomprehensible unless one is immersed in the lexicon of male domination. Men have created the group, the type, the concept, the epithet, the insult, the industry, the trade, the commodity, the reality of woman as whore. Woman as whore exists within the objective and real system of male sexual domination. The pornography itself is objective and real and central to the male sexual system. The valuation of women's sexuality in pornography is objective and real because women are so regarded and so valued. The force depicted in pornography is objective and real because force is so used against women. The debasing of women depicted in pornography and intrinsic to it is objective and real in that women are so debased. The uses of women depicted in pornography are objective and real because women are so used. The women used in pornography are used in pornography. The definition of women articulated systematically and consistently in pornography is objective and real in that real women exist within and must live with constant reference to the boundaries of this definition. The fact that pornography is widely believed to be 'sexual representations' or 'depictions of sex' emphasizes only that the valuation of women as low whores is widespread and that the sexuality of women is perceived as low and whorish in and of itself. The fact that pornography is widely believed to be 'depictions of the erotic' means only that the debasing of women is held to be the real pleasure of sex. As Kate Millett wrote, women's sexuality is reduced to the one essential: 'cunt . . . our essence, our offense.'[1] The idea that pornography is 'dirty' originates in the conviction that the sexuality of women is dirty and is actually portrayed in pornography; that women's bodies (especially women's genitals) are dirty and lewd in themselves. Pornography does not, as some claim, refute the idea that female sexuality is dirty: instead, pornography embodies and exploits this idea; pornography sells and promotes it.

In the United States, the pornography industry is larger than the record and film industries combined. In a time of widespread economic impoverishment, it is growing: more and more male consumers are eager to spend more and more money on pornography – on depictions of women as vile whores. Pornography is now carried by cable television; it is now being marketed for home use in video machines. The technology itself demands the creation of more and more *porneia* to meet the market opened up by the technology. Real women are tied up, stretched, hanged, fucked, gang-banged, whipped, beaten, and begging for more. In the photographs and films, real women are used as *porneia* and real women are depicted as *porneia*. To profit, the pimps must supply the *porneia* as the technology widens the market for the visual consumption of women being brutalized and loving it. One picture is worth a thousand words. The number of pictures required to meet the demands of the marketplace determines the number of *porneia* required to meet the demands of graphic depiction. The numbers grow as the technology and its accessibility grow. The technology by its very nature encourages more and more passive acquiescence to the graphic depictions. Passivity makes the already credulous consumer more credulous. He comes to the pornography a believer; he goes away from it a missionary. The technology itself legitimizes the uses of women conveyed by it.

In the male system, women are sex; sex is the whore. The whore is *pornē*, the lowest whore, the whore who belongs to *all* male citizens: the slut, the cunt. Buying her is buying pornography. Having her is having pornography. Seeing her is seeing pornography. Seeing her sex, especially her genitals, is seeing pornography. Seeing her in sex is seeing the whore in sex. Using her is using pornography. Wanting her means wanting pornography. Being her means being pornography.

NOTE

1. Kate Millett, *The Prostitution Papers*, New York: Avon Books, p. 95.

4.3

SUBJECTS, OBJECTS AND EQUAL OPPORTUNITIES

SUSANNE KAPPELER

Kappeler raises the question of whether equality would be served if men were sexually objectified in the same way as women have been. She argues that this is not the way forward for feminism. The problem is not that pornography represents women as sexual objects but that this form of representation is itself objectifying. She calls into question the distinction commonly made between fantasy representations and sexual behaviour, arguing that the making and consuming of pornography are themselves forms of action.

'I do a lot for feminism,' Gloria Leonard, publisher of the soft-core magazine *High Society*, told me. 'I show women, and men too, that it's all right to be a sex object. That's part of what being a whole person is all about.'[1]

Under the glorious banner of Equal Opportunities we are likely finally to lose sight of what the critique of patriarchy, of sexism, of the objectification of women in representation is about. Good sex vs bad sex does not alter the structure of representation, just as the increasing use of male victims/objects does not.

[. . .]

The feminist challenge to advertising – that it exploits, degrades and objectifies women – is in danger of seeing itself neutralized as an increasing number of inane males are smiling off the posters and pages, clutching bottles of *Brut*. Now Gloria Leonard of *High Society* (an Equal Opportunities Employer) is showing us that it's alright to be a sex object since, look, the men over there are learning to be sex objects too! In the midst of these waves of progress, it might be well to go back to the question of what

From S. Kappeler, *The Pornography of Representation*, Cambridge: Polity, 1986.

it means to turn a person into an object. I shall continue to base my analysis on the model of the objectification of women – the generic object in our culture.

The objectification of women means the simultaneous subjectification of men. The relationship, however, is usually put the other way round, as Simone de Beauvoir notes: 'He is the Subject, he is the Absolute – she is the Other.'[2] Yet the exclusive talk of the 'object', as in the quotation above by Leonard, omits to tell us who is assuming the role of the subject.

In the objectification of women as a gender, the subject, the objectifier, the surveyor of women is the male gender. In the gender equality envisaged by the feminist critique of patriarchy, exploitation of and supremacy over one gender by the other would no longer be possible; it would mean, in other words, the end of exploitation, not 'equal exploitation'. But where the false equal-opportunities ticket is waved at women and men, there is always a third party involved behind the scenes, who will take over the exploiting, oppressing, objectifying from the once supreme male gender. This third party, proffering individual males for sacrifice and promoting individual women to the rank of sacrificers, sees itself as gender-free: it creates a new class, consisting of males and females, the object-class of another analysis. It is increasingly this other powerful subject, behind the objectification of 'men and women' in *High Society*, [. . .] that we have to inquire after in this heyday of equal opportunities. Yet the model of this subject is the male gender, the objectification it operates is modeled on the objectification of women.

The objectification of women is a result of the subjectification of man. He is a pure subject in relation to an object, which means that he is not engaging in exchange or communication with that objectified person who, by definition, cannot take the role of a subject. [. . .] Social relationships are relations between subjects: if there is exchange or communication, each partner is and remains a subject or agent of action, or a subject of speech and communication. The roles are reciprocal, the situation is one of intersubjectivity.

In the structure of representation, the two subjects are the author and the spectator/reader, the white man and his guests. The woman is the object of exchange. This is the dominant relationship, which remains constant across varying 'contents'. There is, further, a scenario of represented action, exchange or communication – in the case of pornography usually 'sex'. It is this represented action scenario which has attracted analysis in the debate about pornography: the feminist observation that the 'sex' is always violent sex. There are, it is true, examples of pornography where the woman is represented as a 'sex object' for the man represented; but there are many other pornographic scenarios where this is not the case. The pornographic image may consist only of the display of a woman – 'no men present'.

[. . .]

Or else the pornographic image may represent the woman as a strong, or willing and delighted participant in the action – as an active subject in the represented scenario. The pornographic representation may show a domineering female abusing a male sex object. It may show two women, in a variety of roles of subject and object, or it may show men in the same variety of roles. Pornography has exhausted the whole gamut of possible commutations of roles within the represented scenario. This is why experts tell us that there is no generalizing as to the victimization of women in pornography. This is also why the rescue of feminist erotica gets hopelessly entangled in the middle of the pornographic spectrum of scenarios: the feminist conference, the convent, the loving lesbians are already spoken for. The scenario itself is the wrong focus for an exclusive analysis of pornography: the structure of representation must be taken into consideration.

[. . .]

As a speaker, I am always present as the subject of my speech: I may represent myself by means of the pronoun 'I' within my utterance, or I may never say 'I' or 'me' at all, and yet I am implicitly present, the author of my speech, the speech the token of my presence. The pornographer is the speaking 'I' of the pornographic representation, and he may or may not represent himself as the subject/master in the scenario of the picture. He is in direct communication with another subject, the spectator or reader – the white man's guest. In the picture or out of it, he objectifies the woman/victim for the reader, the viewing subject who contemplates the object. If the pornographic scenario represents the male master-subject, the woman object is twice objectified: once as object of the action in the scenario, and once as object of the representation, the object of viewing. The former objectification is optional, the latter is always present: it is a structural feature of pornographic representation.

The philosopher with his penchant for abstract symmetry at the expense of social and political factors will tell me that the speaker or the composer of representations may be male or female that the viewer/reader may be male or female, the subject male or female.[3] Such symmetry, however, is only a most philosophical possibility, which has failed to be realized in the history of culture. In the political realm of reality, very different values adhere to the positions of subject and object: the role of subject means power, action, freedom, the role of object powerlessness, domination, oppression. The two roles are not equally desirable. Hence the role of subject constitutes a site for a power struggle.

The history of representation is the history of the male gender representing itself to itself – the power of naming is men's. Representation is not so much the means of representing an object through imitation (matching contents) as a means of self-representation through authorship: the expression of subjectivity. Culture, as we know it, is patriarchy's self-image.

We owe it to the cultural experts, the experts of the arts and of literature, that we are in the habit of contemplating cultural products – masterpieces – as pure aesthetic objects under the banner of aesthetics, rather than as forms of self-expression. [. . .] Today, we have an overwhelming object-orientation in the field of art (and other cultural products), which deflects attention away from the importance of the role of the subject, the producer of art. Instead, the role of the producer has been abstracted to such an extent that the philosopher tells us it is gender-free, androgynous, democratically open to all those talented enough, and that the role of receiver (spectator, reader) is equally neutral. The focus is on the aesthetic object, the work of art, and its aesthetic quality, which derives directly from the concept of beauty.

Although the notion of the aesthetic, as it has been posited by Kant, makes the aesthetic explicitly a function of the subject, we talk of beauty and the beautiful as if they were part of the object, as if they were 'objective'. Let us see how Kant describes this connection. To repeat, aesthetic apprehension consists of

> being conscious of [the] representation with an accompanying sensation of delight. Here the representation is referred wholly to the Subject, and what is more, to its feeling of life – under the name of feeling of pleasure or displeasure – and this forms the basis of a quite separate faculty of discriminating and estimating, that contributes nothing to knowledge.[4]

From this, Kant argues, we can deduce a second principle, that 'the beautiful is that which, apart from concepts, is represented as the object of universal delight.'[5] This is so because, 'where any one is conscious that his delight in an object is with him independent of interest, it is inevitable that he should look on the object as one containing ground of delight for all men.'[6] Since his delight is not based on interest in the object represented, 'but the Subject feels himself completely *free* in respect of the liking he accords to the object' – his liking is without 'reason' and thus disinterested.

[. . .] The claim to universality stems from the fact of the disinterestedness with which the subject regards the represented object. If you think the picture of your mother beautiful, you are excused because you have an obvious interest in and knowledge of the person represented, but your judgement is not aesthetic. If you like the picture of a total stranger, who means nothing to you personally, then your judgement is aesthetic. You may also claim universal validity for your judgement, and demand a similar liking from any other man, with whom you share a common sense – of pleasure and displeasure.

A pretty woman, [. . .] is at the centre of the consideration of the aesthetic. She is, from the start, among the objects. The subjects, for Kant, quite naturally are 'all men' (explicit in the English translation). The position of subject, in principle, is open to all people, but in practice the principle of universal validity has been tested among a limited number of subjects, those in the business of art and literature and taste.

[. . .]

It does not matter if the claim to universal validity has not actually been upheld by philosophers; but the notion of 'disinterestedness' has become a corner-stone among assumptions in the domain of the artistic. Although the aesthetic is grounded in the feeling of pleasure, the feeling of life of the subject, the axiom of disinterestedness allows us to underplay the function of the subject and especially his responsibility, and emphasize the objective. [. . .] Roland Barthes, in the modern age, consolidates the claim of 'the irresponsibility of the text',[7] the irresponsibility [. . .] having shifted, like the feeling of life, from the subject into the aesthetic object – art, the text.

With the twentieth century's professionalization and systematization of the study of the arts and literature – the carving out of expertises – being 'objective' or scientific in method and having a 'specific set of objects (the "texts")' has become and imperative'.[8] The objects themselves, the works of art or the representations are firmly separated from any objects they might represent in the world, separated, that is, from reality, in a sphere of their own: the aesthetic, the artistic, the literary – fiction, fantasy, art. Feminist critique will have to get them out of there again and bring them back into this world for discussion and analysis. The focus on content observed in so many discussions of pornography is a tribute to this object-orientation: we never really ask what the pornographer is trying to 'say' – what, in other words, is his responsibility as an author of a particular communication. Instead, we discuss disembodied ('detached') texts, films or images. The pornographer finds shelter behind his cultured brother, the artist. Like the artist, he is striving to make his product become independent of the mere intelligence (of critique, of understanding), to make it a matter of pure perception, and to get rid of his responsibilities towards his subject matter, the woman 'material'.

There are many kinds of interest, and there are therefore more than one kind of disinterestedness. [. . .] The pursuit of the aesthetic is [. . .] far from disinterested: it is the pursuit of pure self-interest, the pursuit of the pleasure and the feeling of life of the subject.

Women, real and represented, are central to the range of products expected [. . .] to stand on the footing of fine art. Representing to oneself a real woman, stranger though she may be, as aesthetically pleasing is regarding her as such a product, soulless until animated, is objectifying her. By definition the operation has nothing to do with the woman herself – that would be 'interest' – it has solely to do with the feeling of pleasure to be derived from contemplating her. Women are an inseparable part of our understanding of beauty, and they are ubiquitously represented in the fine arts. The fact that men do not in the same way form the core of beauty and do not themselves range among the products expected to stand on the footing of fine art – except in a growing male homosexual sub-culture – leads us to two observations. First, it is a symptom of the fact that men are the Subjects in question, are the cultural authors as well as the cultural audience; and secondly, this might lead us to inquire more deeply into the nature of the feeling of life, of delight and of pleasure that is the hallmark of the aesthetic. Might the disinterested aesthetic pleasure perchance be gendered? Might it even be a version of the sexual?

[. . .]

Turning another human being, another subject, woman, into an object is robbing her of her own subjectivity. The systematic representation of women-objects is not a question of a single subject representing to himself another subject, who happens to be a pretty woman, as an object. In cultural historical terms, it is the male gender, unified by a common sense, who assumes the subject position: as the authors of culture, men assume the voice, compose the picture, write the story, for themselves and other men, and *about* women. The fact that women, as individual subjects, have inserted themselves into the cultural audience (not without a struggle), have apprenticed to the male viewpoint which surveys women as objects and as products of fine art, is itself one of the most fundamental sources of female alienation: women have integrated in themselves, have internalized, a permanent outpost of the other gender – the male surveyor. The male gender, in turn, has extended into the whole space of subjectivity and self-expression – the available 'human' right to freedom of expression. In a patriarchal society, men have spread into and usurped the available space for agency, for power and for action; patriarchal culture validates and replicates this expansion of the male gender into human space. '*Men act and women appear*', writes [John] Berger: subjects and objects. The patriarchal subject constitutes himself through the discourse of culture.[9]

[. . .]

Patronizing the subject position, refusing to grant subjectivity to another subject in interaction, is the fundamental egotism and the fundamental solipsism of the male culture. As Andrea Dworkin notes: 'The power of men is first a metaphysical assertion of self, an I *am* that exists a priori, bedrock, absolute, no embellishment or apology required, indifferent to denial or challenge.'[10] It does not, of course, exist a priori: it is made to look a priori with the help of the cultural self-image, the culture of mankind. It does quite evidently require apology, for why else this repeated apology and self-justification which is the discourse of culture, a culture which, in its careful construction, has the permanent job of editing out, suppressing and silencing any denial and challenge offered to it through the contribution of women? The excavation operation conducted by contemporary feminist scholars reveals not only that such a challenge, such a contribution by women, has existed through most of the history of culture, but that the male producers of the cultural self-image have systematically controlled this contribution through their economic, social and political power, their position of supremacy in the 'public' organization of society which permits them to silence the cultural voice of women.

[. . .]

The fundamental problem at the root of men's behaviour in the world, including sexual assault, rape, wife battering, sexual harassment, keeping women in the home and in unequal opportunities and conditions, treating them as objects for conquest and protection – the root problem behind the reality of men's relations with women, is the way men see women, is Seeing.

The censorship experts are asking for proof that men who consume pornography will go and behave 'pornographically' in the world. What further proof do we need of man's behaviour in the world than his cultural self-representation – the culture from high to low, from hard to soft to aesthetic? The image is made in the image of its maker, after his likeness, and not the other way round.

As usual the pornographer himself is more honest and more astute about pornography than are the cultural experts engaged in defending it. Ron Martin, producer of a live sex show in New York, is asked by his interviewer if he does not think that he degrades women for profit. His reply: 'I know I do. So does *The New York Times*. I have one girl who felt degraded every time she stepped outside. She came here because she was constantly getting hit up by men anyway so why not get paid? Is working here any more degrading than walking down the street?'[11]

In the newspaper we read of the murder of a four-year-old girl by a 45-year-old man, who 'was well-known to [. . .] police as a compulsive child sex offender'.[12]

He had previously sexually assaulted two girls, and 'was charged and acquitted, although indecent photographs of the girls were found in his flat later'.[13] Producing pornography was a part of his sexual assault on the girls' part of his action in the world. If there is any chronology between his criminal behaviour and the representation of it the behaviour comes first, the desire to represent it after. The look through the camera, prefiguring the look at the picture, creating a 'world of fantasy' out of the real, or creating in Kant's words, 'a second nature out of the material supplied to it by actual nature'. Reality is but the raw 'material' for another, 'higher' reality, the reality of the subject. Or are the 'indecent pictures' any less pornographic because they are 'fact' rather than 'fiction', according to the fiction experts?

[. . .]

The male gender's project of constituting male subjectivity is a serious business that has nothing to do with fictional and playful fantasy. It is the means by which the male subject convinces himself that he is real, his necessary production of a feeling of life. He feels the more real, the less real the Other, the less of a subject the Other, the less alive the Other. And the reality he creates for himself through his cultural self-representation is the Authorized Version of reality, the dominant reality for all of us, the common sense which determines what pleases and what displeases.

NOTES

1. Henry Schipper, 'Filthy lucre: a tour of Americia's most profitable frontier', *Mother Jones*, April, 1980, p. 60.
2. Simone de Beauvoir, 'Introduction to the Second sex', in Elaine Marks and Isabelle Courtivron (eds), *New French Feminisms*, Brighton: The Harvester Press, 1981; reprinted from *The Second Sex*, Vintage, 1974, p. 44. The English edition of de Beauvoir's *The Second Sex* appeared in Penguin, 1972.
3. Compare Mary Vetterling-Braggin (ed.), *Sexist Language*, New York: Littlefield Adams, 1981, which is a collection of essays on 'sexism and language' by language philosophers who treat the concept of 'sexism' as asymmetrical.
4. Immanuel Kant, 'From Critique of Judgement', in William Handy and Max Westbrook (eds), *Twentieth Century Criticism: The Major Statements*, New York: The Free Press, 1974, trans. J.C. Meredith, p. 12.
5. *Ibid.*
6. *Ibid.*
7. Roland Barthes, *S/Z*, Paris: du Seuil, 1970, p. 18.
8. Brain Doyle, 'The Hidden history of English Studies', in Peter Widdowson (ed.), *Re-Reading English*, London: Methuen New Accents, 1982, p. 25.
9. John Berger, *Ways of Seeing*, Harmondsworth: Penguin, 1972.
10. Andrea Dworkin, *Pornography: Men Possessing Women*, London: The Women's Press, 1981, p. 13.
11. Schipper, 'Filthy lucre', p. 60.
12. *The Guardian Weekly*, 23 December 1984, p. 3.
13. *Ibid.*

4.4

BLACK WOMEN AND THE SEX/GENDER HIERARCHY

Patricia Hill Collins

Patricia Hill Collins addresses the abuse of black women's sexuality, arguing that an understanding of racism is essential to an analysis of prostitution and pornography: it is not simply that racism compounds sexism, but that racism makes certain forms of sexual objectification possible. She exposes the biological theories and imagery which underpin the idea of black women, and potentially all women, as less than human because they embody animal sexuality.

[...]

For centuries the black woman has served as the primary pornographic 'outlet' for white men in Europe and America. We need only think of the black women used as breeders, raped for the pleasure and profit of their owners. We need only think of the license the 'master' of the slave women enjoyed. But, most telling of all, we need only study the old slave societies of the South to note the sadistic treatment – at the hands of white 'gentlemen' – of 'beautiful young quadroons and octoroons' who became increasingly (and were deliberately bred to become) indistinguishable from white women, and were the more highly prized as slave mistresses because of this.[1]

Alice Walker's description of the rape of enslaved African women for the 'pleasure and profit of their owners' encapsulates several elements of contemporary pornography. First, Black women were used as sex objects for the pleasure of white men. This objectification of African-American women parallels the portrayal of women in pornography as sex objects whose sexuality is available for men.[2] Exploiting Black women

---

From P. Hill Collins, *Black Feminist Thought: Knowledge, Consciousness and the Politics of Empowerment*, New York: Routledge, Inc. 1990.

as breeders objectified them as less than human because only animals can be bred against their will. In contemporary pornography women are objectified through being portrayed as pieces of meat, as sexual animals awaiting conquest. Second, African-American women were raped, a form of sexual violence. Violence is typically an implicit or explicit theme in pornography. Moreover, the rape of Black women linked sexuality and violence, another characteristic feature of pornography.[3] Third, rape and other forms of sexual violence act to strip victims of their will to resist and make them passive and submissive to the will of the rapist. Female passivity, the fact that women have things done to them, is a theme repeated over and over in contemporary pornography.[4] Fourth, the profitability of Black women's sexual exploitation for white 'gentlemen' parallels pornography's financially lucrative benefits for pornographers.[5] Finally, the actual breeding of 'quadroons and octoroons' not only reinforces the themes of Black women's passivity, objectification, and malleability to male control but reveals pornography's grounding in racism and sexism. The fates of both Black and white women were intertwined in this breeding process. The ideal African-American woman as a pornographic object was indistinguishable from white women and thus approximated the images of beauty, asexuality, and chastity forced on white women. But inside was a highly sexual whore, a 'slave mistress' ready to cater to her owner's pleasure.[6]

Contemporary pornography consists of a series of icons or representations that focus the viewer's attention on the relationship between the portrayed individual and the general qualities ascribed to that class of individuals. Pornographic images are iconographic in that they represent realities in a manner determined by the historical position of the observers, their relationship to their own time, and to the history of the conventions which they employ.[7] The treatment of Black women's bodies in nineteenth-century Europe and the United States may be the foundation upon which contemporary pornography as the representation of women's objectification, domination, and control is based. Icons about the sexuality of Black women's bodies emerged in these contexts. Moreover, as race/gender-specific representations, these icons have implications for the treatment of both African-American and white women in contemporary pornography.

[. . .]

I suggest that African-American women were not included in pornography as an afterthought but instead form a key pillar on which contemporary pornography itself rests. As Alice Walker points out, 'the more ancient roots of modern pornography are to be found in the almost always pornographic treatment of black women who, from the moment they entered slavery . . . were subjected to rape as the "logical" convergence of sex and violence. Conquest, in short.'[8]

One key feature about the treatment of Black women in the nineteenth century was how their bodies were objects of display. In the antebellum American South white men did not have to look at pornographic pictures of women because they could become voyeurs of Black women on the auction block. A chilling example of this objectification of the Black female body is provided by the exhibition, in early nineteenth-century Europe, of Sarah Bartmann, the so-called Hottentot Venus. Her display formed one of the original icons for Black female sexuality. An African women, Sarah Bartmann was often exhibited at fashionable parties in Paris, generally wearing little clothing, to provide entertainment. To her audience she represented deviant sexuality. At the time European audiences thought that Africans had deviant sexual practices and searched for physiological differences, such as enlarged penises and malformed female genitalia, as indications of this deviant sexuality. Sarah Bartmann's exhibition stimulated these racist and sexist beliefs. After her death in 1815, she was dissected. Her genitalia and buttocks remain on display in Paris.[9]

[. . .]

Bartmann was used as a pornographic object similar to how women are represented in contemporary pornography. She was reduced to her sexual parts, and these parts came to represent a dominant icon applied to Black women throughout the nineteenth century. Moreover, the fact that Sarah Bartmann was both African and a woman underscores the importance of gender in maintaining notions of racial purity. In this case Bartmann symbolized Blacks as a 'race.' Thus the creation of the icon applied to Black women demonstrates that notions of gender, race, and sexuality were linked in overarching structures of political domination and economic exploitation.

The process illustrated by the pornographic treatment of the bodies of enslaved African women and of women like Sarah Bartmann has developed into a full-scale industry encompassing all women objectified differently by racial/ethnic category. Contemporary portrayals of Black women in pornography represent the continuation of the historical treatment of their actual bodies. African-American women are usually depicted in a situation of bondage and slavery, typically in a submissive posture, and often with two white men. As Bell observes, 'this setting reminds us of all the trappings of slavery: chains, whips, neck braces, wrist clasps.'[10] White women and women of color have different pornographic images applied to them. The image of Black women in pornography is almost consistently one featuring them breaking from chains. The image of Asian women in pornography is almost consistently one of being tortured.[11]

The pornographic treatment of Black women's bodies challenges the prevailing feminist assumption that since pornography primarily affects white women, racism has been grafted onto pornography. African-American women's experiences suggest that Black women were not added into a preexisting pornography, but rather that pornography itself must be reconceptualized as an example of the interlocking nature of race, gender, and class oppression. At the heart of both racism and sexism are notions of biological determinism claiming that people of African descent and women possess immutable biological characteristics marking their inferiority to elite white men.[12] In pornography these racist and sexist beliefs are sexualized. Moreover, for African-American women pornography has not been timeless and universal but was tied to Black women's experiences with the European colonization of Africa and with American slavery. Pornography emerged within a specific system of social class relationships.

This linking of views of the body, social constructions of race and gender, and conceptualizations of sexuality that inform Black women's treatment as pornographic objects promises to have significant implications for how we assess contemporary pornography. Moreover, examining how pornography has been central to the race, gender, and class oppression of African-American women offers new routes for understanding the dynamics of power as domination.

Investigating racial patterns in pornography offers one route for such an analysis. Black women have often claimed that images of white women's sexuality were intertwined with the controlling image of the sexually denigrated Black woman: 'In the United States, the fear and fascination of female sexuality was projected onto black women; the passionless lady arose in symbiosis with the primitively sexual slave.'[13] Comparable linkages exist in pornography.[14]

[. . .]

Certain 'races' of people have been defined as being more bodylike, more animallike, and less godlike than others.[15] Race and gender oppression may both revolve around the same axis of distain for the body; both portray the sexuality of subordinate groups as animalistic and therefore deviant. Biological notions of race and gender prevalent in the early nineteenth century which fostered the animalistic icon of Black female sexuality were joined by the appearance of a racist biology incorporating the concept of degeneracy.[16] Africans and women were both perceived as embodied entities, and Blacks were seen as degenerate. Fear of and distain for the body thus formed a key element in both sexist and racist thinking.[17]

While the sexual and racial dimensions of being treated like an animal are important, the economic foundation underlying this treatment is critical. Animals can be economically exploited, worked, sold, killed, and consumed. As 'mules,' African-American women become susceptible to such treatment. The political economy of pornography also merits careful attention. Pornography is pivotal in mediating contradictions in changing societies.[18] It is no accident that racist biology, religious justifications for slavery and women's subordination, and other explanations for nineteenth-century racism and sexism arose during a period of profound political and economic change. Symbolic means of domination become particularly important in mediating contradictions in changing political economies. The exhibition of Sarah Bartmann and Black women on the auction block were not benign intellectual exercises – these practices defended real material and political interests.

[. . .]

Publicly exhibiting Black women may have been central to objectifying Black women as animals and to creating the icon of Black women as animals. Yi-Fu Tuan [. . .] offers an innovative argument about similarities in efforts to control nature – especially plant life – the domestication of animals, and the domination of certain groups of humans. Tuan suggests that displaying humans alongside animals implies that such humans are more like monkeys and bears than they are like 'normal' people. This same juxtaposition leads spectators to view the captive animals in a special way. Animals acquire definitions of being like humans, only more openly carnal and sexual, an aspect of animals that forms a major source of attraction for visitors to modern zoos. In discussing the popularity of monkeys in zoos, Tuan notes: 'some visitors are especially attracted by the easy sexual behavior of the monkeys. Voyeurism is forbidden except when applied to subhumans.'[19] Tuan's analysis suggests that the public display of Sarah Bartmann and of the countless enslaved African women on the auction blocks of the antebellum American South – especially in proximity to animals – fostered their image as animalistic.

This linking of Black women and animals is evident in nineteenth-century scientific literature. The equation of women, Blacks, and animals is revealed in the following description of an African woman published in an 1878 anthropology text:

> She had a way of pouting her lips exactly like what we have observed in the orangutan. Her movements had something abrupt and fantastical about them, reminding one of those of the ape. Her ear was like that of many apes . . . These are animal characters. I have never seen a human head more like an ape than that of this woman.[20]

In a climate such as this, it is not surprising that one prominent European physician even stated that Black women's 'animallike sexual appetite went so far as to lead black women to copulate with apes.'[21]

The treatment of all women in contemporary pornography has strong ties to the portrayal of Black women as animals. In pornography women become nonpeople and are often represented as the sum of their fragmented body parts. Scott McNall observes:

> This fragmentation of women relates to the predominance of rear-entry position photographs . . . All of these kinds of photographs reduce the woman to her reproductive system, and, furthermore, make her open, willing, and available – not in control . . . The other thing rear-entry position photographs tell us about women is that they are animals. They are animals because they are the same as dogs – bitches in heat who can't control themselves.[22]

This linking of animals and white women within pornography becomes feasible when grounded in the earlier denigration of Black women as animals.

[. . .]

[A]ll Black women are affected by the widespread controlling image that African-American women are sexually promiscuous, potential prostitutes. The pervasiveness of this image is vividly recounted in Black activist lawyer Pauli Murray's description of an incident she experienced while defending two women from Spanish Harlem who had been arrested as prostitutes: 'The first witness, a white man from New Jersey, testified on the details of the sexual transaction and his payment of money. When asked to identify the woman with whom he had engaged in sexual intercourse, he unhesitatingly pointed directly at me, seated beside my two clients at the defense table!'[23] Murray's clients were still convicted.

The creation of Jezebel, the image of the sexually denigrated Black woman, has been vital in sustaining a system of interlocking race, gender, and class oppression. Exploring how the image of the African-American woman as prostitute has been used by each system of oppression illustrates how sexuality links the three systems. But Black women's treatment also demonstrates how manipulating sexuality has been essential to the political economy of domination within each system and across all three.

Yi-Fu Tuan[24] suggests that power as domination involves reducing humans to animate nature in order to exploit them economically or to treat them condescendingly as pets. Domination may be either cruel and exploitative with no affection or may be exploitative yet coexist with affection. The former produces the victim – in this case, the Black woman as 'mule' whose labor has been exploited. In contrast, the combination of dominance and affection produces the pet, the individual who is subordinate but whose survival depends on the whims of the more powerful. The 'beautiful young quadroons and octoroons' described by Alice Walker were bred to be pets – enslaved Black mistresses whose existence required that they retain the affection of their owners. The treatment afforded these women illustrates a process that affects all African-American women: their portrayal as actual or potential victims and pets of elite white males. [. . .] [25]

Prostitution represents the fusion of exploitation for an economic purpose – namely, the commodification of Black women's sexuality – with the demeaning treatment afforded pets. Sex becomes commodified not merely in the sense that it can be purchased – the dimension of economic exploitation – but also in the sense that one is dealing with a totally alienated being who is separated from and who does not control her body: the dimension of power as domination.[26] Commodified sex can then be appropriated by the powerful. Both pornography and [. . .] prostitution commodify sexuality and imply [. . .] that all African-American women can be bought.

Prostitution under European and American capitalism thus exists within a complex web of political and economic relationships whereby sexuality is conceptualized along intersecting axes of race and gender. Gilman's[27] analysis of the exhibition of Sarah Bartmann as the 'Hottentot Venus' suggests another intriguing connection between race, gender, and sexuality in nineteenth-century Europe – the linking of the icon of the Black woman with the icon of the white prostitute.

[. . .]

While the Hottentot woman stood for the essence of Africans as a race, the white prostitute symbolized the sexualized woman. The prostitute represented the embodiment of sexuality and all that European society associated with it: disease as well as passion. As Gilman points out, 'it is this uncleanliness, this disease, which forms the final link between two images of women, the black and the prostitute. Just as the genitalia of the Hottentot were perceived as parallel to the diseased genitalia of the prostitute, so too the power of the idea of corruption links both images.'[28] These connections between the icons of Black women and white prostitutes demonstrate how race, gender, and the social class structure of the European political economy interlock.

In the American antebellum South both of these images were fused in the forced prostitution of enslaved African women. The prostitution of Black women allowed white women to be the opposite; Black 'whores' make white 'virgins' possible. This race/gender nexus fostered a situation whereby white men could then differentiate between the sexualized woman-as-body who is dominated and 'screwed' and the asexual woman-as-pure-spirit who is idealized and brought home to mother.[29] The sexually denigrated woman, whether she was made a victim through her rape or a pet through her seduction, could be used as the yardstick against which the cult of true womanhood was measured. Moreover, this entire situation was profitable.

NOTES

1. A. Walker, 'Coming apart,' in her *You Can't Keep a Good Woman Down*, New York: Harcourt Brace Jovanovich, 1981, p. 42.
2. Scott G. McNall, 'Pornography: the structure of domination and the mode of reproduction,' in Scott McNall (ed.), *Current Perspectives in Social Theory, Volume 4*, Greenwich, Conn.: Jai Press, 1983.
3. Hester Einstein, *Contemporary Feminist Thought*, Boston: G.K. Hall, 1983.
4. McNall, 'Pornography'.
5. Einstein, *Contemporary Feminist Thought*.
6. Offering a similar argument about the relationship between race and masculinity, Paul Hoch suggests that the ideal white man is hero who upholds honour. But inside lurks a 'Black beast' of violence and sexuality, traits that the white hero deflects onto men of colour. See Paul Hoch, *White Hero, Black Beast*, London: Pluto Press, 1979.
7. Sander L. Gilman, 'Black bodies, white bodies: towards an iconography of female sexuality in late nineteeth-century art, medicine, and literature,' *Critical Inquiry*, 12(1), 1985, pp. 205–43.
8. Walker, 'Coming apart,' p. 42.
9. Gilman, 'Black bodies, white bodies.'
10. Laurie Bell, *Good Girls/Bad Girls: Feminists and Sex Trade Workers Face to Face*, Toronto: Seal Press, 1987, p. 59.
11. *Ibid.*
12. Stephen Jay Gould, *The Mismeasure of Man*, New York: W.W. Norton, 1981; A. Fausto-Sterling, *Myths of Gender*, New York: Basic Books, 1989; Zuleya Tang Helpin, 'Scientific objectivity and the concept of the Other,' *Women's Studies International Forum*, 12(3), 1989, pp. 285–94.
13. Jacqueline Dowd Hall, 'The mind that burns in each body: women, rape, and racial violence', in Ann Snitow, C. Stensall and S. Thompson, (eds), *Powers of Desire: The Politics of Sexuality*, New York: Monthly Review Press, 1983, p. 333.
14. Tracey A. Gardner, 'Racism and pornography in the women's movement,' in Laura Lederer (ed.), *Take Back the Night: Women on Pornography*, New York: William Morrow, 1980.
15. Elizabeth V. Spelman, 'Theories of race and gender: the erasure of black women,' *Quest*, 5(4), 1982, p. 52.
16. M. Foucault, *Power/Knowledge: Selected Interviews and Other Writings 1972–1977*, ed. Colin Gordon, New York: Pantheon, 1980.
17. Spelman, 'Theories of race and gender.'
18. McNall, 'Pornography.'
19. Yi-Fu Tuan, *Dominance and Affection: The Making of Pets*, New Haven, Conn.: Yale University Press, 1984; p. 82.
20. Halpin 'Scientific objectivity and the concept of the other,' p. 287.
21. Gilman, 'Black bodies, white bodies,' p. 212.
22. McNall, 'Pornography,' p. 197–8.
23. Pauli Murray, *Song in a Weary Throat: An Amercian Pligrimage*, New York: Harper & Row, 1987, p. 274.
24. Yi-Fu Tuan, *Dominance and Affection.*
25. Any group can be made into pets. Consider Tuan's discussion of the role that young Black boys played as exotic ornaments for wealthy white women in the 1500s to the early 1800s in England. Unlike male servants, the boys were the favorite attendants of the noble ladies and gained entry into their mistresses' drawing rooms, bedchambers, and theatre boxes. Boys were often given fancy collars with padlocks to wear. 'As they did their pet dogs and monkeys, the ladies grew genuinely fond of their black boys' (*Dominance and Affection*, p. 142). In addition, Nancy White's analysis of the differences between how white and Black women are treated by white men uses the victim/pet metaphor (John Langston Gwaltney, *Drylongso: A Self Portrait of Black America*, New York: Vintage, 1980, p. 148).
26. McNall, 'Pornography.'
27. Gilman, 'Black bodies, white bodies.'
28. *Ibid.*, p. 237.
29. Hoch, *White Hero, Black Beast*, p. 70.

4.5

WANKING IN CYBERSPACE
The Development of Computer Porn

Dianne Butterworth

Modern media technologies have made pornography ever more widely available. The newest developments are in the field of computerised images which can be networked all over the world. From a position firmly opposed to pornography, Dianne Butterworth explains recent technological developments, outlines some of the ways in which these have been taken up and speculates on future possibilities.

Pornography is an act of dominance and of sexual exploitation, at the same time as it expresses and reinforces that dominance and justifies that sexual exploitation. One of the primary frustrations of anti-pornography feminists is trying to get a liberal society to acknowledge the harm done to the women *in* the pornography and to women in the sex industry, as well as the harm done through the use of porn by the male consumer. Time and again we encounter the same tired old arguments about pornography being fantasy, as if somehow the women in the porn are merely flickering images on the television/cinema screen.

Now technology is promising the development of 'virtual sex', in which a computer user has 'sex' with a computer program which simulates a woman, a step which will further disguise the harm done to women. It seems the further you get from a real, live woman, the less real the women become, and the fewer consequences for women can be perceived. Each layer or intermediary between the porn consumer/sex industry user and the women 'acting' or portrayed seems to make the use and the abuse of women less real. This technology is the next logical

From D. Butterworth, 'Wanking in Cyberspace', *Trouble and Strife*, no. 27, 1993.

progression in a particular application of computer technology, starting from computer pornography.

TECHNOLOGICAL REVOLUTIONS

Computer pornography has been around since IBM brought out the first mass-market personal computer in 1981. The first type of computer porn was written – excerpts of pornography typed into the computer and distributed as text. As the technology improved, simple, almost cartoon-like, graphical drawings were used; now computer porn is available which is indistinguishable from photographs in the quality of the display.

To get pornography onto a computer, a photograph is digitised, that is, converted into a format which can be read by computer.

[. . .]

To digitise a photograph, it is placed on a colour scanner, a machine sort of like a fax machine hooked up to a computer, which takes a 'snapshot' of the photograph and digitises it in one of several standardised formats. A frame of a video tape can also be digitised, or even a segment of tape. The more complex the image (ie the more colours and the bigger it is), the more storage space the image requires. The storage requirements, particularly for digitised video, have been problematic for the full-scale use of computer pornography. However the technology has improved, and techniques for reducing the size of stored images and video have also improved, making the use of colour graphics and video clips much more widespread.

[. . .]

Film-less cameras are now available which take photographs in digitised format; the camera is then linked up to a computer with a cable and the photos are sent directly to the computer. At the moment, these cameras are only black and white, but when colour cameras are eventually produced, we can probably expect this technology to be used in the production of porn at home in the same way that normal cameras and video cameras have been used.

EASY ACCESS

A computer consultant recently stated in an interview that every large office he had ever been to had pornographic images stored somewhere on the computer system. And with the increasing use of computers in the home, more and more porn will intrude into women's lives. One of the problems with computer pornography is that porn which, in its printed or video form, is relatively difficult (but by no means impossible) to obtain in [Britain] – child pornography, images of women and animals, images of the rape and torture of women – is much more easily accessible in computer format.

The reason is that the majority of computer pornography is distributed via bulletin boards. A bulletin board is a computer with modem (a machine that converts computer data into a form which can be transmitted via telephone lines) and a software program which can handle incoming calls and control the access of the caller to the contents of the computer's hard disk. Bulletin boards usually have an area where you can leave messages, either for specific individuals or for everyone to read. They will also have an area where you (or the person running the board) can leave files that other callers might be interested in. Files on bulletin boards can be 'downloaded', that is, the user can get your computer to retrieve the file from the bulletin board computer via the telephone line. You can also send, or 'upload', files to the bulletin board.

Bulletin boards can be useful information-sharing tools, where people from different areas of the country and across the globe can exchange information or files. [. . .] However, about 10% of bulletin boards in [Britain] have pornographic images on them. There are some which carry only porn.

It used to be that most computer porn was distributed 'free'. Someone would scan in the photo and place it on a bulletin board for others to download. Some bulletin boards, however, now charge a membership fee and/or an hourly connection fee and charge for each image downloaded. This can be a very profitable venture, depending on the type and quality of pornography stored. A recent *Cook Report* on [British] ITV looked at bulletin boards specialising in computer-based pornography. One computer consultant was charging £350 for helping men to access over 10,000 hard-core pornographic images and to set up their own pornographic bulletin board. It was only a matter of time before the commercial pornography producers realised how much revenue they were 'losing'. *Playboy* have successfully sued, for copyright violation, a bulletin board operator in the US for distributing a scanned image from one of their magazines.

The vast majority of pornography at the moment is filmed for video, with a small proportion of photographs for magazines. However, the *Cook Report* stated that the largest producer of pornography in Germany estimates that within 5 years the majority of the porn they produce and distribute will be in computer format. *Penthouse* now have a bulletin board, called 'Penthouse Online', where men can download porn files, 'chat' with the models, and discuss whatever it is that porn users discuss. More recently *Penthouse* have gone one step further.

FROM CONSUMERS TO PRODUCERS

Interactive computer pornography is an alarming, but logical, progression in computer porn – the interactive exploitation of women. Not only does the male consumer look at the porn, he controls it. *Penthouse's* new CD-ROM, called, imaginatively, '*Penthouse Interactive*', holds 45 minutes of digitised video. (CD-ROM is a method of storage which looks like an audio CD, but which stores information in a format which computers can read.) The user plays the role of a *Penthouse* photographer; he chooses which one of three women to photograph, how much (or little) she wears (she strips off the required amount of clothing) and in which position she lies/sits/stands. The user takes a 'photograph', and Bob Guccione (the owner of Penthouse) judges how good (pornographic?!?) it is. The article in *Penthouse* magazine announcing this new product says:

> There is a level of involvement or engagement, of naturalness, that a deeply interactive experience offers. Interactive electronics let you join in, shaping your fantasies to suit your own individual dreams, tastes, and preferences.

Radical feminists have always maintained that pornography affects men's attitudes to women and their propensity to commit violent acts against them. From the not-so-subtle messages about women's proper role and demeanour in sexual intercourse, to the pornographic reinterpretations of reality that occur in porn magazines and videos – 'scenarios' where women react to sexual harassment in the office by turning into insatiable sex-crazed beasts, or where women enjoy rape, or where the casual visit of a door-to-door salesman turns into an orgy – women's experience and reality have been distorted by the propaganda of the pornographers. Interactive pornography means that the consumer is no longer just the consumer, he is, in a sense, the producer as well. Not content with gazing passively at images of women, he can now 'enter into the fantasy' by directing the action.

This latest offering from *Penthouse* is, I believe, just the beginning of a new phase in pornography. Because a CD-ROM can store much more information than the average hard disk (over 360 megabytes, compared to an average of 100 megabytes on a hard disk), it is therefore possible to distribute actual digitised video. This means that the 'action' on this CD-ROM is really that – moving images of women removing their clothes, lying down, and so on. CD-ROMS also have the advantage of not being easily reproducible, partly because of the amount of information stored on them and partly because CD-ROMS cannot yet be copied as easily as floppy disks can.

VIRTUAL REALITY AND 'VIRTUAL SEX'

The next step from looking and interacting with 2-dimensional images and data is looking and interacting in 3-dimensions. Imagine a curved computer screen which is built into the visor of a helmet. This screen fills your entire visual field, even your peripheral vision. Graphics are displayed on this screen; no 'real' visual information can be seen. For example, the 'visor' displays the image of a statue. Sensors in the helmet track the movement of your head in space, and your 'perspective' on the statue changes according to how far the sensors detect you have moved your head or at what angle your head is tilted. With a graphic display realistic enough and sensors that are accurate enough, you can almost imagine that the object you are looking at is real. You can 'walk around the statue', viewing it from the front, side and back, and you can look up and down at the top and bottom of the statue. To all intents and purposes, it is reality you are experiencing – virtual reality' (VR).

You can put on gloves which have sensors on each finger and the palms, and you can 'push' the statue over (as long as the computer program knows that when your hands 'move' to where the statue is 'taking up space', the display should show the statue falling over). At this stage in technological development you might not actually 'feel' your hand touch and push the statue, but scientists are currently working on gloves that not only sense the position and movement of your hand, but through some kind of built-in mechanisms, can give feedback to your hands, simulating touching an object. This means that when you move your hand to where a virtual object is, the gloves would react in some way, perhaps tightening the fabric of the gloves on the pads of the fingers, so that it seems as though you are actually touching the object.

[. . .] [W]hen the film *The Lawnmower Man* was released, the media went into a frenzy of speculation about virtual reality and 'virtual sex' as a consequence of VR. The idea behind 'virtual sex' is that a computer is hooked up to a 'glove' which covers the entire body, and linked up via a phone line to another computer to which someone else is linked. [. . .] I remember some magazines at the time talking about 'virtual sex' as being a boon for those busy executives who travel a lot; they can link up to their partners and 'make love' to them long-distance.

What is actually more likely is that 'virtual sex' would lead to a whole new area of prostitution – women paid to have 'virtual sex' with men. Women have been exploited by technology in the service of male sexuality since the camera was first invented – 'French postcards', 'blue movies', 'dirty videos', 'telephone fantasy lines', computer pornography and, perhaps within 20 or 30 years, 'virtual sex'. (Perhaps men wouldn't even need a full body glove – a 'penis glove' might suffice for the purpose!)

A lot of the hype [is being] talked about this kind of 'virtual sex' as the ultimate 'safe sex'.

[. . .]

Would 'virtual sex' with real women be 'safe' sex? It would, if you believe that the shaping and reinforcing of men's beliefs about women's sexuality and women's reality through the propaganda of pornography has no consequences. It would, if you believe those who say that the sex industry is harmless (after all, the argument goes, those women are being paid, and they look like they're enjoying themselves), that the women in it are expressing their 'true sexuality' and that they have all freely 'chosen' to make pornography or to prostitute themselves.

If, on the other hand, you believe women who say they have been prostituted and pimped and photographed and filmed against their will or under duress, then it is not safe. If you believe 'Third World' women who say they have been trafficked to serve in brothels and strip joints, then it is not safe. If you believe that the current structure of patriarchal capitalism systematically pays women less, restricts them to lower-paid types of jobs, discriminates against them in all areas of the workplace, so that prostitution becomes one of the very few jobs in which women as a group are paid more than men, then it is not safe. If you believe that pornography legitimises men's sexual access to women as a group, disseminates lies and distortions about us and eroticises inequalities of power, then it is not safe. It is, in fact, downright dangerous.

Any technology which promises to lead to an expansion of the sex industry cannot be safe for women.

'VIRTUAL WOMEN'

The first stage in the development of this technology will require two people linked to two computers in order to have 'virtual sex'. The eventual goal, however, is to write a computer program which can 'simulate' a woman – a 'virtual woman'. (For the foreseeable future, this technology is out of reach because it is difficult to write a program which will react realistically to all types of input. Imagine how difficult it would be to program a 'virtual woman' to respond appropriately to all of the various actions a user could dream up.) Users could then act out any fantasies, including violent ones, without 'hurting' a real woman in the act.

[. . .]

One of the harmful ideas that is at the core of all pornography, including so-called 'soft-core' as well as 'hard-core' porn, is that all women are sexually available to any man, at any time, and in any way he wants. This propaganda reinforces men's (and via them, women's) conceptions of the 'inherent' dominance and subordination in sexual and other relations between the sexes.

If interactive computer pornography gives men the illusion of control over the real women in it then 'virtual sex with virtual women' would give men real control over illusionary women. Pornography affects men's ideas about women and thereby their treatment of them. [. . .] It seems logical to me to suppose that the use of 'virtual women' who, in the user's perception, actually *are* real, would reinforce even more strongly harmful perceptions about women and dominance and subordination. How big a step is it from 'acting out' fantasies, violent or otherwise, on women who only *seem* real to acting them out on women who *are* real?

THE TECHNOLOGICAL IS POLITICAL

This may sound like a chapter from a science fiction novel. It is fictional, in that virtual reality technology is still in its infancy. It is science because the technology *is* being developed. Computer pornography exists, VR technology is now being used in the defence industry (of course!) and VR games are already being produced (there is one at the Trocadero shopping complex in London). And sexual exploitation is a reality.

Feminists need to anticipate social and technological developments, to try to influence how they are going to be used and implemented, and to initiate and insist on public discussions on the implications, as we have with reproductive technology. The 'technology club' is a largely male-dominated one, and men are happy for it to remain so. Men have been using computer porn and exchanging it in the 'privacy' of their own realm of technology for a long time, with no dissenting voices to be heard. It wasn't mentioned or discussed publicly until the Campaign Against Pornography brought the issue to light [in 1993]. Since then there have been television programmes, newspaper and magazine articles and radio debates and even a couple of seminars on sexual harassment using computer pornography in universities and schools. The Institute of Data Processing Management has issued guidelines about computer porn.

Women are not consulted in the development phase of new technologies, nor are the implications for women of new technologies ever thoroughly thought out (except insofar as how women can get the toilet cleaner, or cook meals faster). Technology is represented as being an 'evolutionary' process, which arises out of neutral ground or 'the survival of the technologically most useful'. In this view, technology 'just happens' and the good stuff stays, the bad stuff, no-one buys. Radical feminists know that nothing in this world happens which is divorced from its social and political context; that just as the personal is political, so is the technological.

ON THE QUESTION OF PORNOGRAPHY AND SEXUAL VIOLENCE
Moving Beyond Cause and Effect

Deborah Cameron and Elizabeth Frazer

Opposition to pornography sometimes rests on the assumption that it causes sexual violence and abuse. Deborah Cameron and Elizabeth Frazer argue that this view of cause and effect oversimplifies the issues. Drawing on their work on sexual murder, they seek to demonstrate that while there is no direct causal link, pornographic representations do provide ideas and narratives that violent men can draw upon. In particular they emphasise the themes of mastery and transcendence that appear in sexual murderers' accounts of their actions.

What is to be done about pornography? Whenever feminists raise this question – and they have raised it insistently, on both sides of the Atlantic – one particular issue can be counted on to dominate discussion. That issue is: does pornography actually have significant effects in terms of causing violent and misogynistic behaviour? Can we, in other words, establish a firm relationship between the sphere of representation where pornography is located, and the sphere of action in which specific individuals harm other individuals? Any feminist who objects to pornography is immediately challenged to demonstrate such a causal relationship; anyone who doubts that the relationship exists is under pressure to concede that pornography is not a problem. The entire agenda for debate is drawn up in terms of this question.

The purpose of this chapter is to show what is wrong with framing the pornography issue in this way, and to suggest how feminists can move beyond simplistic notions of cause and effect without conceding the argument altogether. Arguments that pornography 'causes' violent acts are, indeed, inadequate. But the conclusion that

From D. Cameron and E. Frazer, 'On the question of pornography and sexual violence. Moving beyond cause and effect', in Co Itzen (ed.), *Pornography*, Oxford. Oxford University Press, 1992.

therefore we should not be concerned about pornography at all is equally unjustified. Representation and action may not be related in a chain of cause and effect, but one can nevertheless discover important and complex connections between them – connections which imply that feminists should indeed concern themselves with the forms of representation that exist in our culture.

The specific case with which we will be concerned here is sexual murder, an extreme form of violence whose catastrophic effects are impossible to deny or minimize; we believe, however, that our analysis can just as well be applied to less extreme instances. By examining the role that representations (primarily, but not exclusively, pornographic representations) play in the lives of sexual killers and in the cultures to which they belong, we hope to indicate new directions for the argument, producing a critique of pornography that does not depend on proving a specifically *causal* link with violence.

[. . .]

[W]e disagree *both* with those anti-porn feminists who see a connection between pornography and violence, but analyse it only in causal terms, *and* with those feminists who have been critical of causal arguments, but who basically do not believe that there is any significant connection to be made between representation and action.

CAUSAL MODELS AND THE CASE OF TED BUNDY

[. . .]

[T]he confession of US serial killer Ted Bundy immediately prior to his execution early in 1989 [. . .] placed great emphasis on the role of pornography in his career as a sexual murderer. He represented himself as an obsessive consumer of increasingly sadistic material, and implied that pornography had been formative of desires which he was ultimately driven to act out in real life. He began with 'milder' forms of deviant behaviour, such as 'peeping Tom' activities, and worked his way up to repeated acts of killing.

Ted Bundy's story postulates some kind of cause and effect relation between what he read and what he did. It draws on certain familiar ideas: that images of torture, rape and murder engender (at least in some people) a compulsion to go out and do likewise; and that there is a progression – its course somehow inexorable – from less to more harmful fantasies and, by association, behaviours.

We may label these ideas about how porn affects its users the COPYCAT MODEL – you see it, then (therefore?) you do it – and the ADDICTION MODEL – initially erotic stimulation is obtained from relatively 'mild' forms of representation, but as the habit becomes established, it requires a stronger stimulus to achieve the same effect, and eventually representation itself is no longer strong enough, so that the user is impelled to act out the stimulus.

If these models are familiar, it is feminism which has made them so. For example, the copycat model is implicit in part of [. . .] the Minneapolis ordinance devised by Andrea Dworkin and Catharine MacKinnon.[1] Among other things, the ordinance provides for victims of sexual violence to sue producers of pornography on the grounds that their product directly inspired an assault.

Let us hasten to point out the uselessness of denying that some incidents of sexual violence do indeed re-enact specific scenarios from pornographic texts with a literalness that might justify the epithet 'copycat'. [. . .] The question we raise is not whether copycat incidents occur, but whether they should be treated as paradigmatic of the general relationship between pornography and sexual violence, or whether they should be analysed as a special case. [. . .] [I]f we treat copycat incidents as paradigmatic we leave most incidents unexplained; that even in the case of clear copycat incidents the causal model is over-deterministic; and that copycat incidents can be explained satisfactorily without treating them as paradigmatic.

The addiction model is perhaps less familiar, though it is often an implicit accompaniment to the copycat model. Lately, though, it seems to have been gaining ground in its own right. [I]t trades on an analogy between the use of pornography and the use of drugs (alcohol, tobacco, narcotics, etc.): all these habits are seen as harmful both to those who indulge in them – the 'addicts' – and to the community which must cope with the anti-social behaviour they engender. Although addiction is viewed as a social problem, there is a new emphasis on the individual within this model; the addict himself can be viewed as a victim whose weakness or inadequacy is exploited by the unscrupulous. We should not be surprised, then, that men find this model appealing when applied to their use of pornography; but we might do well to be suspicious of its depoliticizing implications (since the collective power of men and the institutionalized nature of sexual violence against women are nowhere at issue in this account).

[. . .]

Ted Bundy [. . .] characterized himself as both copycat and junkie.

A serial sexual murderer like Bundy stretches the addiction model to its limits; here we have a habit that got totally out of control. Just as smoking a joint is sometimes depicted as the first step on a slippery slope that leads to the shooting gallery, so in Bundy's case the addiction model posits that looking at pornographic representations was the first step on the long road which led to repeated and brutal killing. Once 'hooked', he could not stop: he was compelled to increase the 'dose' to the point where his behaviour became almost unimaginably destructive.

[. . .]

But what has to be remembered is that when we explain one thing in terms of another we are constructing an essentially metaphorical account. The notion of addiction to pornography is a metaphor; the mechanisms of physiological dependence that characterize, say, cocaine addiction are not directly paralleled in someone who feels a compulsion to look at porn. Feminists are usually very cautious in using 'biological' analogies which imply that aspects of sexuality are 'natural', rather than constructed or indeed chosen: it is therefore necessary to consider very carefully how apt this particular metaphor is.

Nor should we be swayed in this by the fact that Ted Bundy himself thought the metaphor apt. We make this point because it is tempting to believe that Bundy's own endorsement constitutes the strongest possible evidence for the model and for causal explanations in general. From his disinterested position as a complete misogynist, Bundy has confirmed what feminists have been saying for years, i.e. that using pornography can lead to the commission of sexual crimes. [. . .] [W]e should be wary of treating what sex murderers say about themselves as unproblematically true, even when it seems to coincide with our own analysis.

[. . .]

Where does a sex killer's account of himself come from? Not, we suggest, from some privileged personal insight, but from a finite repertoire of cultural clichés which the murderer, like everyone else, has come across in case histories, pop-psychology, newspapers, films and ordinary gossip with family, friends and workmates. At any given time the clichés available are a heterogeneous and contradictory collection; some may carry more authority than others (for instance, we no longer think much of a killer who tells us he was possessed by the devil, though traces of this ancient supernatural account can be seen in the tabloid label 'fiend' used for sex murderers); new clichés may enter the repertoire, challenging or providing alternatives to the existing explanations. Porn-blaming is a recent example.

Let us examine how cultural clichés work by examining one that feminists are in no danger of confusing with 'the truth': the mother-blaming explanation of sexual murder. The idea that sexual killers are revenging themselves on dominating or inadequate mothers is a relatively recent cliché. Although it was found in expert discourse (i.e. forensic psychiatry, criminology) much earlier – its source, in fact, is psychoanalytic theory – it entered popular awareness only in the 1950s and 1960s, by way of cultural products like the Hitchcock movie *Psycho*. At this point, not untypically, the popularized version 'fed back' into expert pronouncements in a circular, reinforcing process. Police in the Boston Strangler case in the 1960s announced that they were looking for someone like Norman Bates, the mother-fixated character in *Psycho*.[2] The actual strangler, Albert DeSalvo, in fact bore little resemblance to this stereotype. But the perception of sexual murder as a consequence of pathological mother-son relations persisted, and during the 1970s became a theme in the testimony of some real-life killers (a striking example is Edmund Kemper, the 'Co-ed Killer' of Santa Cruz)[3] – whereupon it re-entered expert discourse in case-history form. The circle was completed once again.

By the time of Ted Bundy's confession in 1989, a new account had become culturally available: the porn-blaming explanation. This one entered popular awareness in a relatively unusual way, through organized political activity on the part of feminists during the 1970s. It did not replace earlier accounts like the mother-blaming explanation (or any number of other clichés, from the oversexed 'Beast' to the 'split personality' to the 'psychopath'), but it achieved sufficient status in the culture that Ted Bundy could invoke it where Ed Kemper (for example) could not.

That sexual offenders other than murderers use cultural clichés to construct their accounts of themselves is attested by the sociologists Diana Scully and Joseph Marolla who interviewed convicted rapists and found recurring, culturally familiar themes in their narratives.[4] Scully and Marolla call these clichés 'vocabularies of motive' and suggest that rapists use them in order to justify their behaviour and 'negotiate a non-deviant identity' for themselves.

In the case of murderers, of course, the goal is more likely to be negotiating a *deviant* identity. It is hardly surprising to find [. . .] Ted Bundy [. . .] asserting, as he did for a number of years, that his murders had been committed by an 'entity' inside him – when one considers that, in a murder trial, convincing the court that you are incompetent or insane may be literally a matter of life and death. But for the purposes of the argument here it does not matter whether murderers have cynical and self-interested motives in offering their stereotypical accounts, or whether they sincerely believe those accounts to be true. The crucial point is that the accounts *come from the culture*. If they did not, they would make no sense, either to the murderer or to those he seeks to convince.

When Ted Bundy tells us he was corrupted by pornography, we need to ask not whether he is lying but where he got the story. [. . .] [W]e must treat [such] accounts *as accounts*, that is, as discourse, subjecting them to further analysis and, scrutiny. This is what we intend to do with the pornography-blaming explanation of sexual murder.

[. . .]

If a sex killer's endorsement of a particular explanation does not make it true, it does not necessarily make it false either. Nor is an argument automatically false just because its political implications are unpalatable. Surely the fact that Ted Bundy read pornography and attached significance to it calls for comment from a feminist?

We fully accept each of these points, and will respond to them by doing two things. First, we will put forward a general argument against causal accounts of human action. Second, we will try to construct an alternative model of the connections between pornography and sexual violence.

WHAT IS WRONG WITH CAUSAL EXPLANATIONS?

The central objection we have to causal explanations of the relationship between pornography and sexual violence can be stated very simply: causal accounts are completely inappropriate to explain any kind of human behaviour. Indeed, that very common term, human behaviour, has a certain misleading quality. Animals 'behave', impelled by instinct or simple stimuli; inanimate objects can (metaphorically) be said to 'behave', impelled by physical forces. Human beings, however, *act*.

[. . .]

Humans have the capacity for symbolization and language, which enables us – and perhaps even obliges us – to impose meaning on the stimuli we encounter, and to respond in ways which also carry meaning. Human 'behaviour', therefore, [. . .] is not deterministically 'caused'. It needs to be explained in a different way, by interpretation of what it means and elucidation of the beliefs or understandings that make it possible and intelligible.

[. . .]

[A] sceptic might object that the actions of sex murderers are [. . .] exceptional, since they are too bizarre for us to be able to say what understandings make them 'possible and intelligible'. [. . .] But a moment's reflection will show this to be false. Of course not all of us share Ted Bundy's desires; but we are perfectly able to interpret them. We have a category for people like Bundy ('serial sexual killer') and a number of accounts are available to us to make sense of his actions (namely the cultural clichés discussed above). However repellent Bundy's acts, however distant his desires from our own, they are intelligible to us. They do not strike us as pointless and uninterpretable in the way the actions of, say, a severely autistic individual might seem pointless and uninterpretable. The difference between Ted Bundy and the autistic person is the difference between having a language (i.e. a set of socially shared meanings) and not having one. The autistic person's actions defy interpretation because only they have access to the code.

The code of sexual murder was once as uninterpretable as autistic behaviour – in some cultures, it still would be. As recently as 1888, the year of Jack the Ripper, people were at a loss to understand the motivation of someone who murdered and disembowelled prostitutes. It was seriously suggested that the killer wanted to sell his victims' reproductive organs to anatomists for profit; or that he was trying, in a grotesque way, to draw attention to the scandal of slum housing in London.[5] Nowadays we would immediately respond to a comparable set of killings by invoking the category of sexual murder. This account was given by some commentators in 1888, but it had to compete with other explanations (whereas today it would be the obvious, preferred account). And what this shows is that a certain interpretation or discourse has entered the culture and become familiar in the space of a hundred years.

The question we need to ask, then, is where that discourse came from, why it arose at the specific time and in the particular place it did, how it spread and developed subsequently and so on. These would be important questions because, from the kind of perspective advocated here, it is precisely the emergence of a discourse making sexual murder 'possible and intelligible' which creates the conditions for sexual murder to exist on the scale it now does: no longer as an isolated, random aberration but as a culturally meaningful act which an individual might consciously choose to perform.

We may sum up the argument so far by asserting that sexual murder is not a piece of abnormal sexual behaviour determined by innate drives, but a cultural category with a social significance. Sex killers are not responding unthinkingly or involuntarily to a stimulus, they are adopting a role which exists in the culture, as recognizable and intelligible to us (albeit not as acceptable) as the role of 'artist' or 'feminist' or 'hippie'.

What of pornography? Feminist proponents of the copycat and addiction models may be espousing a causal account, but it is not guilty of the biological determinism that pervades many so-called 'scientific' explanations (e.g. the account of sexual deviance which postulates excessive levels of testosterone in offenders). Rather, the 'cause' here is social conditioning through exposure to sadistic representations. And is this not a somewhat different, less objectionable version of the causal model?

The answer, in our view, is ultimately no. This 'social' account too is inadequate because it leaves out the crucial area of interpretation of meaning. The whole idea of conditioning – addiction is simply an extreme form of conditioning – implies a gradual process over which the subject has no control, and in which he does not actively engage (it is done to him, it determines his subsequent behaviour). Here it seems to us there is an implicit behaviouristic (stimulus-response) model in operation. It is taken for granted, for instance, that the addict's compulsion is fuelled by need and not desire, his initial arousal when looking at pornography is rooted somehow in natural/biological responses. At the point where need erupts into action, the behaviourism becomes explicit.

But if once again we compare the use of pornography with the use of narcotics – a comparison to which the addiction model directs us – this account seems less than compelling. A person does not have to interpret a line of cocaine in order to feel certain effects when it enters the bloodstream. S/he does have to interpret the picture of a dead and mutilated female body, along fairly narrow and conventional lines, in order to find it erotic. When someone looks or reads, they are constantly engaging, interacting with the text to produce meaning from it. The meaning is not magically, inherently 'there' in the pictures or the words: the reader has to make it. The text does not independently have effects on readers or compel them to act in particular ways, as if they were passive and unreflecting objects. They are subjects, creators of meaning; the pornographic scenario must always be mediated by their imagination. (This, incidentally, is why pornography calls forth such a variety of responses; why not only individuals, but groups derive such different meanings from it.)

Violent sexual acts, for example murders, are also works of the imagination before they are public events. Both common sense and the testimony of convicted rapists and killers suggest that these acts are conceived, planned, acted out in the imagination, in a way that is active, creative and conscious.[6] To speak of such acts as being 'caused' in the way a virus causes disease, gravity causes objects to fall or a bell caused Pavlov's famous dogs to salivate is to misunderstand their essence, their motivation, the very thing that makes them exciting and desired: in short, it is to overlook their *meaning*.

[. . .]

THE EMERGENCE OF SEXUAL MURDER

We have already indicated that there is evidence to suggest sexual murder was not widely conceived of as a type of phenomenon before the 1880s. As far as we can tell from the historical records available, the kinds of acts which we now call sexual murder, however conceived, were extraordinarily rare before that time too.

[. . .]

Eroticized murder had however been represented in fiction before the late nineteenth century. The sadistic and necrophiliac aesthetic of the Romantic period (i.e. from the late eighteenth century) – its insistent linking of cruelty and death with eroticism and beauty[7] [. . .] was underpinned by an explicit philosophy, whose most relevant exponent [. . .] was the Marquis de Sade.

Sade wrote fictions which also philosophize, and the views he espouses may be summed up as follows. The nature of 'man' is not to be good only, but also to be evil, and there is great (erotic) pleasure to be found in wicked acts. Indeed, it is by *transgressing* the bounds of accepted morality, as embodied in religion, the law and social mores, that 'man' may *transcend* all the constraints that keep him in a state of unfreedom. Murder, the ultimate transgressive act, is both particularly pleasurable and particularly liberating. It gives 'man' *mastery*: over another human being (an Other), the victim whom he kills, but also and perhaps even more importantly over nature, the universe and his own destiny.

[. . .]

The discourse connecting sex, murder, mastery, liberty and transcendence no longer appears as a coherent and revolutionary philosophy, but it is nevertheless familiar enough cultural fare. It is [. . .] woven into [. . .] popular representations, many of which portray the murderer as a rebel and a hero: true crime magazines and journalism, crime fictions, waxwork museums, movies, 'bodice ripper' Gothic novels and, of course, pornography, [. . .] There is a large body of evidence showing that those men who actually do become sexual killers have often immersed themselves in this culture of murder as transcendence and murderer as hero. In *The Lust to Kill* we have argued that the element in murder to which these men are attracted above all is the scope it offers them to become transcendent, masterful heroes who control their own destiny by sheer will.

[. . .]

Sexual murder is enmeshed in a web of discourse: from high art to popular culture to scientific journals to sensational true crime reports, we find a range of meanings with which the imagination of the culture, and of individuals within that culture, can engage. When someone like Ted Bundy plans to commit a murder, he is creatively reworking this whole tradition in the light of his own circumstances.

[. . .]

PORNOGRAPHY

[. . .] [L]et us point out two things which seem to follow from the analysis just put forward.

First, we are suggesting that there is, indeed, a connection between representations and sexual violence. It is not, however, a cause-and-effect relation; it is a relation which turns on the construction of desire. Representations (in which category we include all the forms of discourse alluded to above) have the power not to create desire from nothing, but to shape it in particular ways. Once, there was no general eroticization of murder, no 'lust to kill'. Now, the existence of this 'meaning' is a part of the sexual understanding we grow up with. For this to happen, it was not only necessary that certain individuals should act out the lust to kill. It had first to be imagined, given a form, a set of conventions and criteria. It was discourse which accomplished this, making killing for sexual gratification possible, intelligible, part of the order of things.

Pornography is, obviously, a form of representation. Even if, as we argue here, it does not *cause* sexual violence it may be criticized for its role in shaping certain forms of desire (and not others). As we will try to show in more detail below, pornography occupies an important place in the culture of transcendence/transgression which is so important to our understanding of modern sex crime. It holds this place in virtue of several characteristics: the narratives it constructs, the form in which it renders them and the position it has in our culture as inherently a transgressive genre (though at the same time a pervasive one).

Having said that, though, our second point is that pornography is by no means the only form of representation one would want to criticize in this way, no matter how broadly or narrowly defined. [. . .] Other types of discourse are implicated in the lust to kill. And if we want to ask how the imaginative structures which enable sexual murder can be changed, it is not self-evident that we should concentrate all our efforts on pornography while letting every other form of discourse off the hook.

Nevertheless, it is important for feminists to go on analysing and criticizing pornography, if only because it provides such a clear illustration of the themes (transcendence, trangression, mastery) that are also to be found in the other cultural products through which our sexualities and sexual imaginations are shaped. Let us therefore return to the characteristics of pornography which were briefly mentioned above.

Pornography occupies a somewhat curious position in the cultures where it is prevalent. One of the things which makes it attractive is its inherent transgressiveness: it is illicit, forbidden, a dirty secret. Men writing about the process whereby porn became part of their lives typically tell stories about a submerged, shared male culture into which the adolescent or pre-adolescent is initiated: a furtive passing around of magazines in the playground or the park; secret, snatched readings of material belonging to fathers and older brothers; clandestine visits to sex shops undertaken as a dare. On the other hand, though, pornography must be among the most open secrets our culture has. Its 'softer' forms are all-pervading in nearly all public environments (trucks, billboards, assembly lines, offices, the newspapers and the shops where you buy them).

The result of this paradox is that pornography seems to tell us what we must not do – the scenarios in it are by definition transgressive – but in practice, given that for many people it is the most familiar representation of sexuality, it effectively tells us what we should be doing. Like so-called descriptive sexology, porn has a normative aspect to it; it can be presented as a model of how to do sex, a sort of prototypical narrative or user's manual. And because it purports to be describing the forbidden, the normative model it presents is much more appealing and powerful than something presented overtly as normative, like government 'Safer Sex' guidelines. (An AIDS activist colleague made this point very clearly when he suggested that henceforth pornography should always depict condoms: 'We have to make them sexy' is what he said!)

There is plenty of evidence, especially from feminist research, that pornography is used in this way by many men in heterosexual relations, as a source of narratives whose authenticity and pleasure potential they wish their female partners to recognize. In an in-depth study of sixty women, for instance, Liz Kelly was surprised at how often her informants – most of them quite unfamiliar with the feminist debate on porn – raised this point unprompted. One told her: 'Whatever happened in this magazine we used to have to do it, it was like a manual. I'd think, oh God, I better read it to see what I've got to do tonight.'[8] The women who made these sorts of comments did quite often object to the specific practices and scenarios their partners pressured them to engage in (unsurprisingly, since these most often involved extreme male dominance and female submission). But they also objected, perhaps even more so, to the fact that this mechanical transfer of a scenario from the page or the screen to the bedroom removed all mutuality and interactiveness from sex, leaving no space for the woman to define her own form of pleasure. They disliked being written into someone else's script – their partner's, but also and especially the pornographer's.

It is obvious, of course, that no form of human action can be totally unscripted: everything we do reflects a complex interaction between the cultural meanings and norms we have available and our own individual creativity. There is, then, no culture-free space in which people can come to some wholly authentic and personal sexual expression. What is problematic, though, is the stranglehold pornography seems to have on the available meanings in this particular sphere. Only a certain number of 'authorized versions' are given expression in pornography, and they tend to the 'transcendence' model which feminists would want to criticize.

That the prototypical stories told in pornographic fictions are narratives of (male) transcendence and mastery is obvious enough from content analyses which are available. But it has also been argued that the form of the pornographic representation carries this meaning too. The reader or looker in pornography becomes the Subject of the representation, while the person(s) represented is/are objectified. The Object is Other, existing in relation to the gaze and desire of the Subject. The Subject can project anything he likes on to the Object: fear, acquiescence, active desire, even total dominance (as in fictions for masochists). But whatever the content of the scenario, the Object is written into the Subject's script and he controls her by virtue of that fact.[9] This reassurance that one is a Subject, free and in control, is obtained in pornography as it is in acts of violence like rape and murder, by objectifying and imposing one's will upon an Other.

Of course, we may wish to make a moral distinction between doing this to live individuals and doing it to fictional objects who exist only in words and pictures (though this is to leave aside the fact that models in pornography are real people, and frequently suffer real exploitation in the process of production). But what needs to be emphasized for the purposes of this argument is the similarity of the act from the point of view of the Subject who is writing the script. His perspective is essentially a solipsistic one, in which even 'real' women are rendered imaginary by objectification; it is the Self and its pleasures which become the central focus. From this perspective, looking at porn and committing a sex murder appear as two versions of the same enterprise – the enterprise Susanne Kappeler calls 'subjectification' and we call 'transcendence'. Here is the link between representation and action: a construction of pleasure as necessarily involving transcendence of the Subject's will through transgressive acts negating the will of the Object.[10]

The Marquis de Sade rhetorically asked: 'Do not all passions require victims?'[11] A feminist must surely meet this question with a question: 'Why should they?' Desire could be less solipsistic than this, and less dependent on eroticized relations of dominance and submission. But while pornographic fictions continue to shape our culture's sexual and social imagination more thoroughly and powerfully than competing discourses can, the feminist will be crying in a wilderness.

[. . .]

CONCLUSION

In analysing sexual violence and its links to cultural forms such as pornography, we overlook at our peril the pre-eminent role of imaginative mediation and the creation of meaning. All humans are endowed with the capacity and perhaps the need to interpret and represent their actions, their lives; our possession of consciousness, language and culture ensure that we will impose meaning on even the most fundamental bodily experience. That is not, in itself, problematic. But it does mean we need to move beyond causal accounts of human actions, and look instead at the resources humans bring to their interpretations and representations, the meanings which shape their desires and constrain the stories they can imagine for themselves. For we are clearly not free to imagine just anything; we work both with and against the grain of the cultural meanings we inherit.

In the sphere of sexuality, pornography is a significant source of ideas and narratives. It transmits to those who use it – primarily men but also women – notions of transcendence and mastery as intrinsic to sexual pleasure. These ideas are not taken up only by those who become rapists and killers. On the contrary, they pervade our everyday, unremarkable sexual encounters as surely as they do the grotesque acts of Ted Bundy and his ilk.

In the case of sex murderers (as in many other cases), the extreme, what is perceived as abnormal and deviant, throws light on the normal (of which it turns out to be a version). If we as feminists want to do something about sexual violence, it is precisely the normal and normative sexual practice of our culture that we must change. That means, among other things, that we must be critical of pornography and the other discourses which inform sexual practice, using our imagination to shape alternatives to the pleasures of transcendence and the thrills of transgression. In fact, feminists have been doing this for more than twenty years. But the recent focus of so many writers on causal models of sexual violence (which often imply that the problem is non-normal individuals and extreme sexual practices) is, at least in our view, a retreat from that radical politics of sexuality.

NOTES

1. For an account, see Catharine McKinnon, *Feminism Unmodified: Discourses on Life and Law*, Cambridge, Mass. and London: Harvard University Press, 1987, ch. 14.
2. Gerald Frank, *The Boston Strangler*, London: Pan, 1967; also discussions in J. Caputi, *The Age of Sex Crime*, London: Women's Press, 1988.
3. For a discussion of Edmund Kemper, see Deborah Cameron and Elizabeth Frazer, *The Lust to Kill – A Feminist Investigation of Sexual Murder*, Cambridge: Polity Press, 1987.
4. Diana Scully and Joseph Marolla, cited in L. Kelly, *Surviving Sexual Violence*, Cambridge: Polity Press, 1989, p. 47.
5. Cameron and Frazer, *The Lust to Kill*, p. 125.
6. A pertinent example here is the case of Ronald Frank Cooper, discussed in Cameron and Frazer, *The Lust to Kill*, pp. xiii–xiv.
7. Mario Praz, *The Romantic Agony*, London: Fontana, 1960.
8. Kelly, *Surviving Sexual Violence*, p. 111.
9. The gender of the pronouns here is deliberate, reflecting the fact that men are prototypical Subjects and women generic Objects. However, men can be placed in the object position and women (arguably) in the subject position in relation to pornography; the analysis holds for Subject–Object relations irrespective of gender, but it needs to be stressed that these positions are not neutral in respect of gender.
10. Meryl Altman (whom we thank for her numerous helpful comments on drafts of this piece) has raised the question of whether, if this analysis is right, there can be any objectionable erotic representations at all – the looker/reader will always be Subject, getting the pleasure by objectifying the people in the

story. Altman reads Kappeler's critique of pornography, which focuses on its asymmetric and non-dialogic form rather than its objectionable (e.g. violent or stereotypical) content, as leading ultimately to a rejection of all representation, since the content could be ameliorated but the form presumably could not. She asks if anyone can imagine a world without representation, and whether such a world would not be seriously impoverished.

These are clearly questions of some importance and, as Altman points out, our inability to resolve them leads to ambiguity or maybe even contradiction in the above argument (should we pursue a 'positive politics' of alternative representations, or stick to a 'negative politics' of criticizing existing ones?). Feminist practice over the past five years has shown dangers in both approaches: many women are dissatisfied with the 'repressiveness' of a negative politics, but on the other hand alternative 'positive' representations are easily recuperated to prevailing sexist interpretations. There is little point in creating novel images if we do not at the same time create novel ways of reading them.

We should point out, however, that Altman is a somewhat extreme reading of Kappeler: subjectification/transcendence is not the only actual or imaginable effect of representation, and the representations produced in a 'post-transcedence' culture might have a very different significance (as presumably the representations of 'pre-transcendence' cultures did and do). How to achieve a transformation of our culture and subjectivities is, of course, an enormous problem for feminists. And while we don't think any culture will be without representations and narratives of some kind, it is at least worth posing the question whether it is inevitable or desirable that people should derive specifically sexual pleasure from representations.

11. Sade, quoted by Praz, *The Romantic Agony*.

4.7

LIBERALISM AND THE CONTRADICTIONS OF OPPRESSION

Mary McIntosh

Many modern feminists have misgivings about anti-pornography campaigns. Mary McIntosh argues against a blanket condemnation of erotic representation and for an appreciation of the contradictory ways in which the concept of pornography has been constructed and deployed. She argues that feminists, rather than seeking legislation against pornography, should engage in a politics of subversion. This might include producing feminist 'pornography'.

LIBERALISM IS NOT ENOUGH

The crusade against pornography and its efforts to strengthen legal controls challenge us to rethink what we mean by the slogan 'the personal is political'. If we accept that there is a feminist critique of pornography, if we accept that women's liberation requires a transformation of patriarchal culture, why not campaign to have sexist pornography legally banned? Now of course, there are many problems about defining the category to which this critique applies and about how any new law would actually work. [. . .] But the niggling suspicion remains that those of us who oppose further censorship are libertarians, left over from the 1960s era of 'if-you-dig-it-do-it', who do not recognize the social implications of 'private' individual actions.

[. . .]

[Anti-pornography campaigners] in their more reflective moments [. . .] see this separation of personal and political as the greatest failing of those of us who oppose legislation on pornography. For instance, Catharine MacKinnon and other leading

From M. McIntosh, 'Liberalism and the contradictions of sexual politics', in L. Segal (ed.), *Sex Exposed*, London: Virago, 1992.

crusaders against pornography have contributed to a book called *The Sexual Liberals and the Attack on Feminism*,[1] which takes a principled position against liberalism.

Again, it would be easy to attack the argument of writers like MacKinnon by focusing on its crudest excesses. Their basic position is that every aspect of society is so structured by male supremacy that abstract concepts like choice, consent, equality and freedom are all suspect, as far as women are concerned. This argument has, indeed, a grain of truth, but since they place sexuality at the centre of women's oppression and see it as a practice whose function is to subordinate women to men, some of them recommend withdrawing from sex altogether. [. . .] It would be easy, too, to quote Catharine MacKinnon's statement:

> [The women's movement] knew that when force is a normalized part of sex, when no is taken to mean yes, when fear and despair produce acquiescence and acquiescence is taken to mean consent, consent is not a meaningful concept.[2]

and to point out that this undermines the whole of anti-rape campaigning by merging it with a campaign against intercourse in general. But there remains a nub of argument that must be taken seriously, which lies in their recognition that every aspect of society is interconnected with every other.

The notion of the private as against the public sphere is problematic for feminism, given that we recognize this as a historically developed distinction that was highly gendered in its origins. In the ideology of the emergent middle class, the division of the world into private and public was linked with the flowering of the bourgeois domestic sphere as women's domain and the elaboration of formal organizations and associations as men's. The family home became the model of private life, separated from work and commerce, proudly independent and with its own front door to mark its boundary. The notion of the privacy of family life has been used to justify policies of non-intervention in child abuse and wife-beating. It has often made women lonely and isolated and obliged them to shoulder heavy burdens of care and responsibility. Feminists have wanted to bring these things out into the open and to say that, far from being a sphere of freedom and autonomy, the private family can be a state-protected patriarchy.

[. . .]

All of this means that the 'rights of privacy' that are so favoured in liberal thought are highly problematic from a feminist point of view.

The right to freedom of speech depends upon a distinction between words and deeds that is hard to sustain. That words – and visual images – are powerful in underpinning social institutions is an insight that is not confined to feminism. Social thought over the last two decades has laid great stress on culture and ideology. There has been a recognition that social power at the level of the state is sustained not only by law and force but also by an elaborate system of ideas that make it seem normal and incontrovertible. There has been a growing awareness that racial oppression is to be found as much in the way dominant discourses assume white men as their subject and cast black people as strange and 'other' as in employment discrimination or physical racial attacks. The power of the mass media to whip up issues of public concern and define the political agenda has become more and more apparent. Feminism has brought this sort of concern to bear on understanding women's oppression and there has been a flowering of feminist film studies, literary and art criticism and cultural analysis.

In a more positive and practical way, feminists have sought to transform culture: to get anti sexist books into schools, to publish new magazines for women, to create our own art and writing, humour and drama. Clearly, we have believed in the power of words and images and in the importance of cultural politics. But if the pen is indeed mightier than the sword, should it not be subject to the same controls, licensing and non-proliferation treaties?

In apparent contradiction, though, the term 'liberal' has often been associated with 'reformism' – an orthodox approach to social change through democratic processes and legislation. Feminists have often been ambivalent about orthodox politics and about invoking the state in support of women's interests. On the one hand there has been the view that women are ignored in the political process, denied proper citizenship, and our concerns are treated as 'merely personal'. The project, then, should be to transform official politics to take us into account and to assert a continuity between the politics of everyday life and the politics of party and Parliament. On the other hand, the state has been criticized as irredeemably patriarchal, its apparatuses staffed by men and its policies designed to sustain the institutions that oppress women. The project, then, should be to liberate women, to remove state controls from are.s that affect our lives, like divorce or abortion: 'Not the Church, not the state' women should decide their fate.'

Should women be within the state hierarchies, at risk of co-optation, or mobilizing at the grass roots and sniping from strategic positions outside?

[. . .]

On the whole, the conclusion has been the pragmatic one: there is no general answer; there may be occasions for an engagement with orthodox politics and legislative reforms, but there are also occasions for a more subversive politics of demonstrative actions, self-activity and everyday life.

There are, then, serious problems with the liberalism which had led feminists to assert that 'the personal is political'. On the other hand, 'the political' is not identical with making demands on the state. So the fact that the personal, the sexual, the cultural and [. . .] pornography are 'political' does not necessarily mean that they should be the subject of legislative control. I shall argue, indeed, that the appropriate politics is one of subversion – a kind of cultural guerrilla warfare – because pornography is an inherently contradictory phenomenon.

THE SOCIAL CONSTRUCTION OF SEXUALITY

To work out strategies for feminist sexual politics, we need to understand more about how sexuality and sexual behaviour are formed, how sexual desire – apparently such an individual matter – is shaped by the social context. The anti-pornography campaigners are acutely aware that men's sexual behaviour is influenced by the culture around them, but they usually have very simplistic ideas of the processes involved. Diana Russell, for instance, says:

> My theory, in a nutshell, is that pornography (1) predisposes some men to want to rape women or intensifies the predisposition in other men already so predisposed, (2) undermines some men's internal inhibitions against acting out their desire to rape, and (3) undermines some men's social inhibitions against acting out their desire to rape.[3]

The other 'causes of males' proclivity to rape' that she mentions are 'male sex-role socialization, sexual abuse in childhood, peer pressure and portrayal of women in the mass media'.[4] Her analysis [. . .] of sexuality involves men who have no self-reflection and whose engagement with the cultural complex is completely passive and unselective. So contradictions within that culture become internalized simply as a 'proclivity' that is held in check by internal and social inhibitions. There is no room here even for men to look around them and recognize a wider cultural terrain, and certainly none for such ideas as the 'thrill of the forbidden', perversity, transgression, subversion.[5]

Many anti-pornography crusaders, especially in Britain, are inclined to turn to Russell for their theory. It is a theory in which men are not subjects, except in the sense of 'subjects' in laboratory experiments. At the same time there is a completely opposing theory, most tellingly expressed by Andrea Dworkin, that men are indeed the dominant subjects, the collective subject of 'male sexual domination'. For Dworkin, sexuality is so much a part of this social order that it is no longer conceived as individual or personal at all. She says:

> Men control the sexual and reproductive uses of women's bodies. The institutions of control include law, marriage, prostitution, pornography, health care, the economy, organized religion, and systematized physical aggression against women (for instance, in rape and battery) . . . The ideology of male sexual domination posits that men are superior to women by virtue of their penises; that physical possession of the female is the natural right of the male; . . . The metaphysics of male sexual domination is that women are whores . . . One does not violate something by using it for what it is: neither rape nor prostitution is an abuse of the female because in both the female is fulfilling her natural function.[6]

Here we have a vision of patriarchy as a seamless social totality. But again, as with Russell, there is no sense that there may be contradictions within that totality, and that this may pose problems for a feminist sexual politics. Dworkin [. . .] takes no account of the fact that pornography is banned, seized, burned, kept shamefully under the bed – by men. Nor does she recognize that, far from being considered as an acceptable part of the system, clients and ponces, as well as prostitutes themselves, are hounded and criminalized:

> In the male system, women are sex, sex is the whore . . . Buying her means buying pornography . . . Wanting her means wanting pornography. Being her means being pornography.[7]

So women, too, are completely caught up within this totality. There is no room here for the actual sex worker – only for the 'whore' of men's imagination. Dworkin says: 'The word *whore* is incomprehensible unless one is immersed in the lexicon of male domination',[8] but because her image of society is totalitarian, her solution is utopian: 'We will know that we are free when pornography no longer exists. As long as it does exist, we must understand that we are the women in it.'[9] So she rails against the injustice of being labelled a 'vile whore', but does not engage with the actual politics of prostitution or of women who are 'whores' in a more than metaphorical sense. There is no room here for subversion or destabilization, let alone reform or amelioration.

We need a theory of the social construction of sexuality that is somewhere between what might be called the 'liberal' view that it lies outside the social altogether and the 'totalitarian' view that it is a determinate aspect of a homogeneous social whole. For this purpose, we can turn to the 'social constructionism' that has been developed by lesbian and gay theorists. [. . .]

It starts from the recognition that although homosexual behaviour probably exists in all societies, it is not universally interpreted as being a speciality of a particular type of person: the homosexual. There has been much debate about when this identity emerged in Western cultures. [. . .] What is clear, though, is that there are many complex processes at work but that the stigmatization and punishment of individuals who were beginning to be identified in this way had an important part to play. Doctors, sexologists, psychiatrists, the police, recurrent scandals and moral panics all helped to develop the contemporary notion of 'the homosexual'. So too, of course, did homosexual subcultures and apologias which gradually took root and offered a variety of defensive and offensive strategies.

Now, there are some useful features of this body of theory which may be helpful in understanding heterosexuality as well. One is a clear recognition that the social patterning of sexual behaviour varies from one society to another – so some societies are 'rape prone' while others are 'rape free', as the anthropologist Peggy Reeves Sanday has shown.[10] Another is that although current sexual conceptions are immensely powerful in affecting our identities and behaviour, they do not by any means determine them. Thus there are people who resist classifying themselves as either homosexual or heterosexual and many more who, though they adopt one identity or the other, are nevertheless bisexual in their behaviour, resisting the exclusive sexual orientation that is implied in the social label. Similarly, many heterosexual men do not act out the current hegemonic notions of masculinity; and many heterosexual women resist dominant ideas of feminine passivity, despite Catharine MacKinnon's claim that women's lives are 'seamlessly consistent with pornography'.

A third useful feature of social constructionism is its awareness that the actual social patterning of sexual behaviour is not the same as the culturally and morally approved patterns of behaviour. Just as homosexuality grew up alongside a new emphasis on normative heterosexuality, tied into marriage, procreation and family, so prostitution exists as a separate and specialized institution only because promiscuous, impersonal sex-for-money goes so much against the moral norms and because women are expected to be more monogamous and less sexually active than men.

THE INHERENT CONTRADICTION OF PORNOGRAPHY

It can be argued, also, that pornography represents another non-normative, disapproved phenomenon which has become institutionalized in the form it has precisely because sexual explicitness is so strongly stigmatized. Pornography as a term, and as a phenomenon, is relatively recent in Western history.[11] It would not be a great oversimplification to say that it developed along with middle-class morality in the nineteenth century. As this morality of prudery and sexual restraint displaced both aristocratic licentiousness and the rules of thumb of earlier Christian teaching and rural custom, so a separate space, outside the pale of the new respectability, was created for everything that prudery condemned. It was very typical of the Victorian period to create a deep chasm between respectable and non-respectable, and the image of the Madonna and the Magdalen was often used to divide women in these terms. In the cities prostitution flourished as never before, but was also more sternly punished and stigmatized. Bourgeois morality projected on to prostitutes (as well as the working classes and 'savages') many of the desires it sought to suppress, so it is perhaps not surprising that the term pornography literally means 'a description of prostitutes or of prostitution'.[12]

According to Walter Kendrick, one of the first uses of the word pornography, in anything approximating to its present sense, seems to have been to refer to all those pictures and artefacts unearthed in the excavation of the Roman city of Pompeii which were thought too obscene to be displayed in public and were conserved in a separate collection in the National Museum in Naples – the 'secret museum'. These images were found all over the town, and there were erect stone phalluses at many Pompeiian street corners, but the museum cataloguers of 1866 chose to identify rooms painted with sexual scenes as brothels and to call the locked room in the museum the 'pornographic collection'.

The people excluded from the locked room were women and children and the uneducated in general. When an illustrated catalogue was printed in 1877, it was in an expensive edition which only the wealthy could afford; the genitals were miniaturized or blurred, and the whole text was larded with erudite Greek and Latin quotations – 'the decent obscurity of a learned language'. In this way pornography was born as a genre available to bourgeois men who could declare that their interest was scholarly. So, from the start, the definition of pornography was a highly gendered and class-bound one.[13]

During the course of the nineteenth and early twentieth centuries, the definition of pornography developed and changed with shifts in the boundary of what should be available in public, and particularly what should be available to the most 'vulnerable' and 'corruptible' members of society. In England and Wales, this boundary was succinctly defined in 1868 when Lord Justice Cockburn formulated the test of obscenity to be applied to the 1857 Obscene Publications Act:

> A tendency . . . to deprave and corrupt those whose minds are open to such immoral influences, and into whose hands a publication of this sort may fall.

Ironically or not, this test was first formulated in a judgement against a political tract, in which the Protestant Electoral Union exposed the prurient questions that Catholic priests were said to ask women in the confessional. From the start, then, pornography and regulation were an inseparable couple, and censorship was part of a paternalistic form of patriarchal domination that had its heyday in the Victorian era.

During the twentieth century it became established that scientific and literary merit could outweigh 'obscenity', and the courts were required to take into account the work as a whole, rather than to select out particular passages. The Obscene Publications Act of 1959 says:

> For the purpose of this Act an article shall be deemed obscene if its effect . . . is, if taken as a whole, such as to deprave and corrupt persons who are likely, in all the circumstances, to read, see or hear the matter contained or embodied in it . . . [The defendant shall not be convicted] . . . if publication of the article in question is justified as being for the public good . . . in the interests of science, literature, art or learning, or of other objects of general concern.

Subsequent appeal rulings have further established that shock or disgust by itself does not indicate obscenity, since works which provoke such feelings might actually *discourage* depravity.

The general line of development from the mid-nineteenth century to the present day is that the obscene becomes identified with a particular genre: pornography – that is to say, writing or pictures (and later videos, and so on) that are produced with the purpose of sexual arousal and have no 'redeeming' value. The assumption was that to set out intentionally to produce sexual arousal is despicable, but if the main objective of the work is artistic or scientific and the possibility of sexual arousal is only incidental, then these higher purposes may justify publication. The courts thus undertook to make aesthetic judgements, apparently unaware that class prejudice and aesthetics go hand in hand. The 'educated man' – and nowadays, indeed, the educated woman – can have erotic images packaged with arts and sciences; the uneducated should either do without or make do with the popular press, where they come wrapped up with 'news'. Pornography itself flourishes either as the illegal or restricted 'hard core' or the permitted borderline of available 'soft core'. In both cases it is entirely defined by the laws of obscenity, with the hard core transgressing and the soft core trimming its sails with great precision to stay within the law.

Pornography, then, represents a contradiction within bourgeois Christian morality, in that it exists only because it is condemned. Pornography and censoriousness are an inseparable couple. Until feminism entered the debate, all definitions of pornography depended upon this, and an essential ingredient of pornography was the desire to shock, to cross the boundaries, to explore forbidden zones. Repressive sexual morality always tends to foster and feed its own worst enemies in this way. Struggles over the censorship of pornography have been paradoxical because to defend pornography in public would be at the same time to recognize the morality which defines it as pornographic.

YOU CAN'T GET THERE FROM HERE

Where, then, is the space for a feminist sexual politics in all of this? Feminism has tried to intrude completely new considerations into this long-established contradiction. It has wanted to sidestep the whole question of the boundaries of sexual decency, through which censorship has defined pornography, and to focus instead on the sexually oppressive content of pornography. Some feminists have even wanted to introduce new legal controls on pornography (to extend or replace the existing ones – it is never quite clear). There are many problems with this. One is that since pornography is political, it involves political censorship. Another is that it involves making a political alliance with the forces of bourgeois Christian morality. But even more important is that in accepting the *concept* of pornography, it by definition accepts that morality.

When there is a deep-seated patriarchal contradiction like this, the appropriate feminist strategy cannot be to take one side or the other, but to seek to transcend the contradiction. This calls for a politics of subversion, not of reform. The crusade against pornography has been both utopian and reformist, in that it has imagined a society in which women are free from sexual violence and sought to usher it in through legal constraints on men. It has seen pornography as a branch of patriarchal ideology, whereas I have argued that, far from being the socially approved blueprint for sexual behaviour, pornography is the repository of all the unacceptable and repressed desires of men (even if only for sexual expression outside marriage).

The argument of this essay is that the 'personal' of sexuality is indeed political – that feminists should have a great deal to say about pornography, as about the rest of cultural representations, but that our politics has to take the form of transgression. Transgressive cultural politics can take a variety of forms. In recent years, 'gender-bending' dress – coupling heavy boots with black lace, for instance – has been used by some young women to challenge their elders. Making feminist 'pornography' and declaring ourselves as sexual beings is not simply something that we do for our own pleasure, using such freedom as we have gained; it is also a way of undermining all the oppressive things that sexuality has meant for women in the past. And feminist humour and poetry have immense power to subvert existing discourses by uncovering their contradictions and hinting at new meanings.

[. . .]

NOTES

1. Dorchen Leidholdt and Janice G. Raymond (eds), *The Sexual Liberals and the Attack on Feminism*, Oxford: Pergamon Press, 1990.
2. *Ibid.*, p. 4.
3. Diana Russell, 'Pornography and rape: a causal model', *Political Psychology*, 2(1) 1990, p. 49.
4. *Ibid.*, p. 50.
5. These are terms that have acquired a certain glamour in cultural analysis, but it is important to recognize that even something as unequivocally reprehensible as rape may have some ambivalent and challenging

aspects. It may, in other words, be subversive of an imaginary sexual order, and be perceived as such by some rapists, without justifying it in any way.

6. Andrea Dworkin, *Pornography: Men possessing Women*, London: The Women's Press, 1981, p. 203.
7. *Ibid.*, p. 202.
8. *Ibid.*, p. 200.
9. *Ibid.*, p. 224.
10. Peggy Reeves Sanday, 'The social construction of rape', *New Society*, 16, 1982, p. 1037.
11. For a fascinating interpretation of this history, see Walter Kendrick, *The Secret Museum: Pornography in Modern Culture*, New York: Viking, 1987.
12. *Oxford English Dictionary*.
13. Outside the realm of pornography, too, bourgeois men enjoy the nude women displayed for their delectation in the highly respectable genre of oil painting – see John Berger, *Ways of Seeing*, London: Pelican, 1972, ch. 3.

4.8

PROSTITUTION
A Difficult Issue for Feminists

Priscilla Alexander

Feminists account for prostitution as a consequence of women's subordination. Difficulties arise, however, in maintaining a distinction between a critique of prostitution and a criticism of sex workers themselves. Priscilla Alexander examines some of the problems this has created. She argues that both prohibition and legalisation of prostitutes' activities can cause problems for the women themselves and argues for decriminalisation on the grounds that this offers the best chance of prostitutes controlling their own working conditions.

Prostitution has been a difficult issue for feminists both in the current wave of the feminist movement, which began in the late 1960s, and in the earlier wave which began in the 1860s. As feminists, we abhor the exploitation of women's sexuality by profiteers, and some of us feel, instinctively, that prostitution supports an objectification of women's sexuality and of women, that is somehow related to the pervasive violence against us. In addition, we are defined, by ourselves and others, by our place in the age-old whore/madonna dichotomy. However, there is a growing realization among many feminists that the laws against prostitution, and the stigma imposed on sex work, keep all women from determining their own sexuality.

Few women reach puberty without being aware of prostitution. Many women have at some point thought about engaging in prostitution to pay their bills or to get out of serious debt, although for most it is only a fleeting thought. Many women have prostitution fantasies in which they equate sexual pleasure with depravity and 'badness' on the one hand, or with power on the other hand. Many women equate prostitution

From P. Alexander, 'Prostitution: a difficult issue for feminists', in F. Delacoste and P. Alexander (eds), *Sex Work*, Pittsburgh: Cleis Press, 1988.

with negative feelings about their own sexual encounters with men – for example, when the men are interested in quick, rather anonymous, casual sexual encounters, and the women are interested in more long-term, caring, sexual relationships. The result of such conflicting demands is that many women, at least some of the time, feel sexually used.

[. . .]

Another factor that interferes with a dispassionate view of prostitution is that approximately one out of three women report that they were sexually 'abused' by an adult male before they reached the age of eighteen. In addition, as adults, women face a one in four risk of being raped [. . .] by acquaintances or by strangers. If marital rape were to be included in those statistics, the percentage would be higher. Compounding this abuse is the persistent blaming of the victim with which we are all familiar. [. . .] A standard defense to rape is that the woman was a prostitute. [. . .] This bias is carried into the home as well, particularly in the case of domestic violence: many battering husbands call their wives 'whore' before they hit them, as though the label justifies the act.

[. . .]

In addition to the restrictions and negative experiences that make it difficult for women to view prostitution objectively, prostitution itself is shrouded in layer upon layer of mystique. The male-controlled media, which includes classic literature as well as modern television, movies, novels, and magazines, have largely created an unreal image of the prostitute. On the one hand, the media presents the 'whore with the heart of gold' and the 'sex goddess'; on the other hand, it presents the depraved, degraded prisoner, the sexual slave. Modern pornography has further confused the issue, by misrepresenting women's sexuality, including prostitution. Only recently have prostitutes themselves begun to write about their experiences, or to tell their experiences to other writers.[1] In addition, some feminists have begun to write about prostitution, looking at the patriarchal structures that historically surround prostitution and the role that prostitution plays in contemporary society.[2]

PREVALENCE OF PROSTITUTION

Prostitution has existed in every society for which there are written records.[3] For a long period in history, women had only three options for economic survival: getting married, becoming a nun (earlier, a priestess), or becoming a prostitute. The invention of the spinning wheel, around the 13th Century, enabled a woman working alone to produce enough thread to support herself, for the first time, as a spinster.

[. . .]

At the present time, prostitution exists in every country in the world. Although the forms vary somewhat from place to place – due to differences in culture, economics and law – the institution itself in strikingly similar. A few countries, including Cuba, the USSR, and China, have undertaken large-scale projects to 're-habilitate' prostitutes, and thereby eliminate prostitution. However, some women in all of those countries continue to work as prostitutes, especially in the large urban centers, and especially following an increase in tourism from other countries. Many countries rely on prostitution to provide foreign currency necessary for trade with the technological west.

WHY PROSTITUTION?

Prostitution exists, at least in part, because of the subordination of women in most societies. This subordination is reflected in the double standard of sexual behavior for men and women, and is carried out in the discrepancy between women's and men's earning power.

[. . .]

The specific reasons that prostitutes have given for choosing their work, as revealed in the studies of Dr Jennifer James in Seattle, have included money, excitement, independence, and flexibility, in roughly that order. First person accounts by women in the sex industry often mention economics as a major factor, coupled with rebellion at the restricted and tedious jobs available to them.[4] Dr James and others have also revealed a high incidence of child sexual abuse in the life histories of prostitutes: around fifty percent for adult prostitutes; seventy-five to eighty percent for juvenile prostitutes.[5] The traditional psychoanalytic explanation for the relationship between childhood sexual abuse and later involvement in prostitution is that the child has come to view sex as a commodity, and that she is masochistic. The connection many prostitutes report, however, is that the involvement in prostitution is a way of taking back control of a situation in which, as children, they had none. Specifically, many have reported that the first time they ever felt powerful was the first time they 'turned a trick.'[6] [. . .] It is important to remember that many women with no history of sexual assault become prostitutes (and many survivors of child sexual abuse never work as prostitutes), so the relationship between prostitution and early sexual trauma is far from clear.

A number of authors have also looked at the fact that men and women do not appear to view sex in the same way and that men as a class seem to view sex as power, with rape being the most extreme form of the use of sex as power. Women as a class tend to see sex as nurture, and this generalization is subject to great individual differences. Prostitution also involves an equation of sex with power: for the man/customer, the power consists of his ability to 'buy' access to any number of women; for the woman/prostitute, the power consists of her ability to set the terms of her sexuality, and to demand substantial payment for her time and skills. Thus, prostitution is one area in which women have traditionally and openly viewed sex as power.

[. . .]

DE FACTO LEGALIZATION OF THIRD-PARTY CONTROLLED PROSTITUTION IN THE US

Although prostitution is illegal in most of the United States, a quasi-legalized brothel system has developed in many cities under the auspices of police department. San Francisco is a good example. In the early seventies, the San Francisco Board of Supervisors passed an ordinance regulating massage parlors, and requiring that both the owners of the massage parlors and the workers they employed obtain licenses from the Police Department's Permit Bureau. A conviction on a prostitution-related offense in the previous three years is grounds for denial of the license. Similarly, a conviction subsequent to getting the license is grounds for revocation. In 1981, the Board of Supervisors passed a similar ordinance regulating escort services.

On the face of it, it would seem that the legislation is designed to prevent prostitution; however, according to police testimony at the time the escort service bill was introduced, it is really designed to 'regulate and control' prostitution, not prevent it. In reality, however, it guarantees a turnover of new employees because the police periodically raid the parlors and escort services, and revoke the permits of the women they arrest. The Board of Permit Appeals in San Francisco usually upholds the revocation, even when the charges have been dropped or a judge has dismissed them for lack of evidence (i.e., there was no 'conviction'). After one such raid, I noticed an ad for a massage parlor that promised 'all new staff.'

Interestingly, the same massage license is required, whether the work is 'legitimate' or sexual massage. When a woman applies for the license, the police assume she is a prostitute, and treat her accordingly. When the police raid massage parlors and escort services, and arrest all the women working there, they may not even charge them with prostitution. Instead, they arrest them for minor infractions of the massage parlor licensing code, such as failing to wear an ID badge on the outside of their clothes. Such cases are often dismissed the next morning by a judge who thinks such arrests are a waste of the taxpayers' money and the court's time. Even though there have been no convictions, the women who were arrested lose their licenses and, as a consequence, their jobs. The women who have been arrested do not stop working as prostitutes, however. Perhaps they work in the isolation of their own apartments, advertising in the local sex paper. Perhaps they go out on the street, exposing themselves to much greater risks of dangerous clients and cops. Or they may move to another city, where they don't have an arrest record, or any friends, to apply for another massage license, so the cycle begins again.

PORNOGRAPHY AS A FORM OF THIRD-PARTY CONTROLLED PROSTITUTION

Another version of third-party controlled prostitution has developed as a result of court decisions which, in effect, decriminalize pornography. The proliferation of magazines, books, films, video-tapes, and 'adult' bookstores has been matched by the growth of the live pornography show, in which the line between pornography and prostitution is extremely thin. The legal definition of prostitution in California is 'a lewd act in exchange for money or other consideration.' The courts have held that sex acts for which all participants are being paid by a third party (viewer, pornographic film-maker, etc.), and in which there is no direct physical contact between payer and payee, are legitimate, while continuing to uphold the laws which prohibit the same actions if one participant is paying the other directly. In live pornography shows, including peep shows – where women perform in booths or on a stage separated from their customers by plexiglass windows or coin-operated shutters – as well as more conventional theatrical presentations, the line has all but disappeared. The main consumers of live pornography shows are tourists, and tour buses leave regularly from the major hotels in every city, taking visitors to pornography districts.

New case law is being developed as police charge that the live shows are, in fact, prostitution, while the pornographers contend that they are not, and that the sexual activity involved is covered by the First Amendment. Until recently, I thought there was a strong possibility that the legal struggle surrounding live pornography would result in prostitution laws being struck down, because some producers of live pornography would like very much to be able to become legally involved in prostitution. However, the current political climate in the United States makes such a court decision unlikely.

Moreover, the agitation by anti-pornography feminists, such as New York's Women Against Pornography, has already increased the enforcement of prostitution laws against pornography performers, and the pimping and pandering laws against the producers. The recommendations of the Attorney General's Commission on Pornography (the Meese Commission), which has taken up some of the language of the anti-porn feminists as a smokescreen to cover its real intention of broadening the scope of obscenity prosecutions, are also likely to increase the harassment of prostitutes.

[. . .]

THE LAW
[. . .]

In 1949, the United Nations passed a convention paper that called for the decriminalization of prostitution and the enforcement of laws against those who exploit women and children in prostitution. The paper, which was read to the United Nations General Assembly by Eleanor Roosevelt, has been ratified by more than fifty countries, but not the United States. Most European countries have 'decriminalized' prostitution by removing laws which prohibit 'engaging' in an act of prostitution; although most have retained the laws against 'soliciting' 'pimping' 'pandering' 'running a disorderly house' and 'transporting a woman across national boundaries for the purposes of prostitution.' The United States, on the other hand, has retained the laws prohibiting the act of prostitution as well (except in rural counties in the state of Nevada with populations less than 250,000, which have the option of allowing legal, regulated brothels). Prostitution is also prohibited outright in Japan, and in many Asian countries, including those in which 'sex tourism' is a major industry. It is decriminalized in the [former] Soviet Union, but women who work as prostitutes there are arrested for violating the law against being a parasite (i.e., not having a legally-recognized job).

In addition to laws prohibiting soliciting or engaging in an act of prostitution, and the related issues of pimping and pandering, or procuring, the United States has laws that bar anyone who has ever been a prostitute from entering this country, remaining in this country as a resident, or becoming a citizen. Deportation proceedings on those grounds were instituted in the early 1980s against a French woman who managed a brothel in Nevada, even though the business was perfectly legal.

[Former] West Germany, in addition to decriminalizing the act itself, has developed a variety of approaches ranging from a tightly controlled, single-zone brothel system in Hamburg, to a laissez-faire, open-zone system in [former] West Berlin. Denmark has repealed most of the laws restricting the right of prostitutes to work, and has passed laws designed to help women who want to get out of prostitution.

In Holland, after a prostitute was murdered a few years ago, the government decided it might be a good idea to examine the laws and to see if there weren't ways to reduce the isolation of prostitutes. The government has been working closely with the feminist prostitutes' rights movement – the Red Thread, an organization of prostitutes and ex-prostitutes, and the Pink Thread, a feminist solidarity group. In late 1986, the Dutch government allocated funds to provide the Red Thread with three employees and an office.

The countries with the most restrictive legal systems, including the United States and many countries in Southeast Asia, have the most problems with violence against prostitutes (and women perceived to be *like* prostitutes), thefts associated with prostitution, pimping (especially brutal pimping), and the involvement of juveniles. Conversely, the countries with the least restrictive measures, including the Netherlands, [former] West Germany, Sweden and Denmark, have the least problems. No country, however, is totally safe for prostitutes. The stigma still isolates the women, and the remaining laws still serve to perpetuate that stigma, rather than to dispel it and truly legitimize the women who work as prostitutes.

DISCRIMINATORY ENFORCEMENT OF THE LAW

In 1983, 126,500 people were arrested for prostitution in the United States.[7] This is a 148.4 percent increase over the number arrested in 1973, the year that the prostitutes' rights movement began in this country with the founding of COYOTE. In comparison, arrests for all crimes increased only 35.6 percent. Although the law makes no distinction between men and women and, in most states, prohibits both sides of the transaction, the percentage of women arrested generally hovers around seventy percent. In 1979 it dropped to sixty-seven percent, probably as a result of feminist pressure on police departments to arrest customers as well as prostitutes, but in 1983, it was back up to seventy-three percent. About ten percent of those arrested are customers (usually arrested in a series of raids over a period of a couple of weeks, and then ignored the rest of the year). The remainder of the arrests are of transvestite and pre-operative transsexual prostitutes (i.e., men who, in the eyes of the police, look like women).

Enforcement practices similarly discriminate on the basis of race and class. Eighty-five to ninety percent of the prostitutes who are arrested work on the street, although only ten to twenty percent of all prostitutes are street workers. While approximately forty percent of street prostitutes are women of color, fifty-five percent of those arrested are. The racism becomes even more apparent when you look at the figures on who gets jailed: eighty-five percent of prostitutes sentenced to do jail time are women of color. One student of street prostitution in New York City[8] hypothesized that the reason for the disproportionate number of minority women being arrested was that there was more police activity in the neighborhood of ethnic minorities, where they were more likely to work. What he found, however, was that police were, in fact, more active in white neighborhoods, where most of the prostitutes were also white. He then hypothesized that the racial bias of the mostly white police officers was to blame. My own hunch is that the women of color are mostly likely to be arrested when they drift towards and/or into the white districts. Certainly, prostitution in New York's Times Square did not become a major issue until black prostitutes moved from Harlem to the theatre district as white customers stopped going to Harlem during the racially tense 1960s.

[...]

Enforcement practices vary from city to city, and from time to time. According to a report from the California Attorney General's Office, in 1980, the San Francisco Police Department arrested more prostitutes annually than the police department in Los Angeles, a city more than ten times its size, and with far more visible prostitution on clearly defined strips.

In all cities, there are periods of intense enforcement, followed by periods of relative calm, often seemingly without any clear logic to the pattern. Traditional analysts claim that pre-election politics always demand raids, although since a majority of the population supports a change in the law, it is difficult to see how the crackdowns would help incumbents.

If law enforcement is designed to reduce the amount of prostitution, it has failed miserably. Moreover, crackdowns are generally initiated with a fanfare about how the police are going to rid the streets of violent crime, but crackdowns are actually often followed by an increase in robberies, many of which involve some form of violence, as well as burglaries and other real property crime, as the people who have been dependent on the now-jailed prostitutes seek to replace lost income.

Crackdowns, and arrests in general, tend to reinforce the dependence of prostitutes on pimps, who are often their only friends outside of jail who can arrange for bail, an attorney, child care, etc. Many women who have worked independently before their first arrest are, moreover, recruited into working for pimps by other prostitutes in jail who convince them of the need to have someone outside to take care of business.

Crackdowns also pressure many women to move on to other cities, cutting off their connections with local friends and networks of support, including agencies that could help them leave prostitution if they wanted to. Their isolation in new cities further increases their dependence on pimps, and effectively entraps them in 'the life.'

PIMPS

The legal definition of pimping is 'living off the earnings of a prostitute.' By that definition, those who profit from prostitution include not only the stereotyped pimp with a stable of women, but lovers who shop for groceries and do the laundry, taxi drivers, bell captains, the business-like owners and managers of massage parlors and escort services, madams, and others who personally and directly receive money from prostitutes and/or provide connections between prostitutes and customers. Also included would have to be the publishers of the *Yellow Pages*, newspapers and some magazines, the banks that offer credit cards, travel agents who book sex tours, and a host of corporate entities that are never charged with violating prostitution laws.

When most people think of pimping, of course, they think of bad pimps who lure unsuspecting women into prostitution and physically abuse them when they resist or don't bring in enough money. Most people do not view such violent relationships in the context of relational violence in general, such as violence in marriage. If you consider that about fifty percent of adult prostitutes were either physically or sexually abused in childhood, often by their fathers, it is not surprising that many would find themselves in violent relationships as adults. This is not to condone such relationships, merely to put them into context. Many prostitutes I know say that while they have known some prostitutes who seem to be perpetually victimized, they have known at least as many others who are rarely, if ever, injured or abused.

The battered women's movement has had a profound effect on the consciousness of prostitutes and, increasingly, battered prostitutes are turning to battered women's programs for help. They are often even more frightened to pursue the matter in court than battered wives, but they are beginning to realize that they can, perhaps, have help getting out of the situation. At least some of the time, that is, because too many battered women's programs routinely refuse to serve prostitutes, or if they do, assume that 'prostitution' is the problem, not 'battering.' They refuse, for example, to allow the women to continue to work as prostitutes outside of the shelter, even when other women are expected to continue to work. Some of this may have to do with legal concerns, but in states where homosexual acts are a crime, shelters do not expect battered lesbians to go 'straight' because of the law.

FORCED PROSTITUTION

The issue of forced prostitution is often used to obscure the issue of the right of women to work as prostitutes. Therefore, it is important to discuss this issue separately. At the same time, I want to make a distinction between being forced by a third party (e.g., a 'pimp') to work as a prostitute, particularly where violence or deceit is used, and being forced by economic reality. Most people who work for compensation do so because they need the money – for themselves, for their children. In any society, people make decisions about work based on some kind of evaluation of the options open to them. And most people choose what they perceive to the the best-paying job for their skills. It is easy for other people to judge the nature of the work, but it is up to the individual to make her or his own decision about what work to do. That being said, in the technological western countries, where most women are at least functionally literate and there is a significant array of occupational choice, about ten percent of women who work as prostitutes are coerced into prostitution by third parties through a combination of trickery and violence. This figure appears to be relatively constant in the United States, as reflected in studies done at the turn of the century and current estimates of COYOTE and some other prostitutes' rights organizations.[9] At the other extreme, in India, where there is massive poverty with large numbers of people dying in the streets, and where there are few occupations open to women, seventy to eighty percent of the women who work as prostitutes are forced into the life.

In the Philippines, women's rights advocates estimate that there are approximately 300,000 prostitutes, a large majority of whom work in the vicinity of American military bases, some voluntarily, but many under duress (including being sold into prostitution). Some leave the Philippines to look for other work, or to be married, only to find that the work in the new country is still prostitution. Their isolation is compounded by the fact that, in many cases, they do not have legal immigration papers.

[. . .]

In India, young girls are sometimes sold by their parents to traders, allegedly for service to the 'goddess,' but actually for work in brothels in the major cities. Bombay, a city with eight million inhabitants, has anywhere from 100,000 to 200,000 prostitutes and 50,000 brothels. Again, the prostitutes are rarely able to escape.

[. . .]

Laws against 'traffic' in women, which are supposed to prevent the forced movement of women and girls across national or state boundaries for the purposes of prostitution are, instead, used to keep voluntary prostitutes from traveling. Forced prostitution cannot be addressed until voluntary prostitution is legitimate. Feminist attempts to simply stop it, and to 'rescue' the women who have been so badly abused, are doomed to fail until the laws that punish prostitutes are abolished and businesses that employ them are regulated in ways discussed elsewhere in this essay. Organizations likely to have the greatest impact are those that seek to empower prostitute women to make decisions about their lives, and give them the skills to do so, without making judgments – moral or otherwise – about the work they do.

VIOLENCE AGAINST PROSTITUTES

The danger of violence to prostitutes comes not only from pimps, but from customers and police. A study of street prostitutes and sexual assault found that seventy percent of the women interviewed had been raped on the job, and that those who had been raped had been victimized an average of eight to ten times a year. Only seven percent had sought any kind of help, and only four percent had reported any of the rapes to the police.[10]

Murder is a serious danger to prostitutes, particularly since serial murders of prostitutes are rarely investigated thoroughly by police until at least ten or more women have been killed or until the killer, emboldened by his 'success,' begins to kill 'square' or 'innocent' women.

[. . .]

The police, who are sworn to protect people from violence, are largely negligent when it comes to people who are seen as powerless, and that includes prostitutes. Because prostitutes are seen as having few supporters in the outside world, police – particularly undercover vice officers, – feel free to insult and roughly handle the prostitutes they arrest. Police handcuff their victims from behind, then roughly pull their arms. They demand sex before or during the arrest; and inflict beatings and kickings. They issue specific insults about the individual prostitute's body, and taunts about the how the police officer could get a free blow job with no one the wiser. The arresting officer may suggest that the prostitute give the sheriff a blow job to get out of jail. Few prostitutes file complaints, unfortunately, feeling they have no choice but to accept this abuse as part of the job, and so the few accounts that surface must be seen as symptoms of a much larger problem.

When the law prohibits only soliciting or engaging in prostitution, prostitutes feel that they have some ability to avoid police entrapment.

[. . .] However, in twenty-five states, including California and Washington, recent revisions to the law have made it a crime to 'agree,' or even 'manifest agreement' to engage in prostitution. This means that the customer can initiate all mention of sex and money; if the prostitute merely smiles, the police can say she has agreed.

[. . .]

SEXUALLY TRANSMITTED DISEASES

One excuse often given for the illegality of prostitution is the supposed responsibility of prostitutes for any veneral disease epidemic. [. . .] Countries that have legalized and regulated prostitution often require regular check-ups for venereal and other sexually transmitted diseases. Such programs have had a minimal effect because prostitutes are generally implicated in only a small proportion of venereal disease, at least in affluent, western countries where condoms are easily obtainable. Although one study of prostitutes (done at venereal disease clinics) found that twenty to thirty percent of the women had some venereal disease, a study of Nevada's legal prostitutes found less than two percent to be positive. When Chicken Ranch, the Fayette County, Texas brothel of 'The Best Little Whorehouse in Texas,' was closed, the number of gonorrhea cases rose substantially. This is consistent with the rise in venereal disease following the closing of brothels from 1917–1920. The US Department of Public Health has consistently reported that only about five percent of the sexually transmitted disease in this country is related to prostitution, compared with thirty to thirty-five percent among teenagers.[11]

The studies cited in this section were all done prior to the AIDS epidemic. There have been a number of studies on the rate of infection with the AIDS virus among prostitutes, and it appears that about four or five percent of the prostitutes in the United States, most of them IV drug users or lovers of IV users, have antibodies to the virus.

[. . .]

Prostitutes have always been quite concerned about sexually transmitted diseases. They know, for example, that gonorrhea is asymptomatic among women eighty percent of the time, and that if untreated, it can lead to a life-threatening condition known as pelvic inflammatory disease (PID). Therefore, prostitutes have tended to be quite responsible about being checked for disease to protect themselves, as well as to protect others. They quickly learn to recognize the symptoms of sexually transmitted diseases in men and refuse to have sexual contact with men they believe to be infected. Prostitutes have always made use of any prophylactic measures that have been available, including barrier methods of birth control, such as condoms and diaphragms, and spermicidal jellies and foams. This caution has only increased since the outbreak of AIDS. Even brothel managers, who in the past encouraged women not to demand condoms, by charging more for unprotected sex, are beginning to change to an all-condom policy.

The prostitutes least likely to protect themselves from venereal disease are those who are seriously addicted to heroin and too financially desperate to insist on such precautions. The prohibition of prostitution has not served in any way to solve this problem. What is probably needed, particularly with AIDS, is to educate the customer class, i.e., all heterosexual men, of the need for condoms so they will no longer argue against them.

THE NEED FOR ALTERNATIVES

This country spends an inordinate amount of money to arrest, prosecute, and incarcerate women and men involved in prostitution. [. . .] At the same time, virtually no money is allocated by government or private foundations for programs that would help prostitutes who want to change their occupations or their lives.

Within the criminal justice system, little is spent on rehabilitative programs in women's jails, even relative to the small amount spent for men. There are a few programs for adult prostitutes outside of the criminal justice system in this country (e.g., Mary Magdalene Project in Southern California and Genesis House in Chicago), but not nearly enough. There are also a growing number of programs for juvenile prostitutes, particularly in Minneapolis, Seattle, San Francisco, and New York, but again, not nearly enough.

Any programs set up to help people involved in prostitution must acknowledge and deal with the positive attractions of prostitution. First and foremost is the economic incentive: the average prostitute in this country can gross from about one hundred to two hundred dollars a day, or more, with a great deal of flexibility about hours and days of work. Programs that try to help prostitutes make a transition into low-paid, boring jobs tend to fail.

Transition programs should have ex-prostitutes on their staffs to help deal with sexual stigmatization, and the amount of sexual and physical abuse tolerated in prohibited prostitution.

Shelters for battered women are inconsistent in the way they deal with prostitutes. A few take them in without question, but many would rather not. They might say, for example, that they don't have enough well-trained staff to deal effectively with pimps finding the shelter and demanding 'their' women back. Those shelters that do accept prostitutes as clients, on the other hand, say that 'pimps' are no more tenacious about finding the shelter than 'husbands' or 'boyfriends' of other women. A second concern is that prostitutes 'act out' and need specially-trained staff. A third, flippant, response several shelter workers have given me is that they would be glad to accept prostitutes as long as they didn't 'work out of the house,' the assumption being that prostitutes would be more likely to violate house rules than other women. As more information comes out about the desperate plight of some battered prostitutes, I hope more shelters will take them in. At the present time there is little refuge for prostitutes trying to leave abusive situations.

WHO BENEFITS FROM THE SYSTEM

It is difficult to see how anyone benefits from the present system. At the time the United States prohibition was enacted, it was at least partly in response to feminist concerns about the abuse of women and children involved in prostitution. After an extensive muckraking campaign in the press, exposing the 'horrors' of brothel prostitution, there was much pressure to close brothels.

[. . .]

While the enactment of laws before World War I prohibiting prostitution, pimping, running brothels, transporting women across state lines for 'immoral' purposes, etc., did nothing to reduce prostitution, it did have other effects. Before prohibition, most brothels were owned and managed by women, most of whom had been prostitutes themselves. After the legal brothels were closed, the brothel business went underground and was headed by a male, criminal hierarchy that continues. Most massage parlors and escort services today are owned by men. Closing the brothels also forced many women to work on the streets, subjecting them to greater risks of violence. The basic conditions of women's lives, which caused some of them to choose to work as prostitutes, did not change.

For most of recorded history, prostitution has been set up for the benefit of the customer, no matter what system was in place. The stigma enforced by the prohibition in America is also enforced by systems of regulation that require prostitutes to dress differently or to live and work in special districts, or deny them the right to relationships. The health schemes that require prostitutes to have weekly checks for sexually transmitted diseases are similarly designed to benefit the customer, since there is no equivalent requirement that customers be checked to protect the prostitute, or regulation requiring brothels to provide condoms, disability insurance, workers' compensation, or health insurance. What constantly amazes me is that there is so little variation in the way nations deal with prostitution, under the law, even where there is enormous variation in just about every other aspect of society.

The current system of de facto legalization, in which the workers in massage parlors and other prostitution businesses are licensed by the police, does not reduce the number of women working as prostitutes, it merely registers them as prostitutes with the police, forever.

The number of prostitution arrests increased every year from the time the prohibition was enacted until 1983, which presumably means the number of women working as prostitutes increased accordingly. At the same time, the average age of prostitutes has been dropping in America. In Europe, which has less oppressive systems, the average age is twenty-five, while here it is eighteen. Again, in our youth oriented culture, the system seems to designed to benefit [. . .] the customer.

OPTIONS FOR CHANGE

In 1949, the United Nations called for the decriminalization of the specific transaction between prostitute and customer that is prostitution, while it recommended keeping all related activities a crime. In those countries that have adopted most of the provisions of the convention (most of the Northern European countries), the problems that so plague the prohibited system in this country are less severe. However, the continued prohibition of related activities, such as pimping (living off the earnings of a prostitute), pandering and procuring (bringing prostitutes and customers together, recruiting prostitutes), renting a premises for the purpose of prostitution, keeping a disorderly house, advertising, and soliciting, makes it almost impossible to find a place to work legally, or to engage in the kind of activity that is necessary to contact prospective clients. This leaves the prostitute subject to the exploitation of criminal third parties, landlords, bar owners, bell captains, etc. The pimping and pandering laws are even used to arrest women who work together for safety, even when no money changes hands.

[. . .]

There are two main alternatives to prohibition, generally termed decriminalization and legalization. In Europe, decriminalization is sometimes referred to as abolition, and refers to the abolition or repeal of the prostitution laws. However, the term abolition is also used by some activists, including Kathleen Barry in the United States, and The Abolitionist Society in Europe, to refer to the long-term goal of eliminating all prostitution.

Ideally, decriminalization would mean the repeal of all existing criminal codes regarding voluntary prostitution, per se, between consenting adults, including mutually voluntary relationships between prostitutes and agents or managers (pimp/prostitute relationships), and non-coercive pandering (serving as a go-between). It could involve no new legislation to deal specifically with prostitution, but merely leave the businesses which surround prostitution subject to general civil, business, and professional codes that exist to cover all businesses. Such problems as fraud, theft, negligence, collusion, and force would be covered by existing penal code provisions. Alternatively, existing sections of the penal code could be modified to specifically address the issue of coercion, and business codes could be enacted to require management to provide sick leave and vacation, as well as disability, workers' compensation, and health insurance. Decriminalization of prostitution and the regulation of pimping and pandering, it seems to me, offers the best chance for women who are involved in prostitution to gain some measure of control over their work. It would make it easier to prosecute those who abuse prostitutes, either physically or economically, because the voluntary, non-abusive situations would be left alone.

Decriminalization allows for the possibility that the lives of prostitutes can become less dangerous. For one thing, under a comprehensive decriminalization scheme, it would be possible for prostitutes to join unions and engage in collective bargaining in order to improve their working conditions. It would also be possible for prostitutes to form professional associations, and develop codes of ethics and behavior designed to reduce the problems involved in prostitution as it now exists. Finally, it would be possible for experienced prostitutes to train new prostitutes, so that their first experiences would be less dangerous.

Legalization, on the other hand, has generally meant a system of control of the *prostitute*, with the state regulating, taxing, and/or licensing whatever form of prostitution is legalized, leaving all other forms illegal, without any concern for the prostitute herself. Traditional regulation has often involved the establishment of special government agencies to deal with prostitution.

The brothels in Nevada, for example, are licensed and regulated by the government, and the women who work in them are registered as prostitutes with the sheriff. As discussed earlier, they are severely restricted in their movements outside of the brothel. Independent prostitution is illegal, as is prostitution in massage parlors, for escort services, and of course, street prostitution. The women generally work fourteen-hour shifts, on three-week (seven days a week) tours of duty, during which they may see ten or fifteen customers a day, or more. They have little or no right to refuse a customer (although the management tries to keep out potentially dangerous customers), and they have not been allowed to protect themselves from sexually transmitted diseases by using condoms (although at least two houses in Nevada are now all-condom houses, to prevent AIDS). Because of the grueling aspects of the long work shifts, many of the women use drugs (to help them stay awake and alert or to help them sleep) supplied by the same doctor who performs regular health checks.

Before much can be done to help prostitutes, the laws must be changed. The transaction between prostitute and client must be removed from the purview of the law, and the other laws dealing with prostitution must be reevaluated, and repealed or changed as necessary. Since street prostitution is singled out as 'the problem' it is important for residents, business people, and prostitutes to get together to iron out compromises that take into consideration the right of prostitutes to work without harassment, and the right of other residents and businesses to go about their lives and work without harassment.

In the meantime, until prostitution has been decriminalized, the non-coercive managers regulated, and those who use fraud and force prosecuted, pressure must be put on police and sheriff's departments, district attorneys, public defenders, bail bondspeople, judges, and pretrial diversion and probation programs to improve the treatment of persons arrested under these archaic and oppressive laws.

Should the laws in this country be changed as a result of pressure from men, including well-intentioned civil liberties attorneys, or pornographers with their own motives, there is a good chance that a brothel system will be imposed or that high-class prostitution will be decriminalized and working class prostitution (i.e., street prostitution) will remain a crime, as was proposed by the New York Bar Association in 1985. Unless there is a strong voice pointing out the oppressiveness of brothel systems, both to the women in such a system and to their sisters outside, most people in this country will assume that such a system works to the benefit of all concerned. In a brothel system, prostitution will be kept off the street, and out of the sight of children, they assume, and all in all, it would just be better, safer, and cleaner. The problem is that none of those assumptions are correct, and in exchange for a false sense of security, we would get a punitive system.

Whatever you or I think of prostitution, women have the right to make up their own minds about whether or not to work as prostitutes, and under what terms. They have the right to work as freelance workers, as do nurses, typists, writers, doctors, and so on. They also have the right to work for an employer, a third party who can take care of administration and management problems. They have the right to relationships outside of work, including relationships in which they are the sole support of the other person, so long as the arrangement is acceptable to both parties. They have the right to raise children. They have the right to a full, human existence. As feminists, we have to make that clear. We have to end the separation of women into whores and madonnas.

Our experience with the Equal Rights Amendment and with abortion – not to mention sexual assault, domestic violence, sexual harassment, sex discrimination, lesbian/gay rights, and the rest of the issues on our agenda – should tell us that if we leave the issues up to male legislators and pressure groups, the resulting legislation will not be in our interests. The same is true with prostitution.

Finally, the onus for the abuses that co-exist with illegal prostitution must be put on the system that perpetuates those abuses, and no longer on the prostitutes who are abused. If we ensure that prostitution remains under the control of the prostitutes – and not in the hands of pimps, customers, and police – then we will have given the prostitutes the power, and the support, to change that institution. We will all benefit.[12]

NOTES

1. See Kate Millett, *The Prostitution Papers*, New York: Ballantine Books, 1973; Claude Jaget, *Prostitutes: Our Life*, Bristol: Falling Wall Press, 1980; Roberta Perkins and Garry Bennet, *Being a Prostitute*, Winchester, Mass.: Allen & Unwin, Inc., 1985; Nickie Roberts, *The Front Line: Women in the Sex Industry Speak*, London: Grafton Books, 1986; F. Delacoste and P. Alexander (eds), *Sex Work: Writings by Women in the Sex Industry*, London: Virago, 1988.
2. See Jackie Macmillan, 'Prostitution as sexual politics,' *Quest: A Feminist Quarterly*, 4(1), 1977, pp. 41–50; Mary Elizabeth Perry, '"Lost women" in early modern Seville: the politics of prostitution,' *Feminist Studies*, 4(1), February 1978, pp. 195–214; Kathleen Barry, *Female Sexual Slavery*, Englewood-Cliffs, NJ: Prentice-Hall, Inc., 1979; Judith R., Walkowitz, *Prostitution in Victorian Society: Women, Class, and the State*, Cambridge: Cambridge University Press, 1980; M.S., Goldman, *Gold Diggers and Silver Miners: Prostitution and the Social Life on the Comstock Lode*, Ann Arbor: The University of Michigan Press, 1981; Ruth Rosen, *The Lost Sisterhood: Prostitution in America, 1900–1918*, Baltimore: The Johns Hopkins University Press, 1982; Leah Lydia Otis, *Prostitution in Medieval Society: The History in Languedoc*, Chicago: The University of Chicago Press, 1985; Jacqueline Baker Barnhardt, *The Fair but Frail: Prostitution in San Francisco, 1849–1900*, Reno, Nev. University of Nevada Press, 1986.
3. See Vern Bullough and Bonnie Bullough, *Prostitution: An Illustrated Social History*, New York: Crown Publishers Inc., 1978; Reay Tannahill, *The History of Sex*, New York: Stein & Day, 1980; Emmet Murphy, *Great Bordellos of the World: An Illustrated History*, London: Quartet Books, 1983; Otis, *Prostitution in Medieval History*; Gerder Lerner, *The Creation of Patriarchy*, Oxford: Oxford University Press, 1986.
4. See Jaget, *Prostitutes*; Roberts, *The Front Line*.
5. See Jennifer James, 'Prostitutes and prostitution', in Edward Sagarin and Fred Montanino (eds), *Deviants: Voluntary Actors in a Hostile World*, General Learning Press, Scott, Foresman & Co., 1977; Mimi H., Silbert, PhD, principal investigator, *Sexual Assault of Prostitutes*, San Francisco: Delancey Street Foundation, 1981.
6. See Millet, *The Prostitution Papers*; Jaget, *Prostitutes*.
7. US Department of Justice, 1985.
8. Bernard Cohen, *Deviant Street Networks: Prostitution in New York City*, Lexington, Mass.: Lexington Books, 1980.
9. Rosen, *The Lost Sisterhood*.
10. Silbert.
11. Gary L., Conrad, *et al.*, 'Sexually transmitted diseases among prostitutes and other sexual offenders,' in *Sexually Transmitted Diseases*, Oct. Dec., 1981; Rosen, *The Lost Sisterhood*; Allan Brandt, *No Magic Bullet: A Social History of Venereal Disease in the United States since 1880*, New York: Oxford University Press, 1985.

12. In 1984, the total number of arrests declined, for the first time since COYOTE began keeping track in 1973, to 112,200. There are many possible explanations: unemployment reached its peak in 1982, and has been declining ever since; heavy crackdowns in most cities have encouraged those who could move their business off the street or, retire; fear of AIDS may be discouraging new women from beginning to work as prostitutes. Gloria Lockett, Co-Director of COYOTE, who worked on the street for many of the seventeen years she was a prostitute, says that the percentage of street prostitutes in San Francisco who use IV drugs has increased sharply, which may mean that it is women who don't use drugs who have been able to leave the street or change their occupation.

4.9

PROSTITUTES AND THEIR CLIENTS

Cecilie Høigård and Liv Finstad

Cecilie Høigård and Liv Finstad conducted research into the experience of 26 prostitutes in Norway, and Cecilie Høigård was subsequently involved in research on prostitutes' clients. Both studies feature in the following extracts from interviews in which prostitutes accounts of commercial sexual exchange are set against those of their clients.

FAST FUCK: THE WOMEN'S VIEW OF WHAT THE CUSTOMER BUYS

Eva: 'You don't know how impersonally it all happens. So I'm going to tell you. They don't demand anything from you. You take a taxi down to the street. Then a car stops – you see right away that most of the cars are down there just to have a look. You get into the car and ask him if he wants a trick. It costs so-and-so much, you say. That's fine with him and you tell him where to drive. Then down with one pant leg. The whole thing probably takes about two-and-a-half minutes. Men's sexuality is totally unbelievable, and the worst part is that they come back again and again. Of course they're often sexually excited beforehand – even if you wanted to you wouldn't have time to get caught up in it. It takes ten or fifteen minutes from the time you get into the car until you're back again. I've met some people who you wouldn't have thought needed that kind of contact. Ninety per cent of the men had a wife. I don't understand it; at home, no matter what, they'd have had a better time. I was just an icicle, wanted it over as fast as possible. I think it's unbelievable every time.'

Ulla uses fewer words to describe the same thing: 'They do it to empty themselves. That's all.'

From C. Høigård and L. Finstad, *Backstreets: Prostitution, Love and Money* Cambridge: Polity, 1992.

Several of the women express astonishment at men's sexuality, which they experience as extremely basic.

[. . .]

Pia: '[. . .] I don't understand men's sexuality. They lack feelings. They're controlled by their pricks. They have their brains between their legs, that's what controls all their behavior.'

Most of the customers are married, according to the women. A bad sexual relationship with their wives can explain their behavior:

Hanna: 'The customers are basically assholes. It can't be that great for them either. I'm ice cold, I don't feel anything sexually. But I guess it's not all of them that have a sexual relationship with their wives.'

Vilhelm: 'If they can't eat at home, they have to eat elsewhere.'

Occasionally the women express disgust at married men behaving like this. Particularly if they brag about it as well, like one of Inga's customers: 'Some are completely revolting. There was one bragger who thought he was really hot shit. He told everybody he had an old lady at home asleep. "I'm going out for a little air," he'd told her. That's not right.'

'Emptying himself:' that's the most common way the women describe it. With no more ado. But some men also want to talk. This is number two on the list of customer's motives. Anita: 'Some pay just to talk. They're lonely. I feel sorry for them.'

Some customers are clearly after something more than the quick sexual release. They want their relationship to the prostituted woman to be characterized by more reciprocity. Jane says; 'There are men who ask if they can pay extra to satisfy me sexually. Totally crazy!'

According to Eva, there is a story that circulates among the customers. We're not sure if it has to do with normal vanity or the dream that the impossible will someday happen. 'I'll tell you a story I've heard many times, it keeps circulating. The customers had a strange notion sometimes. They would tell you about a friend, or a friend of a friend, who contacted a prostitute. Then the prostitute had fallen so deeply in love with him that he'd gotten it for free. It's incredible the number of men who came up with that exact same story.'

Other men want long-lasting friendships. Jane: 'Several of the johns have become interested in me and asked if they could help me, if I wanted to move in with them and stuff. Not on your life!'

Boredom in the conjugal bed. Loneliness. Desire for friendship. Prostitution can be a *replacement* for more usual forms of sexuality and companionship. But there are also some customers who do it because they're searching for something special, something that gives prostitution an extra quality other types of sexuality don't have.

Lisa: 'Yesterday I had a really great-looking 20-year-old, I don't understand what he wanted with me. He could score with whoever he wanted whenever he wanted. He said it was more exciting this way.'

Jane: 'There are guys who like excitement. And people who are a little perverse, they think it's exciting to do it up in an office building and at the Seaman's Club.'

[. . .]

The longer you've worked the street the harder it is to turn a trick. Customers want variety.

Inga: 'If you're down there day after day, it's hard to get customers. You're not new and exciting. They'd rather have a new one every time. But there are some who want the same woman too.'

The concept of prostitutes as women who, through their deep insight into physiological reactions, are able to help give birth to love, has little supporting evidence in our research. Katrine's reaction is typical: 'I think that samaritan stuff is a load of shit.'

[. . .]

Piquant fantasies, things that are different: these are also motives. Katrine illustrates men's desire for a little 'thrill' like this: 'I know a woman who advertised. "Younger woman seeks well-to-do woman for morning cuddle." She got tons of answers, but all of them were from men!'

Some men become customers because they want a woman to lend some glamour to their lives. That applies particularly to indoor prostitution.

Kari: 'Last summer I placed my usual ad in the paper about young woman with own apartment seeks well-off man. I got 40–50 answers . . . That's how I get regular customers. Now, half a year later I have two regular customers from that ad. They pay me 500–1,000 each time. They're easy to fool; they let me convince them. I'm maybe going to get a car out of one of them. They're proud, they feel like they're supporting a mistress. But those old, wrinkled men make me nauseous.'

Katrine . . . says: 'Now and then the customer wants to go out and eat dinner first – then the whole thing costs 1,000 crowns. When we go out and eat, the customer tries to pretend he's a man of the world.' Katrine giggles, disdainful of how they don't quite fit the role. 'They've seen in the movies that a man is supposed to suggest something on the menu or order for the lady. So they like to do that. They try to make interesting conversation and play man of the world, but they can't manage. They're incredibly boring. My role is to cast a glow over them, so the older men look like they're out with an attractive woman, who looks expensive. After that, we go to a hotel room.'

Cast a glow over them. Or cast a glow over a gray, ordinary life. Create a little party. Buy something fancy and pleasing – a fancy woman.

[. . .]

Pia mentioned that she didn't need to get dressed up, since the customers weren't very particular. Other women have different experiences. Some customers have fantasy images that turn them on. The whole thing goes faster if you live up to the images. Jane is one of those who dresses up to walk the streets. She has suits or dresses, make-up, huge belts, and sexy underwear. 'Lots of the customers like it if you look like a whore,' she tells me. Elisabeth breaks into the conversation. 'It's either one or the other. Either it's supposed to be little innocent-girl style, or it's supposed be whore-style.' Jane: 'Yeah, that's right. I have a little-girl style too. Then I make myself up to look discreet and innocent. And I wear a wig, the kind with bangs.'

Elisabeth also said something similar. '[. . .] [W]hen I worked down there, I made contact in ways I never used otherwise. It has something to do with the way you walk and your eyes, with your total body language. Not so that everybody around notices it, but that those who are supposed to notice, notice. You know, since I stopped, I haven't gotten a single invitation. [Laughs] I don't think it's because I've gotten old and ugly. It's which signals you send out.'

To look whorish. If a woman looks whorish that's a sign that she is lewd and available. Her physical appearance describes her character and her needs. Therefore the responsibility is hers. Again we see one of prostitution's many paradoxes. When a prostitute gets dressed up as a whore, it does not originate from her own fantasies and needs. She becomes the physical manifestation of men's fantasies and needs. It is men's fantasies about women and sexuality that create the whore. The prostitute creeps into a mold created by someone else.

[. . .]

Most of the customers are average men who want average sexual satisfaction. The women agree on this. Nonetheless, most of them have a good story to tell when we talk about customers who are a little 'special.' A good story: exactly that, precisely that cynical. The women often laugh when they talk about crazy customers. That people can be so screwed up! The laughter can sometimes be mixed with shades of contempt and vengefulness.

[. . .]

Among the more bizarre desires, one is very prevalent: the desire to be little and to be dominated.

Ulla: 'One time I met a john on the street with a really cool car. "Can you be dominating?" he asked. I said I'd try but he wouldn't get his money back if he wasn't satisfied. OK, that was fine with him. I had to beat him while he jerked off. He wanted me to take his sperm in my hand when he came and pour it in his mouth. When he came, I couldn't handle it. I just slapped the sperm in his face and went to the bathroom and threw up. He was satisfied anyway and asked for my phone number.'

Anita: 'In general they're not that perverse. But I had a slave once. He wanted to crawl on the floor and lick my toes. It almost gave me an orgasm; it was fantastic, wonderful.'

For some customers it's important to be bullied along the way. Jane: 'I was supposed to oppress this guy. I was supposed to say, "You fucking piece of shit," and stuff just before he came. Nonsense!'

[. . .]

The other theme that appears repeatedly is tricks involving piss and shit.

Marie: 'A lot of it's really gross. There are a lot of perverse johns, but not that much violence. There was one guy who wanted me to sit on a glass plate and shit. And he'd watch from underneath.'

Jane: 'He was a good-looking upper-class guy. We drove to his house on the west side. He went into the bathroom. Okay, I thought, he's probably washing himself. Then he called for me to come in. When I came in he was lying in a tub full of water. "Take your clothes off and piss on me," he says. "Okay, but then I have to get extra," I said. You get cold from a life like that.'

The pornography industry, which is primarily based on men as buyers, has a number of magazines that focus completely on themes such as these. So the market is there. The prostitution market for 'sinful sex' probably caters to the same needs. Lewd whores dressed as nuns, preferably with a gold cross, surrounded by other religious symbols – this type of pornography also exists. Few things express more directly how puritanism makes its mark on sexuality. Sexuality is sinful and filthy. It can be most successfully aroused when we think of sin and filth. Sin and filth titillate.

[. . .]

There is one 'specialty' none of those we interviewed would service. While they didn't mind having masochists as customers, none of them wanted sadists. It was too dangerous. Randi: 'I've never been beaten but I've gotten lots of offers. Some of them cruise around a lot down there. I've had offers to be scratched lightly, but I wouldn't dare. Suddenly they'd freak, and they'd stick the knife in you.'

The women's fear is well-founded. The prostitution milieu is a violent milieu. A few pimps use violence [. . .] But it is without doubt customers who are responsible for most of the violence against prostitutes. [. . .] The majority of customers are peaceful men. But not all. If the woman has had *many* customers, there is a strong probability that she has experienced customer violence.

WHAT IS HE PAYING FOR? HOW CUSTOMERS EXPERIENCE THE TRICK

We have described the contents of a trick as it is experienced by women in prostitution. How does a customer experience a trick?[1] Does he, for example, know that he is fucking what Eva calls an icicle?

A great way to earn money – maybe

Sometimes it becomes obvious. The women's piecework attitude can be hard to deal with. Frank: 'I was together with one, she was really pretty. It was in the winter, cold and awful. We drove out to the wharf, and she was the one who sucked and was trying. But then she started to complain, "Hurry up already." I said, "No, wait a minute." So she moaned a little, "so fantastic." Then she started again with "aren't you finished yet?" So it didn't work.'

Henry: 'Mostly I go to the Bank Square. They're cleaner and older; I don't chase after young kids. And older women are more controlled and have more practice. The young ones hurry more; I've gotten old enough that I want a little more time. To be honest, it happens that I don't finish. "Come on, come on, hurry up," the younger ones say. You notice that they're waiting for the next man. It's no good saying anything about it.'

Most customers are searching for something that resembles regular intercourse. Then the sexual act is reduced to a one-sided release – his. But if this becomes too blatantly clear, if affects his ability and desire.

Therefore the women do what they can to make the whole process less transparent – acting aroused, groaning, breathing, moving. The women believe that men are easily fooled. But not all men are.

Rune: 'I don't believe they experience sexual pleasure from being with customers. It's just money they're after. They moan and groan like others do, but I think it's mostly acting. When you feel their bodies they don't seem especially excited. They haven't reacted to being touched down there.'

Harald: 'Everything like that from their side is a game, empty gestures – but I've never paid much attention to it. I know it's just a game. And I see it as completely natural; it's the way it should be.'

So some customers see through the game. A few stop being customers for that reason. Others continue. On the other extreme we have customers who are convinced that the women are part of it.

Hugo: 'I think it's wonderful to feel that a woman is coming.'

Extremes are, as a rule, infrequent. It's our impression that insecurity and doubt on the part of the customer go hand in hand with a dream that yes, perhaps, maybe . . . .

Yngvar: 'I don't know, they wail a little, but whether they come, I don't know. They're old hands at the game, after all. There are a lot of them who want to cuddle first, yes, I'd say that most do.'

[. . .]

Tore: 'I feel she's enjoying herself, but I don't actually know what is faking and what is reality. But right then I don't think about it. But anyway I suppose that she's feeling it. But the first one I was with said she had strong sexual needs, and why shouldn't she get something in return, huh? But I've often wondered what kinds of sensations they can have after working three of four years. Maybe they lose the feeling. I think of a machine, it suffers wear and tear after a while. Then I wonder if the same thing happens to women.'

[. . .]

Not fantasy *or* reality. But fantasy *and* reality at the same time, ambiguities and possibilities, layer after layer of contradictory images. It's not at all strange. Few of us have crystal-clear, noncontradictory images when it comes to the more meaningful areas of life.

And it is precisely in the sexual domain that fantasy is used to deepen and strengthen reality. During regular sex, pictures can flicker through the brain – pictures of other people, other sexual organs, other situations. At any rate, for some of us, now and then. The boundary between fantasy and reality is erased. Fantasy becomes a part of the experience. A comparison with masturbation makes it clearer. There *is* a market for inflatable dolls and for realistic vibrators. Sexuality is laden with pictures and imitations. Prostitution can be understood as the last link in a chain of always more lifelike and expensive aids to fantasy: from pornographic photos to mechanical simulations of a woman's sex, to peep-shows and finally to prostitutes.

[. . .]

Men's motives for going to prostitutes are as countless as grains of sand. They go because they desire to be dominated, to dominate, to have anal sex, oral sex, to experience excitement, to be passive, to be active, to get deeper human contact, to be an infant, to be a parent, to scold and be scolded. And much more. The research literature is full of long lists of motives, yet these are not very illuminating. Prostitution is about men's sexuality.

It's important to maintain the connection between men's 'usual' sexuality and men's experiences with prostitution. Prostitution magnifies and clarifies some of the characteristics of masculine sexuality.[2] But if the end result is exclusively a catalogue of the entire panorama of motives for male sexuality, then the structuring of the question and the methodology are wrong. If one primarily wishes to chart men's usual sexuality, then prostitution research is a detour and a skewed point of departure. The approach to the problem should probably be different. Why do some men seek out prostitutes in order to act out their sexuality? What qualities does prostitution have that make some men specifically choose prostitutes?

[. . .]

Many customers placed emphasis on particular sexual acts when they described what they wanted from their prostitution encounter. The acts aren't necessarily very deviant or special; most are acts that very many would see as common elements in a varied sex life. The similarity with the type of sex shown in pornography is often obvious, and some also state that trying out some of the ideas they got from pornography is what prostitution is all about. Tom, a young husband, says: 'Yeah, I've been able to try out what I've read and seen. I want french, and to come in the mouth and between the breasts. I don't get that from my wife. There's more I'd like to try, that I've seen in movies. There was a Japanese movie, and there was this guy who got a soap massage from three girls.'

When these men tell of what they got out of prostitution, they emphasize what happened, the actual acts, and what the woman looked like.

[. . .]

To have sex with *new* women is also an important motive. This desire is easy to fulfill in prostitution. Johan had never been with anyone but his wife before he started to go to prostitutes: 'It's because of curiosity – when a guy stayed virginal in his youth, then he thinks of what he missed by following the straight and narrow. It's fairly banal and simple, getting a little excitement with different figures. . . .'

[. . .]

Many say that they were curious as to what prostitution entailed. It *is* different to just pick up a woman and then pay to have sex with her. For a number of customers there is also something more. Prostitution can play on the myth of the horny, pleasure-loving whore, and on the picture of women who are experienced and skillful in sexual matters. Vegard gets turned on because the women walk the streets, they're 'bold.'

'A bold girl dresses a little temptingly, that's it I guess, that she walks, and she looks horny out on the street, right?'

[. . .]

Frank, too, talks of excitement: 'It's the excitement, that I drive there and find a girl who's good-looking. It's exciting to stop and to hear her steps in high heels. When you've discovered her and – well, the most exciting thing is when you've parked the car and then, maybe in the rear-view mirror, you see that she's coming over, you hear the steps – oh my god, that is so exciting that I get . . . I start to sweat just thinking about it. Then you drive 50 meters down to the bridge at Akershus. And you do it there, so you could be discovered any moment. It's so exciting.'

Curiosity, excitement, and a desire for totally different experiences – these motivations are [. . .] primarily reserved for those who have only been customers once or perhaps a few times.[3]

Almost half of those interviewed pointed out that prostitution is an easy and/or a non-committal solution. Of these, over half are married. For those who are married, their appreciation of its easiness and lack of commitment goes hand in hand with not feeling unfaithful – at least not so unfaithful as they would have if they'd had a relationship which engaged them emotionally. Also, prostitution is easier to hide from the wife.

[. . .]

Paying for it also makes it legitimate to lay aside any expectations of one's own performance. Enjoying oneself is in focus. Some customers want to avoid the mutual sex act: they strive only for a climax. Ivar's pleasure in the fact that his needs come first resonates in his lyrical account of a massage parlor; 'It was obvious that she was a professional, that she was trained in what she did. It was, you might say, carried out in a way that male customers would find agreeable. They give you a wonderful massage, they're really good. There's music there; they massage you up and down your thighs, scratching and tickling you. They start tentatively and then get increasingly more intimate. Stroking your thighs, over the stomach and chest and soaping your penis. It's beautiful. They're well-groomed and refined and agreeable. They're not sloppy junkie whores. They're professionals. They don't get any pleasure from it, it's just routine. But it's a professional routine.' And Jack says: 'Cause she's a prostitute, I dared to let myself flow more with the sexual energy. I didn't need to pretend like anything, or be considerate to her. I abandoned myself to my own needs and satisfied myself, I wasn't the one who was supposed to give her something.'

Sexuality can be tedious. Demands for profundity, stamina, sexual technique, for intimacy and emotions – it's good, for once, to relax with a self-centered climax where the only demand that's made is on the wallet. For some men, prostitution plays the same role as masturbation within the framework of a steady sexual relationship: as something a man (or a woman) occasionally experiences as simply pleasurable, neither dramatic nor ecstatic.

[. . .]

Prostitution can give the customer answers to totally conflicting desires. Prostitution can give both self-occupied pleasure, and the feeling of intimacy and warmth. The reason is that one of the most important things that the customer buys is the power to interpret what is sold – the power to live in his illusions.

NOTES

1. A good deal of the material [used here] originates from the Norwegian customer study: the study was part of a preliminary project for the customer investigation. The study is described at greater length in A. Prieur and A. Taksdal. 'Prostitusjon og mannlig seksualitet,' in *Institutt for Kriminologi og strafferetts smaskriftserie*, no. 1. Oslo: Universitetsforlaget, 1986; pp. 86–101. The method and margin of error is also clarified.

2. See for example, C. Høigård and L. Finstad, 'Der Hurenkunde – ein Spiegelbild', in C. Meyerburg and M.T Mächler (eds), *Männerhaus: Ein Tabu Wird Gebrochen*, Munich: Verlag, Frauenoffensive, 1988; pp. 109–29.

3. See for example, Sven-Axel Mänsson and Annulla Linders, *Sexualitet utan ansikte könsköparna*, Stockholm:carlssons, 1984; Charles Winick, 'Prostitutes' clients' perception of the prostitute and of themselves,' *International Journal of Social Psychiatry*, 84, 1962; and H.R. Holzman and S. Pines, 'Buying sex: the phenomenology of being a john,' *Deviant Behaviour*, 4(1), Oct.–Dec., 1982.

THE PRAED STREET PROJECT
A Cohort of Prostitute Women in London

Sophie Day and Helen Ward

The previous reading illustrates the ways in which prostitutes distance themselves from sex with clients. In this study of London prostitutes, Sophie Day and Helen Ward demonstrate how condom use marks the divide between sex as work and sex as part of a relationship, by showing that the women in their study are much more likely to practise safer sex with their clients than with their partners.

[. . .]

This study was related to a cohort of women who exchanged sex for money (or materials of monetary value).

[. . .]

A cohort study was designed to recruit a hundred female prostitutes who would be seen regularly at the clinic over a period of two years.

[. . .]

The Praed Street Project involved both a structured questionnaire that was administered formally and a series of informal, unstructured interviews on subsequent visits to the clinic.

[. . .]

These methods combine anthropological, epidemiological, and clinical approaches to the study of prostitute women in the cohort. Limitations on one particular perspective were hopefully balanced by the gains to the cohort study as a whole.

[. . .]

Data on condom use reported in the cohort illustrate the relevance of the combined methodology. This illustration does not deal with differences in the cohort, which

From S. Day and H. Ward, 'The Praed Street Project: A cohort of prostitute women in London', in M. Plant (ed.), *AIDS, Drugs and Prostitution*, London: Routledge, 1990.

might be presented in terms of age, work-place, or injecting practices. The focus is rather upon a very general feature of prostitution in London, as reflected in the cohort, which concerns the way that women separate their work from their private lives. The description is based upon women who had sexual intercourse both with male clients at work and with private male sexual partners outside work. It does not, therefore, include a discussion of women who had no private sexual partners or those who had female sexual partners at home.

Many women reported condom use at work when they first attended the clinic. Indeed, many reported condom use long before they had heard of AIDS.

[. . .]

Reports over time during follow-up provide a more general impression of patterns of condom use. One hundred and six women reported, on two or more visits to the clinic, engaging in vaginal sex with clients.

[. . .]

Two points about these reports are important. First, prostitutes reported high levels of condom use before the advent of AIDS. Second, worries about HIV infection have promoted increased condom use. Interview data suggested that peer pressure from other prostitutes provided the major impetus for change, although the project, media coverage, and government health campaigns are likely to have played some role. Since the middle of 1987, prostitutes have also reported that some clients are more willing to use condoms. These points raise the question of why prostitutes were using condoms at work before the advent of AIDS. Information on this subject is not readily collected in quantitative form and data were elicited on the basis of conversations in the clinic.

Prostitutes who attended this project described themselves as 'business girls' or 'working girls' and invariably stressed that the exchange of sex for money was 'work'. This attitude is illustrated by the following conversation. Pseudonyms and literal quotations are used:

Julia: 'I hate that word' (the interviewer had just used the word prostitute).

SD: (Sophie Day): 'Some people say business girls.'

Julia: 'That's even worse. I'm a worker.'

SD: 'Yes, lots of people describe themselves as working girls.'

Julia: 'No. I'm just a worker. You hear "hooker" sometimes. Some of the older ones, who've been around for a while, they call themselves hookers. I'm not working. I'm a worker.'

Many prostitutes stressed the service aspect of their work, suggesting that they stopped men from raping other women or that prostitutes kept marriages intact. Some, usually those who worked as escorts, described themselves primarily as companions or hostesses. Others presented themselves as counsellors, social workers, sex therapists. Such arguments do not seek only to establish prostitution as work but as an *essential* work or service.

[. . .] The prostitutes who visited the clinic were very varied. They originated from eleven different countries and a wide range of work-places and socio-economic backgrounds. They rarely worked together; indeed, one of the more important aspects of prostitution in London is an enforced isolation at the work-place.[1] The women's universal concern to stress that prostitution was a form of work carried all the more significance against this background. This has been elaborated elsewhere.[2]

It is clear from conversations in the clinic that condoms were associated with 'work' among this study group. Certain sexual activities were distinguished by means of condom use and turned into 'work' that had no relationship with a personal or private sex life. One young woman's comments about her work on the street were typical: 'I always use a sheath. I'd commit suicide if I didn't. But I don't use anything else, I couldn't prevent nature.' Other women mentioned a range of protective devices including, at times, a diaphragm, a spermicidal pessary, spermicide, and the oral contraceptive pill as well as a condom. One woman reported that she always put two condoms on her clients, and she stated that they 'never noticed'. She reported that she was currently seriously considering using three condoms during each client contact in order to protect herself from AIDS.

Women often stated that they regarded semen as 'dirty'. Both semen as well as any organisms it might carry were rejected. However, they appeared to take the view that it was only clients who had 'dirty semen' and that it was substances associated with work that must be kept outside their bodies.

Extracts from conversations and interviews in the clinic make it easier to understand why prostitutes use condoms and have always used condoms for many of their working contacts. A number of women said that condoms protected them from sexually transmitted diseases in general and not just HIV infection. They were particularly worried about infections that might cause infertility.

[. . .]

[L]ittle condom use was reported with boy-friends, though a slight increase appears to have occurred. Interviews suggested that increased condom use in the cohort was related to changes of partner and concerns about possible infections. Condoms were also used for contraception. High and increasing rates of condom use at work contrast with little or no use outside work. Eighty-two per cent of the cohort reported no condom use at all in their private lives. These figures can also be understood better in the context of conversations and interviews at the clinic when most women distinguished sex at work from love at home.

Many women were horrified at the thought of using condoms with their private (non-paying) partners. Most said that their relationship would be finished, as illustrated by the following comments from three different women:

> 'We have a very good sex life. It would be spoilt if he wore a sheath. We would be finished.'

> 'I don't want strangers' semen inside. I only drop the barrier with someone I really love.'

> 'How could I? He would be like a client. It's different for people who don't work' (i.e. sell sex).

Much research with female prostitutes has focused only on the domain of work. However, it should be emphasized that women's private lives are equally important. First, what counts as work is established partly through a contrast with the rest of life. Therefore, an exclusive focus upon work provides only a partial perspective on prostitution. Second, reports of high and increasing rates of condom use at work suggest that both women and their clients may be increasingly better protected from HIV infection and other sexually transmitted diseases. It has been suggested that the high rates of partner change associated with work would be related to increased transmission of sexually transmitted diseases. This hypothesis may not be relevant if sex at work is effectively protected through condom use. It may be more relevant to consider prostitutes' non-working lives, which are not associated with high rates of partner change or directly with the sale of sex but which commonly involve unprotected sex.[3] Prostitutes in this cohort were well aware of this possibility. Many women attending the clinic with infections immediately attributed them to their private partners. Approximately half of the women with boy-friends reported that they knew these men had other sexual partners with whom, it was suspected, condoms were not used.

[. . .]

Campaigns to prevent the transmission of [. . .] such diseases will need to be sensitive to the issues noted above. It is important to establish whether findings from this study can be generalized. If they can be, then preventive strategies will need to be directed as much at prostitutes' private lives as their work. [. . .] [A] woman who revisited the clinic [. . .] had moved from soliciting on streets to advertising and working in a flat because, she said, it was safer. She currently used two condoms each time for penetrative sex and one for 'hand relief' (masturbation). She engaged only in 'safer sex' with her clients. She commented:

> It's all right for you [Sophie Day]. You don't work with a gross of condoms by the bed, six days a week. How could I use condoms outside work? . . . The mere thought of putting a condom on a boy-friend or watching him put it on just leaves me cold. I'd rather not have sex.

In fact, this woman later left her boy-friend in November 1988 partly because he had other sexual partners. She had not had a sexual relationship outside work in the previous four months. 'Celibacy' provided a more palatable alternative to the use of condoms outside work.

It is possible that the development of alternative distinctions between different types of sexual activity might make it easier for women to introduce condoms into non-working relationships. Some women did not sell penetrative sex but instead catered for a variety of fantasies, domination, and masturbation. Most women restricted the types of sex which they sold at work. Thus, no one in the cohort was currently selling passive anal sex at the end of 1988. If these other distinctions were developed, condoms might become less central to the demarcation between work and the rest of life. It is possible also that different types of condoms might come to stand for different relationships.

The picture that has been sketched makes it easier to understand why condoms are used at work but also makes it difficult to understand why condoms are not always used at work. A discussion of a third type of sexual partner, in between the casual or new client and the private partner, offers a partial answer to this question. This type of partner is the 'regular client' who pays to see the same woman repeatedly. Regular clients play a central role in a prostitute's career. With 'regulars', women are assured of an income; moreover, they can begin to establish themselves as self-employed businesswomen rather than employees.[4] Money is frequently evaluated in a very different way from the transactions that occur with casual or new clients. Sometimes, regulars do not pay. On other occasions, they agree to meet expenses such as rent, private medical bills, or school fees. An example from the context of AIDS research is illustrative. A member of the International Committee of Prostitutes' Rights was invited to the Fourth International Conference on AIDS in Stockholm during 1988, initially unfunded. She tried to persuade a regular client to pay for her travelling expenses and one of the authors (Sophie Day) was involved in lengthy telephone conversations with this man to explain the purpose of the trip.

Regular clients may also be involved in women's personal lives. Indeed, a small number of women in the study cohort have turned regular clients into private partners. One is now married to an ex-client. In such relationships, women do not see themselves as prostitutes. One woman, for example, gave up work after her boyfriend had, yet again, turned out to be a pimp. She ran away and, later, began a college course. She has reported that she was no longer working even though all her fees were being paid by an ex-customer. Another woman, Tricia, reported that she had stopped work six to eight months previously. After a while it transpired that this meant she no longer worked for an agency. Tricia said:

> I couldn't afford not to work and I couldn't come off the methadone [which she had been using for ten years] because then I wouldn't be able to work. Withdrawing, the punters [clients] would think I was a junkie. I have this friend and he's agreed to support me for a year so now I can afford not to work and to come off the drugs.

This friend turned out to have been a customer who was so worried about AIDS that he agreed to keep Tricia and her son. She also saw another 'client'. This second man was not seen as a client; first, because they did not have 'sex' – 'I just masturbate him' – second, because he did not 'pay' her – 'he just sends me on holidays and things'.

Women in the cohort had different types of sex with regular clients and they did not always use condoms. An analysis was conducted of fifty-seven weeks' sexual history reported by thirty-four women in the last three months of 1987. Only one out of 161 contacts with new or casual clients was unprotected (by condoms) in comparison with twenty-eight out of 134 contacts with regular clients. This contrast was less apparent in data collected during 1988, since more women had begun to insist on condom use with their regular clients.

Patterns of condom use with regular clients provide a partial explanation of the failure to use condoms all the time at work.

[. . .]

NOTES

1. A.A. Sion, *Prostitution and the Law*, London: Faber, 1977.
2. S. Day, 'Prostitute women and the ideology of work in London', in D.A. Feldman (ed.), *AIDS and Culture: The Global Pandemic*, New York: Praeger, 1989.
3. S. Day *et al.*, 'Prostitute women and the public health', *British Medical Journal*, 297, 1988, p. 1585.
4. J. Walkowitz, *Prostitution and Victorian Society: Women, Class and State*, Cambridge: Cambridge University Press, 1980, p. 197.

4.11

SERVING THE TOURIST MARKET
Female Labour in International Tourism

Thanh-Dan Truong

Prostitution, and sex work in general, has become part of the global economy, particularly through the development of sexual tourism. This is particularly well documented in South East Asia, the focus of this study. Thanh-Dan Truong argues that women's involvement in sex-work should be placed in the context of global and local economic and social conditions. Women's work in this sphere can be seen as part of the service sector and an aspect of an international, gendered division of labour.

To understand how specific types of labour are mobilized to serve the tourist industry, the characteristics of the tourist product itself must be taken into account. There are three central characteristics of tourism which affect the organization of production and the mobilization of labour: (1) tourism as 'an experience commodity'; (2) the symbiotic relationship between tourism and advertising; and (3) the unpredictable nature of tourism demand.

The first characteristic of tourism is the combination of services (transport, accommodation, local services) whose quality is experienced essentially at the tourist destinations rather than at the place of purchase, i.e. travel agency bureaux. The salient feature of this 'experience commodity' is the replication in a commercial context of household-based services (hospitality, personal services, accommodation, personal and psychological fulfilment).

[. . .]

[B]eyond standardized requirements such as the safety of means of travel and the comfort of accommodation, the expectation of quality tends to be focused on the personal attention given to the tourist in a wide range of services. Not only must the tourist be attracted by the standard of services offered, he/she must also be entertained and pampered. As noted by several researchers, in some cases, concern over the quality of the tourist experience extends even to the manner in which local citizens treat tourists. This concern can be translated into a public campaign, such as the 'smile' campaign in Jamaica,[1] and 'help the tourist' and 'hospitality campaign' initiatives in several other countries. [. . .] Local cultures are transformed to suit the needs of tourists. In the process, a new homogenized tourist culture has emerged and become highly commercialized. This transformation has been the subject of numerous anthropological studies which have concluded that tourism is a new form of cultural domination.[2]

[. . .]

The second characteristic of tourism is its symbiotic relationship with advertising. As has been pointed out, the tourist market is essentially a 'symbiotic market', which unites under a single concept (conveyed through the medium of advertising) factors that by nature are not directly related to tourism, but become tourist attractions once they are processed into goods.[3] As such, without advertising, the tourist product means little else than household-related services (food, accommodation, rest) provided to the traveller away from home, or landscape and cultural traits, products of nature and human history. With advertising, all these aspects become incorporated into 'the tourist market basket of goods and services'. In this connection, the significance of the ideological constructs of the advertising industry cannot be separated from tourism itself.

Like some other markets of consumer goods, the tourist market is one in which not only supply determines demand, but also one in which the ideological constructs mediated through advertising play a significant role in shaping the demand itself.

Advertising in the tourist industry is a form of discourse. As Uzzell has shown[4] holiday companies attempt to attract holiday makers not through the overt and superficial attributes of holiday destinations portrayed in the brochure photographs, but by utilizing the discourse of advertising to provide the reader with a range of cultural tools with which fantasy, meaning and identity can be created and constructed. In this connection, the ways in which promotional campaigns focus on aspects of hospitality, such as female submissiveness, caring and nurturing as well as sexual temptation, may be considered as part of this discourse sustained by governments and enterprises.

As has been noted by a number of authors, the development of tourism is closely connected with the rise of a playground culture in which sand, sun, sea, sex and servility are the main elements.[5] Images associated with brand names of tour operators and destinations have been developed and quickly propagated through various media. For example, Uzzell[6] notes the advertisements of Club Méditerranée which suggest that a holiday 'may be a chance for you to discover yourself . . . and meet someone special and when the mixing and mingling is done . . . get away somewhere quiet and discover each other'. An image has developed of the Club Méditerranée that it is the place to go for uninhibited sex, lots of food, drink and group recreation, all with little or no contact with the local population except for brief sexual encounters with the native club staff.[7] As *Playboy* describes it: 'for sex, it is Club Méditerranée, hands down. As for Club Méditerranée, most of what you've heard about is probably true, the good along with the bad. There are three club villages in the Caribbean . . . And yes, two of them are sex factories.'[8] Other examples of such advertisements is the case of sex tour operators who offer trips to Thailand and other destinations with detailed descriptions of the kinds of sexual services available and their costs.[9]

Concurrent with this development is the emergence of semi-pornographic motion pictures or pornographic video films, stressing the sexual and exotic characteristics of these cultures, showing how foreign visitors to these countries can enjoy uninhibited sex.[10] Thus, to understand why personalized services, including sexual services are often included in tourist-related services with varying degrees of explicitness, it is essential to bear in mind the power of ideas surrounding the industry itself. This realm cannot be easily separated from material forces which condition different practices of prostitution related to tourism. Particularly in the context of tourism services, the intangible nature of their constitution implies that the effect of advertising is necessarily diffuse while its instrumentality remains central.

The present international information order is such that the Third World has virtually no control over the information produced about its societies, or in Foucault's terms, no control over 'the tactical productivity' of knowledge and power and their 'strategic integration'. As Foucault has pointed out, the power of information is not just a question of ideology. 'It is the production of effective instruments for the for-mation and accumulation of knowledge . . . power, when it is exercised through these subtle mechanisms, cannot but evolve, organize and put into circulation a knowledge, or rather apparatuses of knowledge, which are not ideological constructs',[11] as they are integrated into practice. Many countries which promote sex tourism have allowed segments of their societies to be incorporated into the power-knowledge apparatus of advertising to produce information (with examples of practices) about the trade in sexual services involving the women of these countries.

A third significant aspect of tourism is the unpredictable nature of the demand side. Unpredictability is derived from aspects which are external to the industry such as political and economic instability (e.g. effects of recession on discretionary spending; social and political upheavals at destination areas; the effect of changes in fashion and taste on tourist arrivals). Therefore, on an international scale, business has tended to favour the creation of big groups with sufficient resources to invest in a variety of activities, hedging against a setback in any one branch or geographical area.

[. . .]

By contrast, in the peripheral tourist-receiving countries and particularly in low-income and small-island countries, tourist resorts and hotels tend not to be well-integrated into the local economy. [. . .] Thus, on a local scale, enterprises engaged in the entertainment business, ground tours or other local services generally are not linked financially with other sub-branches of the service sector, as are those originating from industrialized countries. Capital investments of local enterprises are less liquid with few possibilities for diversification. Due to the need for return on capital invest-ment, the perishable nature of services (i.e. rooms and local transportation services which cannot be stored for resale), and the standardization of production, there is a tendency among firms to incorporate more and more services of a 'personal' nature into the travel and tourist product to increase its appeal.

In the production of tourism services, two new categories of wage labour are created. There is a labour category formally employed in the maintenance of the tourist infrastructure (air transport, accommodation, tour operation) and in the provision of services (banking and exchange, etc.), and there is a category of 'casual' labour engaged in providing personal services through the venues of the entertainment industry, which has a dynamic function in attracting tourists. The demarcation between formal and casual occupations only exists in legal terms. In practice, such occupations form a part of a unified economic operation.

The established worker shares a direct relationship with the tourist industry which is determined by wages and other regulations whereas the casual worker shares an indirect relationship through which income is determined by shares of profits, commissions, or other forms of unregulated payment. Female workers may be engaged simultaneously in formal and casual occupations. Under the guise of formal occupations such as hostess, waitress, bartender, masseuse, go-go dancer, etc., female workers may also be engaged in prostitution on their own account. The 'personal' nature of their services means that their work is seen as non-productive. Therefore it can be paid irregularly and is easier to control.

The character of the organizational link between prostitution, sex-related entertainment and tourism depends on the forms of prostitution involved. Sex package tours represent an extreme form of the merging of tourism and prostitution. They involve three main industrial branches namely the airlines, hotels and entertainment establishments, and require a high degree of co-ordination between the branches. Besides sex package tours, there are other forms of prostitution catering to foreign visitors with a different type of linkage to accommodation, entertainment and services (bars, night-clubs, massage parlours). In these cases, services are purchased locally and are not incorporated in the package tours. Sex tourism is then carried out by individual purchase of the means of transport and accommodation, or individual purchase of a package tour. Prostitutes' services are then purchased locally through the agency of various enterprises, for example those providing the services of a 'hired-wife' who comes with a furnished flat for visitors staying for long periods, or, in the case of some hotels, providing information on prostitutes' services available in local entertainment and personal service establishments.[12] Some hotels also provide a selection of sexual services upon guests' arrival as part of their internal commercial practice. In this context, there is no concrete link between tourism and prostitution, except by way of supplying information on prices, locations, and the forms of sexual services available at the destination.

The combined existence of established and casual workers in the sex-related entertainment industry is an outcome of the contradiction between the moral and economic aspects of the industry. Moral concerns impose limits on the degree of public tolerance of forms of entertainment, while economic concerns force governments either to turn a blind eye, or to stimulate the organization of prostitution directly or indirectly. Owing to the composition of vested interests (national, international, and private capital), the mobilization of female labour in the entertainment industry can become integral to government policies as well as to business practices.

For example, in Japan during the period of post-war reconstruction, the government officially praised the *geishas* who served US servicemen as patriotic, for bringing in the foreign exchange needed to rebuild the country. The same happened in South Korea in the 1970s when the *Kisaeng* servicing Japanese businessmen were instructed to 'make sacrifices to get foreign money, and [to see that] this self-sacrifice is a matter of pride for them and for the nation'.[13] Expressed differently, the same logic is found in Thailand and the Philippines, where government officials (under the Marcos regime) publicly made explicit that female sexuality was to be regarded as an economic asset in their tourist ventures for national development.

It is important to point out here that newly emerged ideological mechanisms have enabled the moral justification of the mobilization of female labour for the entertainment industry on a wide scale. To be applicable, these mechanisms combine traits of the female role which are familiar to the traditional society while at the same time reflecting the vision established for the society under transformation. Thus, the ideology of hospitality, servitude and self-sacrifice inherent in the traditional female role is used in combination with the ideology of nationalism and development. The ambiguous nature of ideological mechanisms enables the mobilization of female labour on a large scale while ensuring effective labour control. The glorification of self-sacrifice for the household and nation justifies the act of prostitution, while the criminalization of prostitutes makes labour organization in this area impossible.

Against this background, services which fall into the category of 'personal' and 'informal' but which are nevertheless crucial to the maintenance and development of the travel and tourism industry are to be considered as belonging to an ongoing process of accumulation which takes place mainly from sexual labour. Unprotected by legislation, yet highly integrated in business practices, commoditized sexual services benefit governments and firms from a variety of angles.

For corporations employing a highly mobile male work force, the availability of sexual and household-related services helps reduce the costs of maintenance of needed labour power traditionally provided through family relations. For enterprises such as bars, clubs, and other entertainment establishments, disguised prostitution stimulates clients' expenditure and ensures high profits from sales as well as low or irregular wages. For the international tourism conglomerates, the availability of sexual services as an exotic commodity functions as a source of tourist attraction and helps to fill airplane seats and hotel rooms. National accounts benefit from taxes on accommodation, food, drinks and services. Unlike their flesh, the contribution of prostitutes' labour to this process of accumulation remains invisible.

NOTES

1. L. Turner, 'The international division of leisure: tourism and the Third World', *World Development*, 4(3), 1976, pp. 253–60; H.G. Matthews, *International Tourism: A Political and Social Analysis*, Cambridge: Schrenkamn Publishing Co., 1978.
2. V. Smith (ed.), *Host and Guests: The Anthropology of Tourism*, Philadelphia: University of Pennsylvania Press, 1977; R.E. Wood, 'International tourism and cultural change in South East Asia', *Economic Development and Cultural Change*, 23(3), 1980, pp. 561–81; R.E. Wood, 'Ethnic tourism, the state and cultural change in South East Asia', *Annals of Tourism Research*, 11(3), 1984, pp. 353–74.
3. J. Krippendorf, 'Marketing et tourisme', *Etudes bernoises de tourisme*, Cahier (7), (Berne, 1971).

4. D. Uzzell, 'An alternative structuralist approach to the psychology of tourism marketing' *Annals of Tourism Research*, 11(1), 1984, pp. 79–100.

5. Smith, *Hosts and Guests*; Matthews, *International Tourism*; L. Turner and L. Ash, *The Golden Hordes: International Tourism and the Pleasure Periphery*, London: Constable, 1975.

6. Uzzell, 'An alternative structuralist approach to the psychology of tourism marketing', p. 85.

7. Matthews, *International Tourism*.

8. *Ibid.*, p. 83.

9. K. Barry, *International Feminism: Networking Against Female Sexual Slavery*, New York: International Women's Tribune Center, 1984.

10. A. Stol, *Charter Naar Bangkok*, Rotterdam: Ordeman, 1980. A relation exists between sexual inhibition, sexual violence and the definition of the 'Other'. . . . Discourse on the 'Other', power and practices over the subjugated are inseparable. For example, the pornographic film *Snuff* was advertized by the producers as featuring an actual murder of a prostitute from South America 'where life is cheap'. The idea that the murder was not staged was meant as a sexual turn-on (L. Bell, *Good Girls, Bad Girls: Sex Trade Workers and Feminists Face to Face*, Toronto: The Women's Press, 1987, p. 157).

11. M. Foucault, 'Disciplinary power and subjugation', in S. Lukes (ed.), *Power*, Oxford: Basil Blackwell, 1986, p. 237.

12. Korean Church Women United, *Kisaeng Tourism: A Nation-Wide Survey Report on Conditions in Four Areas, Seoul, Pusan, Cheju, Kyongju*, Research Material Issue No 3, Seoul: Catholic Publishing House, 1984; W. Senftleben, 'Tourism, hot spring resorts and sexual entertainment, observations from northern Taiwan: a study in social geography', *Philippine Geographical Journal*, 30(1 & 2), 1986, pp. 21–41.

13. I. Lenz, *Prostitutional Tourism in South East Asia*, Berlin: Freie Universitat Berlin, 1978, Mimeo; Korean Church Women United, *Kisaeng Tourism*.

COPYRIGHT ACKNOWLEDGEMENTS

1.1   Ann Oakley, 'Sexuality', from *Sex, Gender and Society*, by Ann Oakley, Maurice Temple Smith, 1972.

1.2   Mary Poovey, from *Uneven Developments*, by Mary Poovey, Virago, 1989. Published by Virago Press Limited 1989, 20–3 Mandela Street, Camden Town, London NW1 0HQ. First published by The University of Chicago Press 1988. Copyright © 1988 by The University of Chicago. All rights reserved. Reproduced by permission of Mary Poovey and Chicago University Press.

1.3   Sheila Jeffreys, 'Women's friendships and lesbianism', from *The Spinster and Her Enemies*, by Sheila Jeffreys, HarperCollins Publishers Ltd, 1985.

1.4   Andrea Dworkin, 'Biological superiority: the world's most dangerous and deadly idea', from *Letters from a War Zone*, by Andrea Dworkin, Secker and Warburg, 1988, copyright © Andrea Dworkin, Reprinted by permission of Andrea Dworkin.

1.5   Stevi Jackson, from *The Social Construction of Female Sexuality*, by Stevi Jackson, Women's Research and Resources Centre, 1978.

1.6   Jacqueline Rose, Introduction II, from *Feminine Sexuality*, by Jacques Lacan, ed. J. Rose and J. Mitchell, W.W. Norton, 1982. Excerpts are reprinted with the permission of W.W. Norton & Company, Inc. and Macmillan Ltd. Copyright © 1982 by Jacqueline Rose.

1.7   Luce Irigaray, from *This Sex Which is Not One*, by Luce Irigaray, Cornell University Press, 1985. Translated from the French by Catherine Porter with Carolyn Burke. Copyright © 1985 by Cornell University. Used by permission of the publisher, Cornell University Press.

1.8   Wendy Holloway, 'Gender difference and the production of subjectivity', from *Changing the Subject*, eds Julian Henriques, Wendy Hollway, Cathy Urwin, Couze Venn and Valerie Walkerdine, Methuen & Co., 1984.

1.9   Lynda Birke, 'Animals and biological determination', from *Feminism, Animals and Science*, by Lynda Birke, Open University Press, 1994.

2.1   Anne Koedt, 'The myth of the vaginal orgasm', from *Radical Feminism*, by Anne Koedt, Quadrangle, 1972.

2.2   Janet Holland, Caroline Ramazanoglu, Sue Scott, Sue Sharpe and Rachel Thomson, from ' "Don't Die of Ignorance." I Nearly Died of Embarrassment': Condoms in Context* by Janet Holland *et al.*, Tufnell Press, 1990.

2.3   Adrienne Rich, 'Compulsory heterosexuality and lesbian existence', from *Blood, Bread and Poetry*, by Adrienne Rich, Virago, 1978. Used by permission of Adrienne Rich, Virago and W.W. Norton & Co., Inc.

2.4   Monique Wittig, 'The straight mind', from *Feminist Issues*, Harvester Wheatsheaf, 1992. Copyright © 1992 by Monique Wittig. Reprinted by permission of Harvester Wheatsheaf and Beacon Press.

2.5   Marie-Jo Dhavernas, 'Hating masculinity not men', from *French Connections*, ed. C. Duchen, Unwin Hymen, 1987.

2.6   Cheryl Clarke, 'Lesbianism: an act of resistance', from *This Bridge Called My Back*, eds C. Moraga and G. Anzaldúa, Kitchen Table: Women of Color Press, 1981. Copyright © 1981 by Cherrie Moraga and Gloria Anzaldúa. Reprinted by permission of the author and of Kitchen Table: Women of Color Press, Box 40–4920, Brooklyn NY 11240.

INDEX OF NAMES

INDEX OF SUBJECTS